THE SEDUCTION OF THE OCCULT
AND THE RISE OF THE FANTASTIC TALE

Cultural Memory
in
the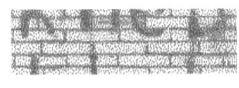
Present

Mieke Bal and Hent de Vries, Editors

THE SEDUCTION OF THE OCCULT
AND THE RISE OF THE FANTASTIC TALE

Dorothea E. von Mücke

STANFORD UNIVERSITY PRESS

STANFORD, CALIFORNIA 2003

Stanford University Press
Stanford, California

© 2003 by the Board of Trustees of the
Leland Stanford Junior University.
All rights reserved.

Printed in the United States of America
on acid-free, archival-quality paper.

Library of Congress Cataloging-in-Publication Data

Mücke, Dorothea E. von.
　The seduction of the occult and the rise of the fantastic tale /
Dorothea E. von Mücke.
　　p. cm.
　Includes bibliographical references and index.
　ISBN 0-8047-3859-9 (cloth : alk. paper) —
ISBN 0-8047-3860-2 (pbk. : alk. paper)
　　1. Fantasy fiction—History and criticism. 2. Occultism in
literature. I. Title.
PN3435 .M83　2003
809.3'8766—dc21　　　　　　　　　　　　　　　2002015101

Original Printing 2003
Last figure below indicates year of this printing:
12　11　10　09　08　07　06　05　04　03

Typeset by James P. Brommer in 11/13.5 Garamond

Contents

Acknowledgments ix

Introduction 1
    Author, Text, Audience, and the Fantastic Encounter   3
    The History of Reading Cultures and the History of Sexuality   9
    Contextualizing the Fantastic   13

1. The Fantastic in the Cultural History of Reading   18
    Cazotte's *Le diable amoureux* and Hoffmann's "Der Elementargeist"   18   *The Devil in Love*   20
    "Che Vuoi?"   22   The Glance Behind the Lure   29
    "The Elementary Spirit"   35   Seduction Through Reading   38   The Passion of the Lonely Reader   42
    Manly Valor and Bachelordom by Choice   49

2. The Aesthetics of Shock and the Poetics of the Perverse   58
    Paranoid Eckbert, Melancholy Emil, and "The Imp of the Perverse"   58   The Limits of Representation   60
    Blond Eckbert's Paranoia   64   Confessions Gone Awry: Eckbert's Paranoia   67   Bertha's Story and the Origin of Sexuality   75   "Rear Window" or "Love Charm"   80
    The Pathology of Aesthetic Subjectivity   84   The Love Charm, the Fantastic, and Seduction by Shock   92   Between Pathology and Amorality: "The Imp of the Perverse"   99

3. The Power of the Artist   109
    Schmolling's Insanity Defense   112   "Das Fräulein von Scuderi"   117   "Automata" and the Simulation of Life   129

4. Artificial Paradise and the Medial Woman　148
"Serapion," "Rat Krespel," "La morte amoureuse," and "Ligeia"　148　Temporality, Ideal Beauty, and Mortality　150　Serapion: Radical Visionary Bliss and the Denial of the Body's Mortality　152　"Councillor Krespel": Narration and Fantasy Between Two Deaths　156　"La morte amoureuse"　169　Ligeia: "Her Large and Luminous Orbs"　180　Poe's Arabesque, or Death by Drapery　187　"Hideous Animation"　192

5. Fantastic Encounters with the Marvels of History　197
"Isabella von Ägypten" and "La Vénus d'Ille"　197　Bella's Blood　199　The Political Mixture of Legend and History　202　Isabella's Sexuality and Femininity　206　The Uses of Blood　212　The Living Past and Its Resistance to Modernization　219　"The Venus of Ille"　224　The Idol's Looks and the Idol's Look　227　The Inspector's Investment　234　Signature, Event, Context: The Narrator's Blind Spot　239

Epilogue, or Turning the Screw from Shock to Fascination　244

Notes　257

Works Cited　273

Index　282

Acknowledgments

Part of Chapter Four, the section on Poe's "Ligeia," has been published previously by *Differences*, and I appreciate the permission to reprint it. During the academic year of 1997–98, I was a fellow at the Center for Advanced Study in the Behavioral Sciences. I am grateful for financial support provided by the Andrew W. Mellon Foundation. I would also like to thank the women's group of the Center, especially Lynn Hunt and Phyllis Mack, for discussing some of the drafts I was working on. At Columbia University, I am grateful for the stimulation and criticism provided by the reading group of the Institute for Research on Women and Gender, with special thanks to Jean Howard, Elaine Combs-Schilling, and Martha Howell.

Two readers have read the entire manuscript for Stanford University Press. Ken Calhoon has been a wonderfully encouraging reader, and Mieke Bal has been a fierce and honest series editor; I thank them both. I also thank Helen Tartar, Mariana Raykov, and Thomas Finnegan from Stanford University Press for their professional help and support.

This book has been written over a long period of time, and many friends, students, and colleagues contributed both to the process and its completion. I am particularly grateful to those dear friends who have read or listened to parts of my argument in the making: Rey Chow, Yvette Christiansë, Jean Cohen, Siobhán Kilfeather, Karin Ohme, and David Wellbery. Caroline Walker Bynum has been a great source of inspiration and encouragement in holding me to high intellectual standards, even when I was not always able to live up to them. Chris Cullens has been an infinitely kind and patient supporter through all stages of the writing of this book. Rosalind Morris has read the entire manuscript and prevented me from giving up in the bleakest moments. Karen Van Dyck has heard and read many parts of the work in progress while keeping up the pace during a decade of morning runs.

Without Maryam Moshaver's superb editorial support and her willingness to discuss many aspects of the argument at great length, and without Daniel Chiarilli's help as a research assistant, I would not have been able to complete the manuscript. I am grateful to Gerrit Jackson for preparing the index. I finished this book while I was serving as chair of the Department of Germanic Languages and could always trust the organizational talent, wit, and good humor of Bill Dellinger and Peggy Quisenberry.

My parents, Horst and Veronica von Mücke, have invited me to write at their home in the Black Forest many summers and given me the joy of hearing Miriam play happily in the yard while her mother was brooding over her computer. As always, Philippe Similon has provided me with the love, assurance, and sense of perspective during the long years when he took on challenges quite different from a mere book manuscript. It is to him that I dedicate this book in gratitude.

AMAGANSETT, NEW YORK, AUGUST 2002

THE SEDUCTION OF THE OCCULT
AND THE RISE OF THE FANTASTIC TALE

Introduction

At the beginning of the nineteenth century, the fantastic tale emerged as a new literary form in German literary history. E.T.A. Hoffmann, one of the foremost exponents of the genre, published several collections of fantastic tales—exploring a range of attitudes from playful irony to sinister fascination with the occult—that earned him the nickname "Gespenster Hoffmann," associating the author with ghosts and specters. A number of his tales were translated and published in France in the 1830s, at a time when French authors had also begun experimenting with the genre. Whereas in France the fantastic tale remained important well into the nineteenth century, in Germany interest in the fantastic subsided by midcentury, only to resurface between 1890 and 1930 in the literary innovations of modernism. Outside of nineteenth-century German and French literature, one finds significant contributions to the fantastic in Russian and American literature. How can we understand and contextualize the emergence of this new literary form?

The fantastic tale is commonly characterized by either "brutal intrusion of mystery into the order of real life" or the reader's hesitation as to how to make sense of seemingly supernatural occurrences that cannot easily be integrated into a familiar model of reality.[1] Both characterizations imply that the fantastic is a narrative founded upon tension between a strange event and a set of possible explanations for it.[2] On the one hand, the fantastic deploys explanations that invoke a model of reality shared by the reader, of commonly held assumptions about the nature of the material and spiritual world and of what can be perceived and known. On the other hand, the fantastic tale's explanations undermine this same model of reality by invoking mystery, occult knowledge, or laws that encompass the supernatural in a way that contradicts assumptions about the natural world and human knowledge thereof. Yet the explanations within the framework of a fantastic narrative do not offer a countermodel of reality with any degree of certainty; instead, they leave open the crucial question of whether or not the challenge to the normal, generally accepted view of reality might be merely the result of the narrator's or protagonist's madness, intoxication, or deception.

This study does not aim to understand the fantastic tale's ambivalence toward strange, possibly supernatural phenomena in epistemological or cognitive terms. Instead, it seeks to understand the fantastic tale as an implicit aesthetic and poetic program that, though hardly addressed in theoretical texts about the fantastic, nevertheless constitutes an integral element of fantastic fiction itself. One sees this aesthetic program in how these tales frame the encounter with an occult phenomenon: as a shock, a shattering of the protagonist's—and by extension the external reader's—certainty; or as a dangerous, disorienting escape into a virtual world of sensuous delights. In this framing, the fantastic tale thematizes and stages a new relationship between a text and its reader. At stake in this aesthetic and poetic endeavor is not just a challenge to available paradigms for making sense of an otherwise unfamiliar world but also, just as strongly, a challenge to the subjectivity of the narrator or protagonist who is encountering this seemingly strange phenomenon. This ultimately implies, also, another challenge to the subjectivity of the reader. Hence, the generic innovation of the fantastic tale can be understood in light of how it intervenes in the cultural history of reading, by proposing a new relationship between a textual representation and the subjectivity of the reader—one that can be captured in terms of shock and excitement, or as the occasion of a flight or escape into fantasy.

Although I approach the fantastic as an intraliterary phenomenon by looking at how an individual tale dwells on problems of perception, communication, and representation—as well as sensual pleasure, mediation, and mediatization—I also show that this literary innovation, in its striking appeal to supernatural or occult forces that appear to interfere with an intrapsychic economy, can be portrayed as a significant contribution to the history of subjectivity and sexuality. On the one hand, I show how the fantastic tale constructed sexuality as a discursive phenomenon—namely, as the individual's ultimate secret and defining feature—that needed to be confessed, analyzed, and treated. On the other hand, I argue that the fantastic tale participated in crucial interventions in the conceptual history of perversion, which prepared the way for a psychoanalytic understanding of human sexuality. Additionally, I show how the formal and aesthetic innovations of the fantastic tale challenged psychological and psychiatric models of its time and addressed the limitations of a consciousness-centered model of subjectivity and agency that anchors and organizes the individual's relationship to her own sensuality as well as her perceptions of the external world and her affective relationship to others. Undermining both instrumental rationality of the optimization of pleasure or gain and the teleology of self-preservation, the strange psychology of the fantastic tale furthermore questions rationalist assumptions of agency as well as commonly held assumptions about the relationship between cause and effect.

To the extent that the fantastic tale focuses on an individual's problematic relationship to sensual pleasure and the individual's alienated relationship toward desire, it elaborates a model of subjectivity that can best be captured by psychoanalytic accounts of sexuality and the unconscious. It is not the goal of this study, though, to argue that the fantastic tale anticipated psychoanalysis. My primary goal is a detailed analysis of individual fantastic tales in terms of their implicit and explicit aesthetic agenda and in relationship to their contemporary context. This contextualization of the fantastic tale does not proceed by way of demonstrating isomorphisms or parallels between extraliterary discourse on madness, sexuality, and perversion on the one hand, and the generic innovations of the fantastic tale on the other. Rather, I pair two kinds of fantastic tales: those that acquired a prototypical status in developing the genre, and those offering a commentary on the genre—either in terms of poetological reflection or with regard to the historical significance and the cultural context of the fantastic. This book addresses how the fantastic tale thematizes its own position in the cultural history of reading; how it relies on and departs from a Romantic philosophy of language; and how it addresses changing ideals of communication and challenges developing theories of madness and models of power.

Author, Text, Audience, and the Fantastic Encounter

How can we isolate and define the aesthetic and poetic program of the fantastic tale as a new way of staging the relationship between a text and its audience? What is new and modern about the fantastic tale's turn to the mysterious, to the limits of knowledge and rational insight? How can the interest in the occult that marks the fantastic tale be distinguished from other kinds of fascination with the limits of human understanding, such as the marvelous? In an article titled "Wonder," Caroline Walker Bynum describes medieval ways of relating to strange, bizarre, and marvelous phenomena. Taking up areas of twelfth-century culture that range from scientific speculation, theological debate, and popular religiosity to entertainment literature, she analyzes how that period dealt with the extraordinary, the marvelous, the monstrous, and the miraculous, in terms of admiration, joy, dread, and wonder. According to Bynum, the rich and intensified fascination of the twelfth century with the marvelous encouraged, and even cultivated and appreciated, an attitude toward the strange and bizarre that was marked by utter respect for manifestations that challenged and exceeded the limits of the known.[3] Whether the extraordinary appears in the form of an elaborate pastry, a sophisticated automaton, or a werewolf, for the medieval observer wonder is a given, and the marvelous is accepted in its singularity and facticity. By contrast, the fantastic tale of the early nineteenth century constructs an encounter with enigmatic phenomena that elaborates the observer's reaction in terms of a fundamental uncertainty and insecurity.

A relatively little-known essay titled "Über Shakespeare's Behandlung des Wunderbaren" (On Shakespeare's Treatment of the Marvelous), published in 1793 by Ludwig Tieck, addresses the fantastic in terms that are significant to this discussion. A leading German Romantic who wrote some of the first fantastic tales, Tieck conceives the fantastic as coming into focus exactly at a moment in history when the marvelous threatens to have disappeared. Tieck's express objective in writing his essay on Shakespeare is to uncover some of the strategies deployed by the great playwright in leading his audience to accept the marvelous—to learn from the great artist literary techniques for recuperating the marvelous for an increasingly enlightened (and hence skeptical) audience. Thus his essay betrays a distinct concern that for his contemporaries the experience of wonder has become deeply problematic, if not entirely lost.

Tieck observes that to persuade an audience to accept magic and ghosts as real, Shakespeare must first of all prevent an allegorical interpretation of the marvelous. The playwright achieves this by creating psychologically realistic characters who offer the audience an identificatory entry into the diegetic universe of his fiction. Furthermore, he has recourse to the low, the comical, and the grotesque, since the ridiculous is easily grounded in everyday reality, and hence can lend credibility to the fiction:

We would often tend to doubt the terrible if it were not that the comical, individualized features that seem to stem from an ordinary reality force us to believe in it. For our judgment gets so confused that we forget the markers by which we usually judge the truth of something; we don't find anything onto which we might fix our eyes; the soul is suspended in a kind of giddiness in which it finally gives itself over to the illusion since it has lost all markers of truth or error.[4]

In this passage, Tieck does not pursue established arguments from the eighteenth-century poetics of verisimilitude, which would have entailed comparing the poetic representation of reality to an extraliterary, unproblematic reality out there. Instead, he makes the distinction between reality and illusion, between truth and error, dependent on "markers" (*Kennzeichen*) within the text itself. Rather than being immediately or intuitively obvious, whatever is to be taken for reality is mediated by signs.[5] Thus the encounter with an apparently inexplicable phenomenon, as addressed in Tieck's essay, involves complex issues of literary mediation that affect the status of the observer, the narrator, and the narratee, as well as the referential dimension of the literary text.

Tieck argues that use of the marvelous is most successful if the audience not only can see what the characters see but is also able to observe *how* the characters see. Frequently in Shakespeare's plays only select characters can see a ghost, whereas other characters deny the reality of the specter:

Only Macbeth can see Banquo's ghost. Along the same lines, Hamlet's mother cannot see her poisoned husband; she believes that the apparition is born of her son's heated fantasy, and the same belief is shared by Macbeth's friends. Though the spectator finds their belief very natural, the poet places the spectator, so to speak, above this kind of enlightenment: [the spectator] sees [the characters'] disbelief as grounded in their closed eyes which are blind to what [both] Macbeth and the spectator can see.[6]

Thus two constructions of reality, one that allows apparitions and ghosts and one that denies their existence, are played against each other and relativize each other. Insofar as Tieck characterizes disbelief in the supernatural as a form of enlightened blindness to other kinds of reality, he reveals his own poetic agenda: a critique of a narrow and ultimately reductionist view of reality.

Tieck celebrates Shakespeare's ability to make his audience forget the aesthetic conventions and enlightened concepts of its own historical period:

For this is the test of any genuine genius, that he knows to win in advance the audience's suspension of disbelief for the boldest fiction and for the most unusual representation. The poet does not depend on our gullibility but on our fantasy; he manages to engage our fantasy, even against our will, to such an extent that we forget all the conventions of aesthetics together with all the concepts of our enlightened century and give ourselves over to the beautiful madness of the poet.[7]

Tieck's account of successful deployment of the marvelous is exclusively phrased in terms of a dual psychological task: making the audience or reader not only forget and disregard but also reconstitute and relativize the commonly accepted markers of the real. The point of reference and ground for a fixed natural order is no longer the world, but the human psyche observing its own workings as it constructs a reality; not just the human psyche in general but the powers of the productive imagination that Tieck calls fantasy. Ultimately, we marvel at the genius of the poet who can return to us the ability to wonder, to be enchanted while lost in the play of our fantasy.

Tieck's essay on Shakespeare articulates some of the central concerns of the literary movement of European Romanticism, summarizing remarkably what is a point of departure for this study—namely, that the fantastic tale arises as an aesthetic and poetic concern out of a historically specific literary interest in the marvelous. To the historian of literature, this Romanticist program is recognizable not only in Tieck's interest in the marvelous as an antidote to narrow, shallow, predictable, and impoverished constructions of reality but also in the textual model that undergirds the genuine reaction of wonder, the admiration of poetic genius. The textual model developed in Goethe's early lyric poetry and institutionalized as the genius poetics of Romantic authorship—a model crucial to Tieck's discussion of Shakespeare—proposes the text as a self-contained system, the product and expression of a self-constituting subjectivity, of an emphatically original authorial persona.[8]

In the course of his argument, Tieck briefly sidesteps Shakespeare to cite a passage from Jacques Cazotte's prototypical fantastic tale, *Le diable amoureux* (The Devil in Love, 1772–1776). This unexpected move not only entails a switch in the object of analytical interest from drama to narrative fiction; it also significantly alters the set of implicit references to the distinctions that define the unity of a text, and its relationship to audience and author. Tieck cites this passage to illustrate the point that the audience's incredulity is best overcome if the literary work makes use of a mixed semiotic universe that provokes a state of uncertainty as to how to discern the markers of the real from the markers of the imaginary. In contrast to his discussion of Shakespeare, Tieck is not in the least concerned with Cazotte's own narrative techniques and stylistic devices. He appears to quote the passage merely for its descriptive value. Indeed, the cited authority who describes this technique of disorientation is not even a literary critic or poet, but a fictional character from Cazotte's frame narrative. Moreover, the technique of disorientation described by the character is not attributed to human agency or skill in producing an artifact, but to the devil and his expert machinations.

The passage Tieck quotes is from the concluding frame narrative of Cazotte's tale, in which the protagonist, Alvaro, is advised by a doctor how to make sense of his strange adventures:

Having beguiled you, he [the devil] then had to appear to you in all his deformity, and acted like a slave premeditating his revolt; he does not wish to leave you any discernible and clear image of himself, so he mingles the grotesque and the awesome, the absurdity of his luminous snails with the alarming vision of his horrible head, in a word the lie and the truth, dream and reality; thus your confused spirit can no longer make distinctions, and may believe that the vision which has beset you is rather a dream occasioned by the vapours of your brain than the effect of his evil doing.[9]

This passage characterizes an observer's reaction not in terms of wonder but as the ambiguity between the scenario of a deception by a supernatural agent and self-deception. The doctor's urgent advice to young Alvaro to give up his mentalist and psychological frame of reference calls for acceptance of the externality of illusion, and the real, concrete nature of all those machinations that produce perceptual, sensory, and sensuous illusions. Moreover, it means that there is a potentially harmful and evil agency behind these effects, a technician of the imaginary who cannot be grasped because he, she, or it does not inhabit the world as we know it. The complex set of illusions that fundamentally disorient the observer have the status of a simulation. It is an illusionary or empty image to the extent that it does not mean, express, or represent anything, yet it is real insofar as the image is caused by external mechanisms that produce powerful effects. Despite the potential for deceptiveness, this simulation nevertheless constitutes a sensuously overwhelming experience.

For Tieck, the fantastic occurs as a transitional stage, in which disorientation of the audience, the reader, or the observer is caused by confrontation with a mixed semiotic universe, one that destabilizes the markers of what is real and what is imaginary. The fantastic calls into question either the observer's sanity and reliability or else the basic parameters of what would have to be taken for reality. Yet the fantastic, as a category defining a distinct group of texts, has not quite emerged for Tieck. The textual model crucial to Tieck's discussion of Shakespeare does not sustain the fundamental uncertainty of the audience since it frames the text in terms of Shakespeare's oeuvre, thus ultimately casting it as the product or expression of an originary authorial persona. Thus the focus on the fundamental uncertainty of the observer, and with it a rudimentary poetics of the fantastic, is embedded in a poetics of the marvelous from which it nonetheless departs decisively.

Tieck's discussion of the fantastic as a strategy of the reader's or audience's fundamental disorientation brings us fairly close to Todorov's by-now-classic characterization of the fantastic. I have shown how in Tieck's argument the focus on the fantastic entailed momentary suspension of his concern with Shakespeare's oeuvre and genius. Todorov as well points out that the fantastic has to prevent a reading that treats the text as a poetic system:

> First, the text must oblige the reader to consider the world of the characters as a world of living persons and to hesitate between a natural and a supernatural explanation of the events described. Second, this hesitation may also be experienced by a character; thus the reader's role is so to speak entrusted to a character, and at the same time the hesitation is represented, it becomes one of the themes of the work—in the case of naïve reading, the actual reader identifies himself with the character. Third, the reader must adopt a certain attitude with regard to the text: he will reject allegorical as well as 'poetic' interpretations.[10]

Todorov states quite clearly that the fantastic elicits a naïve, identificatory reading process that the external reader is to be invited into the diegetic universe as if it were her own world. Furthermore, he argues that as the fictional character's attitude toward her experience becomes an issue of doubt, and as this doubt is thematized, the fantastic fiction recasts and problematizes the reader's identificatory relationship toward the text by refusing to provide a stable system of references. This instability prevents the reader from demarcating the first naïve reading as a purely textual experience; hence it also prevents her from taking a distance from the disturbing experience by recasting it into a process of allegorical translation of textual clues, or by focusing on specific poetic devices that could be tied to an external authorial function. When Tieck departs from analysis of Shakespeare's dramatic techniques and quotes a fictional character from Cazotte's frame narrative, he actually performs what Todorov describes as the fantastic tale's decisive model of a text-audience relationship. Yet Tieck's "staging" of a new relationship by way of Cazotte differs from Todorov's formulation of the boundary conditions of the fantastic by casting it in terms of a dangerous erotics. It is Cazotte's model of satanic seduction that must be pursued if we want to understand the emergence of this facet of the fantastic tale's aesthetic and poetic program.

The History of Reading Cultures and the History of Sexuality

Tieck's essay enables us to situate a radically destabilized observer position within the context of the Romanticist effort to reenchant the world. Moreover, the key distinctions that set the fantastic apart from the overarching Romanticist project are clearly outlined. We have seen how Tieck's quote from the tale by Cazotte illustrates the bewildering, disorienting status of illusion as a complex semiotic construct that can be characterized as a media-technological effect, an external image or simulacrum that stands out in terms of its overwhelming sensory and sensual impact on the observer. Quite apart from the former's observations, Cazotte's tale in its own right touches on numerous other key issues that justify its status as a prototypical tale. In its decisive refusal of a purely mentalist, psychological explanation of a state of illusion, the few lines quoted above from Cazotte's tale mark the devil's apparition as part of a scenario of simulation and seduction that can be spelled out in terms of both its media technological context and its position vis-à-vis the history of sexuality.

Cazotte's framing of an encounter with the devil echoes the apparition of the devil in the German and English *Faustbooks*. Already in these texts, dating from the late sixteenth century, the devil appears at the moment when the avid reader and scholar Faust is most intensely absorbed in the virtual reality of print culture. The devil takes Faust onto a flight of fancy as he presents to him the illusion of being a pure spirit who can instantly travel through time and space to exotic sites of sensory delight. In other words, the experience of the supernatural and the sensory delights of the devil's magic can be read as a reflection on the temptations and cultural effects of what was then still the new print technology. In the *Faustbooks*, just as in *The Devil in Love*, the devil appears as a technician of the imaginary. However, in Cazotte's tale the devil is erotically charged—an alluring simulation, an object of desire and fear, and a desiring subject. Here it is not the novelty and temptations of print culture per se that are addressed by the scenario of satanic seduction, but the private, absorbed, identificatory reading of fiction that had become the dominant mode of escaping into virtual sensuality.[11]

In Cazotte's fantastic tale, the scenario of satanic seduction, with its mysterious erotic charge, is not merely the framing of the fantastic tale vis-à-vis the escape into the virtual delights of printed fiction. If the protagonist's hesitation to dismiss his experience as illusory is the result of having been seduced by some mysterious devil, he is no longer merely passively registering external phenomena; nor is he arbitrarily constructing his own world. Instead, it is his status as a subject and object of desire that is foregrounded. Cazotte casts Alvaro's adventures into the frame of satanic seduction; the young man is not just a passive victim of an external illusion or deception but framed as a subject who has responded to the lures of the devil, and who in turn has desired something from the devil. Thus the scenario of satanic seduction transforms the observer's uncertainty from a cognitive or epistemological problem into a moral or psychological one, as he negotiates a mysterious want or desire, for an unknown, evil, but alluring Other. This aspect of the observer's uncertainty is further elaborated in the conclusion of the tale, when the doctor advises the disconcerted protagonist that the only cure for his frightful experience and state of uncertainty can be found in his marriage to a nice girl.[12] The doctor's diagnosis of Alvaro's experience therefore appears to be one of a perverse desire in need of normalization.

For the longest time, perversion—an individual's unnatural behavior or desire—has been considered in a moral and theological tradition as an expression of humankind's fallen state and a marker of volition, the freedom to turn away from the love of God. Even within a secular context, in the philosophical anthropology of Herder and Kant in the late eighteenth century, we can find a model of human freedom that is informed by this tradition. Whereas for Kant or Herder animals are bound to their respective environments in terms of instinctually regulated response, human beings are deprived of instinctual guidance and marked by radical openness to the world of the senses. This openness means that there is no natural, predetermined, instinctually regulated need directing mankind's perception of and interaction with the world; humans have to constitute this world through language and culture in the first place.[13] Kant's interpretation of the story of the fall is one of humanity breaking away from instinct or the voice of nature. According to Kant, eating the fruit from the forbidden tree of knowledge originated from Eve's desire for something that her luxurious imagination made attractive to her. On the basis of this first and fatal action, the development of human reason, freedom, and history became possible.[14]

Only in the late eighteenth century did what was then the emerging medical subspecialty of psychiatry begin to displace the predominance of the moral register through its approach to madness as a mental illness.[15] Although by the end of the eighteenth century madness was beginning to be considered and treated as a disease, the forms of mental aberration on which early psychiatry focused were not related to the patient's sexual behavior, erotic object choices, or modes of desiring.

The moralizing view of perversion changed only by midcentury. A medical dictionary from 1842 defines perversion as "one of the four modifications of function in disease: the three others being augmentation, diminution, and abolition." By way of connecting perversion to the notion of function, this definition implies that the pathological disturbance consists in turning away from a naturally given end or purpose. Specifically, sexual perversion implies that there is a well-defined human need for sex that has its appropriate means of being satisfied.[16] This medicalization of sexual practice had decisive implications. As long as sexual behavior was strictly considered a matter of choice, it could be judged in moral terms (and even be legislated). By the end of the nineteenth century, the Viennese professor of psychiatry Richard von Krafft-Ebing (1840–1902), author of the famous *Psychopathia sexualis* (1886) and of works in the field of forensic psychiatry, wrote a short essay advocating decriminalization of homosexuality. In it he argues that homosexuality should be considered a degenerative neurotic disease, or, as he adds in parentheses, a perversion but not a vice or perversity, as another parenthetic comment explains.[17] Krafft-Ebing's distinction between perversion as disease and perversity as lewd behavior works with and transforms this new medicalized concept of perversion as a diseased basic function, which he defines as an individual's disturbed mode of desiring that does not necessarily need to result in specific action. What is new in Krafft-Ebing's take on perversion is that he models a mode of desiring not just as an individualizing principle but also in view of a principle of latency.[18]

With regard to the psychiatric discourse on perversion, Freud's *Three Essays on the Theory of Sexuality* was a groundbreaking intervention, making the case that the dividing line between the normal and the pathological is arbitrary, and most of all an issue of convention.[19] By the end of the collection's first essay, on perversion, Freud has not only dissolved the sharp distinction between the normal and the pathological but cast an even more fundamental doubt on the concept of what is considered normal. He has shown that many supposedly perverse features of sexual behavior are constitutive elements of what would usually be called normal sexual behavior. This leads him to the conclusion that there is no such thing as one unified, normal, and natural sex drive. Rather, this supposedly normal sex drive is made up of many elements. Neither the object nor the aim, and not even the nature of pleasure, can ultimately be fixed. Once he has thoroughly deconstructed the evolutionary teleological model of a healthy, quasi-instinctual sex drive, he asks how a sex drive should be thought of differently. Rather than seeking a model for development of the sex drive in the prehistory of the species and some evolutionary master plot, Freud turns to the beginnings of the individual's history. Examining this phase of human life leads him to argue that so-called perversion is not a sign of degeneration but an anthropological constant. What is more, in his essay on the sexuality of children, he shows that so-called perversion is in fact the very essence of all of human sexuality: if there is such a thing as the human sex drive it is radically perverse, insofar as it has neither a definite aim nor a definite object. According to Freud, human sexuality is both radically perverse and always in need of normalization.

This sketch of the history of perversion merely captures one aspect of the complex history of sexuality to the extent that it indicates a conceptual trajectory, away from a moral approach to behavior that was considered unnatural toward pathologization of perversion in terms of a dysfunctional drive, and finally to dissolution of the guiding distinctions between the natural and the perverse in the psychoanalytical concept of human sexuality as polymorphously perverse and subject to a complex process of both normalizing and potentially pathological transformations. In my summary, I have merely highlighted two decisive interventions in the history of sexuality in nineteenth- and early-twentieth-century psychiatry; the history of sexuality is far more complex than that, involving many more discursive practices. As a nineteenth-century construct, it plays a crucial part in the sciences of mankind, the policing of families, and the hermeneutics of the individual.[20] Against the assumption that the nineteenth century was marked by general repression of anything related to sexuality, by pervasive Victorian prudishness, Michel Foucault has argued that it was precisely during this period that human sexuality was produced as a modern, discursive phenomenon—

that is, as the secret principle by which an individual organizes pleasures of the flesh and fantasies thereof. This study proposes to examine the role of fantastic literature in shaping the concept of subjectivity on the basis of a generalized notion of sexuality as perversion.

My central thesis for the study of the emergence of the fantastic tale is that this kind of literature can be contextualized in terms of the history of sexuality and individuality as well as narrative short fiction's exploration of an aesthetics of intensity and shock resulting from its own media-historical position. Thus I analyze how the fantastic tale participates in the growing relevance that is given to an individual's secrets and the speech genres of the confession on the one hand, and the poetic and aesthetic deployment of latency, mystery, and shock on the other. In other words, this book investigates how the literature of the fantastic played a crucial role in negotiating conflicting models of subjectivity within the context of nineteenth-century notions of the normal and the pathological, the free and the instinctually (or "naturally") driven. Thus the study of fantastic literature can produce insight into a genealogy of the model of subjectivity that has been theorized only with the aid of the psychoanalytical notion of sexuality and the unconscious.[21]

Contextualizing the Fantastic

Being based on a characterization of the fantastic tale as the narrative elaboration of a mode of uncertainty vis-à-vis a seemingly supernatural event, most attempts to understand the historically specific phases of its occurrence have primarily sought to situate the fantastic tale in relation to other, extraliterary challenges to commonly accepted models of reality. Pierre George Castex's classic study of the fantastic tale in France contextualizes the emergence and endurance of the fantastic primarily in view of interest and knowledge on the part of occultist writers and practitioners who were then popular. Equally, a study by Marianne Wünsch argues that in German literary history the fantastic tale flourishes whenever the general cultural climate is open to occultist theories, which also call into question our basic assumptions about the nature of the material and spiritual world, the conditions of their interaction, and the extent and limits of human knowledge thereof. By contrast, Tzvetan Todorov concludes his structuralist approach to the genre with the statement that the fantastic has an inherently transgressive character; it relies on breaking down distinction and opposition, it thematizes concerns that are otherwise censored in the larger cultural context, and ultimately it must be viewed as an expression of the literariness of literature. Todorov also compares the fantastic to psychoanalysis and argues that the arrival of the latter has made the former obsolete in its historically specific function.[22]

The argument in all these studies moves from defining the generically decisive feature that identifies an individual literary text as a fantastic tale or fantastic novel to discussing the fantastic as comprising a certain body of texts, a cluster or series that constitutes some kind of unity for which they seek to find a historically specific context, or a set of more general cultural conditions that explain the specific emergence or disappearance of this literary genre. Whereas Castex discusses the fantastic in view of the chronological development of individual authors' literary careers and the lines of influence and exposure of these writers to each other and to occultist theories and practices, Wünsch argues that the majority of early modernist fantastic texts are unified in their adherence to a more or less coherent spiritist, occultist worldview, a syncretist system combining elements from a range of available contemporary occultist sources. Thus, according to Wünsch's analysis, the relationship between extraliterary occultist theory and practice and its use in fantastic literature is not one of an easy parallelism or isomorphism; she portrays the body of fantastic texts as the distillation of a common occultist worldview that, beyond this literary formation, does not exist as a coherent discourse.

Other book-length studies of the fantastic construct a literary corpus to which is attributed a historically specific function, which can be discussed and criticized in terms of a specific ideological agenda. Tobin Siebers situates the romantic fantastic in the intellectual context of Romanticism's rebellion against rationalism and the Enlightenment. He portrays the romantic fantastic as a sentimental return to superstition culminating in condoning victimization and social violence.[23] By contrast, Rosemary Jackson attributes to the fantastic a liberatory, subversive function insofar as she detects in it "a desire for something excluded from cultural order—more specifically, for all that is in opposition to the capitalist and patriarchal order which has been dominant in Western society over the last two centuries."[24] José B. Monléon, however, argues that "the exposition of the repressed is not necessarily a subversive act, if by subversion is meant a challenge to the causes of repression, a defiance of order, an assault on dominant ideology . . . the fantastic played exactly the opposite role: that is, the defense of the status quo and the preservation of economic order."²⁵ In contrast to these approaches, however, I demonstrate that the fantastic cannot be subsumed under one ideological umbrella.

Deborah Harter's approach to fantastic narrative as engagement with the poetics of the fragment is a notable exception in this series of books attempting to historicize the fantastic by way of inscribing it within a more or less unified ideological agenda. She conceives of the fantastic narrative as a complementary aesthetic and poetic program in the overall nineteenth-century literary concern with realism: "The dream of material completeness that often defies yet fundamentally defines the realist enterprise is countered here [in the fantastic narrative] by a seeming delight in reproducing reality in its 'pieces,' where even the human body succumbs to morselization."²⁶ Thus Harter's study, like my own, focuses on the fantastic's particular staging and engagement with a text-audience relationship, which, according to her focus on and selection of fantastic tales from the mid- and late-nineteenth century, can be characterized by the thematics of the fragmented human body, a fantasy that is related in complex fashion to the ideal of the unified subject in that it both supports and subverts it.²⁷

This book differs decisively from the majority of full-length studies of the fantastic. Instead of taking a sudden leap from the isolation of the generically distinctive features of the fantastic to conceiving of it as a homogenized entity whose social, or ideological, function could then be historically contextualized, this book puts more emphasis on how the fantastic arises as an aesthetic and poetic program at the time of its first emergence, spanning the period from Cazotte's *The Devil in Love*, to the publication of fantastic tales by German Romantics, and the French rediscovery of Cazotte and their further development of the genre in the 1830s and 1840s. This study does not present its argument through analysis of isolated themes or narrative devices but instead proceeds by analyzing entire fantastic tales: How is the relationship between a text and its audience staged? How is the reader's identificatory relationship to the fiction shaped and thematized? The insight that can be gained from reading individual fantastic tales in their entirety consists in a more nuanced understanding of how the fantastic tale participates and intervenes in a larger aesthetic and poetic agenda by addressing such questions as the nature of art and representation, the role and function of the artist, the nature of pleasure and entertainment, and the role of the reader. The goal of this book is not to revise what has become the corpus or canon of fantastic tales, but rather to focus on one segment of this corpus (from the early nineteenth century) and analyze a group of fantastic tales in terms of their relationship of congruence and divergence as well as commentary. It is in this last function—commentary on the fantastic as an aesthetic and poetic project—that I will leave the focus on German and French tales and bring in two texts by Edgar Allan Poe.

Although this book denies a unifying ideological agenda to the fantastic tale, it nevertheless argues that this literary innovation participated in producing a subjectivity that is intricately embedded in the history of sexuality. My study is primarily organized not as a chronological argument but in terms of those systematic and thematic aspects that allow discussion of key fantastic texts within the emergence of nineteenth-century sexuality. However, I do propose an overarching trajectory for the emergence of the fantastic tale within nineteenth-century literary history. I argue that the fantastic tale arises at the limits of the culture of sensibility, at a moment in the cultural history of communication when a relationship of similarity and perfect openness and frankness is no longer considered the unquestioned basis of a friendship or love relationship, but when the other's opacity and potentially dark secrets become attractive, seductive, and fascinating.[28] I then show that once the fantastic has been established as a literary form (and even a fashion) of its own, it can be framed within a growing consumerist, journalistic interest in escapist fiction, which defies any alignment of art's function with a pedagogical, didactic, or moral agenda. It is in this context that the function of the artist as a powerful technician of the imaginary, as well as the thematization of the mediatization of the world of the senses becomes a guiding concern for the fantastic tale. I conclude my study by analyzing the fantastic tale's relationship to its own position in history, how it uses its own generic conventions to engage with the nineteenth-century reorganization of the past.

Chapter One, "The Fantastic in the Cultural History of Reading," pairs an analysis of Cazotte's prototypical tale *The Devil in Love* with E.T.A. Hoffmann's retelling of this tale in the context of the Napoleonic Wars. Chapter Two, "The Aesthetics of Shock and the Poetics of the Perverse," deals with Tieck's "Der blonde Eckbert" and "Liebeszauber" in relationship to models and ideals of language, subjectivity, and communication as they are addressed in the frame narrative of Tieck's collection *Phantasus*, and also as they are addressed by the subversive, antipsychiatric, discursive performance of Poe's "Imp of the Perverse."

Chapter Three, "The Power of the Artist," focuses exclusively on texts by E.T.A. Hoffmann. First, I analyze a legal document that Hoffmann wrote in his function as the judge of an appeals court charged with evaluating an insanity defense case. Then I show how his prototypical detective story, "Das Fräulein von Scuderi," addresses the limits of the traditional juridico-discursive system in view of the changing role and function of the artist. Finally, I focus on his "Die Automate," a tale that examines the artwork-audience interaction as the product of the artist as a powerful and sinister technician of the imaginary.

Whereas Chapter Three concerns itself primarily with models for the role and function of the artist, Chapter Four, "Artificial Paradise and the Medial Woman," returns to the question of the fantastic tale's reflection on its relationship to models of artistic and technological mediation. I analyze tales that focus on a specific artistic medium in its relationship to the human body: the mad visionary who believes he has survived his own death (Hoffmann's tale about Serapion), the sinister musician who confounds the body of a violin with the voice of his beloved daughter (Hoffmann's "Rat Krespel"), and the provincial monk who escapes into the virtual world of a Venetian nobleman's extravagant lifestyle with the aid of a vampire (Théophile Gautier's "La morte amoureuse"). I conclude the chapter with an analysis of Edgar Allen Poe's "Ligeia," a tale that spells out the connection between the vision of otherworldly bliss and plenitude and the reanimated corpse of the beloved woman as the concretization of the imaginary materiality of the signifier.

For the final chapter of the book, "Fantastic Encounters with the Marvels of History," I have selected Achim von Arnim's "Isabella von Ägypten" and Prosper Mérimée's "La Vénus d'Ille", two tales that each portray an inexplicable, occult event as an intrusion into an otherwise "realistic" diegetic universe and that contrast this fantastic dimension with the referential dimension of historical documents or archeological finds. My analysis of these two stories shows how the fascination with the occult specific to the fantastic tale is not at all some nostalgic construction of a lost era that still knew marvels and wonder but—if these stories are read as historical self-portraits—an elaboration on the nonsynchronicity and heterogeneity of the modern era.

1

The Fantastic in the Cultural History of Reading

Cazotte's *Le diable amoureux* and Hoffmann's "Der Elementargeist"

Although Jacques Cazotte's *Le diable amoureux* (The Devil in Love) had little literary impact at the time of publication, retroactively the story was considered the generic prototype for French and German fantastic tales.[1] A quick glance at some of the reactions to Cazotte's novella from the time of its publication, however, reveals the spectrum of textual models that were applied to this tale before it became firmly associated with a corpus of fantastic tales. Cazotte's own contemporaries praised *The Devil in Love* as a *badinage ingénieux* (ingenuous banter) and emphasized its *gaieté* (lightheartedness), associating the work with the tradition of light entertainment literature that was cultivated by the playful *conte de fée* (fairy tale) and the more erotically charged *conte oriental* (oriental tale).[2] By contrast, the French Romantics would later approach the text in the hope of uncovering in it clues to occult secret societies and practices (and to the author's personality). This direction in the reception history of Cazotte's novella was initiated by Gérard de Nerval's edition of *The Devil in Love* in 1845. Nerval's edition foregrounded an interest in Cazotte as a man, detailing his eventual conversion to Martinism (despite his rejection of the revolutionary agenda of the *illuminati*) and his abiding loyalty to the king, which led him to the guillotine in 1792.[3]

In his book-length study, Dietmar Rieger argues that although the author was indeed well-versed in the gallant entertainment genres of his time, Cazotte's contemporaries ignored the moral interest of the story that extends beyond the fairy tale's simple code of good versus evil, and the story's psychological realism, which was much closer to the eighteenth-century novel than to the stereotypical characters of the fairy-tale tradition. Rieger concludes that *The Devil in Love* must be read as an antiphilosophical *conte morale* (moral tale), one that, far from aiming at the dissemination of Enlightenment ideas, in fact warns the reader against dangerous innovation and change, advising him to hold on to the stability of the *ancien régime*. Rieger attributes the fact that Cazotte's contemporaries as well as his nineteenth-century critics did not pursue the moral message of the story to the story's psychological realism and its ability to make the reader identify with the fictional universe.[4] This conclusion, however, disregards the psychological realism of an Enlightenment tradition, developed in the wake of the *conte morale*, that posits the human observer as the final authority for the distinction between what is real and what is illusion. It can, on the contrary, be shown that Cazotte's text invokes and marks this psychological realism as a set of conventions for constructing a reality that has no more authority or claim to certainty than one encompassing supernatural forces.

In the afterword to the second and revised edition of 1776, Cazotte refers to his novella as

An allegory, where the principles are in conflict with the passions: the soul is the battlefield; curiosity initiates action, the allegory is twofold, and the readers can perceive this with ease.

We will not pursue this explication further. One remembers how at age 25, while leafing through an edition of Tasso's complete works, one happened upon a volume that contained nothing but the explanations of the allegories of *Jerusalem Delivered*. One was careful not to open the book. One was passionately in love with Armida, Herminia, and Clorinda; and would lose the all-too-agreeable chimeras if these princesses were reduced to the status of simple emblems.[5]

Cazotte brackets the allegorical dimension and, casting himself into the role of the reader, characterizes the desire for a psychologically realistic fiction as an erotic longing, as the desire to be in love with charming chimeras. He draws attention to the reader's desire to escape from the restraints of reality and invites his reader to follow the fictional protagonist's path of seduction. Yet we must take into account that in Cazotte's own tale the seductively alluring chimera is not, as in Tasso, just a beautiful fiction of an idealized feminine subject, but a deception, an intoxicating illusion produced by a devil.

The object of the protagonist's erotic longing with which Cazotte invites the reader to identify therefore appears as deeply problematic and threatens to undermine the basic distinctions that support what would be considered a normal psychology.

The argument of this chapter proceeds in two steps. First, I focus on the fantastic tale's decisive generic feature, its elaboration of a fundamental doubt or hesitation in both the protagonist and reader. I trace this innovation in Cazotte's *The Devil in Love* as the staging of a new text-audience relationship that is framed as a seduction by a mysterious other. This phase of my argument shows how Cazotte's tale departs from a "normal" or "typical" love story, how it problematizes and thematizes both the object of the protagonist's longing and the aim of his engagement with his strange lover as it details the protagonist's (and by extension the reader's) departure from a world of psychological normalcy. I then turn to E.T.A. Hoffmann's retelling of Cazotte's *The Devil in Love* in his fantastic tale "Der Elementargeist" (The Elementary Spirit, published in 1821), which both contextualizes the new text-audience relationship in the cultural history of reading and activates the model of the seduction by a mysterious other in its own plot. Finally, I show how Hoffmann's fantastic tale about his protagonist's interpellation by Cazotte's fantastic tale is framed as an aesthetic and poetic agenda that addresses a particular phase in the history of sexuality and male subjectivity—namely, the moment when bachelorhood became a historically viable option.

The Devil in Love

The plot of Cazotte's tale can be briefly summarized as follows.

Alvaro, the young narrator, is a Spanish captain in the king's guard at Naples. One evening, as he sits drinking in a tavern in the company of friends and strangers, the conversation turns to the Cabbala and cabbalists. By evening's end, an old man, Soberano by name, proposes to initiate him to the world of supernatural spirits. A few nights later, Alvaro, together with Soberano and two of his friends, heads to the ruins of Portici, where Soberano, after drawing a magic circle around Alvaro, gives him an incantation with which to call Beelzebub. Despite Alvaro's skepticism, the incantation produces an apparition. A huge camel's head, bathed in light, appears and confronts him with a question: "Che vuoi?" In an effort to master his discomfiture, Alvaro commands the apparition to take the shape of a spaniel, which the phantom readily obeys. Alvaro then orders an elaborate dinner, during which the phantom reappears, first as an elegant page, then as a beautiful singer, and finally as Biondetta, who insists on remaining in Alvaro's service.

Alvaro and Biondetta leave for Venice, where he takes up gambling. Biondetta saves him from his gambling debts by showing him an infallible system of winning. He distracts himself with an affair with the courtesan Olympia, who, overwhelmed by jealousy when she discovers Alvaro's ties with Biondetta, attempts to have her rival stabbed to death. Attending to the injured and convalescent Biondetta, Alvaro is overcome with tenderness and remorse; he promises to marry her, though he refuses to consummate their relationship before the official ceremony. When Biondetta tries to seduce him, he flees her and embarks on a journey to Spain, ostensibly to obtain his mother's consent to his intended marriage. Biondetta, however, catches up with him and attempts to seduce him in a barn, where they have taken refuge from a thunderstorm. She finally succeeds when their carriage breaks down in a village, not far from the estate of Alvaro's mother, where they find only a single vacant room to spend the night. As Alvaro surrenders at last to Biondetta's charms, she invites him to call her by her real name, Beelzebub. At the mention of this name, Alvaro's senses are overwhelmed by the visual and aural phenomena of the fateful night of the incantation at the ruins of Portici, and he loses consciousness. Biondetta is gone when he comes to his senses. His mother, upon hearing his story, summons a doctor from Salamanca, who assures Alvaro that he will be cured of this devilish apparition as soon as he marries a nice woman. However, the doctor also insists that Alvaro would be utterly mistaken if he were to believe that his experience with the devil was a mere hallucination.

The story can be divided into two halves. In the first part, the phantom tries to make Alvaro fall in love with him/her by fulfilling all his wishes and by making himself/herself indispensable. For most of the second part, Biondetta tries to seduce Alvaro into consummating their relationship. Whereas the first part of the story focuses on the protagonist's problematic relationship with his lover as an object of love, the second part concentrates on the problematic aim of the union between the two.

At the center of the story is not just uncertainty as to whether Biondetta is a dream woman, entirely a figment of Alvaro's imagination, or a real devil who can assume whatever shape pleases him; there is an equally strong fascination with the devil's own desire—as the story's title, *The Devil in*

Love, clearly indicates. Furthermore, the final frame narrative, which concludes with the doctor's advice for Alvaro to marry, highlights an even more problematic desire, for the doctor does not explain Alvaro's state as the result of a natural, instinctual longing for sexual gratification, but as the real effect of his seduction by the devil. The doctor's proposed cure for Alvaro's condition, that of a healthy and normal marital life, is not based on a natural, instinctual model of sexuality but is offered as cure and correction of a perverse desire. Indeed, the doctor insists on the devil's facticity and reality as something urgently to be reckoned with, for Alvaro is master neither of his fantasy nor of his desires—both have been produced for him by the external agency of the devil. This perverse sexuality to which Alvaro has fallen victim is thus produced by the intertwining of the order of knowledge, represented by Soberano, and the order of desire, represented by the devil.

If seduction is the overall goal in this story's narrative program, it is not simply the seduction of the protagonist by a woman/devil that would culminate straightforwardly in an erotic encounter; rather, the trajectory of seduction that this text proposes needs to be understood in its departure from a traditional erotic program. In the first place, Alvaro plays the passive part that is traditionally coded as feminine; he is in the position of the beloved whose resistance must be overcome. The lover, or devil, makes the confusion of gender roles even more complex as he shifts from a male to a female sexual identity, using femininity as a lure for the purposes of seduction. Once Alvaro has fallen in love, however, the lover is referred to with exclusively feminine pronouns and articles, except for the final scene in which she/he reveals her/his true identity as a masculine devil. In the second place, the obstacle to the union of the lovers is entirely on the side of Alvaro. His resistance is first made to be the result of his uncertainty about Biondetta's identity; then it is tied to his fear of losing his own identity. The two stages of his resistance and attraction to the devil, however, might be two sides of the same coin, the result of Alvaro's interpellation as a subject of an alienated desire, his response to the frightening question bellowed by the camel head, "Che vuoi?"

"Che Vuoi?"

In the beginning of the story, the initiation into occult knowledge is announced as a test of the protagonist's bravery. Alvaro is told that if he can control his anxiety he shall command the world of the spirits, and in the darkness of night among the ruins of Portici he summons the devil exactly as instructed by Soberano and the initiates:

A flood of light more dazzling than that of day pours in through the opening; a camel's head, as hideous in size as in shape, appears at the window; the ears in particular were disproportionately large. The odious phantom opens its muzzle and, in tones fitting with the rest of the apparition, answers me: "Che vuoi?"
All the surrounding caves and vaults echoed back the terrible "Che vuoi?"
I wouldn't know how to describe my situation; I wouldn't know what upheld my courage and prevented me from falling into a faint at that sight [à l'aspect de ce tableau] and at the even more dreadful sound which echoed in my ears.
I felt the need to rally my forces; a cold sweat was threatening to dissipate them; I steadied myself. The soul must indeed be many-mansioned and prodigiously resilient; a multitude of feelings, ideas and reflections touch my heart and pass through my mind and make their impression all at once.
The revolution is achieved, I master my terror. I fixate the spectre boldly.
"What do you mean, oh brazen one, by appearing in this hideous guise?"
(English translation, slightly altered, 34–35; French, 59)

As Alvaro recounts the events of his initiation, the past-tense narrative abruptly shifts to a dramatic present; the first person narrator depicts the sudden and strange apparition, with its overwhelming effect of sensory overstimulation, as an unassimilated mass of visual and aural data. He returns to the past tense only to capture the apparition's voice echoing in the cave, and later to describe his sensation of breaking out in sweat. Moving into the subjunctive to express his inability to describe, understand, or even manage his confusion, he then branches out (in an atemporal present) into a universalizing aside about the marvelous capacities of the human soul. A renewed onslaught of internal perceptions and reflections returns him to the dramatic present. Through these temporal distinctions, the observer position of the protagonist and narrator is fragmented and splintered: as the master of ceremonies in a conjuration scene he is addressed by a phantom and responds to this address; as the principal character in the narrative he perceives his environment and reacts to his observations; as narrator he tries to articulate and communicate a past experience; and finally as speaker he speculates about the make-up of the human soul and the prodigious resilience it must command for processing and managing this kind of frightening encounter.

The detailed present tense description of the narrator's subjective reactions invokes the conventions of psychological realism typical of the epistolary novel of the eighteenth-century culture of sensibility. Yet whereas that genre operates with a model of sensations and feelings that are eminently representable and communicable from person to person in all their precision and nuances, here the human soul appears as an unfathomable spatial structure in which echoes rebound and in whose vastness a flood of images circulate. This model of the human soul's interior spaces mirrors the description of the external scene of the dark vaults, cavities, and ruins of Portici, where the strange encounter with the devil takes place. Thus the distinction between internal and external perceptions is radically suspended not only for the protagonist within the diegetic universe of the tale but also for the reader in his attempt to recreate the narrated observations in terms of aural and visual hallucination.

The description of Alvaro's initiation into occult knowledge must be not only viewed in terms of its elaboration of a complex observer position but also analyzed along the lines of a dramatic exchange. A character calls "Beelzebub," and in response a hideous camel head bathed in light appears at a window and shouts "Che vuoi?" to which the character, after he has overcome his initial shock, replies: "What do you mean, oh brazen one, by appearing in this hideous guise?" This exchange of phrases can be described as a mutual calling or hailing in which the apparition of the one who is called fundamentally and aggressively questions the caller's identity and legitimacy. The irony of this scene of initiation into secret knowledge is evident insofar as the neophyte does not acquire knowledge or insight at all; instead, he is overwhelmed by the appearance of something he does not understand. Despite its potentially comic overtones, the scene culminating in the camel head's "Che vuoi?"—echoed both externally by the vaults and cavities of the ruins and internally by the frightened Alvaro—must also be read in terms of its elaboration of an affective register of fundamental shock and anxiety. Through these repetitions the simple question "What do you want?" ricochets back and forth, producing more questions: What do you demand from me? What do you really want by calling me? What are you lacking that I am supposed to give you? Who are you to command something from me?

The protagonist manages to control his fear and master the situation only by rephrasing the echo and readdressing it to the apparition. His courage, however, is the audacity of an impostor who, having overcome the initial shock that his incomprehending articulation of a magical summons has nevertheless produced an effect, follows this up with a lengthy sequence of commands. Fantasy and enjoyment are his dominant concern as soon as he has staved off his anxiety and taken up his position of impostor, confident that all of his demands will be obeyed and all of his wishes will materialize.

The events that immediately follow the incantation scene pursue exactly this performative model of magical thinking, attributing to mere thoughts or words the power to create an external material reality. Alvaro commands the camel head to appear in the shape of a spaniel, and his wish is immediately executed: "My confidence had soared to the point of audacity: I leave the circle, I hold out my foot, the dog licks it; I make a gesture to pull its ears, and it rolls over on to its back as though to ask forgiveness. I saw that it was a little bitch" (English translation, slightly altered, 36; French, 60). Then Alvaro orders an elaborate banquet from the dog, who reappears as an elegant page. During the banquet, he commands the page to furnish entertainment for him and his friends. The page reappears in the shape of a beautiful singer. Indeed, all of Alvaro's orders are executed "more promptly than a scene being changed at the Opera. The walls of the vault, previously black, dank and moss-covered, took on a gentle hue, a pleasing form: we were now in a hall of mottled marble, roofed with a semi-circular arch supported by columns. Eight crystal girandoles, each with three candles, cast a bright even light" (36; 62).

The effect of this instant realization of all wishes is what one might call with Freud *Realitätsverlust*, the sense that what poses as reality no longer seems real. What Alvaro observes loses the character of external reality. Even so, this passage does not present events as merely imagined or hallucinated. Apart from making the events appear as the instant realization of Alvaro's private wishes, the passage also emphasizes the theatrical technologies the devil has at his disposal (floodlights, a turning stage). In view of all the theatricality and artificiality in the scene, the illusionary aspects of the camel's head and the spaniel, the palace and the banquet, and the handsome page with his subsequent transformation into a charming woman singer are not discarded as an individual's mental imagining but are marked as illusions that have real, material existence.

Finally, the phantasmatic scene issuing from the initial incantation of the devil must also be analyzed as an apotropaic gesture. The sequence of Alvaro's extravagant wishes, with their instant realization, is supposed to hold an utterly frightening apparition at bay and control the frightening echo of the "Che vuoi?" The camel head per se does not mean anything; we can read it, though, as it appears in the series of other apparitions by which it is replaced, a series in which the persistent feature is the alternation between male and female: Camel head—female spaniel, male page—female singer—male/female page. First in this series is the little dog, which Alvaro requested as a more pleasing substitute; the isolated, cut-off body part of the camel is replaced by the whole body of a dog, and the physical detail that stands out to Alvaro's perception is the absence of a penis (when the dog rolls over, he notices that the spaniel is a little bitch). The manner in which the little spaniel satisfies Alvaro's wish for a more pleasant sight marks the anxiety motivating the demand as castration anxiety. He demands to see the more pleasing shape as a reassurance of a bodily wholeness, of a body that has not been and cannot be mutilated. Yet it is also noteworthy that the assurance afforded by the sight of the little bitch is apparently limited to the realm of animals and foreclosed to the realm of speaking subjects. As soon as he articulates new demands, sexual differentiation reemerges and the spaniel's reassuring female shape is transformed into the ambiguous gender identity of the page, who ultimately displays his pleasing femininity as the alluring guise of an Other.

It is Lacan's and not Freud's model of castration that corresponds to the initial scene of the devil's incantation. We are not dealing with a castration threat and anxiety in the context of the Freudian family romance, and not with the protagonist's incestuous wishes, but with his confrontation with a threatening loss of self and consciousness as he articulates some want or demand that he does not know, in a language given to him by others, by means of which he commands an Other's appearance. Lacan, who attempts to capture the specific nature of the human subject as marked by sexuality and the unconscious with the conceptual tools of structuralist linguistics and anthropology, reformulates the psychoanalytic concept of castration as symbolic castration, as a "lack in being" that is introduced through the speaking subject's position in language.[6] Hence I propose to read this first scene as the phantasmatic solution to the shock of symbolic castration, a shock that comes about by one's becoming a speaking subject unwittingly. When we don't know what we are saying and can't be at the origin of what we want, we want or lack insight into what is expected from us: "Che vuoi?"

With Alvaro's response to the apparition's question "Che vuoi?" his initiation under Soberano's guidance into the order of knowledge is transformed into an initiation—now with the complicity of the occult force he has conjured—into the order of desire. This new initiation is completed in a reversal that takes hold of Alvaro's consciousness when he comes to see himself no longer as the subject, whose desires are immediately fulfilled, but as the object of the desire of a mysterious other. This final stage is described in the conclusion to the banquet scene, one initially framed in terms of Alvaro's growing confidence in his magical capacity to control reality through his wishes and demands and thereby to overcome the terrible reality of the thundering echoes of the apparition's question. For a while, Alvaro entertains himself with impressing his companions, their fascination and desiring glances being in the direction of the page Biondetto: "The page is everywhere at once, and the service never flags for an instant. I cast a covert glance in his direction: imagine Cupid decked out as a page; my companions were ogling him in their turn with looks bespeaking mingled surprise, pleasure and disquiet" (English translation, slightly modified, 38; French, 63–64). It is noteworthy that Alvaro's entertainment is focalized as an enjoyment of the others' desire he wants to believe he can control.

In an attempt to impress his companions even more, he demands to hear a mysterious Signora Fiorentina sing, whereupon Biondetto leaves and a beautiful woman appears with her harp and performs for the company. "I was moved to the depths of my being, and almost forgot that I was the creator of the charms which ravished me. The singer addressed the tender expression of her recitative and song to me. The fire of her gaze pierced through the veil; its sweetness and persistence were indescribable; those eyes were not unknown. At last, fitting together the features as the veil allowed me to glimpse them, I recognized in Fiorentina that rascal Biondetto; but the elegance of her figure was shown to much more striking advantage in the guise of a woman than in the costume of a page" (40; 63–64). The status and nature of desire is radically altered when Alvaro recognizes the handsome page in the guise of the beautiful opera singer. It is at this moment he is singled out as the object of desire of a mysterious other. The "Che vuoi?" of the camel has been transformed into the implicit question asked by Alvaro: "What does she/he want from me?"

Alvaro's command of supernatural forces seems secure until suddenly his safe observer position is questioned: an alternate and unsuspected "reality" (the page Biondetto), emerges from beneath the wished-for illusion (the singer Fiorentina), making him the object of a previously unsuspected gaze. Until that moment, he could imagine himself as the all-powerful producer of a show for the entertainment of his companions; now the show appears as someone else's production aimed at him. It is still a show, but there now appears a lurking reality that makes of the show no longer just a product of his imagination or the scenario of his own wish fulfillment. This supposed reality is the glance from the eyes underneath the veil. It is from this point that the narrative program of the story evolves. Alvaro's episodic adventures narrate his experience of himself as the object and subject of desire of a beautiful feminine form who might also be the devil in disguise. The devil is in the place of the real, a site that is inaccessible to the symbolic construction of reality; the devil is also at the site of some unmentionable, excessive, obscene enjoyment.

This fantastic tale is situated exactly at the point where the linguistic constructedness of reality is felt in its relation to the order of desire. In his seminal essay "The Subversion of the Subject and the Dialectics of Desire," Jacques Lacan obliquely refers to *The Devil in Love* by citing the phrase "Che vuoi?" to indicate the position of the phantasmatically invested Other (such as the analyst).[7] Lacan's recourse to Cazotte can be taken in two ways. On the one hand, it can be viewed as a witty and obscure literary allusion adumbrating one element of his larger argument: that the human subject's approach to knowledge can never be neutral or natural but is always linguistically mediated and thereby utterly imbricated in the order of desire. On the other hand, Lacan's reference to Cazotte suggests that the fantastic played a decisive role in elaborating a problematic subjectivity that challenged the rationalist models of a unified, consciousness-centered human subject. In the latter sense, Lacan's cryptic citation can be taken as a historical insight into the fantastic tale's generic innovation, marking the performative dimension of this new literary genre in terms of a new text-audience relationship, its unsettling seduction of the reader.

The performative force and function of this "Che vuoi?" is in the ability to call attention to the strange, presumably supernatural apparition produced as the result of the protagonist's incantation both by asserting the external existence of the phenomenon as alien, other, unknown to the protagonist, and by questioning the protagonist's initial demand, command, or incantation in view of a lack, want, or underlying desire. In addition, the performative dimension of Cazotte's "Che vuoi?" is that it addresses the protagonist and first person narrator of the tale and can also be taken as a metonymy for the fantastic tale's generically decisive framing of a supernatural encounter. In this sense, the question extends to the reader of the tale, who can neither attribute this phrase to a definite external agency or source nor disavow it as the result of a merely subjective phantasmatic realization of a wish. Instead, the reader is placed by the fantastic tale in a position analogous to its protagonist and narrator in the sense that she is puzzled, pleased, disoriented, and frightened by her confrontation with the loss of precisely those distinctions that would ordinarily stabilize her perceptions, observations, and sensations. In brief, the "Che vuoi?" isolates the fantastic as the interpellation of a subject subjected to an alienated desire.

The Glance Behind the Lure

Until the crucial turning point in the story, when Biondetta is stabbed by a rival and lies bleeding before him, Alvaro manages to resist all of the devil's attempts to seduce him into considering him or her as his beloved. Alvaro is attracted and fascinated but refuses to conceive of Biondetta as an object of love that would satisfy his desire. He refuses to believe in the existence of a woman who might suddenly disintegrate into the insubstantial effects of a light-and-sound show. Just before the crucial stabbing, however, there is a reversal in his apprehension of the distinction between what constitutes an illusion and what constitutes reality.

Alvaro is suddenly aroused to irresistible suspicion at the sight of Biondetta—whom he spies through a hidden opening in one of his closets—sitting alone in her room, improvising at the harpsichord in a transport of reverie and meditation. This scene of apparently antitheatrical absorption appears to Alvaro as the index of utter deception and manipulation:

I can see Biondetta seated at her harpsichord, arms crossed in an attitude of profound reverie. She broke the silence.
"Biondetta! Biondetta! He calls me Biondetta. It is the first, the only tender word he has ever uttered."
Again silent, she seemed to relapse into her reverie. Then she places her hands on the harpsichord I had seen her mending. She had a closed book before her on the stand, and now she is playing an introduction and singing softly, to her own accompaniment. (English translation, slightly modified, 62; French, 84)

The passage continuously slips in and out of the dramatic present tense. The narrator/protagonist presents his observations as if he were beholding a picture from a position of presumed neutrality and objectivity. Moreover, this picture displays all the elements of the eighteenth-century genre painting, of a scene from everyday life in which the subject is portrayed in an intimate and natural setting, unaware of being the object of a beholder's gaze, utterly absorbed in an activity.[8] Biondetta is not performing; she is merely expressing, confiding her innermost desire to be loved by Alvaro, as she improvises at her harpsichord and mourns the loss of Alvaro to a rival, the courtesan Olympia.

In spite (but perhaps also because) of all the markers of antitheatrical absorption, Alvaro refuses to take what he sees at face value as an immediate reality and a natural and spontaneous expression. He repeats Biondetta's song of longing for him, suddenly noticing the song's effect on him:

The sound of her voice, the melody, the implication of the lines and the turn of phrase all throw me into ineffable confusion.

"Extravagant being, dangerous imposter," I cried, hastily retreating from that place where I had stayed too long. Could anyone don the traits of truth and nature more skillfully? How fortunate I am not to have discovered this keyhole before this day! How eagerly would I have come here to intoxicate myself, how I would have contributed to my own self-deception! I have to leave, to go to the Brenta to-morrow at the latest, indeed this very evening! (English translation, slightly altered, 64; French, 88)

At the moment Alvaro registers the impact that the scene and song have on him, and as he realizes he can maintain neither neutrality nor distance toward his perceptions but is instead utterly overwhelmed by them, he tries to pull back and reestablish his position of critical and neutral observer by focusing on the constructedness and conventionality of the scene, on its successful deployment of the techniques of verisimilitude.

Yet when Alvaro prides himself on having a superior, external point of view, immune to the working of desire, he is also utterly duped. He congratulates himself for "seeing through" the conventions of authenticity and the antitheatrical theatricality of the scene. But this assumed pose of the superior observer contrasts comically with his panic reaction: If Alvaro is immune to deception, why does he have to flee precipitously? He has to flee ("I have to leave, to go to the Brenta to-morrow at the latest, indeed this very evening!") because, in reading the peephole tableau as a lure meant to ensnare him, he has precipitated himself into an observer position, in which he is framed as the object of the devil's desire. He leaves the inn on the run from a threatening reality that he has constructed in the act of seeing through it.

When Alvaro sees that the image of the submissive woman pining away for him is nothing but a deceptive tableau or lure held out to him by the Other, he thinks he can extrapolate what kind of object of desire he

The Fantastic in the Cultural History of Reading 31

must be for the Other.[9] Note that at this stage—as he is observing himself reacting to the other's expression not as authentic but as cleverly deployed artistic, rhetorical, and poetic conventions of verisimilitude—for the first time he fully posits an agency in total control of the symbolic order by which he is addressed; he switches from seeing Biondetta's status as a mere other to conceiving of her as a construction of the Other. Ironically, it is precisely by assuming the position of a supposedly neutral observer who does not fall for this woman—when he claims to know what the Other wants, what is behind the Other, and what he is for the Other—that he identifies himself with the object of the Other's desire. Once he has turned himself into the object of the devil's desire, then it should come as no surprise that he cannot flee, that the devil's emissaries are after him, pursuing him. This is what happens when he leaves the inn:

> It would have been impossible for me to await nightfall in my inn. I went out and walked at random. At a street turning, I thought I saw Bernardillo going into a café, Bernardillo who had been with Soberano on our walk to Portici. "Another phantom!" said I; "they are pursuing me." (English translation, 65; French, 88)

Alvaro's position of knowledge, insight, neutrality, and caution against deception leads him into paranoid hallucination.

The subsequent narrative continues to unfold the logic of his false position of insight—his erroneous assumption that he can see through the devil's disguises, that he can distinguish the devil's lures from what is real. Wandering through the streets and canals of Venice, followed by Biondetta, he suddenly finds her stabbed by the henchmen of the jealous courtesan Olympia:

> By the light of the torch I discover Biondetta, pale, steeped in her own blood; dying.
> My state couldn't be depicted. Any other thought is effaced.
> All I can see is a woman adored, the victim of an absurd prejudice, sacrificed to my vain and extravagant temperament and crushed, hitherto, by the most cruel insults.
> I rush forward, calling for assistance and vengeance at one and the same time. Attracted by the noise of these events, a surgeon appears, I have the wounded creature transported to my apartment and, for fear that sufficient care might not be taken, I myself share the burden.
> When they had undressed her, and I saw the lovely body bleeding from its two gaping wounds, both seeming to threaten the sources of life itself, I said and committed a thousand extravagances. (English translation, slightly modified, 66; French, 89)

The contrast between the picture of Biondetta as he perceives her through the peephole and the description of his reactions to the sight of the wounded Biondetta could not be stronger. The former is a self-contained tableau, which he rejects as a cleverly engineered lure; but now he is faced with the wounded, bloody, unclothed body of an unconscious creature whose two gaping wounds seem to threaten life itself. Alvaro's reaction to this sight is a series of hysterical outbursts, a crushing feeling of guilt for the attack on her, and a desperate effort to help save her, culminating in "a thousand extravagances," a rapturous phrase evoking an almost unmentionable, excessive enjoyment.

Now, the machinations of the devil are equated with a media-technological mix of deceptive data, and the real is equated with a bleeding body: "Do I indeed see here what I took to be a many-coloured phantom, I wondered, a mass of shining vapours assembled purely to impress my senses? Surely she was mortal, just as I was, and was dying because I had always refused to heed her, because I willfully exposed her to danger. I am a tiger, a monster" (English translation, 67–68; French, 90). These are two separate worlds, one of insubstantial and deceptive constructs and the other of perfect sense-certainty. But this opposition, which for Alvaro is phrased as the distinction between illusion and truth, is grounded in his trust in the independent reality and certainty of his senses. The foundation of his certainty actually remains the same, whether he rejects the tableau of Biondetta at the harpsichord or embraces the bleeding creature with complete abandon. To the extent that his rejection of the tableau leads him to assume an observer position from where he becomes the Other's object of desire (a move spelled out by the paranoid interlude), Alvaro's acceptance of Biondetta as a mortal woman also means his embrace of the devil.

In terms of its narrative presentation, the stabbing sequence represents the opposite of the neatly framed tableau, the picture of the absorbed woman that could have been painted by Greuze or Chardin. The reader of Alvaro's tale is not presented with a direct description of the stabbing or the condition of the victim, but merely with the narrator's incoherent and chaotic reactions to it. Rather than calling this scene a "representation" of something, it would make more sense to describe it as a disruption, a shattering of all previously established interpretive frames. Thus the sight of the wounded female body is now the site of lust and murder, guilt and passion. Although captivated by this sight, Alvaro is subject to an intense excitement; his actions seem aimless and diffuse and are not clearly addressed to any specific other. He seems overwhelmed by some polymorphously perverse sexuality. His subsequent acceptance of Biondetta as a mortal woman whom he plans to marry but with whom he refuses to have sex must be read as an apotropaic gesture through which he wards off the danger of relapsing into this kind of excessive, radically destabilizing enjoyment, a strategic move that alone guarantees his position as the protagonist and narrator of the tale.

Biondetta counters Alvaro's concern about obtaining his mother's consent to their union with an argument that echoes the language of the *philosophes*:

With you, prejudices are born for want of enlightenment and, whether through a process of reasoning or not, they render your conduct as inconsistent as it is bizarre. While subjected to real duties, you impose others upon yourself which are unnecessary or impossible to fulfill; in a word, you seek to stray from the true path in the pursuit of the object whose possession you most desire. Our union becomes dependent on the will of others. Who knows if dona Mencia will find me of sufficiently high lineage to ally myself with the house of Maravillas? And would I not feel belittled were I to have to secure you from her instead of possessing you of your own accord? Is it a man destined for great knowledge who is speaking to me, or a child just out of the mountains of Estremadura? (English translation, 74–75; French, 96)

The contrast between Alvaro's loyalty to a traditional marriage and Biondetta's advocacy of a modern, enlightened love between individuals is not phrased in typical terms from the culture of sensibility, which would portray it as a conflict between traditional alliance politics (where the parents choose the suitable partner) and young lovers who are free to follow their hearts. Alvaro perceives in his love for Biondetta not a danger to his family interests but a potential danger to himself. He uses social constraints against premarital sex as a welcome aid in sustaining his identity as a desiring subject.

Until the end of his story, Alvaro refrains from giving way to his desire, from seeking the ultimate enjoyment that Biondetta offers to him, fearing that should he sleep with her she would suddenly revert to her initial satanic nature. He clearly distinguishes her from an erotic object such as the courtesan Olympia with whom he could entertain an erotic relationship of sensual pleasures. Indeed, the manner in which Biondetta is set apart from the world of "normal" sensual pleasure is what defines and secures the narrator's and protagonist's position vis-à-vis the world of sense and the realm of the senses.

My analysis of Cazotte's tale has isolated primarily two sets of scenes, the first from the initial conjuration of the devil up to Alvaro's being struck by the singer's gaze, and the second from the narrative sequence that leads to Alvaro's acceptance of Biondetta as a mortal woman. The novella's final scene, before Alvaro arrives at his mother's estate, recapitulates decisive elements from these two narrative sequences and fuses them with one another. The protagonist is confronted with a phantasmagoria that entails the ultimate collapse of all the previous distinctions he had shored up to differentiate himself as an observer from the objects of an environment that he observed—namely, the distinctions between an observing consciousness and its environment, between illusion and external reality, between inner and outer, and between an externally produced lure and a subjective wish.

When Biondetta draws Alvaro into bed with her, undresses, and tells him who she really is, the bizarre scenario of the initial evocation of Beelzebub is suddenly repeated: the camel head, strange and strong effects of light, luminous snails, and a disembodied, thundering voice, shouting: "Che vuoi?" The main difference between the light-and-sound show at the beginning of the story and its reappearance at the end is that in the aftermath of Biondetta's stabbing, what had initially appeared to Alvaro as a frightening and surprising vision within the realm of opera and illusionistic tricks is now, at the climax and end of his seduction, fused with unrepresentable, totally physical, bodily immediacy. In the pair's first (and final) sexual encounter, the two previous shocks are repeated and combined; the polymorphously perverse excitement over the sight of the stabbed Biondetta is just as much present as the hallucinatory engrossment of the first vision. What has disappeared for the duration of the final scene, however, are the moments of doubt, hesitation, and suspicion, and along with them anything resembling a separate observer position or any distinct image; the devil has completed his work of seduction exactly as the doctor describes it.

This leads us back to the analogy between the devil's strategy of seduction and the genre of the fantastic tale. If Alvaro's confusion and enjoyment are considered from an "external" point of view such as the doctor's, then the climax of Alvaro's relationship with the devil can be compared to a synesthetic media fantasy of a total work of art, in which the work of art cancels all the distinctions among beholder, artistic illusion, and reality by way of an immediate transformation of visual and acoustic data into nervous impulse and physiological reaction. To put it crudely and anachronistically, the story culminates when an illusionistic fiction produces the powerful effect of cyberspace pornography.

At this point, it is possible to recall those features of the fantastic tale that are already part of Cazotte's story and that become crucial for the fantastic tale of the nineteenth century. Broadly, the story's main interest lies in what I have called the intertwining of the order of knowledge and the order of desire. This happens at the critical turning points of the narrative, whenever a perceived reality is portrayed as the product of a dangerous or risky desire. The content of the perception is in response to a wish, not as a daydream would be, but in such a way that the narrator or protagonist has to question the nature and reality of his articulation of a demand or wish in the first place ("What lies behind the perceived illusion that corresponds to my wish? What gave rise to it? What does the Other want from me by presenting that kind of illusion?"). One might also describe this moment as the destabilization of an observer's position that occurs when a perceived reality is understood not just as a potential illusion but also as a potentially clever installation. This shock to the observer position entails two components. First, the observer is confronted with desire as an unknown. Second, the intensity of the potential illusion, which disrupts all previous interpretive frames, becomes both the site of an intense shock and the site of utter enjoyment, an excess of stimulation that cancels the distinction between the perceiving consciousness and its environment.

The second element of the fantastic is related to the first by the tale's commentary on the power of illusion. I have tried to emphasize the extent to which almost all the scenes that strike the narrator/protagonist as powerful illusion are concretely described as media technology (the comparison of the wonderful banquet among the ruins of Portici with a successful operatic stage design; the similarity of the peephole scene with the beholder's position in front of an eighteenth-century genre painting that successfully creates a state of antitheatrical absorption). What is interesting about the semiotic and aesthetic status of these "scenes of beholding an illusion" is that the illusion the beholder witnesses does not have the status of a representation of a possible reality. Instead it is a simulation of a reality. This posits if not a devil—then the figure of an artist who is not just the producer of an artifact or the maker of a representation but rather a powerful seducer and a master technician of the imaginary.

"The Elementary Spirit"

In 1821, almost fifty years after the publication of Cazotte's *The Devil in Love*, E.T.A. Hoffmann wrote "Der Elementargeist" (The Elementary Spirit). The story is related to Cazotte's tale in terms of a complex intertextual and historical commentary. The frame narrative is set in November 1815. After having participated in the battles of June of that year, which brought about Napoleon's decisive defeat, Albert, a Prussian officer, rides east from Lüttich to Aachen in the vague hope of finding his fellow officer and long-lost friend, Viktor. Accidentally, he runs into Viktor's servant, Talkebarth, who leads Albert to a nearby estate where Viktor was living as guest of a baron and baroness. The baroness had nursed him back to health after a head injury he suffered in 1813 when, on his way to join the Prussian troops, he had fallen from his horse. Albert is invited to stay for the night. After the hosts retire, Viktor spends most of the night in conversation with Albert, telling him of his infatuation with the middle-aged lady. Viktor confides that he has come to the conviction that the baroness is an incarnation of the elementary spirit in Cazotte's *The Devil in Love.*

Viktor's autobiographical story, recounted to Albert in the course of an evening at the baron's house, constitutes the main part of "The Elementary Spirit." In an effort to show his friend how his life has come to mirror the events of Cazotte's fantastic tale, Viktor tells the story of his early adulthood, his education and reading experiences, and his early military career, in addition to the two-year period of his separation from Albert during the war. The following morning, Viktor decides to leave the Baron's estate with Albert and returns with him to their former military circles in Aachen. But despite Albert's urging, Viktor remains aloof from society, believing that his past experiences have acquainted him with pleasures too exquisite ever to be matched in marriage and domestic bliss. Thus Hoffmann's protagonist and narrator, much like Cazotte's, is marked by a problematic desire. Here, though, the frame narrative contrasts Viktor's voluntary bachelorhood with other models of masculinity, especially the patriotic and martial version of manly valor.

"The Elementary Spirit" can be read as a commentary on both Cazotte and the cultural contexts surrounding the fantastic tale. As already indicated in the title, in Hoffmann's tale the supernatural encounter is with a spirit, not with the devil. The devil, in fact, is reduced to a figure of speech in the frame narrative, as for instance when Albert, commenting on Viktor's obsession with the baroness, tells him that his infatuation with the middle-aged matron is so ridiculous that one might as well wish to be possessed by the devil ("daß man darüber des Teufels werden möchte")[10]; or when Albert, annoyed by one of Talkebarth's pranks, wishes him to the devil. The comic figure of Paul Talkebarth in Hoffmann's setting replaces the benevolent helper figure of the mother (the source of stability and traditional values in Cazotte's tale). The manservant speaks a bastardized French, swears by good Christian values, and keeps quoting the advice of his friend Liese, who can tell fortunes from coffee grounds. Cazotte's tale polarized two distinct positions toward the supernatural and the fantastic by casting Alvaro's temptation as a choice between the traditional values of the ancien régime and the satanic seductress who takes the position of an Enlightenment philosophe. But Hoffmann, by introducing the devil as a mere colloquialism or figure of speech and the elementary spirit as the incarnation of a literary character, invokes a dimension of self-reference and self-reflection typical of Romantic wit and irony. Viktor's belief in the baroness's "higher nature" can be read as expressing an early Romantic program that aimed at restoring a sense of wonder to the familiar, banal, and disenchanted world of everyday life. Thus the protagonist's encounter with an elementary spirit is presented much less as a potentially moral story about temptation than as a story about the specific cultural and historical circumstances that would underscore such a desire.

Unlike Alvaro, who is characterized by his traditional ties to his mother and the family estate, Viktor is marked by a typically modern anomie. From Viktor's autobiographical recounting to Albert, the reader learns that he pursued a military career without real commitment or passion, and that he received little formal education but was an autodidact and deeply affected by Goethe's *Werther* and Schiller's *Robbers*. When he read Schiller's unfinished *Ghostseer*, his penchant for the occult greatly increased. His reading experience came to define and dominate his entire life such that acquaintances from his real life appeared to him as incarnations of literary characters. Thus a mysterious Irishman, Major O'Malley, seemed to him first an incarnation of the sinister helper and dubious mentor figure of the Armenian in Schiller's *Ghostseer*. Later, as if having discovered the true literary source of the character, the same O'Malley appears to him as an incarnation of Soberano, the mentor figure from Cazotte who initiated Alvaro into the occult. Along the same lines, he is convinced that the middle-aged baroness is an incarnation of Cazotte's elementary spirit.

If Viktor's desire for the elementary spirit and its incarnation in the person of the baroness is marked as a Romantic desire for the reenchantment of the world, his autobiographical narrative specifies this desire as the mentality of a sociologically specific generation. Traditionally, the second sons of the impoverished nobility joined either the army or the expanding Prussian bureaucracy; still, it was from this same layer of society that many Romantic poets were recruited. With respect to cultural history, Viktor's narrative highlights the intense reading experience associated with the culture of sensibility and the literary production of the *Sturm und Drang* (Storm and Stress), especially in such works as *Ghostseer*, which steers Viktor toward the occult and prepares his later identification with Cazotte's *The Devil in Love*. Yet Viktor's identificatory reading habits are not analyzed through the typical eighteenth-century pedagogical concern with a so-called *Lesesucht* (addiction to the print medium), such as that explored at great length in Karl Philipp Moritz's psychological novel *Anton Reiser* (1785–1790). Rather, his powerfully transformative reading experience is presented in terms of its sexualizing, seductive impact. This results in a problematic desire that thoroughly informs the protagonist's individuality and idiosyncratic relationship to reality. What is more, the intimate exchange between the two men—Viktor's conversation with his friend Albert about his frightening, enlivening, and sexualizing encounter with the elementary spirit—can itself be read as occupying the place of a sexual relationship.

Whereas Cazotte's tale develops its fantastic plot of Alvaro's adventures with Biondetta out of one initial scene in which the protagonist, a curious neophyte experimenting with occult forces, invokes the devil with an incantation, Hoffmann's tale elaborates a portrait of a susceptible, highly sensitized reader who is drawn to the occult by progressive awakening of inner affinities. As opposed to only one, there are actually three "conjuration" scenes in "The Elementary Spirit." In what follows, I analyze them as a series of experiments with spirit mediumship, in which the magical formula is not merely an element of occult knowledge and practice but is also composed of elements that belong to a thematic repertoire concerned with practices of writing, reading, and poetic production. Hence incantation and commerce with a mysterious spirit, in Hoffmann's tale, cover the spectrum of meanings associated with that term, from a supernatural being to the human mind, representing both an inspired creation and the mentality of an age.

Seduction Through Reading

In the first conjuration scene, Viktor is not a central player at all, but merely a witness. One evening, when he is drinking with two friends, a young peer and an older captain, an Irish major by the name of O'Malley joins them. The captain asks O'Malley "whether he would not do well by contradicting the silly rumour, that he commanded mysterious powers, and thus, in his own person, check the foolish superstition, which by no means accord[s] with an age so enlightened" (English translation, 281; German, 681). The major rebukes the captain, calling him an extremely uneducated fellow who insists on believing that the world can be reduced to his own limited experience as a mere mortal being. The captain concedes that there might very well be higher spiritual beings, but he insists that "any communication with an unknown spiritual world [is] contrary to the very conditions of humanity, and therefore impossible." O'Malley, in response, challenges his interlocutors to sit down and write "an epic as noble and as superhumanly great as the *Iliad*" (282; 682), thus comparing spiritual mediumship to poetic talent: "I tell you, the intercourse with higher spiritual natures depends on a particular *psychic* organisation. That organisation, like the creative power of poetry, is a gift which the spirit of the universe bestows upon its favourites" (282; 682). The first conjuration scene is therefore announced both as a challenge to the captain's philistine, self-satisfied misunderstanding of the Enlightenment and as an experiment in spirit mediumship which is likened to poetic inspiration.[11]

On the night of the autumnal equinox, O'Malley takes the three friends into the deep woods, to the ruins of a cellar. When the captain discovers that instead of a book of magic formulas O'Malley has taken along *Peplier's French Grammar*, he attempts to ridicule him. O'Malley calmly replies: "Do you think that my power requires such paltry crutches as especial mystical forms, choice of a particular time, a remote awful spot— things which paltry cabalists are in the habit of employing for their useless experiments? In the open market-place, at every hour, I could show you my power" (284; 685). In other words, what is at stake is O'Malley's spirit mediumship, a particular power that is supposed to be independent of superstitious practices:

"O'Malley ranged us in a half-circle, threw off his cloak and shirt, so that he remained naked to the waist, and opening the book began to read as follows, in a voice that more resembled the dull roaring of a distant beast of prey than the sound of a human being: 'Monsieur, pretez moi un peu, s'il vous plaît, votre canif.—Oui, Monsieur, d'abord—le voilà, je vous le rendrai.'"

"Come," said Albert, here interrupting his friend, "this is indeed too bad! the dialogue 'On Writing,' from *Peplier's Grammar*, as a formula for exorcism! and you did not laugh out and bring the whole thing to an end at once?"

"I am now," continued Victor, "coming to a moment which I doubt whether I shall succeed in describing. May your fancy only give animation to my words! The major's voice grew more awful, while the wind howled more loudly, and the flickering light of the torches covered the walls with strange forms, that changed as they flitted by. I felt the cold perspiration dripping on my forehead, and forcibly succeeded in preserving my presence of mind, when a cutting tone whistled through the vault, and close before my eyes stood something—"

"How?" cried Albert. "Something! What do you mean, Victor? A frightful form?"

"It sounds absurd," continued Victor, "to talk of 'a formless form,' but I can find no other word to express the hideous something that I saw. It is enough to say that at that moment the horror of hell thrust its pointed ice-dagger into my heart, and I became insensible. At broad mid-day I found myself undressed and lying upon my couch." (English translation, 285–86; German, 687–88)

That the magic formula is a French phrase about borrowing a penknife, which Albert calls the dialogue "On Writing," comically highlights the framing of this scene as one about poetic production. Furthermore, after Albert interrupts him, Viktor's announcement of his inability to describe the subsequent events to which he was witness emphasizes this thematic recasting of Cazotte's conjuration scene. Viktor has to appeal to Albert's fancy to give animation to his words; besides reproducing a template for a polite, grammatically correct exchange about a writing tool, he can do no better than to describe a sequence of disjointed visual and optical data and a physiological reaction. Immediately after this exchange, the inset narrative returns to the specific shock Viktor experienced when confronted with something real and external for which he had no interpretational frame: a formless form, something distinct that was, however, nothing.

If we look at the first conjuration in the light suggested by O'Malley, as a scene about poetic production, we note that it has produced nothing beyond the unstable observer position that is so typical of the fantastic tale. Still, Peter von Matt, in what constitutes one of the most extensive readings of this tale, argues that this scene is crucial to understanding Hoffmann's position on creativity. According to von Matt, most of Hoffmann's fictions thematize two distinct aspects of producing a work of art. One aspect pertains to the visionary act of a creative imagination, rooted in the genius aesthetics of the Storm and Stress period and most memorably invoked in Hoffmann's tale about the mad visionary Serapion.[12] Concurrently, though, Hoffmann emphasizes the concrete material artifact (production of which requires expert knowledge and skill), embodied by the many craftsmen and mechanics who populate his fiction. Although a young man like Viktor might well be endowed with a "poetic spirit" that he first discovers when reading Goethe and Schiller, there is as yet nothing that would ensure its realization. Von

The Fantastic in the Cultural History of Reading 41

Matt's reading emphasizes that the first conjuration scene lacks any external object that might serve as the medium of conduit for Viktor's poetic spirit, through which he might externalize his visionary powers. Hence Viktor's impulse for creative expression in the first conjuration scene remains thwarted, insofar as the creative urge can only be developed with the aid of some external object of love.[13]

It is not until the second conjuration scene that an external object is introduced, in the shape of a magical doll that O'Malley fabricates for Viktor to summon the "elementary spirit." In von Matt's reading, this doll is the external object by which the aspiring poet can proceed to externalize his poetic potential. Before the second conjuration scene, however, Viktor undergoes a profound transformation, which offers clues with regard to the nature and function of this magical external object, clues that von Matt's reading does not fully take into account.

Viktor has almost forgotten his previous adventure in the woods with O'Malley when he happens to read Cazotte's tale *The Devil in Love*. He describes Cazotte's effect on him as a total transformation of his subjectivity. Already prior to his encounter with Cazotte's tale, Viktor was immensely influenced by his identificatory reading habits. Now, however, the experience of reading appears to him in a totally new and hitherto unprecedented intensity:

> I have every right to claim that I was entirely innocent. For neither my reason nor my imagination has ever occupied itself with the relationship of a man to a woman. It was only now that the mystery of an unexpected sensuality was awakened in me. In the scenes of the most dangerous, most gruesome love, which the poet described in the most glowing colors of life, my pulse was beating; a consuming fire streamed through my nerves and veins. I could see, hear, feel nothing but that supremely alluring Biondetta. Like Alvaro, I succumbed to the lustful torture. (my translation; German, 690)

Viktor's experience as a reader is described in two separate registers. The first is an initial encounter with the idea of sex, an original loss of innocence, the exposure of his understanding and imagination to something new and exciting. It is noteworthy that his reading experience is rendered not by means of distinct images, thoughts, or emotions—not in a cognitive, psychological, or sentimental register—but as an intense physiological reaction. The second register is the reader's or Viktor's identification with the content of what he has read. This aspect emerges when Albert interrupts Viktor and asks to be reminded of the ending of Cazotte's tale. Viktor's cryptic reply is that Albert will eventually learn the ending by listening to the outcome of his friend's own life story. Characterizing Cazotte's book as a "magic mirror," Viktor explains that the early part of his life had already been under the sign of that text; the sinister O'Malley from the military academy was in fact none other than the mysterious Soberano who had tempted Alvaro with the occult arts.

In its overwhelming impact on his past and future life, Viktor's reading of Cazotte's tale can be called a conversion experience. The overpowering physiological impact of the book, as it awakens him to the mysteries of an unexpected sensuality, turns him around, utterly transforms him, and causes him to throw overboard all his prior vows to avoid O'Malley. Cazotte's text seems to epitomize the magic and power of the print medium, as it leads Viktor to reinterpret all his previous life experience. Hoffmann situates Viktor's reading experience of the fantastic at the culmination of that historical phase in the cultural history of reading during which print had become the dominant medium; absorbing the silent reader into a work of fiction had become a habitual mode of reading. But the description of Viktor's reading experience also marks a departure from the culture of sensibility and the Enlightenment paradigm of representation. Instead of an effortless translation of the book's contents into mental images, which could be assembled into a hallucinatory ersatz reality, Cazotte's text produces a powerfully physiological reaction, a strong sexual arousal that cancels the distinction between external and internal perception. Rather than a simple mirror, Cazotte's book is called a magic mirror; instead of representing a reality, it produces one, situating this type of reading at the limits of an aesthetics of representation.

The Passion of the Lonely Reader

When Viktor confides to O'Malley the confused desires awakened in him as a result of his encounter with Cazotte's tale, the major declares the actual content of the book to be immaterial. Viktor should, however, take this experience as a sign that a powerful spirit was trying to get in touch with him. Peter von Matt interprets O'Malley's words as an authorial hint that what was actually at stake was Viktor's coming to terms with his half-acknowledged poetic spirit. To realize his poetic spirit, the artist must first fall in love with an external object, an embodiment of beauty, which he subsequently has to give up, recognizing the beauty of the concrete love object to be a mere projection of his own internal creative potential. Only then is he ready to become a true artist. Whereas von Matt reads the scene about the fabrication of the teraph (the magic doll) as the first step in the artist's process of self-realization, I would interpret this scene in view of how it refers back to Viktor's experience of reading Cazotte, how it reiterates Viktor's interpellation as a reader.

The fact that O'Malley conjures the teraph out of some drops of Viktor's blood heated on a metallic mirror above the flames of his stove repeats the two fundamental elements from Viktor's own description of his reading experience of Cazotte's tale: there, Viktor's physiological excitement was described as a fiery liquid running through his veins, but now there is actual blood and fire; there, Viktor called the entirety of the book a magic mirror, but now O'Malley, using the magic mirror, fuses Viktor's blood into the little figure of the teraph. The elements out of which the teraph is fabricated schematically duplicate and externalize the elements from Viktor's description of his experience of reading Cazotte. In that sense, the teraph embodies and externalizes Viktor's reading fantasy; that is, the teraph is not an other, not quite an independently existing external object.

How is this little doll supposed to summon the elementary spirit? O'Malley instructs Viktor to hold the teraph close to himself and focus on his desire while looking into the mirror that O'Malley unveils before him, while pronouncing a magical formula.

Scarcely had half the syllables passed my lips, than an ugly, madly-distorted face grinned at me spitefully from the mirror. 'In the name of all the devils, whence come you, you accursed dog?' yelled O'Malley behind me. I turned round, and saw my Paul Talkebarth, who was standing in the door-way, and whose handsome face was reflected in the magic mirror. (English translation, 290; German, 695)

This second conjuration mockingly invokes Cazotte's text by repeating and demystifying key elements from its prototype. The magical formula; the ugly, madly distorted face that Viktor sees; O'Malley's figures of speech, "in the name of all devils" and "the accursed dog"; and the "handsome face" that recalls the attractive page all hark back to Alvaro's conjuration scene. Viktor referred to Cazotte's book as a magic mirror, and O'Malley claimed that he would unveil a magic mirror before Viktor. The reflection of Talkebarth in the mirror, however, reveals it to be a perfectly ordinary, banal, real mirror that simply reflects what is in front of it. Its surprising production of an unexpected, alien sight can be entirely accounted for in terms of an optical technology.

The image of the magic mirror framed as a particular optical technology can also be read as an ironical commentary on the "specular moment," a key metaphor of Romantic love and communication that goes back to Goethe's early lyrical poetry of the 1770s. It is articulated in Goethe's "May Song," of which I shall quote the last four stanzas:

> O Mädchen Mädchen,
> Wie lieb' ich dich!
> Wie blinkt dein Auge!
> Wie liebst du mich!
>
> So liebt die Lerche
> Gesang und Luft,
> Und Morgenblumen
> Den Himmels Duft,
>
> Wie ich dich liebe
> Mit warmen Blut,
> Die du mir Jugend
> Und Freud und Mut
>
> Zu neuen Liedern,
> Und Tänzen gibst!
> Sei ewig glücklich
> Wie du mich liebst.

> O maiden, maiden,
> How I love you!
> How your eye gleams!
> How you love me!
>
> Thus the lark loves
> Song and air,
> And morning flowers
> The heaven's fragrance,
>
> As I love you
> With warm blood,
> You who to me youth
> And joy and spirit
>
> For new songs,
> And dances give!
> Be eternally blissful
> As you love me.

This mutual look of love producing a circular exchange between Nature and new songs in Goethe's poem testifies to an epochally new codification of intimacy; it is also one of the first articulations of a radically new lyrical poetry. It lays the groundwork for what was to become the typically Romantic model of the genius whose originary constitution of subjectivity posited its source in what David Wellbery calls the specular moment of the mutually loving, symmetrical exchange of looks.[14]

Hoffmann's story cites this crucial cultural paradigm of the poetic genius by invoking the magic of the specular moment and also radically analyzes and perverts this trope of poetic inspiration and love. The aspect of nature is altogether absent. The loving look of the beloved is not immediately given; it is an effect that depends on the concrete technical apparatus of the mirror. Only when Viktor actually recognizes the familiar face of his loyal servant can he refer to it with mild irony as handsome. Before, when he sees it as an unexpected apparition in the mirror, it is a frightening, ugly grimace. Instead of magically conjuring up the look of the beloved as the confirmation of a self-constituting poetic subjectivity, Viktor's look into the mirror opens up a radical gap between his desired vision and what he actually sees.

If we compare the first and the second conjuration scenes, we notice that in spite of their differences they both end in Viktor's momentary confrontation with the apparition of a frightening alterity: in the first scene there was the "formless form," and in the second the unexpected and madly distorted face. Both encounters repeat the frightening apparition of the camel head from Cazotte's tale. Whereas that protagonist responds to the frightening apparition by demanding a more pleasant shape, a banquet, and musical entertainment—all of them distractions that for a while allow him to mistake himself for the all-powerful producer of these pleasant illusions—Hoffmann's protagonist retreats to the realm of his private (reading) fantasies as he plays with his little doll:

The Devil Amor, Biondetta—all was forgotten; I thought only of my Teraph. For whole hours I could look at the little doll as it stood on the table before me, and the glow of love that streamed through my veins seemed then, like the heavenly fire of Prometheus, to animate the little figure which grew upwards with lustful longing. But this creation [*Gestaltung*] vanished as soon as I had thought it, and the unspeakable anguish that cut through my heart was associated with a strange anger that impelled me to fling the doll away from me as a miserable, ridiculous toy. Yet when I grasped it an electrical shock seemed to dart through all my limbs, and I felt as if a separation from the talisman of love would annihilate me. I will openly confess to you that my passion, although the proper object of it was an elementary spirit, was directed among all sorts of equivocal dreams towards objects in the sensible world that surrounded me, so that my excited fancy made now this, now that lady, the representative of the coy salamander that eluded my embrace. (English translation, slightly altered, 290; German, 695–96)

Unlike the mythological Prometheus, Viktor does not create human beings. Nor does he, like Goethe's Prometheus, give shape to the human capacity of self-fashioning; instead, he animates a little doll.[15] The teraph, here referred to as a talisman, is never described in any physical detail as an object of a specific shape (*Gestalt*); rather, Viktor calls it a *Gestaltung* (a shaping, a formation, something in process). The teraph seems to have retained some plasticity in the sense that it can change its size and form. To a certain extent, Viktor's narrative suggests that all that is at stake in his wondrous interaction with the magical idol is some kind of daydreaming associated with masturbation. Read along those lines, the animation of the little doll, described as a lustful tumescence, appears to be the externalization of the physiology of an erection.

Nevertheless, one might also want to pursue what is entailed by the little doll's status as a magical object, as a particular object of fantasy, an object that was made of the key elements of the protagonist's reading of a fantastic tale. One might call the teraph a "transitional object," a technical term from Winnicott's theory of how the separation between child and mother, between itself and its environment, is negotiated through the child's attachment to one particular object. This transitional object (which can be anything from a piece of cloth to a stuffed animal or a doll, or the child's own thumb) provides comfort because it is easily available to the touch and allows the child to hallucinate the presence of the mother. It is the object by which the child can feel whole; it is also the first object that gives rise to fantasy and play. The transitional object is both "created" and "found" by the child. It is neither entirely part of the child's internal world, nor entirely part of external reality. It serves, however, as the central mediator between the two, particularly as it survives the child's aggressivity.[16] (Viktor can fling it away as a ridiculous toy.) Although the transitional object is frequently used for oral stimulation and gratification, its sexual charge must not draw attention to itself if the activity of play is to endure. This is how we can account for the "failure" of the teraph, for the manner in which Viktor's *Gestaltung* vanishes with the climax.

According to object relations theory, the transitional object mediates the separation from the mother and allows libidinal investment of other love objects. Once this transition has been successfully accomplished, the transitional object loses its significance. To conceive of the teraph in terms of Winnicott's transitional object could allow one to frame Viktor's autobiographical narrative as a story of libidinal development, to compare and contrast his obsession with the little doll with a narrative of sexual normalization. Indeed, up to a certain point Viktor seems to progress along this path of "maturation" when he finds himself attracted to a particularly beautiful countess. Upon learning about his obsessive preoccupation with the teraph, she confiscates the little doll. He accepts her invitation to visit her at night and lets himself be led by a servant through the spacious palace into a wonderfully decorated room:

"There I was to expect the countess. Half overcome by the fumes of the sweet scents that wound through the chamber, trembling with love and desire, I stood in the midst of the room. All at once I was hit, a glance darted through my innermost being like a flash of lightning—"

"How!" cried Albert, "a glance, and no eyes! And you saw nothing?" "Another formless form!"

"You may find it incomprehensible," said Victor, "but so it was; I could see nothing, and yet I felt the glance deep in my bosom, and a sudden pain quivered at the spot O'Malley had wounded. At the same moment I perceived upon the chimney-piece my little image, grasped it, darted from the room, commanded the terrified servant, with a threatening gesture, to lead me down, ran home, awakened my man Paul, and had all my things packed up." (English translation, slightly modified, 291–92; German, 697–98)

Albert's interjection calls attention to the fact that Viktor's narrative again culminates in a shocking, painful encounter with a radical alterity, a formless form. The glance without eyes retains the annihilating power of the formless form from the first incantation scene of being something in external reality that has not the subjectivity-affirming status of a definite object, and it repeats the grimace from the mirror as a glance that denies the comforts of the loving look. This sudden apparition of the gaze is new and different because it is entirely embedded in the environment in which Viktor expects to find ultimate sexual satisfaction. The description of Viktor in the middle of a room that appears to have been "decorated by the god of love" literally situates him center stage and thus integrates him into a picture, a vision or fantasy of enjoyment of an Other whose desire he cannot know. In that sense the "glance without eyes" from the countess's apartment (a lady who had the reputation of being a loose woman) reiterates the disturbing "Che vuoi?" of the camel head. Responding to the countess's demand, Viktor does not find a loving other but is confronted with the Other's desire. From there he withdraws into the comfortable phantasmatic exchange with his little doll. The teraph becomes his recourse and comfort when he faces an objectless desire and the radical uncertainty of an observer whose subjectivity is wounded or split as he recognizes himself as the object of an inscrutable gaze, a gaze without eyes, the object of the Other's desire.

One could also compare the countess with the courtesan Olympia from Cazotte's tale and say that Viktor, like Alvaro, flees a "normal" or "natural" sexual relationship to preserve his attachment to the fictional Biondetta. In this sense, Viktor's attachment to the teraph represents a departure from a model of a supposedly normal satisfaction of desire, a means by which his status as desiring subject is preserved. After Viktor's flight from the countess, he withdraws to his room and falls asleep. On awakening, he sees for the first time the apparition of the beautiful salamander, a lovely woman clad in red silk. They embrace and caress each other, and he listens to her melodious voice; but before they consummate their relationship, she vanishes, or evaporates like the *Gestaltung* of the animated teraph. Waking up in the morning, he finds himself holding the little teraph in his hand.

This kind of encounter is repeated over several weeks. Viktor calls the vision Aurora—the same name that Alvaro uses for Biondetta when he is finally convinced of her status as a mortal woman. Against von Matt's claim that during this phase Viktor has come close to the breakthrough of realizing beauty as a projection of his own creative potential, my reading suggests that the potential development of the protagonist's poetic talent never becomes an agenda in its own right but is only brought up to be differentiated from another libidinal development, namely, the strange desire and sexuality of a reader who has been seduced by reading fantastic fiction.[17]

The conclusions of Viktor's inset narrative and the frame narrative both evoke, but at the same time depart from, that of Cazotte's tale. Viktor ends his story by telling Albert how one night the apparition demanded that he renounce the bliss of an unknown beyond if he desires actual consummation of their relationship. In exchange for an overpowering experience of satisfaction, Viktor is indeed willing to give up his desire, his objectless yearning. But Talkebarth interrupts his solitary commerce with the supernatural spirit and saves him from irrevocably losing his soul to the devil. From then on, the elementary spirit remains hidden from him until she returns to him as he is recovering from his head injury at the baron's estate, "glorified—purified in the fire of Heaven," in the shape of the matronly, safely married baroness (English translation, 296; German, 705). Though he leaves the baron's estate and returns to Aachen, he refuses to be drawn out of his bachelorhood; the tale's very last sentence reads, "The colonel remained unmarried" (298; 707).

Hoffmann's ending makes it clear that the fantastic, with its investment in the supernatural and opposition to a commonsensical approach to reality, is based on a problematic desire and relationship to pleasure:

> Whether it was that I had been mystified, and, by wicked means, made to serve some unknown end, or whether an evil power really tried to tempt me, this much is certain, that though the past has not cost me the bliss of the beyond, it has deprived me of the paradise of love. Never can that time return, when I felt the highest earthly felicity, when the ideal of my sweetest, most transporting dreams, nay love itself, was in my arms. Love and pleasure have vanished, since a horrible mystery deprived me of her who to my inmost heart was really a higher being, such as I shall not again find upon earth! (English translation, slightly modified, 297–98; German, 707)

Cazotte's story leaves it open as to whether Alvaro will eventually follow the doctor's advice and get married. This normalizing move is clearly rejected by the ending of Hoffmann's story: Viktor's relationship to pleasure and his past sexual dreams are made into a feature that permanently defines his fate, that marks him as a man who no longer hopes for love and satisfaction in this world. His loyalty to the exquisite joys of love that he believes he has known is a retrospective, nostalgic creation. It is what strengthens his resolve to abstain from the satisfactions of marital life and to hold on to his desire. His deliberate choice of a bachelor existence affirms his desire as a want that cannot be satisfied. In the history of sexuality, bachelorhood by choice rather than failure is a recent option, one that became available primarily to members of the social class to which Viktor belongs.[18]

Manly Valor and Bachelordom by Choice

So far, my reading of Hoffmann's "The Elementary Spirit" has shown how the protagonist's supernatural encounters are contextualized with regard to the reading habits of the culture of sensibility and to the recoding of intimacy as it took shape in the myth of the self-constituting subjectivity of the genius. The specular moment from Storm and Stress poetry, however, in Viktor's conjurations of an elementary spirit is merely evoked as part of a temporary illusion. It does not become part of an economy of poetic productivity. Where then does the search for the elementary spirit lead? How are we to understand Viktor's refusal to accept a beautiful wife as the answer to his desire?

In the remaining pages of this chapter, I argue that the desire for the elementary spirit can be understood in the cultural historical context of the Napoleonic Wars that links Viktor's and Albert's narratives. It is not only Viktor who is marked by his encounters with and yearning for a powerful spirit; this longing is also present in his friend Albert as he recollects the expectations that guided him while riding from Aachen to the battlefront in May 1813. His enthusiastic hopes on his way to battle are projected onto the flowering meadows, which in turn contrast with the barren, cold, and gray autumnal fields of his return:

He thought how, a few months before, he had travelled on the same road, in an opposite direction, and during the loveliest season of the year. The fields then bloomed forth luxuriantly, the fragrant meadows resembled variegated carpets, and the bushes in which the birds joyously chirped and sung, shone in the fair light of golden sunbeams. The earth, like a longing bride, had richly adorned herself to receive in her dark nuptial chamber, the victims consecrated to death—the heroes who fell in the sanguinary battles. (English translation, 268; German, 659–60)

Albert transforms the battlefield deaths of the soldiers into a hero's reception by a longing bride in her richly adorned nuptial chamber, prefiguring for the reader the scene of an ultimate sexual fulfillment in the sensuously decorated chamber of the loose countess whom Viktor flees in horror. Contrasting these two scenarios of ultimate enjoyment, we can glimpse the distinction between Viktor's flight and final choice of bachelorhood and Albert's nostalgic remembrance of the patriotic dream that led him into the final phase of the liberation wars.

Indeed, the frame narrative of "The Elementary Spirit" contrasts Albert's and Viktor's experiences as alternative encounters with the "spirit of the age." This spirit marked its generation as inspired poets—enthusiastic readers but also visionary patriots and Romantic dreamers. Like Viktor, Albert believes he has encountered a spirit. The German word *Geist* covers a wide spectrum, ranging from mind, spirit, and mentality to apparition and ghost. A four-volume work appearing between 1806 and 1818, by Ernst Moritz Arndt (1769–1860), entitled *Geist der Zeit* (Spirit of the Times), was one of the most influential propagandistic works elaborating the myth of a "new nation," a proud, antifeudal, and antiparticularist German nation, unified in its armed resistance against the French.[19] Whereas Viktor's awakening to the spirit occurs through his reading of the early works of Goethe and Schiller, Albert's is situated in his memory of the last days of the military campaign:

The battle of Issy now rose brightly before Albert's soul; he thought of things that, as it seemed, he had not observed, nay, had not been able to observe during the fight. Thus the faces of many individual officers and men appeared before his eyes, depicted in the most lively manner, and his heart was struck by the inexplicable expression, not of proud or unfeeling contempt of death, but of really divine inspiration, which beamed from many an eye. Thus he heard sounds, now exhorting to fight, now uttered with the last sigh of death, which deserved to be treasured up for posterity like the animating utterances of the heroes of antiquity.

"Do I not," thought Albert, "almost feel like one who has a notion of his dream when he wakes, but who does not recollect all its single features till several days afterwards? Ay, a dream, and only a dream, one would think, by flying over time and space, with its mighty wings, could render possible the gigantic, monstrous [*ungeheure*] unheard-of events that took place during the eighteen eventful days of a campaign that mocks the boldest thoughts, the most daring combinations of the speculative mind [*Geistes*]. Indeed the human mind [*Geist*] does not know its own greatness; the act surpasses the thought. For it is not rude physical force, no! it is the spirit [*Geist*] that creates deeds as they have happened, and it is the psychic power of every single person, really inspired that attaches itself to the wisdom and genius of the general and helps to accomplish the monstrous and the unexpected." (English translation, slightly modified, 269; German, 660–61)

Certainly, what Albert "remembers" does not have the status of an eyewitness account, as he is aware that in the heat of battle he could not have attended to his observations. Instead he conjures up before his mental eye the faces, words, and sounds of the dying soldiers. There is no narrative component to his memory; nor does it bear the traces of his own affective response to what one would expect to be expressions of individual agony and horror.

Albert's battlefield dream memory can be contrasted with Hoffmann's own account of his first visit to a battlefield, from his diary entry of August 29 after the battle of Dresden in 1813:

A list of the naked bodies of Frenchmen in a mass grave, of maimed and torn-apart bodies of Russians—of a soldier whose head had been torn off—of horses and everything mixed up and thrown into a wild disorder—on many an unmaimed face one could still see the rage, the grim fury of the battle—one had been just about to take out a fresh cartridge in order to reload when he was hit by death—A

Russian officer, a wonderful, handsome youth (at most 23 years old) still held his sabre above his head in his right hand and this is how he became stiff with rigor mortis—A cannon ball had hit him on the chest at his left arm, tore off the arm and smashed his chest—his death had been easy.[20]

The contrast between the two battlefield accounts could not be stronger. Instead of the horror and chaos of fragmented bodies, Albert's remembrance of the dying soldiers is unified into a testimonial to the heroic spirit. First he attempts to capture the battlefield experience in terms of the Greek ideal of "immortality," of the fame of those who died valiantly in battle; then he compares his account to the secondary elaboration of a dream. In the comparison with a dream—something that is not bound by the constraints of time and space—he slides from his own experience into idealist speculation, to a transcendental consideration of the conditions of the possibility of victory, and then to speculative conjecture about what gave rise to the events of the last eighteen days of the campaign. He finds the answer in an inspired collectivity in which each individual's enthusiasm is fused into a powerful force that gives rise to such events of world historical significance.

Juxtaposing Albert's remembrance of the battle of Issy and Hoffmann's own account of his first view of a battlefield at Dresden brings out the immense ideological charge of Albert's vision, one that became central to the first mythopoetic stages of German nationalism. It evokes the tremendous spiritual force of the collective effort emphasizing both the importance of the individual fighters and their joint achievement. In addition, it captures the patriotic spirit that inspired the liberation wars, that found its most popular, concrete, and detailed articulation in the writings of Arndt and the gymnastics movement of Friedrich Ludwig Jahn (1778–1852). Yet it is of equal importance that Albert's vision is marked as a "dream," and that this dream is opposed first by the autumnal and barren landscape through which he rides back east on November 20, 1815, the day when the peace treaty between France and the allied forces that had fought against Napoleon was signed, and then by the sudden appearance of Talkebarth, who intercepts Albert and leads him to his friend Viktor at the nearby estate of the baron and baroness.

Considering the temporal spacing and seasonal contrast, one might note that the content of Albert's dream vision and the melancholy surroundings of his return ride parallel Napoleon's midsummer defeat (the Battle of Waterloo ended on June 18 and the Battle of Issy on July 3, 1815) and the restoration that followed. One might then conclude that the narrative frame marks the present as that moment in then-recent history when the enthusiastic patriots' political hopes for continuation of the liberal reforms begun by von Stein were thoroughly disappointed. If the November landscape and the isolated, sleepy, and self-satisfied existence of the baron are indeed indicative of the era that followed the peace treaty, it is furthermore important to note that Hoffmann wrote "The Elementary Spirit" precisely when, in his capacity as a Prussian civil servant and judge, he was called into a committee charged with investigating and prosecuting the "demagogues," enthusiastic patriots who felt betrayed by the political developments after the liberation wars and who became political activists rebelling against the restored government. Hoffmann was put into the position of having to work for the prosecution of the political opposition. Against the pressures of the ministry of justice, he fought for the civil rights of Jahn, who had been incarcerated and charged with planning to assassinate the chief of police.[21]

Especially if we consider Hoffmann's frequently expressed contempt for the philistine atmosphere of the restoration (which found its culmination in his 1822 novel *Meister Floh*, which was censored and which led to Hoffmann's being accused of demagoguery), we must also note that his critical position has nothing in common with the patriotic nationalism of Arndt or Jahn. Indeed, I argue that Albert's patriotic enthusiasm serves as a foil for Viktor's quest. Albert's dream of heroic patriotism is not only contrasted with the November landscape but actually cut off by Talkebarth, who assumes the same function of interrupting and undercutting an enthusiastic union with the spirit as when he intercepts Viktor's look into the mirror, or when he prevents Viktor's final union with the elementary spirit. The frame narrator uses Talkebarth as a leading character in the comic episodes, such as the mock heroic passage about the accidental slaughter of the baron's poultry, to undermine the seriousness and the pathos of Albert's heroism.

Paul Talkebarth is primarily characterized by his speech, which is interspersed with bowdlerized French expressions, such as "Zermannöre!" (sur mon honneur) or "Zackermannthö" (sacre nom de dieu) (English translation, 270; German, 662). "Talkebarth's fine French phrases—the gentle reader has already been made acquainted with some pleasant curses—were current, if not through the whole army, at any rate through the corps to which his master was attached. Every trooper who came to quarters in a village cried to the peasant with Paul's words, 'Pisang! de lavendel pur di schevals!' [Paysan, de l'avoine pour les chevaux]" (271; 664). Thus this sympathetic comic character embodies everything that the nationalist propaganda needed to reject with hatred and moral indignation, in its attempt to give shape to a unified German culture, spirit, and character.

In his essay "Über deutsche Art und über das Welschtum bei uns" (On German Manner and Frenchness Among Us) from volume IV of *Spirit of the Times*, Arndt goes on for many pages condemning the evil influence of the French language and French manners as something that has already managed to corrupt, falsify, feminize, and weaken the simple, truthful, and manly German national character.[22] Indeed, Arndt goes so far as to call the French language and spirit that has infiltrated German culture a devil that needs to be exorcised: "This devil is too powerful, he has eaten himself so deeply into our more noble parts that he will not be easy to exorcise. One can at least get rid of the French overcoat and manner of bowing, the French headdress, the little boxes for cream and bottles for smelling salts from Paris" (my translation).[23] Talkebarth is not a devilish figure but quite the opposite, an exorcist who drives away the evil spirits. He chases away the devilish apparitions of Biondetta and O'Malley in the inset narrative, and he interrupts Albert's patriotic pathos and seriousness. One might argue that through the character of Talkebarth Hoffmann's tale reverses the issues; if the hatred and abjuration of anything French were all that was left of the patriotic spirit from the liberation wars, and if this hatred of the French became the only hope for creating a German national body and spirit, then what needed to be exorcised was not all things French but the xenophobic nationalism of the restoration period itself.

Sir Walter Scott's influential and unsympathetic review of Hoffmann did not appear in the *Quarterly Review* until 1827, five years after the German author's death. Whereas Scott bemoans Hoffmann's misled genius, busying itself with fantastic tales that are at best of pathological interest instead of spending his energy on realistic descriptions of scenes from the Napoleonic wars, the frame narrative of "The Elementary Spirit" actually sets the two options (battlefield account and fantastic tale) side by side and removes any moral reproach from the latter genre. Thus Scott's juxtaposition of useful and instructive battlefield eyewitness reports with the frivolous genre of the fantastic tale is already an issue in the frame of "The Elementary Spirit." Moreover, if there is anything frivolous about either genre, it is the complacent sensationalism associated with the desire for bloody battlefield accounts that Hoffmann represents in the character of the baroness: "The baroness assured him, with a smile, that there was nothing prettier than tales of war and murder; while the baron, who had rejoined the party, said that he liked to hear of battles when they were bloody, as they always reminded him of his hunting-parties" (my translation, 297; German, 670).

The narrator points out that although Albert was initially annoyed by these remarks trivializing his war experiences, he eventually "unfolds before Viktor's eyes the entire horribly sublime painting of that terrible battle, which at once destroyed all the hopes of the one who had dreamed himself ruler over the world" (my translation, 297; German, 670). However, the narrator does not retell anything from Albert's narrative. Apart from calling that story a "horribly sublime painting" and speaking of Albert's "glowing enthusiasm," he merely focuses on the audience's reactions: Viktor, entangled in the wool of the knitting baroness, lost in his own dreams, does not take in a word of Albert's story; the baron falls asleep, and the baroness, apologizing for her fatigue, suggests that they leave the two friends alone. Thus the frame narrative of "The Elementary Spirit" marks the place for the historically significant battlefield account but leaves this space blank. Instead of Albert's story, the reader of Hoffmann's tale is presented with Viktor's fantastic tale. In other words, as if prefiguring Scott's criticism and refuting it in advance, the main part of the narrative (the inset fantastic tale told by Viktor) takes the place of the history painting.

The fantastic tale is not merely contrasted to the sublime historical narration of Napoleon's final defeat; it is made into an equivalent or substitute. Moreover, Albert's solitary recollection of the battles on his ride toward Aachen is cast in nuptial imagery and the poetic terminology of enthusiastic inspiration. Thus the semantic fields of *Sehnsucht, Tod, Brautgemach, Geist, Begeisterung* (longing, death, nuptial chamber, spirit, and enthusiasm) connect Albert's characterization of the heroic battlefield deaths with important elements from Viktor's fantastic romance narrative. Finally, the themes of the battlefield memory and ultimate enjoyment are recalled in the ending of the tale. The penultimate paragraph, preceding Viktor's final decision to remain unmarried, concludes as follows:

Albert's reflections on his ride from Liège to Aachen have shown the deep seriousness and glorious significance with which he grasped the events of that fateful time. On the journey to the Residence, whither the two friends now returned, he succeeded in completely delivering Victor from the dreamy condition into which he had sunk, and, while Albert depicted in the most lively colours and brought to his friend's mind all the monstrous occurrences that the days of the last campaign had brought forth, the latter felt himself animated by the same spirit as that which dwelt in Albert. And although Albert never ventured upon long contradictions or doubts, Victor himself now seemed to look upon his mystical adventure as nothing but a bad dream. (English translation, slightly modified, 297; German, 707)

If this paragraph had concluded the tale, Viktor's mystical adventure would have had the status of a mere nightmare or an escapist fantasy. We should note, however, that his dream is countered not by supposed reality but by Albert's recollection about the last days of the campaign, which in the introduction to the story also was explicitly compared to a dream—one like the patriotic vision that inspired the liberation wars. One could also say that Viktor leaves his own mystical adventures behind when he enters Albert's dream. Even so, the story's last paragraph, confirming Viktor's refusal to get married, emphasizes that ultimately he does not subscribe to Albert's dream. This second closure affirms Viktor's loyalty to his own recollection of his mystical adventures in his opposition to nuptial bliss. Whereas Albert embraces and glorifies death on the battlefield as the ultimate fulfillment of patriotic longing and human happiness, likening it to marrying the most beautiful woman, Viktor has come to separate desire from fulfillment.

With Hoffmann's "The Elementary Spirit," the genre of the fantastic tale has been situated within European culture, from the late Enlightenment of the 1770s to the restoration after the Napoleonic Wars. The enthusiasm of a generation of young men was kindled by the identificatory, intense reading experience of the popular literary products of the Storm and Stress, the late Enlightenment fascination with the occult that yearned toward the limits of rational insight, and the early Romantic discontent with the habitualized forms of everyday life. Everything that pertains to the literary production of German classicism (such as the works by Schiller and Goethe written after 1795)—the literary movement contemporary to Romanticism that took a critical stance toward the identificatory enthusiasm of the Storm and Stress and the Romantic transfiguration of everyday life—everything that elaborated a model of aesthetic distance and autonomy is carefully elided. We also note a growing nationalism, which found its first concrete manifestation in the liberation wars and their subsequent glorification, a "spirit of the times" conjured up and disseminated in such publications as the eponymous work by Arndt. Hoffmann links both of these cultural hallmarks: Albert's patriotic enthusiasm in the frame narrative, and Viktor's identificatory reading experience in his "confession." He presents both types of "spiritual encounter" as sexual fantasies of an ultimate fulfillment; death on the battlefield becomes the earth's nuptial embrace, and Viktor longs for union with the fiery salamander.

Furthermore, Hoffmann situates Cazotte's tale within the history of sexuality. He draws attention to the ending of Cazotte's novella, marking its conclusion with the doctor's advice that Alvaro should marry a young woman his mother would choose for him as a normalizing move that his protagonist, Viktor, explicitly rejects. Moreover, the idea of marriage that Viktor rejects is not limited to that of the normalizing measure that would bind him to a monogamous relationship, nor to a traditional parental arrangement (the recommended option for Alvaro). Indeed both, the Romantic definition of marriage as exclusively defined by love and the Enlightenment definition of marriage as based on friendship and common interest, are unacceptable to Viktor. He renounces marriage for quite modern and radical reasons: out of fidelity to the type of ultimate bliss he believes he has known, and from refusal to accept substitutes. His renunciation of marriage thus becomes an affirmation of his desire, so that his sexuality is elevated into an identity-granting feature shaped by his individual memory as well as history. What is more, Hoffmann makes the fantastic the all-important catalyst in his protagonist's sexualization. Whereas the traditional path of seduction would have taken its beginning from the actual sight of the object of desire and been followed by a concrete series of actions (approach, touch, and so on), Viktor's seduction is initiated by his physiological reaction to Cazotte's *The Devil in Love*.

A complex commentary on the historical contexts for the fantastic, Hoffmann's "The Elementary Spirit" unfolds the genre's qualities in terms of a seduction through reading. His poetological tale not only characterizes the pragmatic dimension of the specific reading experience of the fantastic as a radical transformation of the reader's subjectivity into a new kind of sexuality—a fundamentally problematic relationship to pleasure and desire—but also explores the political aspects of that culture's longing to be united with the spirit of the occult. As the analysis of the frame narrative has shown, Hoffmann dissociates the fantastic from any particular ideological agenda, such as the rabidly xenophobic patriotism of the Napoleonic Wars or the philistine complacency of the Restoration. In the last chapter of this study, I explore what appears here as Hoffmann's insight into the fantastic, namely, that this generic innovation cannot be subsumed under one ideological umbrella.

2

The Aesthetics of Shock and the Poetics of the Perverse

Paranoid Eckbert, Melancholy Emil, and "The Imp of the Perverse"

In his essay about Shakespeare's use of the marvelous, Tieck outlines a poetics for a modern era, for which the marvelous must be produced by inviting the reader's acceptance of the fiction in terms of the conventions of psychological realism, but without allowing the reader to discard seemingly supernatural occurrences as a mere hallucination or deception of the fictional character.[1] The fantastic tales that Tieck began to write shortly thereafter make use of this technique of unsettling the reader. As detailed in his Shakespeare essay, his own tales also invoke both the register of the marvelous and the conventions of psychological realism to suspend the reader's "normal" sense of reality; yet they aim not merely at the sensation of marvel or wonder but at a far more violent shock to the reader's sense of certainty. This shock can be discussed in terms of how it undermines an Enlightenment model of representation and communication. But insofar as the shock arises from the protagonist's (and by extension the reader's) confrontation with a potentially supernatural, overpowering, and occult force that appears as both strangely external and alien and intimately familiar and embedded in the psyche's motivational deep structure, it can also be captured in terms of a psychoanalytical understanding of sexuality and the unconscious.

Heinz Hillmann describes the effect of "Der blonde Eckbert" (Blond Eckbert, written in 1795) as driving its reader into madness.[2] This fantastic tale remains Tieck's most famous and widely translated story. By contrast,

"Liebeszauber" (Love Charm, written in 1811 and translated by Thomas De Quincey) never achieved popularity and was considered essentially violent.[3] Both tales were published in Tieck's collection *Phantasus* (1812), which uses as the context for the fantastic tales an ongoing conversation among a group of friends about nature, representation, art, and friendship. Indeed, as I show in the first section of this chapter, the fantastic tale, as framed by Tieck's *Phantasus*, emerges in response to an acute awareness of problems of mediation and communication.

Hoffmann, in "The Elementary Spirit," contextualizes the problems of mediation with references to the cultural history of reading and the political history of the Napoleonic Wars. By contrast, Tieck, in both the frame narratives of *Phantasus* and the fantastic tales themselves, projects the destabilized observer position onto the background of a Romantic philosophy of language that, insisting on the linguistic constructedness of reality, radically undermines the historically older Enlightenment paradigm of representation. Even so, this focus on the vanishing ideal of linguistic transparency does not result in mere epistemological concern with what can be known and represented; instead it highlights a crisis of trust, on the part of the culture of sensibility, in the possibility of sympathetic understanding, and of promoting understanding and proximity by way of sharing one's own story. In several of the texts that I discuss in this chapter, this problem of communication is crystallized in focusing on the speech genre of the intimate confession.

Whereas traditionally the autobiographical genre of the confession relies on the assumption that one can know and communicate the secrets of one's psychic life, the fantastic tales that are the focus of this chapter bring this presupposition radically to question. "Blond Eckbert" makes use of autobiographical narration only to show that the speaker can neither entirely know his own story nor control the effect that the act of confession may elicit in himself or in the addressee. Instead of improving mutual understanding and promoting friendship and proximity, the scenario of intimate confession results in violence, madness, and death. In "Love Charm," the protagonist's hope of confiding his secret love of his beautiful neighbor to his close friend is bitterly disappointed, and instead of an autobiographical tale the reader is given a direct view of the protagonist's psychic state through the poems he composes. Moreover, the reader is drawn into psychological speculation over the protagonist's extreme asocial nature through conversations in which he expresses his abhorrence of music and dance. "Love Charm" posits aesthetic hypersensitivity as the cause of the protagonist's violent outbreak of madness.

Both stories characterize the protagonist's violent break out of a state of melancholic isolation as a total disregard for the rational concerns of self-protection and self-preservation, driven by the irresistible force of an unconscious sexuality. They both focus on the strange impossibility of intensifying the intimacy of a friendship, or of consummating a love relationship. The protagonist's pathological or problematic relationship to another—whether friend or beloved—is addressed, analyzed, and talked about in the diegetic context of the tale; yet these acts of confession, these communications, seem to exacerbate and intensify rather than resolve the problems and tensions. This peculiar take on an individual's sexuality invites two approaches: one historical, to the discursive construction of sexuality as a problematic form of desiring; and the other psychoanalytical, to sexuality as fundamentally different from any instinctual organization.

In the last section of this chapter, I turn to Edgar Allan Poe's intriguing pseudoscientific treatise, "The Imp of the Perverse" (1845). Neither a fantastic tale nor a narrative about love or friendship, this text might at first seem unrelated to the concerns of this chapter. But insofar as it argues for the existence of a radically irrational drive to disregard any calculus that would aim at the optimization of pleasure, gain, or self-advancement, and insofar as it attempts to illustrate and prove the existence of this bizarre urge—which it calls "the imp of the perverse," compelling a most peculiar and shocking confession of a murder—Poe's text can be read as a commentary on the novelty and the provocative nature of a powerful compulsion that is conceived as a departure from the natural and the instinctual, the emergence of which I discuss in Tieck's tales as the construction of a radically perverse sexuality. In Poe's text the literary construction of perverse behavior and desires can be distinguished from the traditional moral approach to perversion and contrasted with the nineteenth-century psychiatric and psychological attempts to pathologize perversion. On a performative level regarding its use of the confession, Poe's "Imp of the Perverse" addresses the aesthetic and radically amoral dimension of perversion that emerges with the supposedly new sexuality of the fantastic tale.

The Limits of Representation

The introduction to the framing narrative of *Phantasus* addresses the end of the representational paradigm of language.[4] Speaking out against the Enlightenment ideal of transparent communication, perfect confidence, and mutual exchange of the most intimate confessions, Ernst, one of the characters of the group, formulates an altogether novel model of friendship:

> What is so heavenly about friendship, is to lose oneself entirely in the beloved object; to anticipate, right next to all that is familiar, so much that is strange and mysterious; to respect with heartfelt belief and noble confidence also that which is not understood; to gain soul through this love and to give soul to the beloved! How crude is the life of those—and how they forever inflict pain on themselves and their friends—those who understand, judge, and measure themselves so completely and unreservedly, in the illusion that this will bring them closer! What this means is to cut down trees, to level hills and to deviate brooks in order to have a clear view, to gain in communication and connections—and it means also to destroy a beautiful romantic park in the process. (25–26)

The enjoyment of friendship consists, according to Ernst, in some form of estrangement from oneself that entails confronting the limits of understanding. With the park metaphor, he highlights the necessity of cultivating and controlling a friendship and also emphasizes a level of judicious artifice in expressing friendship that, allowing the other to remain opaque in his alterity, respects and adapts to the local particularities, thus protecting the other from reckless confession of intimate truths. Another character, Anton, further develops this germinal idea:

> What you are addressing, Anton said, this touches on the issue not only that it should be allowed but that it should be necessary that friends should have secrets that they do not share with each other. It also explains the strange phenomenon that one would confide something to a certain friend that one would not share with the person with whom one is even more intimately involved. There is an art to friendship as there is in all things, and perhaps the lack in friendship that is mourned all over stems from not recognizing friendship as an art. (26)

In the course of this opening discussion, therefore, friendship itself comes to be defined as one among the many arts that are of concern to the aesthetic and poetological discourse of the frame narrative.

Throughout the conversation in the introduction to *Phantasus*, gardens and parks are used as a metaphor for comparing approaches to the more general problem of mediation and communication.[5] The nature of a garden or park cannot be discussed apart from its specific mediation (a bridging, a framing, a separation, a preparation, and so on) between the alterity of the adjoining nature and the familiarity of the domestic architecture. Translated into poetological issues, this observation raises a crucial question: If we always construct reality through the linguistic filters and perceptual schemata of our everyday culture, how can we ever be capable of glimpsing of what is truly other; how can we comprehend what underlies these filters? The garden or park becomes in this context a model of an approach to art that can propose another language, one that aims at access to the other as truly other.

The end of the frame narrative's introduction to the first volume of *Phantasus*, which primarily contains the fantastic and marvelous tales, further elaborates this problem of the modality of access to alterity. Anton points out that there are two ways of experiencing nature. The first is the kind of experience in which the beholder enjoys the beauties in nature that reflect his own inner disposition. However, in this kind of contemplation it is not the strangeness or newness of the encounter that is at issue, but an aesthetic experience of beauty that is based on the mutual mirroring of the beholder's interiority and the external surroundings—in other words, affirmation of the harmony of the beholder's own faculties. The second way of experiencing nature, is the possibility of "an unsuspected rapture that falls from the skies into our heart, which it opens up to an unknown enthusiasm" (112). This experience has nothing to do with the beholder's inner disposition. It is, to a certain degree, independent of the beholder and can only be described as something like a "revelation," a confrontation with alterity that happens at best only "twice or three times" in a lifetime. By sheer rarity of occurrence, therefore, this second mode of experiencing nature is impossible to translate as an aesthetic or poetic program.

These, however, are not the only options, for Ernst articulates yet another possibility for an encounter with alterity. This access lies in minimally displacing one's attention, and it is here that we glimpse a rudimentary poetics of the fantastic:

Even the most beautiful environment has its specters that cross our heart; even the most beautiful environment can unleash such strange anticipations, such confused shadows through our fantasy [*Phantasie*]; that we try to flee them by seeking refuge in the bustle of the world. This is how poems and fairy tales arise in our inner nature; this is how, with the aid of these figures, we try to populate the immense emptiness and the terrible chaos, and to decorate the unpleasant space; these fictions, however, will then not be able to deny the imprint of the character of their producer. In these fairy tales of nature [*Naturmärchen*] the lovely is fused with the terrible, the strange with the childish, and it stirs our fantasy into a poetic fury [*Wahnsinn*], which it tries to unbind and set free in our interiority. (112–13)

Whereas the initially mentioned harmonious experience of the beauty of a natural landscape relies on the mutual mirroring of an inner disposition, and the composition and sequence of external stimuli and perceptions, this passage directs our attention to the kind of operation of linguistic and perceptual filtering that ensures such harmony. The limits of our knowledge ("strange anticipations") and the uncertain contours of our perception ("confused shadows") become specters that suddenly transform beauty that had been familiar into something uncanny. The experience of radical alterity does not arise from a revelation (in the familiar guise of a sunrise, for example) but as sudden estrangement from the harmonious and familiar, and confrontation with emptiness and terrible chaos. Out of this anxiety comes sudden loss of orientation and inner fragmentation; out of this encounter with alterity we produce "fairy tales of nature"—that is, fantastic tales. They are motivated—and we see this principle in operation in the discussion of "Blond Eckbert" yet to come—by flight from the loss of reality, by an attempt to reconstruct access to the world ("we try to populate with these figures the immense emptiness and the terrible chaos and to decorate the unpleasant space"). This kind of poetic production is, in contrast to lyric poetry about the beauties of nature, not an expression of a harmonious subjectivity but the result of a minimal shift in attention from the inspiration of nature to the functioning of language itself, which is, in Tieck's words, the vehicle of a "poetic fury."

How does this shift in attention work? These figures that "unbind and free" the poetic fury inside us have a specific relationship to language. These fairy tales are allegorical in the romantic sense, insofar as they insist on an indirect mode of expression emphasizing a heterogeneous semiotic repertoire that mixes "what is lovely with the terrible" and "the strange with the childish." Enlightenment semiotics understands by allegory those signs that are clearly marked as signs—that is, signs that emphasize the conventionality of the code. This is why Enlightenment aesthetics, so interested in the transparency of the signifier, rejects allegorical signs because they disrupt the aesthetic illusion.[6] Romanticism, by contrast, develops an entirely different relationship toward allegory; it is especially because allegory directs our attention to the linguistic construction of reality that it is readmitted into the repertoire of poetic devices. Its definition and function, however, are fundamentally changed. For Tieck, allegory always means an additional strategy by which a text is shown to be a linguistic and subjective construct.[7]

The poetics of the fantastic arises in the context of a Romanticist aesthetics and philosophy of language, and in light of awareness of the linguistic and cultural constructedness of subjectivity and reality. It is especially in an instance when language manages to convince us of the self-evidence of the commonsensical that it proves to be just as limiting as the most idiosyncratic kind of madness or delusion. The power of art in creating access to alterity, then, must not be sought in the attempt to find a more direct or faithful access to alterity, but rather in the emphasis it places on what is strange, distorted, and grotesque in something that was known to be beautiful and harmonious. To a certain extent, the poetics of the fantastic tale then moves rather closely to a modernist poetics of defamiliarization. The observer position of the fantastic tale is one for which the self-evidence of what used to be taken for reality has disappeared; it is also the position of a beholder for whom the harmonious and the beautiful are merely fragile guards against an otherwise chaotic, disturbing intrusion of overwhelming impression and perception. Still, the disruption of harmony and beauty itself, despite shocking and threatening aspects, can also become the domain of the aesthetic, albeit a radically new aesthetic of terror and shock.

Blond Eckbert's Paranoia

On the surface, "Blond Eckbert" (originally published in 1796) can be seen as a fairy tale with an underlying theme of revenge: Eckbert (who, with his wife, Bertha, lives an extremely secluded life in his castle in the woods) invites his only friend, Walther, to stay overnight. After dinner, he asks Bertha to tell their guest the story of her childhood and youth. Bertha's narrative takes up almost half the novella. She tells how she was raised in poverty and how she suffered from an abusive father who would angrily blame her for clumsiness in domestic tasks, to the point that she finally ran away. Exhausted, hungry, and lost in the woods, Bertha met an old woman, who took her to an isolated hut in the forest. Bertha learned to take care of the old woman's household, to look after her little dog and her exotic bird, which sang a beautiful song about the loneliness of the woods and which laid eggs filled with jewels. Periodically, the old woman would embark on a long journey, leaving Bertha to mind the little menagerie. Bertha's secluded life seemed peaceful and idyllic to her, until she learned to read and began yearning for the larger world. One day, before leaving on another trip, the old woman warned Bertha not to stray from the right path. But not long after her departure, Bertha tied up the little dog to keep it from following her, took the bird, and left the woods. After aimlessly wandering around, she suddenly found herself in the village of her early childhood, where she learned that her parents had died. She continued traveling, living off the sale of the jewels from the bird. One day the bird, who had been silent since their departure from the woods, suddenly started to sing again. In a fit of panic, Bertha killed the bird. Soon after, she met Eckbert, who resembled a young knight she had read and dreamed about in the days of her seclusion in the woods. She decided to marry him and follow him to his castle.

Immediately after Bertha ends her narrative, Eckbert begins to distrust Walther and to regret the gesture of intimacy that, he now feels, besides revealing the source of their wealth was not even appropriately appreciated by Walther. Bertha too is eaten up by worry and wonders how Walther could possibly have known the name of the old woman's little dog, which she had been unable to remember when she was telling him her story. Soon after, on a stormy winter day, Eckbert takes his crossbow and goes into the woods to hunt. At a distance, he sees his friend Walther; before fully realizing what he is doing, he aims and shoots him. When he returns home, he learns that his wife has died during his absence.

Plagued by guilt and loneliness, he seeks distraction and begins a friendship with a young knight named Hugo. Although he fully suspects that the discovery of Walther's murder may destroy Hugo's friendship for him, Eckbert nevertheless confides in him. From that moment on, he feels increasingly distrustful of Hugo. Suddenly, he begins to believe that he can see Walther in Hugo. He fears for his sanity and decides to travel. Having lost his way, he seeks directions from a peasant who also resembles Walther. He climbs a hill, hears the song of the exotic bird, and encounters the old woman from Bertha's tale. The old woman demands that he explain what became of her dog, her bird, and her jewels. She tells him that his friends Walther and Hugo were none other than she herself, and she reveals to him that Bertha was his sister. Eckbert falls to the ground and dies in a transport of madness.

The story is striking in its bold mixing of the generic conventions of the fairy tale, for which the supernatural and the marvelous are accepted in their facticity, with those of the psychological realism of the eighteenth-century novel, in which the supernatural and the marvelous are explained as the protagonist's deception or delusion. The omniscient narrator, who recounts Eckbert's story, portrays the protagonist as a melancholic, deeply troubled about his mental stability and health, and thus initially invokes the conventions of psychological realism. By contrast, Bertha's story, recounted in the first person, includes the most typical elements of the fairy tale genre in the narrative of her wandering, and in finding her way to the old woman who lives in the woods with her dog and her exotic bird, suspended in time, in the solitude of a miraculous space. Also typical of the fairy-tale ending is the conclusion of Bertha's story as she marries the knight of her dreams, who takes her away to his castle. However, before commencing her story she draws attention to its fraught, ambivalent, generic nature when she asks Walther not to mistake her tale for a fairy tale but take it for a true account of her childhood and youth.

Insofar as Bertha's narrative weaves heterogeneous elements into her mysterious tale, however, it departs from the formulaic nature of the fairy tale. The idyllic fairy-tale setting in the woods is contrasted with the harsh realism of her poor upbringing. Furthermore, the rendering of Bertha's story as a first person narrative, interspersed with nuanced passages of introspection and self-reflection, invokes conventions of psychological realism that undermine those of the traditional fairy tale. Finally, the manner in which Bertha's narrative is integrated into the story as a whole, the extent to which it is not concluded with its telling but exerts an ominous and powerful influence over subsequent events, transforms the issue of possible confusion over generic markers from a purely literary question into an issue of how far generic markers and linguistic conventions exceed the conscious control of the speaker or narrator.

In its two-part structure, one might say that the fantastic tale commences after the happy ending of the fairy tale. The remote fairy-tale setting of Bertha's story, far from being safely separated from the narrative that follows, irreparably ruptures the protagonists' lives, causing Bertha's death and catalyzing Eckbert's anguished paranoia in the events that ensue. At the very end of the tale, Eckbert, lost and half mad, finds his way to the suspended, miraculous, sylvan space of Bertha's childhood, hears the magical song of the exotic bird, and learns from the old woman the fatal truth about his life and origin. Hence Eckbert's frantic wandering sketches out a return to a remote and menacing place of origin that, by its fairy-tale markers, stands in contrast to the tale's psychological realism.[8]

Finally, the conventions of psychological realism are undermined not merely at the level of the plot (by the strange concatenation of events and the final conclusion of the tale) but also in the omniscient narrator's manipulation of the reader's own approach to language and communication. On the one hand, he steers the reader's expectation toward clarification and revelation, suggesting that the tale will ultimately offer a comprehensive explanation of the mysterious events and enigmatic psychic dispositions of its characters, recruiting, so to speak, the reader into a rationalist, enlightened approach to language and representation. On the other hand, the omniscient narrator also addresses and problematizes this model of language, which takes for granted that it is possible to provide a transparent account of an external or psychic reality by foregrounding the dependency of any perception of reality on its linguistic construction and also by ominously adumbrating the pragmatic effects of communication as lying far beyond the conscious knowledge and control of the speaking subject.

It is this radical subversion of the subject's position vis-à-vis language, representation, and communication that guides my reading of "Blond Eckbert." First, I focus on how the frame narrative portrays his strange psychic disposition culminating in murder, madness, and death. In this phase of my argument, I make the case that this story's account of the genesis of the protagonist's persecution anxiety anticipates certain key elements of a psychoanalytical approach to paranoia (though without schematically mapping Eckbert's madness onto Freud's Schreber analysis). In the second part of my analysis of "Blond Eckbert," I turn to the narrative of Bertha's transition from childhood to adulthood. To a certain extent, this story about the loss of innocence and exit from the paradise of childhood resonates with anthropological and pedagogical discussion of sexuality from around 1800. Nevertheless, insofar as Bertha's story thematizes how her very position as a speaking subject is marked by a blind spot, and how she ultimately produces her sexuality in the telling of her story and is barred from access to this story (she does not know the truth about her incestuous marriage), the model of sexuality suggested through Bertha's narrative clearly departs from its contemporary discursive context and, like Eckbert's paranoia, anticipates a psychoanalytical understanding of the unconscious.

Confessions Gone Awry: Eckbert's Paranoia

In the course of his expository introduction to the tale, the narrator briefly abandons his focus on the characters of the tale and branches out into a psychologizing and universalizing aside, as he speculates about the wish for intimacy and better understanding through communication:

There are hours in which man feels grieved that he should have a secret from his friend, which, till then, he may have kept carefully hidden; at such times, the soul feels an irresistible drive [*Trieb*] to open itself wholly [*sich ganz mitzuteilen*], to disclose even its innermost recesses to a friend, that he may grow even closer in friendship. It is in such moments that tender souls make themselves known to each other; and at times it will happen, that the one recoils from the acquaintance with the other.[9]

The narrator invokes transparency and intimacy, the communicational "deep" values of the Enlightenment culture of sensibility, only to hint that ultimately these values might not be realized, and that total openness might actually not bring people closer but alienate them from each other.

In the narrative that follows, sharing an intimate secret and revealing a hidden truth turn out to have a disastrous effect. Bertha's telling of the story of her youth ultimately leads to her own death; it also triggers Eckbert's paranoia, Walther's murder, and finally Eckbert's desperate and misguided attempt to reassure himself of the truth and stability of Hugo's friendship with the confession of Walther's murder. Significantly, the final blows to Eckbert's sanity and life also come in the form of a series of revelations, but this time from the old woman who reveals her own identity as both Walther and Hugo, and Bertha's identity as Eckbert's sister. By the end of the tale, the destructive potential of disclosing secrets has been fully unleashed.

Whereas in the introductory frame narrative Eckbert is portrayed as a melancholic who might harbor some mysterious secret, which the reader expects will be elucidated through Bertha's tale, the entire second part of the frame narrative—far from explaining the cause of Eckbert's secluded lifestyle and mysterious melancholia—compounds the tension with its single-minded focus on his persecution anxiety. The crux of this tale lies precisely in this transformation of a withdrawn melancholic into a violent, mad character in desperate search of friendship and intimacy. The fantastic nature of the tale issues from the strange effects that occur in the aftermath of the intimate confession of another's autobiographical story told at the bidding of the eponymous hero. It is here that Tieck's tale both invokes and radically subverts the communicational and rationalist paradigm of the Enlightenment culture of sensibility, transparency, and understanding. Somehow, Bertha's story in lieu of Eckbert's is supposed to intensify the intimacy between the two men. Moreover, through Eckbert's vehement and obsessive focus on Walther's reaction to Bertha's story, the telling of Bertha's tale is reframed as something quite different from an innocent confidence, for it appears as an affectively highly charged demonstration of trust; indeed, it becomes a declaration of love that Eckbert perceives as having been rejected. As soon as Walther has thanked Bertha for the story and bid them goodnight, Eckbert is deeply troubled and cannot fall asleep as he begins to suspect and distrust Walther.

Eckbert, reacting to Walther's apparent indifference, maintains the same intensity of affect and exclusivity of attachment toward him, but the nature of his emotion has now turned from love to hatred. Moreover, his hatred of Walther is not acknowledged as such; Eckbert suddenly begins to see in his former friend an oppressive presence.

> Walther had been for many years his sole companion; and yet now this man was the only mortal in the world whose existence pained and oppressed him. It seemed as if he should be gay and light of heart if only that one being could be removed from his path. He took his crossbow, and in order to distract himself, went hunting. (142)

The narrative makes it clear that Walther's visits decreased significantly after the night of Bertha's story telling; it suggests Eckbert's own strange psychic economy as the exclusive cause for feeling oppressed by Walther's existence. Moreover, the wording of the actual killing emphasizes how unaware Eckbert's action is: "Without knowing what he was doing Eckbert aimed; Walther looked around and silently made a threatening gesture. But the bolt was released and Walther fell" (142). Both timing and agency are strangely suspended. To a certain extent, the phrase suggests it was his unaware aiming at Walther that produced the perception of the threatening gesture and that the bolt was released at the same time. Eckbert's perception and action seem to be exclusively dictated by his own subjective emotional economy; yet the nature of his own feelings seems to be only partially accessible to him. Within this context, Eckbert's feeling of oppression at Walther's very existence appears as a defense mechanism against repressed anger stemming from unrequited love.

After he returns home from the murder, he finds out that his wife has died during his absence. His feeling of calm and relief immediately after the murder gives way first to guilt and then to a generalized state of anxiety that "some unhappy event" might occur. For a while, he lives in great solitude but eventually seeks the distractions of the city:

> He longed for a friend to fill the void in his soul; and yet, when he remembered Walther, he would shudder at the thought of meeting with a friend, for he felt convinced that, with any friend, he must be unhappy. He had lived so long with

his Bertha in lovely calm; the friendship of Walther had cheered him through so many years; and now both of them were suddenly swept away. As he thought of these things, there were many moments when his life appeared to him as some strange fairy tale [*seltsames Märchen*], rather than the actual history of a living man [*ein wirklicher Lebenslauf*]. (English translation, slightly modified, 43; German, 143)

Eckbert's psychic state is characterized in terms of a total loneliness and worldlessness that is contrasted with the positively marked solitude of his marital life. It is not for a new wife, though, but for another friendship that he longs, a hope that is immediately overshadowed by fear that this yearning for intimacy would make him unhappy. Any intense human friendship appears to him in light of his failed friendship with Walther, and his fear that the total love that he needs might remain unreciprocated; that he might again be struck by anger and hatred and feelings of persecution at the hands of his new friend. Within this paranoid pattern, how can he assume responsibility for his actions? He can only remember the dear friend who "cheered him" for so many years, but not the killing. His friend, like his wife, seems to have been "suddenly swept away" from his life. Thinking of the recent past, his life appears unreal to him. Moreover, Eckbert's vanishing sense of agency and reality articulates itself in his perceiving his own life like a text for which the generic conventions have been radically switched; instead of being subject to the narrative conventions of an actual curriculum vitae (*Lebenslauf*), his life now appears subject to the conventions of a strange fairy tale.

The new friendship with Hugo repeats and emphasizes key elements of his association with Walther. At the moment when their new friendship has reached a degree of unprecedented intimacy and trust, Eckbert wants more. He cannot be content, for fear that "Hugo loved him only by mistake, that he knew him not and was unacquainted with his history" (143). Thus "on a solitary ride, he disclosed his whole history to Hugo, and asked if he could love a murderer" (143). Significantly, Eckbert's confession is not phrased as a demand for understanding; nor is it motivated by the wish for release from an oppressive sense of guilt. Rather, the demand for recognition and love is marked as a shocking transgression, of confronting a friend with his own repressed past. He wants to be loved as a murderer; he wants to possess him exclusively by making him share the burden of his darkest secret.

Indeed, it does not suffice that Hugo listens sympathetically and tries to console Eckbert; as soon as they are in company, Eckbert's persecution anxiety reemerges, this time as fully formed paranoia:

But it seemed to be his doom that, in the very hour of confidence, he should always find materials for suspicion. Scarcely had they entered the public hall, when, in the glitter of the many lights, Hugo's expressions had ceased to please him. He thought he noticed a malicious smile. He remarked that Hugo talked only very little to him, that he talked with the others, and seemed to pay no heed to him. In the party was an old knight, who had always shown himself hostile to Eckbert, had often asked about his riches and his wife in a peculiar manner. It was with this man that Hugo was conversing; they were speaking privately, and pointing towards Eckbert. The suspicions of the latter seemed confirmed; he thought himself betrayed, and a tremendous rage took hold of him. As he continued gazing, suddenly he discerned the countenance of Walther, all his features, the form so well known to him; and as he continued to look he was convinced that it was none other than Walther talking to the old man. (English translation, slightly modified, 44; German, 144)

Again, a transgressive demand for total love is issued at the outset in the form of an intimate confession, followed by jealousy and anger, which is quickly transformed into the feeling of being persecuted by the object of unrequited love. All of this is brought on by the apparent indifference and insufficient response of the listener.

The emergence of Eckbert's paranoia when he comes to perceive himself as being persecuted by Walther, who now suddenly seems to peer at him through Hugo's face, shows a structural affinity with Freud's model of paranoid symptom formation. Freud characterizes the paranoid's external perception of the agent of persecution ("He persecutes me and hates me") as the substitution and projection of an internal perception ("He will betray me, I don't love him, I hate him, I want to kill him").[10] Clearly, we can note this pattern in Eckbert's relationship to Walther as well as in his relationship to Hugo. Moreover, the psychoanalytical model of repression seems to be called for if we are to account for the intensity and reversal of affect, the hatred that is projected outward. Yet whereas Freud argues that the delusional persecution anxiety ultimately can be understood as the defense against homosexual fantasy,[11] I argue that Eckbert's paranoia is not the result of "repressed homosexuality" but rather the result of repressed sexuality.[12]

In "Blond Eckbert," the stress is not on a presumed pathology of same-sex desire but a deeply disturbing sexuality, and the story depicts various stages of its emergence through Eckbert's actions. Whereas initially it is announced to Walther in the wish (at first sight, harmless) to intensify his friendship, the repetition of the scenario of the intimate confession in Eckbert's relationship to Hugo retrospectively reveals this harmless wish as part of a powerfully compulsive pattern of an unconscious libidinal economy, which culminates in his becoming someone driven to express something he does not, or even cannot, know and who is overwhelmed by the effects of his own speech. In "Blond Eckbert," sexuality arises in and through the protagonist's desperate but failed attempts at communication, as he attempts to break out of his melancholic isolation. It becomes such a deeply disturbing issue because it is profoundly aligned with the speaking subject's exposure to limited control over language and desire.

Already in the passage in which the narrator describes Eckbert's anxiety-tainted longing for intimacy and friendship after Walther's death, we have noted how his psychic state appears to him as a switch from the generic conventions of a curriculum vitae (by which one would narrate the actual story of one's own life as a responsible agent) to the fictional conventions of a bizarre fairy tale. By abandoning the register of psychological realism and concluding in the generic register of the fairy tale, the end of the tale performs for the reader of the tale the same exchange of generic convention. It is in the register of the fairy tale that Eckbert's tormented life finds its end, as he is confronted with the old woman's revelation that she was none other than Walther, Hugo, and even the peasant from whom, lost in his mad wanderings, Eckbert asked for directions. It is the old woman who reveals the secret of his and Bertha's life, their transgressive, incestuous relationship, the truly significant intimate secret that they cannot have known. Even so, despite the invocation of mysterious forces or occult laws that in proper fairy-tale fashion would have suspended the commonly accepted natural order, the conclusion of this tale does not allow the reader to maintain a safe distance from its disturbingly mad and violent character.

Eckbert's death is depicted by the omniscient narrator as drowning in madness: "Eckbert lay mad and dying on the ground. In dull, hollow confusion he heard the old woman speaking, the dog barking, and the bird repeating its song" (English translation, slightly modified, 46; German, 146). However, the assumption of psychological realism conjured by this description is undermined by the old woman's "explanation" of Eckbert's paranoia. Instead of countering paranoid perceptions and fears with an account of how he could have been misled in perceiving Hugo's and the peasant's likeness as identity, the old woman actually confirms Eckbert's suspicion: not only did these people look alike, they actually were the same person, namely, herself. In the story's concluding passages, Eckbert's deep underlying fear that his two friends have been one and the same person loses the status of a mad illusion that lies in opposition to reality and becomes instead the truth from which he has tried in vain to flee.

Eckbert responds to the revelation of the old woman's identity with the despairing sigh that sums up his life: "In what frightful solitude [*in welcher entsetzlichen Einsamkeit*] have I passed my life!" (English translation, slightly modified, 45; German, 145). Although the old woman's revelation of her identity seems to assert the order of the fairy tale and take back the option of a psychologically realistic explanation of Eckbert's perceptions as mere delusion, his reaction to her revelation and her telling him that he was living in incest reintroduces a psychological register—albeit one that no longer gives primacy to a consciously acting and reflecting subject, but one that posits a subject whose life is determined by an unconscious sexuality. His phrase echoes the solitude of the woods (*Waldeinsamkeit*), the key term of the bird's song that weaves together the story's fairy-tale elements introduced in Bertha's tale. Eckbert's outcry, however, reverses the positively connoted term into its opposite, into a frightful isolation that recalls the "void of his soul" after Walther's death, when, losing his sense of reality, he saw himself living in a strange fairy tale.

As this anguished cry against his life's fearful solitude sums up the fundamental truth of his existence, it retrospectively marks his paranoia less as a pathological anxiety and delusion than as a failed attempt to involve himself with external reality and his fellow human beings. In other words, in light of the old woman's revelation, Eckbert's paranoid relationship to Walther and Hugo can no longer be seen as mad flight from the external world and social reality, but instead as a reaction against total isolation, a program for perceiving external objects by way of renewed affective investments, and hence as a construction of reality. Cast in this light, Eckbert's paranoia seems to illustrate what Freud characterizes in these words: "what we take to be the product of illness, the delusion, is actually an attempted cure, a reconstruction . . . the human being has regained a relationship to the people and things of the world, often a very intensive relationship, that now might be hostile whereas before it used to be loving. . . . What noisily announces itself to us is this process of a cure that takes back the repression and returns the libido to the people from whom it had been taken away."[13]

The fantastic ending of the story does not leave the reader hesitating as to whether the protagonist is mad and merely imagining things, or whether these strange occurrences are to be taken for real. In this sense, the story's ending does not fit with Todorov's characterization of the genre that identifies the fantastic element as lying in the reader's hesitation between two explanatory possibilities. The fantastic element in "Blond Eckbert" lies in the moment of disillusionment itself, when the truth, far from opposing Eckbert's fears, actually confirms them. Both the emergence of his delusion and the moment of disillusionment mark the perception of reality as an affectively anchored construct. Eckbert's life, characterized by a terrible isolation from which he has desperately but vainly tried to escape, is furthermore deemed a fateful and incestuous fixation by the old woman's lapidary addendum: "And Bertha was your sister." Thus Eckbert's life is reframed in view of his transgressive, albeit unconscious, sexuality.

"Blond Eckbert's" deployment of its generically innovative feature (intermingling the conventions of the fairy tale with those of psychological realism) confronts the reader with a protagonist who is powerfully governed by some complex occult force best captured by the psychoanalytical concept of an unconscious sexuality. In my reading of the frame narrative's portrait of Eckbert's paranoia, I have shown how his descent into madness is accompanied both by his feeling that his sense of reality is overtaken by the generic markers of the fairy tale and by his encounters of incompletely repressed aspects of his past, which are crystallized in the figure of Walther. The final apparition of the old woman actually combines these features; she can be seen as a personification of the strange fairy tale and a figure for the return of the repressed.

Along these lines, the figure of the old woman may also be read as an embodiment of the effect of the fantastic tale, the uncanny, which Freud discusses in view of E.T.A. Hoffmann's "Der Sandmann." According to Freud, the reader's uncanny feeling results from a confrontation with the repressed childhood trauma of the castration threat.[14] As already indicated in the context of my discussion of Eckbert's paranoia, I would like to refrain from jumping to a premature conclusion about the precise nature of this repressed sexuality. Specifying this repression in terms of repressed homosexuality or a repressed castration threat would take as ahistorical constants aspects of the complex field of human sexuality that are subject to particular historical institutions and discursive practices such as particular constellations of the nuclear family or the pathologization of same-sex desire. Instead, I prefer to further pursue my double focus on the fantastic tale's generic innovation and analyze its production of sexuality as a specific construct within the larger history of nineteenth-century individuality and subjectivity on the one hand, and on the other its analytical take on sexuality anticipating key psychoanalytical insights that approach sexuality and the unconscious from within a poststructuralist focus on the subject's position in language. This double focus seems particularly warranted in analyzing Bertha's inserted tale. As I show later, this story oscillates between a psychologically realistic autobiographical narrative and a fictional fairy tale, and furthermore it suggests an allegorical and universalizing dimension in that it can be read as a story about the exit from paradise, a version of the fall and an account of original sin.

Bertha's Story and the Origin of Sexuality

Bertha introduces her story with these words: "You must not take me for somebody too forward, . . . my husband says that you have such a noble manner of thought that it would be unjust to keep something hidden from you. Only do not take my narrative for a fairy tale, as strange as it might sound" (127). Apparently, she is aware of the generic confusion that governs her narrative; her own story seems to be cast in the same light as Eckbert's take on his life when his memory of the recent past is struck by the repression of his true relationship to Walther and when his sense of reality seems to be lost as he begins to see himself as part of a strange fairy tale. Even so, she attempts to deny the fairy-tale markers that signal her limited access to her own story by asserting its truth value. Significantly, it is only Eckbert who, after her death, at the end of his own life learns the principal secret about Bertha's youth: that he was her brother and that the people she took to be her parents were only her foster parents. Again, sexuality appears as an individual's most intimate and crucial secret, one that wants to be communicated but is also barred from conscious access. This aspect of Bertha's story is brought out when Walther, her interlocutor, indeed does not take her story for a mere fairy tale but accepts it as a true story and even asserts her story's referential dimension by recalling the little dog's name. It is at this confrontation with what has been repressed in her story that she is overcome with fright and ultimately dies of a nervous fever.

Many interpretations have read Bertha's narrative as a story about the loss of innocence and exit from the paradise of childhood.[15] In the hut of the old woman in the woods, Bertha knows neither lack nor strife nor discouragement. All her needs are satisfied. No sooner does she learn to read than her imagination is pushed beyond the limits of her narrow surroundings.

She begins to dream about love, the world, and meeting a handsome young knight. Initially, her innocence prevents her from understanding the old woman's warning not to depart from the right path. But soon she makes the connections: "I would only have to wait for the absence of the old woman, take the bird and the jewels and leave to find the world about which I had read. At the same time this might enable me to meet the extremely handsome knight who was still in my memory" (136). What triggers her departure from the innocent and protected life at the old woman's is her excited fantasy, a reaction provoked in part by the old woman's mysterious words of warning not to depart from the right path, and in part activated by the vague ideas she has elaborated for herself on the basis of the partially understood romances she has been reading.

Why should such a harmless tale about a young girl's sexual awakening be framed as a story of the fall? How might it claim to compete with the account of original sin, the origin of evil or free will from Genesis? To answer this question, a brief glance at contemporary accounts of the emergence and role of human sexuality might prove helpful.

Around 1800, we find discussion of sexuality in the new field of pedagogy, in the form of anxious warnings that young girls must be protected from excessive novel reading. Too much reading might excite their imagination and encourage the supposedly dangerous practice of masturbation.[16] A second discourse addressing the issue of sexuality is that of philosophical anthropology, which focuses chiefly on the powers of the imagination. Here, the distinctly human desiring capacity, though portrayed as a perversion of a natural or instinctual order, is positively interpreted as the condition of the possibility of freedom and rational progress. Kant, for example, even explicitly casts his hypothetical account of the "origin" of human freedom in man's radically open desiring capacity into the frame of an *explication de texte* of Genesis.[17] What both of these otherwise quite unrelated discussions have in common is their focus on human sexuality as something that is neither naturally given nor instinctually programmed, something quite unrelated to reproductive behavior or specific erotic practices but instead intimately linked with the human imagination and desiring capacity and perceived as radically open and prone to external influence and distortion.

Bertha's narrative resonates with these contemporary accounts of sexuality and fuses them. With regard to the pedagogical anxiety over too much novel reading, Bertha's narrative seems to confirm the validity of these warnings; she is indeed led to disregard the simplicity and happiness of her secluded existence in that from her reading of romances she wants to seek the alluring image of the handsome knight. From the discourse of philosophical anthropology, Bertha's autobiographical story borrows its allegorical and universalizing dimension, the depiction of an irretrievably lost mythical past, free from need or strife, from which she was expelled only because of the activity of her imagination and her strangely vague desiring capacity. Bertha's narrative casts her original sin, her first act of transgression, as her reaction to the old woman's warning not to stray from the right path. At first, she does not at all understand what the old woman might have meant by this injunction. But gradually, while elaborating the fantasies she acquired from her reading, she remembers the old woman's warning and "understands" it in that she realizes she can act on her fantasies and depart from her enclosed world in the woods.

Similar to the philosophical and anthropological insistence on the absence of instinct and the openness of the human desiring capacity, Bertha's story also situates the fall in the discovery of some perverse, strangely aimless and objectless sexuality. However, in her case the awakening of sexuality does not give rise to reflection or rational development. Moreover, by attributing a crucial, catalyzing function to her encounter with enigmatic signifiers (the mysterious warning and the books she cannot yet understand), Bertha's tale reframes and specifies the anthropological model of a radically undetermined human desiring capacity in a manner that suggests an ontophylogenetic parallelism. In light of Bertha's account of the fall, the general human condition, as marked by human entry into a fundamentally perverse sexuality and desiring capacity, is reactivated and rehearsed in the development of each individual.

Young Bertha is seduced by texts, by romance novels that she cannot fully comprehend, and is further lured and fascinated by the mysterious warning of the old woman. This scenario of an individual's sexualization by means of seduction by an enigmatic signifier can be compared with Jean Laplanche's psychoanalytical model of the emergence of human sexuality and the unconscious.[18] According to Laplanche, the psychoanalytical concept of sexuality need not be grounded in the historically specific family romance of the Oedipus complex; rather, it should be viewed as a more universal anthropological condition. Laplanche situates the complex development of human sexuality and the unconscious in the modalities of the youngster's dependency on adult care, and the circumstance in which the growing human child is necessarily exposed to articulation of adult sexuality.[19] He emphasizes the fundamentally asymmetrical communicative situation that arises if a child is confronted with adult sexuality. On the one hand, articulation of adult sexuality far exceeds the child's capacity to integrate what it sees or hears into its own psychic economy. On the other hand, owing to the affective charge of the articulation, the child cannot just ignore it. To the extent that adult articulation of sexuality cannot be mentally or emotionally processed, it can neither be fully remembered nor forgotten; instead, it becomes a reservoir of repression. According to Laplanche, it is this encounter with an enigmatic signifier that has the long-term and far-reaching effect of producing human sexuality and creating the unconscious.

The part of the story that is told by the omniscient narrator after Bertha has concluded her tale does not, as in Eckbert's case, focus on her transgressive, incestuous sexuality but on her forgetting the name of the little dog. Even in her narrative she draws attention to the "strange" manner in which she remembers her life at the old woman's hut in total isolation from all human contact, where the two animals impress her as if they were old friends: "I have never been able to recall the strange name of the dog, though I used to call him by it so frequently" (134). It seems obvious that forgetting the dog's name is a form of repression motivated by feelings of guilt, for despite her love for the little creature she was willing to leave him behind in the hut where he might have starved, to pursue some vague erotic fantasies. Nevertheless, she does not repress the memory of the little dog altogether, merely its name: *Strohmian*, based on the verb *strohmern* (to be aimlessly wandering around), could be associated with her own "straying from the right path," her departure from the old woman's hut prompted by her awakened sexuality. Articulation of sexuality in Bertha's story (the narrative of her departure from the old woman's hut) produces a verbal or textual deficit; the repressed and hence the unconscious emerge together with sexuality in the subject's displaced relationship to language and to its own history.

The frame narrative, in its insistence on the dog's name, foregrounds the framing of Bertha's sexuality through her position as a speaking subject who is subject to the unconscious. Moreover, the frame narrative elaborates Bertha's repressed sexuality in Walther's harmless-sounding statement, "My lady, I thank you, I can very well imagine you with the strange bird and how you were feeding little Strohmian" (140), which provokes her anxiety and finally her death of a nervous fever. What is shocking and upsetting in Walther's response to Bertha's narrative is the manner in which his formulation repositions her vis-à-vis her own story. If he had not added the detail omitted from her own narration, his commentary could be understood as praise of Bertha as a storyteller. But mentioning the name suddenly turns her story from a verbal construct that lends itself to being visualized by its addressee into a description of a scene that might indeed have been actually observed by somebody else. Bertha's own position is, retrospectively, radically altered. As long as Walther is merely the absorbed, engaged listener, Bertha alone is in the position of control in conveying what happened, what was reality, and what could and could not be seen. But at the moment when Walther returns to her the repressed name of the dog, she becomes the object of the gaze of an unknown other; she loses the exclusive claim to represent external reality in the narrative rendering of her story. Suddenly, her narration becomes a limited construction of reality that furthermore is affected by her unconscious.

Both the omniscient narrator's tale about Eckbert and the inserted narrative of Bertha's youth end in the death of the two protagonists. In each case, the fatal outcome is provoked by the protagonist's encounter with the limits of a subject who believes himself or herself capable of observing, controlling, and representing a stable external reality, through confrontation with sexuality and the unconscious in the return of the repressed. Whereas the content of Bertha's confession can be read as her sexualization through an enigmatic text or speech by an other, the pragmatic effects of it on the relationship between Eckbert and Walther characterize this kind of autobiographical speech as a seductive and enigmatic text. "Blond Eckbert" frames and stages the confession of the secret as a site of intimacy and seduction, and it marks this speech situation as potentially dangerous and harmful.

In my reading of "Blond Eckbert," I have shown how the subject's sudden confrontation with her or his unconscious sexuality is integrated into both the plot of this fantastic tale and its critical take on the Enlightenment ideals of transparent communication and neutral observation. One might wonder to what extent Tieck's fantastic tale, especially in its strange and troubling conclusion far exceeding an aesthetics of the marvelous, could be captured in the sense of an aesthetics of shock. That this can indeed be the case I show in my analysis of Tieck's "Love Charm." This fantastic tale situates its shock to the presumably neutral observer position within an aesthetic model that challenges traditional models of beauty and harmony by juxtaposing them with an aesthetics of sensory intensity. Moreover, as its mysterious title indicates, this narrative investigates the close nexus between aesthetic and erotic pleasures and constitutes a model for the seductive and sexualizing effects of shock.

"Rear Window" or "Love Charm"

According to Lothar, a character from the frame narrative of *Phantasus*, the tale titled "Love Charm," stands out for its "shrill coloring."[20] The reaction of the group, after hearing the story, divides along gender lines. The ladies of the company express their shock and protest against a story in which "the most cherished and familiar characters are suddenly transformed into strangely spectral beings" (240). The ensuing debate over the terrors of the fantastic tale programmatically announces its break with the culture of sensibility. The male poets from the frame narrative defend the fantastic and argue that everyday reality is actually "a lot more horrible, because there is no poetic mediation of the terror" (242). Manfred reminds his interlocutors of the execution of Urbain Grandier in Loudun in 1634. Although the judges were convinced of the defendant's innocence, Grandier was cruelly tortured and finally burned at the stake as the entire enlightened nation looked on: "and this atrocity was committed fairly close to our days, in the days of philosophy (not during the so-called Middle Ages)" (242). All the spectators could do was pity the tortured victim. Through this aside to intellectual history, Manfred seems to condemn the age of philosophy and rationalism, as well as the ensuing Enlightenment culture of sensibility, as a failure. It was ineffective in improving the morality of the times, and it actually prevented intervention in a just cause by encouraging people to indulge in an impotent display of pity.

The sentimental genres are held partially responsible for this pseudoenlightened attitude that allows self-satisfied consumption of terrible spectacles. Manfred goes on to mock the sentimental "family portraits" of eighteenth-century bourgeois tragedy as well as advice literature for women, together with their idealizing portrait in the contemporary novel. What appears under the guise of a gendered polarization in the debate over "Love Charm" is rejection of the Enlightenment belief in the pedagogical mission of art. Neither literary works nor pedagogical examples can improve the world through a sentimental education. Instead, the fantastic tale comes onto the stage under a "realist" banner, as a project that attempts to face up to the cruelty and terror of everyday reality.

In many ways, "Love Charm" lends itself particularly well to comparison with "Blond Eckbert." As in the earlier tale, the protagonist is also marked by a peculiar psychic affliction; like Eckbert, Emil seeks to confide his secret to a close male friend. Unlike "Blond Eckbert," however, in which the protagonist attempted to shock his friend Hugo into loving him by asking whether he was capable of loving a murderer, in "Love Charm" the confession of the protagonist's intimate secret to his best friend never takes place. In this tale, it is the external reader who is made the exclusive witness of Emil's voyeuristic obsession with his strange and beautiful neighbor from across the street. Yet the reader's exposure to Emil's secret activity acquires a position functionally analogous to the scenarios of intimate confession in "Blond Eckbert." As in the earlier story, we also find here a sudden reversal and shockingly violent disruption emerging from an apparently innocent activity. In contrast to "Blond Eckbert," "Love Charm" not only adumbrates the protagonist's psychic affliction in much greater detail but also explains his pathology in aesthetic terms as an exaggerated anxiety of contact with external stimuli. In other words, "Love Charm" deploys shock at the level of plot and also examines the relationship between the *affective* consequences of shock—its ability to arouse strong love or hatred—and an *aesthetics of shock*, its ability to reorganize an individual's relationship to his or her sensibility and approach to pleasure and forms of enjoyment.

From the start, the principal protagonist's morbid interiority and aesthetic hypersensitivity is contrasted with the exuberant, gregarious cheerfulness and sunny (though somewhat superficial) disposition of his boyhood friend, Roderich. Emil is brooding and reclusive, and he has a contemplative nature that abhors, above all things, music and the noise of human merrymaking. Roderich, by contrast, loves nothing more than to take part in every frolic and adventure. The two, though sharply critical of one another's views and attitudes, are nonetheless inseparable in their bond of friendship. Unlike Eckbert, Emil's desire to confide in his friend is at the core not isolation or alienation but a disturbance within his extremely sensitive inner equilibrium, for which he seeks advice.

The story begins, against the background of a carnival being held in the town, with Emil impatiently awaiting the arrival of Roderich, with whom he has made an appointment to discuss his secret. He has become infatuated with a beautiful young woman whose movements he can spy from the window of his room across the alley. Instead of pursuing the normal occupations of a wealthy young man in his position, he spends most of his time in his room watching her as she tends to a young child, and as she prepares herself in the evening for bed. As he waits for Roderich, annoyed by his lateness, he composes a poem about the beauty of his beloved and the effect that the sound of her singing has on him. Roderich finally arrives, much later than expected and with a friend in tow. Roderich is dressed in a Turkish costume and on his way to a masked ball. He has no time for Emil's confidences but hurriedly attempts to persuade him to don a costume and join the festivities. Emil declines the invitation, upon which Roderich borrows his black cloak, ostensibly to hide his costume while he visits a church on his way to the ball. He asks Emil to keep his Turkish dagger for fear that it might prove dangerous in the topsy-turvy world of the carnival, and leaves the disgruntled young man to his solitary musings.

Emil remains for some time at his window, but soon the young woman across the street extinguishes her light. In the hope of finding the face of his beloved stranger in the crowd, Emil decides to go to the ball. On his way through the crowded streets, attracted by the stillness of a church, he enters. As he contemplates the works of art of the past, he witnesses a bizarre transaction taking place between an ugly old woman wearing a red bodice and two cloaked male figures. The old woman, whose face he first mistakes for a mask, receives money from the men, and discusses a magical ritual requiring human blood that has power to produce a charm that can provoke overwhelming love or hatred. Incensed by the audacity of conducting this kind of transaction in the sanctity of a church and in front of a statue of the Madonna and child, Emil quickly leaves. Briefly, he enters the ball but cannot find his beloved among the few unmasked faces. He hurriedly withdraws, leaving Roderich and his friends astonished at his strange psychic disposition. Back in the safety of his room, Emil sits down to compose another poem, expressing the wild and violent sensations and feelings that the masked ball has aroused in him. Having completed his poem, he steps to the window. His beloved has returned, and he watches her as she prepares for sleep. Suddenly the horrible old woman from the church enters the picture. He witnesses his beloved holding the imploring and struggling child as the old woman with one hand cuts its throat and collects the blood in a silver bowl she holds in her other hand. A fearful dragon head appears from behind the two women, and with a black tongue it slurps up the blood. Suddenly, its brilliant green eye pierces Emil's gaze; he loses consciousness and falls to the ground. A few hours later, Roderich finds the seemingly lifeless body of his friend.

The story resumes at a festive outdoor breakfast gathering in the country. Through the conversation among the guests, the reader learns that the celebration is for Emil's wedding; that he miraculously recovered from a severe nervous fever accompanied by nearly total amnesia; and that he met a beautiful woman, with whom he quickly decided to get married and move to his newly acquired country estate. The guests describe the beauty of the bride in such detail that the reader is led to suspect that she might be the mysterious stranger whom Emil was in the habit of watching from his window. Emil tells Roderich that for some inexplicable reason he cannot be happy; he is deeply disturbed by a conversation he overheard between his beloved and another person who had asked her whether, now that she had obtained exactly what she had wished for, she was finally content. Roderich attempts to cheer up his friend by taking him down to the village, where they witness the wedding procession of a beggar couple. Whereas Roderich's friends amuse themselves by mocking the grotesque couple, Emil, disgusted by this behavior, throws a bag of money to the groom and withdraws with feelings of utter abjection and guilt as to the uselessness of his life of luxury.

A wedding ball is planned at sunset. Unbeknownst to Emil, Roderich has hired musicians for the occasion, contending that his friend, on the threshold of this momentous step toward a new life, must be aided in the transition with music, grotesque costumes, and masks. The bride leaves the guests to change for the ball, and Emil follows to watch her dress. In the meantime, Roderich, disguised as an ugly old woman and wearing a red bodice just like the one worn by the bride's old woman servant, leads the group of musicians upstairs past the invited guests, disappearing behind a door. Suddenly the bride, half dressed and drenched in blood, runs through the door, Emil after her with a dagger in his hand, followed by the old woman who was his bride's servant. The old woman and Emil struggle, cling to each other, and finally fall over the rail in front of the guests. Emil expires in Roderich's arms.

In the narrative presentation of "Love Charm," the psychological trauma sustained by the principal character is reflected structurally in the two-part division of the tale. The first part abruptly ends with the shock of witnessing the ritual child murder, a shock that occasions a narrative caesura in the text. The second part, culminating in the bloody conclusion of Emil's wedding celebration, appears as the protagonist's reenactment of the repressed scene of the child murder. Thus, within the diegetic universe of the story Emil seems to have been led to act out the same scene to which he was a traumatized witness. But the omniscient narrator's psychological perspective of the protagonist's mysterious melancholia and its sudden eruption into bloody violence is not worked out in terms of a coherent biographical narrative. Rather, Emil's violent act is prepared for in the manner in which his melancholia is adumbrated as an extreme, potentially pathological aesthetic sensibility.[21] This aesthetic dimension of Emil's pathology is most clearly depicted in the two poems he writes on the night of the carnival.

In the following section, "The Pathology of Aesthetic Subjectivity," I analyze how Emil's concern with beauty is cast in the light of a psychopathology. This phase of my argument focuses primarily on Emil's poems, which strangely motivate and prefigure the violent reversals of the narrative. The second part of my analysis, "The Love Charm, the Fantastic, and Seduction by Shock," deals with those elements of the tale that prevent the reader from attributing the violent ending of the love story exclusively to Emil's pathology; this constitutes the generically decisive feature of this tale. Ultimately, I argue that this tale is a complex account of the pragmatic dimension of the fantastic tale in terms of the reader's seduction through a shocking encounter—that the fantastic tale works a love charm on its reader, so to speak.

The Pathology of Aesthetic Subjectivity

In the structural economy of "Love Charm," Emil's two poems comment on his momentary psychic disposition by crystallizing his inner state as a particular form of aesthetic sensibility; each poem also proleptically announces the traumatic plot reversals by focusing on the transformation of the aesthetic pleasure of contemplative calm into the frenzied lust of total self-abandon. The first poem stands in lieu of confiding his secret infatuation to Roderich, passing from a description of his beloved's plastic beauty to his inner agitation at hearing the sound of her voice. This voice is an imagined construction, which he has never heard. The second poem immediately precedes the shocking child murder across the street and is a whirling cacophony of sounds, images, and sensual abandon. One might say that both poems function as windows, completely analogous to the window through which Emil witnesses his beloved's movement, giving the reader a direct and presumably unmediated view of the state of Emil's soul.

Before exploring in greater detail the manner in which the two poems come to hold a key position in preparing Emil's sudden eruption of violent madness, it is worthwhile to consider how the narrator implicitly enlists the external reader of the tale in coming to terms with Emil's strange disposition in medical and diagnostic terms. The narrator proceeds by way of a dialogical setting, in which a nameless, unspecified character at the masked ball asks Roderich (who has just held forth on Emil's joyless existence and inability to tolerate the distractions of the carnival), "So he is a melancholic?" (223). Roderich responds "Not really" and claims that he is merely spoilt by his upbringing and, though fundamentally good-hearted, remains unfortunately impervious to Roderich's attempts to change him. Thereupon the nameless listener suggests: "Perhaps he should see a doctor," to which Roderich replies: "It is one of his whims . . . to entertain a supreme contempt for the whole medical art. He will have it that every disease is something different and distinct in every patient, that it can be brought under no class, and that it is absurd to think of healing, either by attention to ancient practice or by what is called theory" (English translation, 446–47; German, 223).[22] The unnamed listener, who might be considered a placeholder for the external reader of the tale, attempts to view Emil's disposition either in light of traditional humorology or in light of the newly emerging medical subspecialty of psychiatry, which attempts to "cure" mental diseases. According to Emil's understanding, however, a psychic disease cannot be accounted for in light of a nosological taxonomy but must be understood in its particularity—how it is an expression of a particular subject's individuality. Insisting on the individual's particularity, Emil's position invokes the approach to psychology and mental illness that was promoted by Moritz's *Magazin der Erfahrungsseelenkunde*, which attempted to study the multiple aspects of the human soul by gathering detailed individual life stories.[23]

This foray into individualizing and particularizing approaches to a psychic affliction notwithstanding, in explaining Emil's solitary ways and asocial character the narrative emphasizes not his melancholia but a self-protective defense mechanism caused by his acute aesthetic hypersensitivity. Emil's aesthetic permeability is articulated in his abhorrence of music, his flight from the noise of crowds and merrymaking, and the fearful assault on his imagination of masks and disguises. His aesthetic sensibility aims at a particular inner harmony; what he calls beautiful does not refer so much to the object of contemplation as to the feelings aroused in him upon contemplating that object. To the extent that Emil's aesthetic experience seeks a contemplative calm, a certain self-sufficient harmony of his faculties, it could be compared to Kant's analytic of the beautiful. Significantly, though, in contradistinction to Kant, Emil's aesthetic sensibility pathologizes Kant's model of the beautiful in that it is both deeply interested and potentially diseased.

Emil's refusal to accompany Roderich to the carnival ball is for Roderich a sign of "sickness." Emil justifies his reclusiveness as a necessary caution against the dangers of music. Music evokes in him all those internal and external perceptions that he tries to hold at bay through his focus on the beautiful. He describes the world of sound as a world of "specters, masks, and furies [*Gespenster, Larven und Furien*]" (215), phenomena that are not clearly defined in their ontological status, which might be real or imagined, which might hide or else reveal something frightful underneath, and which deeply trouble the observer's sense of certainty and self-sufficiency. Roderich remarks that even in childhood Emil had an extreme abhorrence of perfectly harmless spiders and other vermin. Emil's response is significant both in its vehemence and in its universalizing claims about the nature of the true lover of beauty:

"Harmless [*unschuldig*] you call them," cried Emil, now quite untuned, "because you have no repugnance toward them. To one, however, who feels the same disgust and loathing, the same nameless horror, that I feel rise up in his soul and shoot through his whole being at the sight of them, these miscreant deformities, such as toad, spider, or that most loathsome of nature's creatures, the bat, are not indifferent or insignificant: their very existence is directly at enmity and wages war with his. In truth, one might smile at the unbelievers whose imagination is too barren for ghosts and fearful specters, and those births of night [*Geburten der Nacht*] that we see in sickness, to take root therein, or who stare and marvel at Dante's description, when the commonest everyday life brings before our eyes the most terrible and distorted models of these horrors. Yet, can we really and faithfully love the beautiful, without being terrified at the sight of such monstrosities [*Fratzen*]?" (English translation, 439; German, 215)

The last sentence points out the relationship between the beautiful and the horrific. Aesthetic susceptibility appears as a defense against the sudden disintegration of everyday reality. Only those who are aware of and threatened by the proximity of nightmares and madness are truly capable of appreciating beauty, because they need the beautiful as an armor. The art form of music represents the greatest danger to Emil's sense of harmony because it penetrates and disrupts this protective shield that ensures a clear distinction between the external world and his interiority.

The entire narrative of the first half of the tale evolves out of Emil's strange hypersensitivity. Apart from the conflicts and discussions between the two friends, the narrative comprises Emil's musings in front of the window, his yearning for the sight of the beautiful woman attending to the child, and his brief excursion into what is for him the much-abhorred frenzy of the carnival ball. The two poems elaborate at great length two distinct aesthetics and models of pleasure, which can each be related to two forms of aesthetic involvement: tranquil contemplation of the beautiful beloved, and an agitated state of reckless abandon. The thematics of love frames and connects these states, both of which are evoked in each poem in such a way that the tension between the two allows the pleasures of peaceful contentment to be suddenly transformed (especially in the second poem) into the lust of frenzied ardor.

The opening six stanzas of the first poem conform to the conventions of the traditional love lyric. The speaker praises the beauty of the song of the nightingale, the moonlight, the perfume of the linden trees and the roses; but even more beautiful is his beloved, in the evening as she prepares for sleep:

> Wie sie die Flechten löst und bindet,
> Wie sie im Schwung der weißen Hand
> Anschmiegt dem Leibe hell Gewand
> Und Kränz' in braune Locken windet. (212)

> As she loosens and binds her braids,
> As she swiftly with her white hand
> Smooths the bright gown to her body
> And winds crowns into her brown locks.

The last two stanzas, however, effect a sudden reversal in the direction of the relationship between the observer and the observed. The beloved uses her voice to catch the sounds of her lute:

> Sie einzufangen schickt sie Klänge
> Gesanges fort, da flieht mit Scherzen
> Der Ton, such Schirm in meinem Herzen,
> Dahin verfolgen die Gesänge.
>
> O laßt mich doch, ihr Bösen frei!
> Sie riegeln sich dort ein und sprechen:
> Nicht weichen wir, bis dies wir brechen,
> Damit du weißt, was Liebe sei. (213)

> To catch them she sends forth tones
> Of song, but jestingly they flee
> To find refuge in my heart,
> Whereto her songs pursue them.
>
> O, let me be free, you evil ones!
> They bar themselves within, and say:
> Till this be broken, here we stay,
> That thou mayst know what 'tis to love.

Of all things, it is the singing voice of the beloved addressed to the loving admirer that becomes a threat and that invades him as an alien, evil intruder. As long as he merely looks at her desiringly, he can enjoy a self-sufficient peace. But her singing, the musical expression of her desire, suddenly disrupts his contemplative calm, as the sounds penetrate his protective armor.

Emil's second poem elaborates this conjunction of music, love, and violence in much greater detail. The first stanza describes the effect of the dance music of the masquerade as an unleashing of sounds that (as with the first poem) expresses agitation and fear of the pain of music, which threatens to unleash the fettered madness.

> Dazwischen Flöten singen,
> Und Pfeifentöne springen
> Mit gellendem Geschrei
> Zwischen dröhnenden tönenden Geigen
> In rasender Wut herbei,
> Das wilde Gemüt zu zeigen,
> Und grimmig zu morden das stille kindliche Schweigen. (224)

> In the midst of all flutes are singing,
> And the tones of pipes are springing forth
> With shrill clamor
> Among the droning violin sounds
> To approach in raging anger,
> To reveal the wild state of mind,
> And fiercely murder
> The quiet childlike silence.

The second stanza evokes the dance, the brilliance of the lights. Now, suddenly, music in its shriller, intensified mode can actually render the experience of pain insignificant.

> Wir tummeln uns näher und dichter,
> Es jauchzt in uns das wilde Herz;
> Lauter tönet
> Grimmer dröhnet
> Ihr Zimbeln, ihr Pfeifen! betäubet den Schmerz,
> Er werde zum Scherz!—(225)

> In the tumble we get closer and closer,
> The wild heart within us jubilates;
> Resound more loudly
> Drone more grimly
> Ye cymbals, ye pipes! Bedull all pain,
> Till it become a jest.

The static model of pleasure based on equilibrium, satiety, and aesthetic contemplation has here been subjugated by a dynamic eruption of a sensory stimulation, the sheer intensity of which can anesthetize the experience of pain.

This transformation of the initial source of pain into an engine of overpowering abandon that is no longer abhorred but eagerly embraced foreshadows the third stanza, which addresses the beloved: the fragility of the mortal beloved's beauty does not become the occasion for the plea of the traditional *carpe diem*; rather, it becomes the occasion to imagine a wholesale embrace of the ephemeral and transitory brevity of mortality. The stanza reverses the position of the observer and that of the observed, as the immobile skull being cast as witness to the airy lightness of the poet, released from the shackles of fear and sorrow:

> Du winkst mir, holdes Angesicht?
> Es lacht der Mund, der Augen Licht;
> Herbei, daß ich dich fasse,
> Im Schweben wieder lasse;
> Ich weiß, die Schönheit bald zerbricht,
> Der Mund verstummt, der lieblich spricht,
> Dich faßt des Todes Arm.
> Was winkst du, Schädel, freundlich mir?
> Kein Kummer mir, nicht Angst und Harm,
> Daß du so bald erbleichest hier,
> Wohl heut, wohl morgen.
> Was sollen die Sorgen?
> Ich lebe und schwebe im Reigen vorüber vor dir. (225)

Thou beckonest me, beauty's daughter?
The mouth that laughs, the eyes that light;
Come closer that I grasp you,
And in my gliding let go again;
I know that beauty is soon destroyed:
The mouth is silenced that lovely speaks
As you are embraced by the grip of death.
Skull, why beckon you so friendly to me?
I have no grief, no fear, no sorrow,
That you so soon are paling here.
Be it today, be it tomorrow,
Wherefore these sorrows?
I live and swiftly glide past you
In a round dance.

The fourth and fifth stanza describe a crescendo in the interaction between the lovers:

Heute lieb ich dich,
Jetzt meinst du mich;
Ach, Not und Angst sie lauern
Schon hinter diesen Mauern,
Und Seufzer schwer und tränend Leid
Stehn schon bereit
Dich zu umstricken;
Froh lass uns blicken
Vernichtung an und grausen Tod;
Was will die Angst, was will uns Not?
Wir drücken
Im Taumel die Hand,
Mich rührt dein Gewand,
Du schwebest dahin, ich taumle zurück—
Auch Verzweiflung ist Glück.

Aus diesem Entzücken,
Und was wir heut lachten,
Entsprießt wohl Verachten
Und giftiger Neid;
O herrliche Zeit! (226)

Today I love you,
Now you turn to me;
Ah, harm and fear are lurking
Already behind these walls,

The Aesthetics of Shock and the Poetics of the Perverse 91

> And heavy sighs and tearful sorrow
> Are already prepared
> To tie themselves around you.
> Let us cheerfully face
> Destruction and cruel death;
> What can this fear, this sorrow do to us?
> We press
> In the frenzy our hands,
> I am touched by your gown
> You glide along, I tumble backwards—
> Even despair is happiness.
>
> From this delight,
> And what today has made us merry,
> There can emerge both scorn
> And poisonous envy.
> O glorious times! (see also de Quincey, 449)

The two poems, flanking his brief foray into the carnival, with its dreaded hurly-burly of music and masks, function as two windows disclosing the inner transformation taking place in Emil's psychic and aesthetic economy. The model of pleasure in the first poem is characterized by careful protection of an inner equilibrium, minimization of tension, and an attempt to maintain the isolation of a cocoon of familiar comforts, that is radically transformed into a new and reckless model of pleasure derived from the subjugation and destruction of the first. A state of extreme tension, the violent shattering of a contemplative calm, a state of being painfully overwhelmed by intense stimuli is turned into a scenario of ultimate intoxication, a bacchantic dance of death and the pleasurably painful encounter with another's desire and alterity.[24] In articulating this transformation of the pain of overstimulation that follows the traumatic destruction of a protective shield into the new pleasures of excitement, intensity, and tension, the poem announces the logic of pleasure that will dictate the succession of the two shocking, overwhelming encounters that jointly make up a scenario of the emergence of sexuality.[25]

The poems are the key to the two shocking scenes that seem to spiral out of them. In both poems, the pattern of reversal is triggered by a reversal of address. In the first poem, it is the beloved's desire and song that penetrates Emil's heart; in the second, it is first the beloved and then the skull that reverse the gaze. In the actual narrative, this reversal is echoed when Emil's peaceful contemplation of the girl's evening preparation is suddenly shattered by the sight of the child's murder, and it concludes in the reversal of the gaze when the monster's eye penetrates his brain. In addition, the first poem describes the effect of the music from the ball in the image of the murder of a quiet childlike sleep ("Und grimmig zu morden das stille kindliche Schweigen"), a metaphor in reference to which the actual child murder appears as the concretization. The reader is thereby led to wonder whether the subsequent narrative will continue to follow the logic of the poem; whether this brutally shocking destruction of calm, harmony, and innocence, which in the poem is turned into a fiercely violent dance of love and death, will be equally carried through in the narrative about Emil's wedding that follows upon his sight of the murder of the child. Indeed, this is the case in the second part of the story, which ends:

> Roderich took his dying friend in his arms. He had found him in his wife's room, playing with the dagger. She was almost dressed when he entered. At the sight of the hated red bodice his memory had rekindled; the horrible vision of the night had risen upon his mind; and, gnashing his teeth, he had sprung after his trembling, flying bride, to avenge that murder and all those devilish doings. The old woman, ere she expired, confessed the crime that had been wrought; and the gladness and mirth of the whole house were suddenly changed into sorrow and lamentation and dismay. (English translation, 463; German, 240)

This concluding paragraph connects the horrible scene that Emil watched through the window with the bloody ending of the wedding. Emil suddenly recognizes in his bride the perpetrator of the "devilish artifice" of that horrific night. Insofar as the two traumatic and climactic scenes in "Love Charm"—the child murder and the stabbing of the bride—both are embedded in a context of the protagonist's economy of sensuous pleasure and desire, they jointly constitute a scenario of the emergence of sexuality from within a pathological aesthetic subjectivity.

The Love Charm, the Fantastic, and Seduction by Shock

The conclusion of the story prevents the reader from writing off Emil's view of the ritual child murder as mere hallucination since it asserts the agency of the old woman who confesses her crime before she dies. Restrospectively, the reader is reminded of the significance of passages he or she might have overlooked, such as the conversation Emil accidentally overheard as he lingered in the church on the way to the masquerade: "Can it then be,

Alexia, that such rites and forms of words—as those old stories, in which I never could put faith, tell us,—can fetter the free will of man, and make love and hatred grow in the heart?" (English translation, 442; German, 219); or the words addressed to Emil's bride on the morning of the wedding, namely, that she should be happy now that her wish has been fulfilled. The repressed horrific vision of the beloved as the accomplice in the ritual murder of the child appears, in retrospect, as a scene in some way associated with seduction, for the reader has been informed early on of the beautiful stranger's intentions on Emil in a phrase that might easily have been overlooked or taken for a metaphor: "He knew not that she also would often spy on him in the same state of intoxication [daß sie eben so trunken zu ihm hinüber spähte]; nor did he suspect what wishes were forming in her heart, of what effort, of what sacrifice she felt herself capable, so she might but attain to and possess his love" (217).

All of this might still lead the reader to imagine simple complicity between the beautiful neighbor and the old woman, Alexia, in preparing a kind of magical potion or brew made of human blood. Yet the tale makes reference only to a ritual, an act, a deed that, together with the beautiful neighbor's reciprocal spying, puts the nature of the love charm sharply in question. This magic seduction, the "charm," appears to shun the cloak of secrecy. Neither a figment of Emil's diseased imagination nor a simple element within a more extensive magical preparation, the ritual of the child's murder appears as a deliberate rear-window staging, intended for Emil's eyes. The love charm is therefore nothing other, nothing less, than the display of the brutal murder of the child, with the intent to seduce.

How can the mise-en-scène of a ritual child murder function as a love charm, or a means of seduction? What is the underlying logic of this shrill and shocking scene? Given Emil's bizarre economy of desire and pleasure, how does this scene produce and organize sexuality? What is the ontological status of the green monster that appears behind the two women as they collect the child's blood in the silver bowl? We have already noted in the previous section that Emil's aesthetic sensibility is a self-protective armor, an outgrowth of a morbid psychic permeability. His aesthetic hypersensitivity, and his concomitantly strong repugnance of ugliness, is thus marked as having a pathological origin. We have also noted that his fine-tuned suggestibility, when in the grip of a painful stimulus that penetrates his protective armor, acts as a kind of resonator producing a frenzied but liberating effect, and eventual wholesale self-abandon to the overpowering excitement of the moment. The moment of sexualization consists in this transition from a homeostatic organization of pleasure aiming at a state of minimal tension to an organization abandoning itself to the pleasure of intensity and excitation.[26] The scene of the green monster enacts precisely such a sequence.

Upon his return from the ball, Emil finds his frustrated longing to see his beloved assuaged. Sheltered in the refuge of his room, he becomes fully absorbed in admiring her movements as she appears to calm the agitated child in her arms. The realization of the brutal horror he is witnessing thrusts itself upon him without warning, and the effect of the shock is compounded by the sight of the monster lapping up the child's blood from the silver bowl. The reversal of the gaze that leads to Emil's loss of consciousness is described in great detail. Emil is transfixed as he watches the monster: "its black tongue licked up the spirting red blood, and a green sparkling eye shot over into Emilius's eye, and brain, and heart, so that he fell at the same instant to the ground. He was senseless when found by Roderich some hours after" (English translation, 451; German, 227). The gaze of the monster overturns the neutrality of Emil's position as observer and in so doing binds him to the sacrificial ritual. Echoing the passage from his first poem in which the beloved's singing voice, by addressing him, violently pierces his protective shield of quiet contemplation, the scene enacts the reciprocation of Emil's desire by transfixing him as the object of the desire of another. As the monster's gaze fixes itself on Emil's watching eyes, it penetrates his "brain and heart," thus rupturing the screen that has protected Emil from external overstimulation and has guaranteed the wholeness and integrity of his narcissistic subjectivity.

One might explain Emil's loss of consciousness and subsequent amnesia as the result of a sudden sensory overstimulation that, rather than arousing him to frenzied abandon, leaves the end result of the love charm ritual unconsummated. It remains to be underlined, however, that neither is the fantastic element of the tale—the appearance of the monster—a mere hallucination; nor is Emil's presence at the window at the time of the staging of the murder an accidental and unwanted voyeuristic indiscretion. Rather, the transverse link that is established in the locking of the monster's gaze with Emil's draws him into the economy of the sacrificial scene that constitutes the essence of the love charm itself.

The wedding celebration rekindles the unfinished business of the traumatic scene of the child murder. A bridegroom is expected, on his wedding night, to initiate a sexual relationship with his bride. The consummation of love in Emil's wedding takes its cues from the repressed traumatic encounter. The themes of penetration, piercing, and stabbing have recurred throughout the plot in both metaphorical and psychological registers. Already in the first part of the tale, Emil has toyed with the idea of stabbing someone when Roderich, after having arrived late to his rendezvous and frustrated his friend's urgent need to share his confidences, entrusts his Turkish dagger to Emil and takes off to join the carnival. Emil tries to swallow his anger and disappointment, to "fix attention on the laughable side of his friend's behavior. After a while his eyes rested upon the shining, finely-wrought dagger, and he said: 'What must be the feelings of a man who could thrust this sharp iron into the breast of an enemy! but oh, what must be those of one who could hurt a beloved object with it.' He locked it up, then gently folded back the shutters of his window, and looked across the narrow street" (English translation, 440; German, 217). This fantasy of stabbing can be read as a substitute for the hoped-for intimacy of confession as he struggles to forget his anger. The musing on the dagger also prefigures the murder of the bride.

Emil's behavior on his wedding night is not exclusively "explained" as acting out the horrid sight he witnessed from his window. That vision anticipates the change from a rational, self-protecting organization of pleasure to something fundamentally perverse. Sexuality in this story is cut off from any supposedly natural, biological, and binary sex or gender system of reproductive behavior, arising instead in the shocking confrontation with alterity that, in its destruction of a fragile self-sufficiency, disrupts models of pleasurable harmony and destabilizes markers of identity. This is further supported through the ambivalent figure of the ugly old woman by means of which this text mobilizes anxieties of sexual undifferentiation and hence brings home to the reader that this "perverse sexuality," which, though not grounded in any natural binarism, is nevertheless not gender-neutral. The figure of the old woman is introduced in two contexts: first as the threatening old witch who is the beautiful neighbor's helper, and next as Roderich's disguise on the wedding night, a disguise he chose in an attempt to aid his friend in the transition from one stage of life to the next. In both cases, the ugly old woman is the helper figure without whom the love relationship would never go beyond the stage of self-sufficient contemplation. She becomes, so to speak, the all-important catalyst for the sexualized relationship to the other.

Throughout the story, Roderich is portrayed in the function of the normalizing helper figure, the friend who attempts to pull Emil out of his melancholia and isolation, and the friend who wants to safely marry him off. During the wedding celebration, Roderich explains the rationale and function of the masquerade, with its grotesque disguises and shrill music to the guests around him, as a cultural form that mediates and aids the newlyweds in their move to the radically unfamiliar matrimonial state. He then shows off to his friends a marvelous red bodice, costume, and mask that his tailor obtained from some old woman who probably sported it at a witches' gala. This is what he will wear in a surprise masquerade procession to the newlyweds' bedchamber.

With his love of music, dance, and masks, Roderich entertains a lighthearted attitude and believes it is possible to safely contain the frenzied, unpredictable world of the carnival (even though he felt obliged on the fateful night to leave the Turkish dagger behind with Emil). This belief, grounded in the conviction that it is ultimately possible to distinguish truth from appearance, is radically undermined in the conclusion of the tale. In the first part of the story, when Emil stops in a church on his way to the ball sees the old woman, he "fancied at first it must be some tasteless mask that had strayed there by mistake; but he was soon convinced by the bright light that the old, brown, wrinkled face was real and no imitation" (218–19). But in the passage in which Roderich shows off his disguise, we learn that the ugly mask that he has acquired came with the costume. Did the figure Emil encountered in the church then wear a mask after all? Moreover, what are we to make of Roderich's request to borrow Emil's black cloak so that he could visit a church on his way to the ball? These questions remain unresolved and further unsettle the reader's presumed sense of certainty. In the end, it is not the celebration of carnival but rather the celebration of a wedding that culminates in the shocking dissolution of identity and certainty, thus replacing the stability of the institution of marriage.

On the wedding night, when the two figures of the old woman are present, it is not his bride's servant but Roderich's mask that recalls for Emil the horrid vision of the murdered child that triggers his murder of his bride. It is not that he mistakes his friend for the old servant; rather, he fuses the two images. Only if we see how the two are one for him can we understand the strangely redundant formulation that describes the killing of his bride: "But he had already furiously pierced her bosom, and cut through her white neck" (English translation, 463; German, 240). The piercing echoes Emil's sadistic revenge fantasy vis-à-vis Roderich (as the object of love and hatred) when he looks at the Turkish dagger his friend has left behind, and cutting through the neck echoes the ritual murder of the child. The figure of the ugly old woman ties together the various aspects of Emil's sexualization and perversion, which ultimately end in the deadly final embrace: "The old woman had clasped round him to tear him back: he struggled with her, and hurled himself together with her over the railing; and they both fell, almost lifeless, down at the feet of the relations who had been staring in dumb horror at the bloody scene.... Roderich took his dying friend in his arms" (English translation, 463; German, 240).

The ambivalent relationship between sadistic and masochistic impulses, as well as the emotional ambivalence of love-hatred, is far more carefully elaborated with respect to the friendship between Emil and Roderich than with respect to the other sex. To argue that the heterosexual relationship in this novella takes its cues from a homosexual relationship misses the point in the same way in which it is anachronistic to speak of Eckbert's repressed homosexuality. Yet Emil's relationship with Roderich does have a strong sexual component, if by sexuality we do not mean a type of desire that is oriented to the same sex or other sex but instead this fundamentally perverse organization of pleasure. Prior to any fixed sex or gender system, this perverse kind of pleasure seems to originate through contact with another's alterity, be it a male friend or an unknown beautiful woman.

*

In both stories, "Blond Eckbert" and "Love Charm," we encountered the elaboration of a fundamentally perverse sexuality. Each narrative presents a story about the emergence of the protagonist's bizarre sexuality in a shocking encounter, whether with an enigmatic text, the unconscious, or the sexuality of another. This encounter can only be described within a post-Enlightenment model of language that considers language constitutive of both subjectivity and reality. In contrast to the aesthetics of German classicism, in the Romantic fantastic the relationship to alterity becomes much darker and more problematic. The classicist ideal of a self-sufficient, calm, and stable contemplative subjectivity, as we find it in Herder or Schiller, for instance, appears as an extremely fragile construct that can only temporarily be upheld at the cost of excluding all alterity. In the threat to this contemplative calm and self-sufficiency, a threat that can arise at any moment because it consists of a minimal shift of attention onto the fragility of the reality construction, we find the possibility of a new, radically different organization of pleasure that arises from the shattering of the all-too-fragile ego boundaries. The aesthetics of the fantastic tale explores this sensuality of shock, tension, and intensity, which almost a hundred years later informs the psychoanalytical understanding of a polymorphously perverse human sexuality.

Tieck's "Blond Eckbert" portrayed the protagonist's desire to break out of his isolation by way of confiding his darkest secret to his intimate friend, Hugo, as an overwhelming and irresistible urge, despite his awareness that acting on this impulse might not bode well. Bertha is equally driven to disregard her own best interests, to give up the peaceful and protected environment of the isolated hut in the woods to pursue some strangely vague desire. In "Love Charm," the urge to act against his own best interest is developed in view of the protagonist's initial overcautiousness with respect to all external disturbances or stimuli, which, however, tips over into its opposite, into a frenzied state of total self-abandon and violence. To the degree that these stories invoke the register of the fairy tale or the supernatural, they propose to cast the protagonist's compulsive violence as part of a larger pattern of occult powers and forces and thereby introduce an explanatory schema that prevents clear attribution of an individual's conscious agency. At the same time, these stories tend to pathologize and individualize the protagonist's compulsion and perceptions as grounded in his libidinal economy of repressed affect.

In my reading of Tieck's stories, I have argued that to a certain degree the portrait of an individual's motivational deep structure matches or anticipates that of a psychoanalytical understanding of the unconscious and sexuality. I have also drawn out some parallels between the fantastic tale's construction of a fundamentally perverse human sexuality and desiring ability and the philosophical view of perversion around 1800. Both philosophical anthropology and the fantastic tale depict perversion and the human capacity for desire as radically open and free from what would be determined by natural needs or self-interest. However, only the fantastic tale attributes to this an overpowering force. Kant's anthropology, by contrast, makes this perverse desiring the key element propelling the human being beyond the dictates of instinct. In brief, what is new in the fantastic tale's construction of sexuality is its depiction as a force that resists conscious and rational intervention, that might lead to such a bizarre act of violence and destruction that it can no longer be accounted for in terms of the instinct of self-preservation.

By way of concluding this chapter, I turn to Poe's "The Imp of the Perverse" as a text registering the novelty of this quasi-instinctual urge that, though having all the force of an instinct, radically undermines the traditional understanding of instinct insofar as it does not fit into a teleological model of self-preservation. Poe's text brings this notion of a quasi-instinctual urge to a paradoxical climax by depicting it as an instinct that—in relentless pursuit of self-destruction—overrides all the instincts of self-preservation. Finally, Poe's "Imp," like "Blond Eckbert," elaborates this perverse impulse as the strange compulsion to confess a crime. In contradistinction to Tieck, though, the act of confession no longer aims at intimacy with another person but stands on its own, autonomous and self-sufficient like a perfectly executed work of art.

Between Pathology and Amorality:
"The Imp of the Perverse"

Published in *Graham's Magazine* in 1845, "The Imp of the Perverse" stems from a time in which psychiatry was beginning to conceive of perversion in terms of pathology rather than morality. Whereas philosophical anthropology around 1800 decoupled human sexuality from an instinctual model and emphasized the indeterminacy of desire, later nineteenth-century psychiatry reactivated the notion of instinct when it tried to articulate a functional model of the sexual drive in analogy to the role played by hunger in the alimentary function.[27] A pathological disturbance of hunger could be an exaggeration or diminution of the function (such as bulimia or anorexia), or its craving for an inadequate object. Analogously, a diseased sex drive was conceived of as an exaggeration of the function (nymphomania), diminution (impotence, frigidity), or direction toward "unnatural" objects (those not serving an overall procreative function). Hence it was in the slot of the unnatural object choice that such perversions as pedophilia or fetishism were accommodated.

One of the first steps towards this functionalist, teleological model in psychiatry was the attempt to connect basic mental functions with a physiological site or organ. This kind of research was begun by the so-called phrenologists, among them Karl Spurzheim (1776–1832). Now, it is exactly this functionalist approach to the "faculties and impulses—of the *prima mobilia* of the human soul" that Poe's "The Imp of the Perverse" attacks, and with great conviction.[28] Poe begins his text with the polemical statement that

> The phrenologists have failed to make room for a propensity which, although obviously existing as a radical, primitive, irreducible sentiment, has been equally overlooked by all the moralists who have preceded them. In the pure arrogance of the reason, we have all overlooked it. We have suffered its existence to escape our senses, solely through want of belief—of faith;—whether it be faith in Revelation, or faith in the Kabbala. The idea of it has never occurred to us, simply because of its supererogation. We saw no need of this impulse—for the propensity. We could not understand, that is to say, we could not have understood, had the notion of this *primum mobile* ever obtruded itself; we could not have understood in what manner it might be made to further the objects of humanity, either temporal or eternal. It cannot be denied that phrenology, and in good measure, all metaphysicianism have been concocted *a priori*. The intellectual or logical man, rather than the understanding or observant man, set himself to imagine designs—to dictate purposes to God. (268)

The critic assumes the position of the empiricist indicting the metaphysical assumptions of an anthropocentric teleology that has guided even the latest paradigm claiming to account for the human faculties and impulses. He does so in a mockingly moralist tone, accusing this kind of functionalism of being hubris, of trying to second-guess God's thoughts rather than study his works. By attacking the teleology of Nature inherent in this functionalism as a form of bad metaphysics, the critic suggests a radically different possibility: a natural order that neither obeys rational principles nor makes sense, an anthropological makeup that does not fit into a natural order.

The writer of "The Imp of the Perverse" takes the trouble to illustrate and parody the functionalism of the phrenologists:

> In the matter of phrenology, for example, we first determined, naturally enough, that it was the design of the Deity that man should eat. We then assigned to man an organ of alimentiveness, and this organ is the scourge with which the Deity compels man, will-I, nill-I, into eating. Secondly, having settled it to be God's will that man should continue his species, we discovered an organ of amativeness, forthwith. And so with combativeness, with ideality, with causality, with constructiveness, so, in short, with every organ, whether representing a propensity, a moral sentiment, or a faculty of the pure intellect. (268)

The description of appetite in the dual image, the coupling of the biologistic "organ of alimentiveness" and the dramatically religious "scourge," brings out in its utter incongruity the clash between a quasi-religious metaphysics and modern scientific pretensions. The arbitrary series of the heterogeneous set of supposedly psychic faculties, moral dispositions, and mental operations furthermore ridicules the scientific claims.

Drawing on the first two examples that serve to establish the basic paradigm of this functionalism, hunger and sex drive, the essayist points out that this kind of functionalism admits of two basic principles or motives for human action: preservation of the self and preservation of the species. If, then, the critical voice of this essay proceeds to undermine the edifice of phrenological theory and—as quickly becomes quite clear—all other prior theories of the human soul, it does so by attacking the exclusive validity of those two principles. The imp of the perverse—the force that drives us to act without any motive, or the ability to do wrong for wrong's sake—is, according to the writer of this piece, "a radical, a primitive impulse—elementary" (269), a fundamental force that can in no way be subsumed under "combativeness."

> The phrenological combativeness has for its essence, the necessity of self-defense. It is our safeguard against injury. Its principle regards our well-being; and thus the desire to be well, is excited simultaneously with its development. It follows, that the desire to be well must be excited simultaneously with any principle which shall be merely a modification of combativeness, but in the case of that something which I term *perverseness*, the desire to be well is not only not aroused, but a strongly antagonistical sentiment exists. (269)

By designating the imp of the perverse as a radically self-destructive impulse, the writer of this essay does not merely add a third drive to the two already existing ones; rather, he actually questions the entire functionalist edifice.

After these general statements about the existence of a fundamentally perverse impulse, a drive to disregard self-interest and reason, the writer goes on to offer examples that should resonate with everybody's introspective experience. First, he describes how the temptation of torturing one's listener through circumlocution prevails in spite of the desire to please and the availability of concise language. Then he uses an example about procrastinating on a task until the deadline is imminent. The last example evokes the passionate urge to hurl oneself down a precipice. This suicidal urge is not a determination to end one's life, but merely resistance to the voice of reason: "And because our reason violently deters us from the brink, *therefore* do we the most impetuously approach it" (270).

All of these examples share two features. On the one hand, the action is never motivated by pursuit of well-being, pleasure, creaturely comfort, or self-interest in any form. In this sense, it is comparable to Kant's notion requiring that an act of freedom transcend any consideration of self-interested instrumental rationality. On the other hand, the writer also makes it clear that just as the first example is not about the pleasure of torturing one's interlocutor but merely about the irresistibility of the idea of doing so, the second example rejects the force of duty, and the third the force of reason. Thus there is nothing left of the Kantian model of freedom. The nonpathological, radically non–self-interested nature of this impulse (in a Kantian sense) does not promote rational insight into one's duty; if anything, it draws force exactly from opposition to reason and duty. After all, the imp of the perverse remains a basic impulse, an almost irresistible force, a compulsion that gives shape to symptomatic behavior and actions.

After exposition of the general relevance of his discovery and its illustration by way of these commonly observable phenomena, the writer of this piece proposes a new rationale for the first part of his text. Until this point, the reader has been led to assume that the piece was written from purely scientific interest, that the first person singular refers to the neutral speaking position of the objective writer/observer of modern science, a speaking position that is emptied of all individual subjectivity. Now, the speaker informs the reader that the entire scientific discourse served the particular purpose of establishing the proper framework for classifying and understanding the writer's very own, personal position. The writer fears that unless the role played by the imp of the perverse in the economy of human faculties is properly understood, the reader might take the author of this text for mad, whereas in fact he is merely a victim of this impulse. He tells his reader that this discourse on the imp of the perverse gives him the "faint aspect of a cause for my wearing these fetters, and for my tenanting this cell of the condemned" (270). However, not until the reader has been through the second part of the text can this phrase be understood in a literal sense as concretely referring to the fact that the piece was written in a prison cell on the day before the writer's execution for a murder.

In view of the perspective of the scientific discourse about the nature of human desire and motives, the confessional narrative would actually represent a rare and powerfully convincing example illustrating the writer's hypothesis with respect to this irresistible driving force. His previous examples of the operation of this fundamental force—in circumlocution, procrastination, and the fascinating lure of the abyss—might still be refuted, the first two rather banal examples falling to the argument that rhetorical clumsiness and laziness might just as well cause the behavior as the imp of the perverse. The last, and crucial, example about the attractiveness of self-destruction suffers from the shortcoming that it can only be confirmed by one who, though susceptible to the urge, ultimately does not succumb to this impulse, a fact that weakens such a testimony considerably. The best witness for the impulse to self-destruct would have to be someone's authentic account of carrying out a successful suicide. Obviously, the speaking position of this kind of witness is nearly impossible, since with few exceptions it must come from beyond the grave, from someone already dead. It is the construction of this impossible speaking position that is performed in the second half of the "The Imp of the Perverse," a narrative about confessing a capital crime, spoken by a criminal from death row on the eve of his execution.

The second part of the text, an autobiographical narrative, describes how the imp of the perverse led the first person narrator to confess the successful, undetected murder of a relative. This confession is supposed to have resulted from an elemental, radical impulse, hence to represent the satisfaction of a quasi-instinctual urge. What is rather interesting about this scenario of indulging the imp of the perverse, however, is both its complexity and the fact that the satisfaction of such an elemental drive is shifted entirely to the discursive level. It involves successful deployment of the institutional apparatus of the legal system and successful performance of the speech genre of the confession in that context. This performance is explicitly and proudly acknowledged in the concluding sentences of the text: "They say that I spoke with a distinct enunciation, but with marked emphasis and passionate hurry, as if in dread of interruption before concluding the brief but pregnant sentences that consigned me to the hangman and to hell. Having related all that was necessary for the fullest judicial conviction, I fell prostrate in a swoon. But why shall I say more? To-day I wear these chains, and am *here*! To-morrow I shall be fetterless!—but *where*?" (271).

This testimony to the imp of the perverse constitutes a complex and rare discursive performance and rhetorical achievement: documentation of a successful suicide by the one who has already set in motion the mechanism of this suicide. Indeed, this report of a successful suicide is relished with a certain pride and insistence on its artistic virtuosity. By contrast, the moral register, even though we are after all dealing with the confession of a crime, is hardly touched upon at all. There is only one brief reference to the writer's guilt: "And now my own casual self-suggestion, that I might possibly be fool enough to confess the murder of which I had been guilty, confronted me, as if the very ghost of him whom I had murdered beckoned me on to death." The casual self-suggestion that he might confess his murder becomes, insofar as its irrational, nonsensical, self-destructive aspects correspond so perfectly to the imp of the perverse, an overwhelmingly powerful urge or compulsion. This, at least, is the argument of the text. When the writer introduces guilt and the ghost of the victim, it is not—as would be expected along the lines of a more traditional explanation—how a serious crime should produce the desire for confession, or how the confession might somehow stop the ghost of the victim from persecuting his murderer. Quite to the contrary, the urge to confess is in total agreement with, and on the same side as, the ghost of the victim; to put it more strongly, the latter is a personification of the former. Thus, what a more traditional moral discourse would take to be expression of the powers of conscience here becomes mere acting out of a perverse impulse.

The circumstances of the emergence of this perverse impulse to confess are detailed at some length. Initially, the murderer is happy about the successful execution of the deed, and the fact that it remained entirely undetected gives him a "rich sentiment of satisfaction" as he "reflected upon" his "absolute security." But this sense of security, expressed in the sentence "I am safe," gradually becomes a mere phrase that he repeats to himself, which over time and almost imperceptibly becomes an annoying "ear worm": "It is quite a common thing to be thus annoyed with the ringing in our ears, or rather in our memories, of the burthen of some ordinary song, or some unimpressive snatches from an opera. Nor will we be the less tormented if the song itself be good, or the opera air meritorious. In this manner, at last, I would perpetually catch myself pondering upon my security, and repeating, in a low under-tone, the phrase, 'I am safe'" (271). Note that his annoyance lies with the obsessively repeated phrase, not with the actual feeling of security. The comparison to the song or snippet of an aria that, regardless of its actual aesthetic merit, by sheer repetition becomes intolerable suggests that what is called for is a formal, aesthetic innovation: "One day while sauntering along the streets, I arrested myself in the act of murmuring, half aloud, these customary syllables. In a fit of petulance, I re-modelled them thus: 'I am safe—I am safe—yes—if I be not fool enough to make open confession!" (271) The self-suggestion that provoked the imp of the perverse emerges almost accidentally, in a perfectly external and almost playful fashion by "re-modelling" a sentence; it is unrelated to any kind of remorse or moral consideration.

To a certain extent, one could argue that the confessional part of the text breaks with the convention of religious confession in its utter disregard for a moral code. It maintains from this discursive set of conventions only the nonsentimental, minute attention to psychological detail. By making the entire narrative half of the text into an ingeniously executed testimony to the imp of the perverse, and by emphasizing the success of this as a performance, what would ordinarily have been evaluated in terms of a moral code is actually measured according to an aesthetic code. The criteria for this aesthetic code are not those of the beautiful versus the ugly, but those of the effective versus the ineffective performance; and those of the new, interesting, unique, and shocking speech act versus the endlessly repetitious phrase.

The discussion of the actual murder is equally nonsentimental, kept in a neutral, objective tone and free of moral consideration. If anything, the murder is even described with a certain amount of pride as the most exquisitely accomplished crime, introduced by the hyperbolic phrase: "It is impossible that any deed could have been wrought with a more thorough deliberation" (270). What makes his murder so exceptionally successful is the fact that it does not leave traces. He killed his relative, who loved to read, while in bed in his ill-ventilated chamber, with a poisoned candle. The idea for this kind of murder had come to him from reading some French memoir. This murder is fastidiously nonbloody, and there are no sensationalist details. Whereas the act of murder is cleansed of gore and violence, the shock element of the text is entirely shifted over to the confession itself. In this respect, it is entirely different from the slaughter described by Thomas De Quincey in his "Murder Considered as One of the Fine Arts." In terms of the elegance of its execution, however, Poe's "Imp" lends itself to comparison with De Quincey's text insofar as the latter author provocatively argues that once a murder has occurred, once it is in the past and there is no chance of averting it or saving a life, one might just as well consider the murder in terms of the technical perfection of its execution—meaning, in aesthetic rather than moral terms. Poe's text contains no graphic account of violence, nor is there any association of violence with sensations of pain, pleasure, excitement, and lust. In this it constitutes a marked contrast to "Blond Eckbert" and especially "Love Charm." Poe's markedly unbloody account of a murder can be, however, read as a critical reaction to the sensationalism of popular journalism.[29]

At a fairly abstract level (of drawing attention to how specific discursive genres imply a certain observer and subject position), this text recapitulates some central aspects of use of the confession that I have traced in the fantastic tale's portrayal of a perverse sexuality as the individual's secret. In Poe's text, the urge to confess designates a fundamentally perverse impulse. Insofar as it radically undermines any consideration of instrumental rationality, it frames confession as a compulsion that cannot be accounted for with a model conceiving of basic drives in terms of natural functions. Consequently, as the expression of a basic and radically perverse impulse, the confession in Poe's text cannot acknowledge—indeed, it actually cancels—any moral and spiritual authority.

The act of confessing is merely the acting out of a perverse impulse. Nevertheless, it is also a most exquisitely rare rhetorical achievement, as it bears witness to this perverse impulse in an almost unheard of purity. This is accomplished by grafting the writer's personal, intimate confession onto the neutral, expository prose that constitutes almost the entire first half of the text. If there is any shock involved, it is the surprise sprung on the reader whose generic expectations are radically questioned in this unexpected transition from the *I* of the neutral observer to the emphatic subjectivity of the criminal on death row. Consequently, this text posits an aesthetic order comprising "interesting," novel effects and based on a perfectly accomplished performance that is radically cut off from a moral order—a decoupling that is central to many fantastic tales.

Whereas the fantastic tale draws its central, defining feature from the fundamental uncertainty of an observer position, from the observer's blind spot and the ultimate lack of control over his own story, "The Imp of the Perverse" stages this blind spot and lack of control in terms of masterful execution of the compulsive confession. The reader of Poe's tale is thoroughly disoriented through the manner in which the text fuses the subjectivity of the participant's perspective with an initial speaking position that invokes the neutral subject of the scientific observer. What constitutes the basic uncertainty for the fantastic tale in Poe's text is assigned a definite place in a (pseudo-) scientific discourse. To the extent that this discourse parodies the phrenological paradigm and, in a more general sense, radically subverts the neutral, scientific-observer position, it also undermines the basic parameters of the map it proposes.

By depicting the curious imp of the perverse both as a fundamental human faculty and a quasi-instinct that could cancel any instinctual behavior, Poe's text undermines the basic conceptual grid that was to guide the nineteenth-century distinction between what was to be considered normal and natural and what was pathological. Furthermore, Poe's text not only draws attention to the lacunae of scientific discourse but also—by mimicking and "emendating" scientific discourse—shifts the site of discovery and innovation from the field of science to literature and the arts. In all of these aspects, Poe's newly discovered or constructed imp shares the subversive features of the fantastic tale's elaboration of a fundamentally perverse sexuality, which indeed was theorized only much later by the scientific discourse of psychoanalysis.

Even so, there are also aspects in which the fantastic tale's construction of sexuality must be distinguished from Poe's fictional imp, especially those in which the fantastic tale—even far more radically than Poe's pseudoscientific treatise—departs from traditional psychological concepts. Thus, whereas Poe still argues within a "faculty" psychology (a model that attributes various basic capacities to the human psyche), even though the imp of the perverse can undermine all the other faculties, the occult force or motivational deep structure that fatefully determines the behavior and affects of the protagonists from Tieck's fantastic tale by contrast cannot clearly be cordoned off or localized as an intrinsic psychic force or drive, for it emerges through language and in intersubjective contact. It is the individual's deepest and darkest secret that seeks expression and even confession, but it can also never be entirely known. The perverse sexuality of Tieck's characters emerges as a highly particular modification of subjectivity through encounters with a mysterious alterity, encounters that are perceived as both shocking and overwhelming.

In my analysis of Tieck's fantastic tales, as well as in my discussion of the framing narrative of his *Phantasus*, I have attempted to highlight how his poetics of the fantastic is based on a radically new aesthetics. Founded on a Romantic philosophy of language, Tieck's aesthetics of the fantastic critically examines the pathological nature of the harmonious and beautiful and proposes a countermodel of shock and intensity, confrontation and novelty that is to replace or at least supplement the traditional values of harmony steeped in recognition of the familiar. Here too, Poe's text is a helpful commentary that brings out aesthetic concern and rhetorical achievement as something radically free of moral considerations. Indeed, Tieck and Poe are involved in decoupling the aesthetic and the moral, in asserting that the beautiful and the good are not necessarily congruous. Furthermore, both authors somehow privilege novelty over beauty. However, Tieck's critique of received notions of harmony and beauty, as well as his concern with alterity, still seems to issue from an ethical impulse and concern with the other's alterity, from an ethics rooted in a critique of the sentimental ideal of linguistic transparency. By contrast, Poe's text, not at all concerned with an ethics of communication, is much more interested in issues of formal mastery. Thus, for instance, the confession in Poe's text that suddenly replaces neutral scientific discourse is no longer soliciting anything from its addressee; it appears as a perfectly self-sufficient and closed-off document or textual artifact.

3

The Power of the Artist

In the fantastic tales discussed so far, we noted a preoccupation with the protagonist's desire and understanding of pleasure as part of an individualizing, enigmatic, and potentially pathological feature, one that, particularly in the fictional universe of Tieck's fantastic tales, can erupt into utterly irrational and violent action. Tieck's fantastic tales challenge received notions of rationality and accountability by begging the question as to how one would understand the human inability to resist such a powerful desire or quasi-instinctual urge. Is the lack of this faculty a pathological condition, or is it a moral deficiency? Obviously, for the realm of fiction these questions do not need to be answered. However, during this same historical period, in the field of criminal law these questions about the limits of accountability assumed pressing urgency. In the early nineteenth century, practitioners and scholars of law debated the criteria and procedures that would guide the decision as to whether a killer can be tried for murder if he were shown to be mentally deficient or deranged.

The legal debates surrounding the insanity defense in the early nineteenth century mark an epochal threshold, a moment when the sciences of the individual—psychology and psychiatry—came into contact with the juridical domain.[1] When courts called upon the expert advice of psychologists or psychiatrists to define the mental status of a defendant, the juridical concepts of human rationality came into potential conflict with those of psychiatry or psychology. According to which criteria would a judge evaluate or dismiss expert opinion? Certainly, to the extent that this last question continues to be debated even today, the historical transformation described by Michel Foucault as the transition from an older regime of juridico-discursive power to a modern predominance of biopower (exercised over populations and individuals with the help of medicine, pedagogy, and the psychosciences, as well as demographics and public health) is far from complete. However one might describe the completion of this historical transformation, only its inception is of interest in this chapter, for it is in the beginning of this transformation that the fantastic tale can be situated.

As the fantastic tale elaborates an observer position at the limits of rationality, it raises issues about human agency and responsibility that challenge both the traditional models (originating in contemporary juridical discourse) and the newly available psychiatric accounts of mental deficiency, now understood as pathology. In this respect, the fantastic tale's fundamental uncertainty refuses to commit to a clear distinction between the framing of a bizarre psychic disposition resulting in mad or violent behavior as either a moral choice or failure and its framing as pathological disturbance. Moreover, as a result of this refusal, the fantastic tale articulates a third option: conceiving of the human motivational deep structure as both natural and irrational. It allows for a characterization of the human desiring capacity in terms of a departure from instinctual determinism—as Kant would have had it—without, however, launching on an idealist trajectory that would necessarily inscribe it within the development of reason. Instead, the fantastic tale characterizes this human desiring capacity—with its potential to generate bizarre interests, strange pleasures, and mad behavior—as the cause of pathological distortion, and as the site for normalizing intervention quite similar to the conception, one hundred years later, in Freudian psychoanalysis, of a polymorphously perverse human sexuality.

A fitting introduction to the concerns of this chapter is an important case from the history of legal debate over the insanity defense, the murder trial of Daniel Schmolling, in which E.T.A. Hoffmann presided in his capacity as appellate court judge. A key element in this case is the psychiatric diagnosis of *amentia occulta*, the clinical label designating a latent form of madness that articulates itself exclusively in an utterly irrational urge to commit an otherwise unmotivated deed. The label *amentia occulta* stands, in a way, for what Poe was later to refer to in his fiction as the "imp of the perverse." In contrast to Poe's "imp," however, *amentia occulta* does not designate a general human faculty, but instead a pathological condition for which medical experts can account neither for its genesis nor for its cause.

In this sense, *amentia occulta* designates an unknown that marks the limits of both psychiatric and juridical rationality.

Thus to begin this chapter with a discussion of *amentia occulta*, from the history of the insanity defense, allows me to contrast the literary production of sexuality as it is embedded in the aesthetics of the fantastic tale with contemporaneous extraliterary discourse. Specifically, this discussion shows how little the literary production of sexuality—as the key to the motivational deep structure of an individual—hinges on extraliterary parallels or isomorphisms, and it highlights both its radicality and its novelty by framing the question of the power of art, and alongside that the new role and function of the artist. The transformative role of the artist is the main focus of the chapter, in my analyses of Hoffmann's "Das Fräulein von Scudéri" (Mademoiselle de Scudéri) and "Die Automate" (Automata).

The discussion of "Mademoiselle de Scudéri" pursues this study's inquiry into the historical contexts for the fantastic tale. Written in 1818, just after Hoffmann's involvement in the Schmolling case, "Scudéri" proposes a pathogenic model for the same kind of criminal impulse that, in light of contemporary psychiatric models, would have to be labeled by such terms as *amentia occulta* or *idée fixe*. Though not a fantastic tale per se but rather a detective story, this story invokes the register of the fantastic in its proposed model of shock, trauma, and seduction, which is supposed to explain an occult, mysterious, or latent form of madness. Moreover, the tale, which attributes a vital function to the artist both in the discovery of the mysterious murderer's identity and in the subsequent implementation of this kind of psychological knowledge, can be read as a historical commentary on the transition from a juridical regime of power to the regime of biopower. The story encapsulates this transition by way of naming and modeling its eponymous heroine after the historical persona of the *précieuse* courtier and novelist Mlle. de Scudéry—and by addressing the crisis of power through an excursus on the history of the expanding police force and its implied threat to the king's sovereignty.

"Mademoiselle de Scudéri" addresses the question of exactly how a work of art or an artist could have such an eminently transformative influence primarily from an external perspective in its historicizing portrait of the artist's relationship to traditional and newly emerging forms of power. Addressed to a far lesser extent, however, are questions pertaining to the precise nature of the work of art or the aesthetic experience; these questions are dealt with in the second part of the chapter, where I turn to Hoffmann's "Automata." This latter text, written in 1814, explores at great length and in great detail the relationship between life and art. In the form of a dialogue about art's relationship to life and nature, it engages aesthetic debates that, through the vehicle of a fantastic tale, narrativize the relationship between artwork and beholder, by casting its protagonist as someone thoroughly perturbed and ominously transformed in his encounter with a mysterious artifact. This effect of the artifact on the protagonist leads him on a potentially mad quest for the presumed agency behind the powerfully transformative aesthetic experience, the person who traditionally would have been the artist. Thus, whereas "Mademoiselle de Scudéri" situates its artist in the historical centers of power, in close contact with the king and the police force, "Automata" by contrast casts the artist figure into a sociologically more marginal position in which he conducts his all-important work offstage. Within the register of the fantastic, this text explores a new role of the artist: that of a technician of the imaginary invested with the power granted to him by virtue of his phantasmatic position as the agency behind the scenes.

Schmolling's Insanity Defense

On September 25, 1817, Henriette Lehne was found with severe stab wounds in the Hasenheide outside Berlin. According to the victim's statements, her lover, a tobacco-rolling apprentice named Daniel Schmolling, was the perpetrator, testimony confirmed by Schmolling himself. On the day following the stabbing, the woman died of her wounds. During the first legal investigation, the thirty-eight-year-old Schmolling made an extensive confession. He said he had decided to kill his lover three weeks before the actual deed. Incapable of naming a motive, he merely claimed that the thought that he must carry out the deed would not leave him in peace. This claim gave reason to request a medical examination of the defendant. A psychiatric expert, Dr. Merzdorff, stated in his opinion that Schmolling had committed the deed during a fit of *amentia occulta* and, while carrying out the stabbing, "was entirely deprived of the freedom to determine his own actions according to reason ... ," though his faculties were in no way impaired by alcohol or passionate affect.[2] On medical grounds, the counsel for the defense requested that the defendant be exempted from all punishment, but nonetheless be taken into police custody. The criminal court of Berlin, however, requested the death penalty for Schmolling, arguing that although in principle the motive for a deed had to be taken into account in a juridical evaluation, it nevertheless was not the task of the judge to account for the absence of a motive. The court felt that a judge must begin with the premise that any human being is able to resist the temptation to commit a crime; whoever fails to make use of this ability is subject to the laws of punishment, and only a person who can be proven not to possess this ability can be exempted. Insofar as the expert had not offered medical reasons as to why Schmolling might have been unable to resist the urge to commit the crime, the accused was to be held accountable and punished. The case was appealed, and Hoffmann, in his function as judge, rejected the appeal, finding Schmolling accountable for his actions and refusing him exemption from the death penalty on account of insanity.

In his lengthy legal opinion, Hoffmann does not simply evaluate Dr. Merzdorff's individual expertise; rather, he takes on the entire field of psychiatric theory about the types of madness that do not manifest clearly in recurrent and observable physical and mental symptoms. Before discussing the medical literature, however, Hoffmann pauses for a philosophical aside:

> It is not granted to the human being involved in worldly life to fathom the depth of his own being. If the philosopher loses himself in speculations about this dark subject matter, the judge must hold on to that which has been established by unambiguous experiential data. Human freedom, considered from a metaphysical point of view, can never influence the practice of legislation and jurisdiction. When human freedom is considered from a moral point of view, i.e., the faculty to determine one's will and its practical articulation according to a moral principle (*arbitrium liberum*), this kind of freedom is presupposed whenever penal sanctions are applied, and any doubt with regard to this has to be substantiated and convincingly presented to the judge if he is to take it into account. (Segebrecht, 109)

With this statement, Hoffmann radically departs from contemporary legal-philosophical and forensic psychiatric positions as he apodictically asserts the limits of human self-knowledge.[3] Not only the rationalist legal scholar Feuerbach but also the entire psychiatric literature of the time presupposes knowledge of the self, the human ability to reflect on one's actions and to be aware of one's motives, as long as one is sane. It is exactly the absence of this insight into action and motive that leads the legal investigator or psychiatrist to question the mental status of the defendant. In this case, it is the fact that Schmolling's own motive was an utter enigma even to himself that leads to the request that he be examined by a forensic psychiatrist. But before Hoffmann even begins to debate the validity of the diagnostic term *amentia occulta*, he is already committed to the view that complete insight into human motives and actions is impossible.

Hoffmann's discussion of *amentia occulta* offers an overview of his contemporaries' accounts of latent psychic forces toward which he maintains an acutely critical position with which, ultimately, Hoffmann's fictional narratives about enigmatic behavior can be contrasted. Psychiatric literature, according to his overview, offers three options for classifying an irrational, unfathomable type of violent action that is supposedly caused by an "automatic drive" or "blind instinct" (Segebrecht, 109)—options whose terms indicate an unfree state, though without impaired understanding. They are partial insanity caused by an *idée fixe*; periodic insanity that articulates itself in an unpredictable, sudden, murderous outbreak of fury; and hidden madness, for which Hoffmann cites Ernst Platner (1744–1818), a professor of medicine and philosophy: "*amentia occulta*, a hidden kind of madness, is the inclination and impetus of a suppressed will to violent action; it secretly desires and brings about such an action as if it would mean the alleviation and liberation from what oppressed it."[4]

With regard to the first two diagnoses, Hoffmann has no principled objection. But he critically reviews the psychiatric literature to show that among the actual examples listed by the psychiatrists there are at least some instances of the presence of physical symptoms, or strong indications of a disturbed general mind-set, or both. People suffering from an *idée fixe* display their obsession openly: "This kind of madness is very frequent, since the *idée fixe* is usually so abnormal that it strikes even the most untrained observer as being easily recognizable" (Segebrecht, 110). The examples of a sudden murderous outbreak imply the presence, according to Hoffmann, of general physical symptoms that indicate an abnormality of the organism. Because two of the three diagnostic categories that are applied to madness without delirium are applicable to easily recognizable pathological phenomena (such as forms of mental illness that clearly manifest themselves in a partially abnormal obsession or a periodic, physiologically induced loss of the powers of the mind), Hoffmann argues that the diagnostic *amentia occulta* is ultimately an empty term, unless its meaning can be collapsed with Reil's "Wuth ohne Verkehrtheit," or Pinel's "manie sans délire, marquée par une fureur aveugle," in which case, however, there would after all remain in evidence—according to the examples of these authors, though against their own definition—strong proof of a disturbed mind (an *idée fixe*) or of physical causes and symptoms.

To summarize the main issues of this psychological debate of the 1800s: besides the obvious kinds of madness that manifest themselves in delirium, there are variations of madness that border on the normal or that allow the insane to pass for mentally healthy, either because in general the symptoms of insanity do not easily reveal themselves as unusual and irrational fixations or because the afflicted person appears deceptively healthy. The extreme form of this kind of latent madness is *amentia occulta*. For the expert, a diagnosis of *amentia occulta* supplies an explanation for an otherwise inexplicable deed. If Schmolling had been sane, he would not suddenly have decided to murder his fiancée without knowing why. He had no good motive, none that would fit into a model of either instrumental rationality or passionate action. According to the experts, therefore, Schmolling's unexplained deed must have been an expression of madness. According to Hoffmann, however, Schmolling's lack of motive is perfectly in line with what marks the human condition in general; no human being has complete access to self-knowledge.

What can be learned from this discussion of *amentia occulta* is that the available discourses of psychiatry, psychology, law, and philosophy come into irreconcilable conflict once the motive of a crime is not apparent. In the Schmolling case, we witness the clash of a legal pragmatics that excludes speculation over an unknown motive from its decisions, with a medical psychiatric literature that—though it cannot yet fully theorize this latency—nevertheless marks this as its specific territory. Crucial to Hoffmann's position is not his final recommendation, which merely reaffirms the decision of the first legal investigation, but the manner in which he dismisses the position of medical experts.[5] He radically questions the distinction between the normal and the pathological, on the grounds that the opaqueness of motive constitutes an anthropological condition that is inapplicable to the individual case of abnormality or pathology. Thus he claims the mysterious unknown for the realm of philosophy and—as I demonstrate shortly—for the realm of art.

The manner in which Hoffmann concludes his legal document after having rejected the insanity defense is also relevant. Here, he rewrites the case in light of an accepted rationality and normality, enabling us to localize the precise contrast between the evaluation of a case of this kind in the framework of a legal discourse and the appearance of such a case in the realm of fiction. Hoffmann carefully cites and analyzes Schmolling's statement describing how he conceived of the murder and committed the crime.

He detects in the young man's articulation of his anxiety over the idea of murdering his fiancée not evidence of a blind urge but the rudiments of moral awareness, and the ability to distinguish between good and evil. Hoffmann situates Schmolling's inability to resist this temptation in his "loose" lifestyle, his wantonness and immoderate habit of drinking. According to Hoffmann, the most experienced psychologists agree that for coarse or nervously exhausted people, wantonness can easily turn into a murderous lust, though he adds that this area of psychology should not concern a judge who has to remain within the realm of established facts. Then he conjectures that Schmolling might also have been moved by economic worries, the dread that since Lehne was pregnant she would no longer have supported Schmolling materially but instead would have expected him to support her. Hoffmann concludes his speculation about motive by citing Feuerbach, who was then the reigning expert of legal psychology:

All transgressions have their psychological cause in sensuality, to the extent that human desire is driven by the attempt to gain pleasure in a certain action itself or by means of a certain action. This sensual impulse is cancelled by the fact that everybody knows that his deed will inevitably be followed by an unpleasant result, a displeasure far greater than the dissatisfaction that would have resulted from not following the impulse. (Segebrecht, 124)

To anchor the position of the law, Hoffmann grounds his conjectures on what would constitute a supposedly normal motive for a crime like Schmolling's in this overall rationalist model of an economy of pleasure and pain, which allows consideration of the deed and its motivation purely through the defendant's habits, in a calculus of loss and gain. The nature of his relationship to his lover is thus reduced to instrumental concerns: she is an object of pleasure and a potential obstacle to obtaining other pleasures. In accordance with this paradigm, Hoffmann demands that Schmolling be held fully responsible for the murder.

The case of Schmolling illustrates both the logic and the limits of the paradigm of legal psychology in its instrumental, rationalist account of an economy of pleasure and pain. Furthermore, it also illustrates the claims of the emerging psychiatric discourse in its effort to define the boundaries between the normal and the pathological in view of some latent, unconscious, or enigmatic psychic force that does not fit this rationalist paradigm. Nevertheless, just as the problematic definition of pleasure cannot enter into considerations of legal psychology any more than the problematic relationship between pleasure and desire can, it also remains excluded from the psychiatric literature. However, it is precisely this dark and mysterious area, indicated by Hoffmann the judge as the reserve of metaphysical speculation rather than psychiatric expertise, that becomes a central concern of fantastic fiction.[6] The issue is not just how the fantastic tale would correct or supplement existing psychological and psychiatric models of human motivation and the structure of desire, but also, and more important, how this new knowledge is to be obtained and implemented.

"Das Fräulein von Scuderi"

Hoffmann began working on *"Das Fräulein von Scuderi"* in the spring of 1818, just six months after Schmolling's stabbing of Henriette Lehne, and published the tale in 1820. To a certain extent, the plot of this story can be summed up as the plot of a detective story.[7] The eponymous heroine, named and modeled after the well-known seventeenth-century novelist, manages to unravel a series of terrible murders that the newly created Paris police force is unable to solve. She is the only person to whom the sole suspect, Olivier Brusson, is willing to confide. Brusson has been incarcerated and charged with a string of murders after he was found at the home of the goldsmith and jeweler Cardillac, who had been stabbed to death. During his questioning by legal investigators, Brusson, an apprentice of Cardillac's, denies any guilt in the jeweler's death but refuses to extend further information about a series of other stabbings that have suddenly ceased since his arrest. Only to the old lady Mlle. de Scudéri (his mother's foster mother, who had cared for him during his early childhood) is he willing to reveal the truth: all the murder victims were customers of Cardillac's who had commissioned pieces of jewelry from him. It was Cardillac himself who, to steal back his own creations, murdered his former customers. On the night of his death, he was on one of his nightly excursions in pursuit of a former client and was stabbed by an attacker appearing suddenly out of the dark. When the police arrived, Brusson was merely trying to save the life of his master, whose daughter, Madelon, he hoped to marry.

When Brusson first learns of Cardillac's nocturnal murders, his love for Madelon prevents him from divulging her father's secret. Later, it is the desire to protect the girl's memory of her dead father that seals his lips. When Scudéri witnesses Brusson's arrest at Cardillac's house and sees the despair of the young and beautiful Madelon as she vouches for her lover, she is instantly and intuitively convinced by this image of pure love and innocence. Brusson's confession only confirms the truth of her initial intuition. But what can be done with this knowledge?

The story marks an irreconcilable conflict between an isolated insight into the truth of an individual (Brusson's manifest innocence from Scudéri's viewpoint) on the one hand, and an opposing juridical system that establishes the guilt of a defendant by reconstructing the defendant's moves and whereabouts, with the aid of witness accounts, more or less forced confessions, and other forms of evidence, on the other. Scudéri seeks the advice of Pierre Arnaud d'Andilly, the most famous lawyer in Paris, telling him of Brusson's innocence without betraying the young man's confidence. D'Andilly explains that the procedure of legal investigation, which includes torture, was not at all cruel but only in accordance with the duties of the judge. Even he would not dare to argue for an exemption from torture. Nor should she approach the king in this matter, because the king could not possibly grant mercy to a criminal who represents a danger to the people, and this ultimate means of appeal would be wasted. The lawyer hereby emphasizes the degree to which the power of the sovereign is bound up with the juridico-discursive system itself. The monarch has power of life and death over an individual; it is within his power to sign a death sentence or grant a pardon. Yet because his power is itself legitimated by the juridico-discursive system, he must remain within its bounds and cannot intercede on behalf of a subject who represents a threat to the collective body. In this instance, even the power of the absolute monarch is limited.[8] The only hope is for some new kind of evidence that might stall the proceedings. In such an instance, if Mademoiselle de Scudéri were to appeal to the king, he would be justified in relying on his inner conviction instead of conceding to the legal evidence.

Shortly after Brusson confides in Scudéri, the needed evidence arrives. Count Miossens, chief of the royal guard, reveals that he is Cardillac's murderer. The count tells Scudéri that he connected the jeweler with the stabbings when Cardillac asked suspicious questions about Miossens's plans to deliver some commissioned jewelry to his lover. Miossens, wearing armor under his vest, had stabbed Cardillac at the moment when he attempted to attack the count from behind. As d'Andilly explains it to Scudéri, however, this supporting evidence does not help Brusson's legal case. True, it confirms that Brusson was not Cardillac's murderer and that the other killings were actually executed by Brusson's master, but according to the law Brusson is still guilty by association for allowing Cardillac to continue his murderous activities instead of reporting him to the police. Nevertheless, the new evidence now warrants an appeal to the king.

The narrative detour that relates the legal issues and complications that must be overcome before Scudéri can actually approach the king to implore his pardon of her foster grandson draws attention to the extent to which Scudéri's notion of innocence is incompatible with the legal definition of an accused who is not guilty. Knowing the identity of the jeweler's real murderer, and obtaining his testimony as to Cardillac's stabbing of his customers, will not legally free Brusson from responsibility for the series of murders; nonetheless, in this case, the king might be persuaded to weigh Brusson's motive—his loyalty and pure love for Cardillac's daughter—against his unwitting complicity in the jewelry murders. To pardon Brusson, the king will have to go beyond the limits of the juridico-discursive system and subscribe to a new model of power, one that would give much more value to an individual's motive and secret desire than to his actual deeds. Indeed, if Scudéri succeeds in moving the king to pardon Brusson, the old lady will have accomplished nothing less than the king's recruitment into the new form of power that conforms to Foucault's model of biopower.

My plot summary of this tale as a detective story has allowed the introduction of its crucial thematic concern with the transformation of the juridical regime of power by way of the artist's intervention. Yet the artist's transformative power is not merely articulated at the level of the plot; it is also enacted vis-à-vis its reader, through the manner in which the tale is told. It is through the perspective of Scudéri, acting as the story's focalizer, that the reader encounters the shock of the events, their initial incomprehensibility, and the gradual revelation of the underlying truth. Before the story reaches the point at which Scudéri resolves the murder mystery and sets out to seduce and overwhelm the king with her powerful performance, the reader is already seduced into a new approach toward what might constitute an individual's guilt or innocence. Moreover, it is not only through confronting the reader with shock and incomprehension that the story enacts the transformative power of art; it also reflects on the powerful effects of the incomprehensible in the fantastic explanation of the origin of Cardillac's criminal obsession. In the following pages I trace in greater detail the role of Scudéri as the tale's focalizer, as advocate of a new hermeneutic of the individual, and as powerful artist. Finally, I examine the function of the vignette about Cardillac that locates the hidden source of his murderous obsession in his mother's transgressive desire.

The story begins *in medias res* as an unknown, mysterious visitor vehemently requests to see Mademoiselle de Scudéri in the middle of the night. When he is not admitted to her presence despite his violent paroxysms of despair and his threatening brandishing of a jeweled dagger, he leaves, entrusting the old lady's maid with a little box containing jewelry and insisting that his night-time intrusion is a matter of life and death. Some months later, Scudéri is accosted in her carriage by a young man whose countenance is vaguely familiar, but whom her attendant immediately recognizes as the night-time intruder. With violent haste he throws a note into the old lady's lap before disappearing into the crowd. In the note, he implores Scudéri to instantly return the jewels to René Cardillac. With increasing unease, she sets out the next morning to Cardillac's house with the intention of returning the jewels and is witness, amidst a mob of onlookers, to the scene of an arrest. A man in chains is dragged out of the house while a beautiful young girl heartrendingly pleads his innocence. Scudéri learns that the jeweler has been murdered, that the weeping girl is his daughter, and that the man arrested and taken into police custody is her fiancée. She takes the girl, Madelon, home with her and is all too willing to be convinced of the young man's innocence after she questions the girl about the events preceding her father's murder. Moved by Madelon's innocence and ardent love, Scudéri asks to meet the murder suspect in prison, hoping to assist him in his defense, but she faints in recognizing him as the young man who threw the note into her carriage the day before; the same who her attendant insisted had intruded into her house months ago with the box of jewels.

Suddenly, in her mind Brusson is associated with the jewelry murders; she is torn between feeling personally deceived and grasping for new hope as she remembers her initial impression when she saw Madelon's inconsolable grief at Brusson's arrest:

Many things that had previously been regarded as evidence of innocence and purity now became proof of wanton maliciousness and studied hypocrisy. Madelon's heartrending lamentations, the tears of anguish, might well have been pressed from her, not by her mortal dread of seeing her sweetheart bleed—no!—but at her own death at the hands of the executioner. . . .

She cursed the destiny that had granted her so many years in which to strengthen her belief in truth and virtue, only, in her old age, to destroy the beautiful picture that had illuminated her life. . . .

Mademoiselle de Scudéri was pierced to the heart by Madelon's voice and once again deep within the inmost depths of her soul there dawned the feeling that there was a mystery involved and that Olivier was innocent.[9]

In addition to the authenticity of the young girl's compassion, Madelon's beauty, youth, and virginity come to signify innocence for Scudéri, not just hers but metonymically also Brusson's. Through Scudéri's perspective, Brusson's innocence is constructed in analogy with a beautiful girl's sexual innocence.

Before the confession of Count de Miossens finally settles the issue of Cardillac's murder once and for all, and while Mademoiselle is still grasping for hope of Brusson's innocence, Desgrais, an officer of the mounted police, calls on her to ask for assistance in their investigation. He tells her that Brusson, beside himself with anguish after her abrupt departure from the prison, swore his innocence of Cardillac's murder but insisted he would confide in none but the old lady. At first she protests: "'What?' cried Mademoiselle de Scudéri indignantly. 'Am I to become an organ of the tribunal, am I to abuse the trust of this unfortunate man and bring him to the scaffold? No, Desgrais! Even if Brusson were an accursed murderer, I could never so deceive him. I wish to know nothing of his secrets, which would anyway remain locked in my breast like a holy confession'" (English translation, 245; German, 820). Nevertheless, she agrees to allow Brusson to be brought to her house. This quasi-official involvement with the Brusson case marks the beginning of her participation in a historical transformation of power.[10]

It is in this meeting that all the mysteries of the affair are brought to light. Gazing at the desperate Brusson, the old lady is again troubled by a vague feeling of recognition, and stirred by the conviction of the young man's essential goodness. Brusson now reveals his identity as the son of Scudéri's foster daughter, the little boy she had idolized before they were separated following his mother's move to Geneva. It is also here that Brusson tells of his discovery of Cardillac's secret, his silence and unwitting complicity in the murders, the deeply buried and horrific source of Cardillac's compulsion, and how it was at the jeweler's urgent bidding that he delivered the box of jewels originally intended for Henrietta of England to Scudéri's house, believing, as indeed Cardillac believed, that only the old lady would be safe from his murderous compulsion. Only when Brusson detected signs of a resurgence of Cardillac's desire to repossess the jewels did he approach her in her carriage with the note of warning.

After Brusson's confession, Scudéri lets him be reunited with his lover for a few moments before the police take him back to prison. The narrator dwells on this scene: "Had Mademoiselle de Scudéri not already been convinced of Olivier's innocence, she must have been convinced of this now as she saw them both forgetting, in the rapture of profound and sincere love, the world, their misery, and their indescribable torment. 'No,' she called, 'only a pure heart is capable of such blissful forgetfulness'" (English translation, 261; German, 840). The tableau of Madelon and Olivier's self-sufficient love becomes for Scudéri the token of their pure hearts. Theirs is an otherworldly love, one that is free of worldly misery and suffering. It transposes a model of religious love into the sphere of human love. The love of this couple, in Scudéri's view, is the expression of a pure desire and innocent enjoyment, free of transgressive passion and the pleasures of the flesh; a love sustained by loyalty and commitment to the nuclear family. This love emblematically stands for the state of their soul, the hidden kernel and truth of their characters. It is both a decorporealized and an individualized and psychologized sexuality. What is more, through the narcissistically invested perspective of the virginal grandmother, it is embodied by Madelon's youthful beauty and grief. Thus innocence is related to the entire personality, to a state of the soul, as opposed to the legal sense in which *innocent* merely means not guilty. For the entire period between Scudéri's visit to the prison and Brusson's being brought to her house by the police, as she contemplates the possibility of his guilt, it is in view of Madelon's looks and expressions that she tries to decide whether she can confirm her suspicion or whether she has reason to hope. In the end, it will also be Madelon who "seals" the effect of Scudéri's appeal to the king.

Scudéri, as the focalizer of the story, not only establishes the truth behind the mysterious crimes but also inaugurates a new model of how an individualized psychological account can supplement or even replace the traditional juridical position toward the defendant or prime suspect. Yet her unraveling of the murder mystery is accomplished in the context of the domestic setting of the bourgeois family, in which she assumes the role of the sympathetic listener and confidant guided by sentiment and inner conviction. From the very beginning of the story, however, she also appears in a contrasting, public role. The story makes it clear that the précieuse Scudéri is a friend of the king's mistress and a regular guest at the court. Two encounters with the king, however, make her stand out among the other courtiers; in both she has an immediate impact on his exercise of power. The first narrative segment detailing her encounter with the king is preceded by a historical excursus about the increase of crime, creation of a police force, and the changing nature of crime. It marks a historical moment when the effective interventions of the new police force have produced so many political repercussions that the king's power seems to be threatened. As a result, in spite of the new, inexplicable, and unsolvable string of mysterious jewelry murders, he is unwilling to create yet another and even stronger police force. This crisis of power is the historical background for the first of Scudéri's encounters with the king, in a scene in which the sovereign turns to the old lady for advice. The monarch is at a loss for an answer when the courtiers, alarmed at the continuing rash of unsolved murders, demand renewed expansion of the police force. Scudéri's high-flown interjection "un amant qui craint les voleurs n'est point digne d'amour" offers him an excuse to ignore the courtiers.

Even though Mademoiselle's glib remark does not ultimately solve the problem at least it deflects the issue and buys the king time. Furthermore, it associates the novelist with the sovereign in a maneuver for an exercise of power that is somehow in competition with the expanding power of the police. In this sense, this scene prepares Scudéri for her role as the protagonist of the detective story—as an ancestor of Miss Marple, if you will, who competes successfully with, and often stands in opposition to, the official police force. Finally, this scene interpellates the king as the protector of love. The courtiers illustrate the urgency of their demand by pointing out how, unless the police force is strengthened, they risk their lives as they deliver gifts of jewelry to their paramours. Though the king's pardon will indeed be pronounced in the name of love, it is (as I show later) a love utterly different from the frivolous erotic pleasures of courtly society.

Initially characterized as a witty, précieuse *salonière*, Scudéri takes up the function of the maternal ear and hermeneutically trained psychologist in the middle part of the story, when she establishes and elaborates her own notion of Brusson's innocence through listening to Madelon and later to the accused. In this role, she contributes decisively to the transformation of power, to the construction of individuality and truth by way of the genre of the individualized, intimate confession. During that phase, she competes and collaborates with the police force; in so doing, she might very well confirm Brusson's innocence in Cardillac's own death. She can furthermore assemble a psychologically convincing and sentimentally appealing picture of Brusson's suffering of having become witness to Cardillac's murderous obsession. But because Brusson is undeniably (though unwillingly) implicated in the murders committed by Cardillac, her knowledge and psychological insight is utterly pointless, unless there is a decisive change in the dominant juridical regime to make it possible that her notion of Brusson's innocence can be weighed against his guilt. To effect this transformation of power, she has to assume yet another role and recruit the king into the régime of biopower.

The transformation entails changing the mode of a sovereign's power from one displayed in the moment of an execution or the suspension of a death sentence to one in which he is a representative of a power that takes into account the motives and family circumstances of a defendant, thus demonstrating active interest in the quality of life of a subject who has been released from prison. This form of power corresponds exactly to what Foucault termed biopower, an "enlivening" power that manifests itself in demographics, health, and family politics. In her final confrontation with the king, the transformation she effects in him is of this kind. He pardons Brusson and thus frees him from prison and threats of torture and execution, but he also grants to the young Madelon a significant dowry to ensure that the young couple is able to leave Paris. The story marks the extent of this epochal transformation of power quite consciously through the juxtaposition of two culturally overdetermined cities. To ensure their happiness, the couple is obliged to leave the Paris of the ancien régime. They choose to move to the hometown of Brusson's father (and Rousseau's republican hometown), Geneva.

In her final confrontation with the king, Scudéri no longer appears as a maternal ear, psychologist, or confessor. Nor does the story hint that she would have tried to win over the sovereign by pity. The poetics of sentimentality, of the epistolary novel and bourgeois tragedy, have no place at court. Instead, Scudéri has to assume the role of a powerful artist who can exercise a profound influence on her audience. Carefully dressed, in solemn black, and wearing Cardillac's jewelry, she immediately manages to attract the attention of the king. The narrator primarily describes how Scudéri "stages" her narration, which culminates in an overwhelming, shocking, and transformative effect on the king. By contrast, the content and precise wording of her speech seems less of an issue:

> The King, overwhelmed by the violence of the most lively life that glowed in Scudéri's speech, did not perceive that it actually was about the hated Brusson trial, to him so horrible. He could not utter a word; he could only express his inner movement by an occasional exclamation. Before he realized what he had learned, beside himself over the unheard of, and still incapable of sorting it all out, Scudéri had thrown herself to his feet and implored him to have mercy on Olivier Brusson. (English translation, slightly altered, 267; German, 847–48)

This is not the scenario of somebody who is being moved by a sentimental narration, but one in which the listener is violently overwhelmed and seduced. The force of the affect displaces the content of her narration; all representational claims are canceled by "the violence of the most lively life that glowed in Scudéri's speech."[11] In a poetological tradition, the hyperbole of Mademoiselle's speech, in its combination of fire imagery with a heightened vitality, echoes the Prometheus legend, which has informed the ideal of the artist as genius ever since the *Sturm und Drang*.

In Hoffmann's own work, the fire-and-life imagery serves two functions. It is a central element in an almost formulaic repertoire that marks a metapoetic dimension within his fiction (the violence of art, speech, music, and the like), and it is used on the diegetic level to narrate a traumatic encounter. Here, as in so many other passages in Hoffmann's work that make use of this imagery, we are dealing with a model of overstimulation, an overload of sensory input that accomplishes the transformation of an aesthetic scenario into one of sensual excitement.

The story's culmination in Scudéri's seduction of the king into biopower demarcates a new function for the artist. The tale's subtitle ("A Story from the Age of Louis XIV") must not be mistaken as a narrow historicist approach to the artist of the seventeenth century. Rather, the references to the historical novelist Scudéry and the crisis of absolutist power in light of an expanding police force offer a commentary about a much broader historical transformation that reaches all the way into the modernity of Hoffmann's nineteenth century. This conclusion can be reached by analyzing Scudéri's performance or intervention in communicative situations with respect to the cultural historical moment that each of them represents.

There are three distinct phases from the history of aesthetics and poetics that can be associated with Scudéri. First, there is the seventeenth-century courtly salon culture of the précieuse, oriented toward the connoisseurs of rhetorical performance ("un amant qui craint les voleurs n'est point digne d'amour"). The second phase encompasses the mid-eighteenth-century bourgeois culture of domesticity and sensibility, in which Scudéri assumes the role of the mother, whose sympathetic ear produces the intimate confession, the truth about Brusson and the Cardillac murders. Within this phase of the history of poetics and aesthetics, the figure of the artist is entirely pushed to the background in favor of this period's ideal of poetic illusion and transparency, making the literary product real by presenting it as an authentic letter or a family "docudrama." The final phase is that of the Romantic artist, who fundamentally transforms reality. This is the new artist Scudéri, who with her carefully timed and staged performance transforms and seduces the king and the style of power through her overwhelming speech.

This kind of seduction aims exclusively at the sexualization of the one who is seduced, and by no means at anything related to what would count as sexual activity; it is with this purpose in mind that Scudéri takes the beautiful Madelon, the attractive icon of innocence, with her to her court appearance. The narrative draws attention to this marked departure from the erotics of the ancien régime. Exactly at the moment when Scudéri has finished and the beautiful girl is brought upon the scene to seal the effect of her speech, a brief narrative segment signals the enduring force of the alternative to this new kind of sexuality, the older model of courtly erotics:

> The King seemed to be moved by the wonderful beauty of the angelic child. He gently raised the girl and moved as if to kiss the hand he was holding. He let it fall and looked at the precious child through eyes wet with tears which testified to deep emotion. La Maintenon whispered softly to Mademoiselle, "Isn't the little thing the very image of La Vallière. The King revels in the sweetest memories. Your game is won!" Despite La Maintenon's having spoken softly, the King appeared to have heard. A blush came to his face; he cast a glance at La Maintenon: he read the petition which Madelon had given to him and then said, gently and kindly, "I find it easy to believe, dear child, that you should be certain of the innocence of your beloved, but let us hear what the *Chambre Ardente* has to say about it. . . . "
>
> To her terror, Mademoiselle de Scudéri noted that the recollection of La Vallière, as propitious as it had appeared at first, had changed the King's intention as soon as the name had been mentioned by La Maintenon. It was perhaps felt by the King that he had been rudely reminded that he was about to sacrifice stern justice to beauty, or that he was like a dreamer who discovers that the beautiful image created by sleep quickly disappears even as he prepares to embrace it when he is awakened by a loud call. (English translation, 268; German, 849)

Maintenon's mere mention of her predecessor's name threatens to destroy the effect of Scudéri's speech. As soon as the beautiful Madelon is compared with a former mistress, she is placed in an altogether different context, the one of ancien régime erotics, the pleasure of bodies and more-or-less secret affairs conducted outside the bonds of marriage. Through the comparison with La Vallière, Madelon is placed in the rank of objects of pleasure, abolishing the aura that previously defined her as a phantasmatic object of yearning, the embodiment of the Romantic dream of an innocent sexuality. This scene, which immediately follows on Scudéri's effort to recruit the king into the new regime of biopower, spells out what this shift entails. It necessitates abandoning the traditional erotics of the flesh with its system of concubinage in favor of the Romantic yearning for a pure and unreachable object of desire. This is further confirmed when the king finally is persuaded; he puts Madelon out of his reach by releasing Brusson from prison on condition that the young couple leave Paris.

How closely the new type of the artist, such as Scudéri in her pivotal encounter with the king, is related to the nineteenth-century history of sexuality can also be seen in the "explanation" of Cardillac's secret. The same mysterious urge that makes him an extraordinary artist, an artisan whose creations bear a "signature," also turns him into the murderer of his customers.[12] As we have seen in the Schmolling case, neither the legal psychology nor the forensic psychiatry of Hoffmann's time had a model that could easily accommodate this combination of a hidden motive, of some mysterious quasi-instinctual drive and its articulation in violent crime; Cardillac does not seem obviously mad, disturbed, or ill, nor does he commit his crimes within the then-accepted legal psychological model of an instrumental reason that aims at optimized pleasure. The absence of this kind of motive is also why the police—who can only think of such motives as profit, a hereditary scheme, or political machination—cannot connect the mysterious jewelry crimes to Cardillac.

Now, it is exactly at the borders of the models then available for explaining some mysterious force leading to criminal activity that Cardillac's mystery is situated. Where psychiatry could have merely provided the problematic diagnostic label *amentia occulta*, Hoffmann's tale actually proposes an explanation, taking the form of an inserted quasi-fantastic tale that is to be the key to understanding Cardillac's strange behavior. It is found in the transgressive desire of Cardillac's mother, who, when she was one month pregnant with him, was attracted by the brilliant necklace of a proud courtier who had pursued her in the past, and whom she had rejected. Now, noticing her desiring glance he approached her anew; they secretly met and embraced. As she reached out to touch the necklace, he suddenly sank to the ground, dragging her down with him. She was pinned to the ground, caught in the rigid arms of a corpse. Cardillac's mother recovered from that shock, despite the severe trauma she suffered, but the fetus was indelibly marked by the encounter, and Cardillac lived his entire life under the curse of an unquenchable desire for jewelry. This is what first led him to become a jeweler and goldsmith, but eventually his desire, perversely following the scenario of his mother's encounter, was twisted into compulsion, theft, and murder.

The story of Cardillac's mother can be read in the tradition of superstitious beliefs about the supernatural influence that can be exerted on a fetus if a pregnant woman beholds a picture with intense desire. Texts by Tasso and Montaigne, as well as Lessing, come to mind. Hoffmann, however, gives this traditional myth a new twist, one that moves it from the realm of the supernatural into that of the unconscious and sexuality in the modern psychoanalytical sense. The irrationality of the horrible crimes and the terrible compulsion leading up to them can be explained neither by an early nineteenth-century model of madness nor by some supernatural force, and certainly not by any rational economy of pleasure or profit. Instead, the irrational nature of the crimes leads to another irrational narrative explanation: the story of Cardillac's mother, which is, in fact, less an explanation than an enigmatic narrative about a traumatic encounter. Its explanatory value vis-à-vis the string of crimes consists in positing a prototype, model, or "primal scene" for an encounter: marking Cardillac's killing of his customers as repetition of the terrifying embrace in which his mother was caught, it gives his obsession for repossessing the jewelry from his customers the character of an illicit sexual compulsion. Situating Cardillac's mysterious behavior during his adulthood in a prenatal encounter introduces a strange model of how external events might influence a person's psychic organization.

I have used the term *primal scene* for the vignette of Cardillac's mother because it contains two of the elements essential to justifying this technical expression. First, it cannot be stated with certainty whether the scene actually happened, or whether it was merely fantasized. In any case, it left strong traces and must have meant a strong disruption. Second, if the scene is somehow witnessed by the little unborn creature, it must have been incomprehensible and utterly enigmatic. Whereas the traditional superstition operates with a model of "programming" the fetus with a special mark or feature that is singled out by the mother's desire, Hoffmann's primal scene programs not through content but through its shocking, disruptive, and enigmatic character. Whereas in Tasso's *Gerusalemme liberata* the African queen gives birth to a white baby after having too intensely contemplated a picture of a white horse, in the case of Cardillac the message that sets his desire in motion is far greater, far more unreadable and enigmatic than the luster of the jewelry alone. Equally undecipherable to the fetus is the heavy charge of the mother's sexuality and unconscious desires. Thus, the primal scene of the mother tells a story of the origin of sexuality and perversion as the result of a necessarily traumatic—because always precocious—encounter with an enigmatic signifier, the adult unconscious and sexuality.[13]

In "Mademoiselle de Scudéri" there are two senses in which the production of sexuality can be understood. Through the conversational genre of the intimate confession, when Brusson tells Scudéri his secret in the form of Cardillac's mysterious obsession, sexuality becomes a discursive construct in the manner analyzed in Foucault's argument about sexuality in the nineteenth century, where it becomes the central feature determining the identity of a person. Furthermore, sexuality emerges as a result of a necessarily traumatic seduction, as a departure from and perversion of instinctual satisfaction that goes back to earliest infancy. In this latter sense, we can connect the fantastic explanation of Cardillac's murderous obsession, his sexual perversion going back to a prenatal encounter with the mother's desire, with other shock encounters in the story, examples being the story's opening scene, in which Brusson violently, unexpectedly, and inexplicably attempts to see Scudéri in the middle of the night; or Scudéri's sudden assault on the king; her overwhelming presentation of the solution to the jewelry murders; pleading the case of Brusson's innocence with "the violence of the most lively life"; and supporting her point with the help of Madelon's seductive beauty. As we have already seen in the previous chapter, the model of a seduction through shock describes the character (cognitively and affectively highly ambiguous, though aesthetically exciting and pleasing) of the mysterious event that is at the core of the fantastic tale. In the next section, I pursue in greater detail the implications that this new role of the artist has for the communicational model underlying the poetics of the fantastic: How does this new role of the artist challenge contemporary ideals of the artwork-beholder interaction?

"Automata" and the Simulation of Life

As opposed to the vitalism of such medical scholars as Georg Ernst Stahl (1660–1734), who sought the principle of life in the *anima* or soul and opposed mechanistic and materialist explanations of life, physiologists and neurologists in the mid-eighteenth century such as Albrecht von Haller (1708–1788) began to articulate a system of material, organically based life forces (such as reproduction, secretion, propulsion, and also irritability, and sensibility) that became the markers by which living organisms can be hierarchically distinguished from one another, as well as from inanimate matter. In the latter part of the eighteenth century and the early nineteenth century, these physiological concepts of life force—especially irritability and sensibility—found further elaboration in medical theories of bodily and mental disease, in the experimental branches of physiology and neurology, and in the holistic metaphysical speculation of Romantic medicine.[14]

Apart from this cluster of physiological concepts of life, the mid-eighteenth century saw an altogether different appeal to life, liveliness, or vividness that was part of an aesthetic and poetological discussion belonging to the semiotics of transparency. In this context, it was an artifact, a representation, that was supposed to create "lifelike" presence for the reader or beholder, making him or her forget the dead materiality of the actual verbal or visual construct. Instead of keeping those two disparate domains of physiology and aesthetics apart, the poetics of the fantastic actually fuses together elements from both realms. So far, we have seen how the disturbing, disruptive encounter at the core of the fantastic tale posits this experience as an enlivening event that generates a heightened sensibility—the result of overstimulation or intense irritation that produces pleasurable pain, or painful pleasure. This intensified sensibility has been discussed in terms of the seduction or sexualization of the reader or beholder. What remains to be shown is how this transposition of a physiological cluster of concepts into the realm of the aesthetic manages to affect the more traditional aesthetic models of the "liveliness" of a work of art.

This section, devoted to Hoffmann's "Automata," a story that he wrote and first published in 1814 in the *Allgemeine Musikalische Zeitung* and later included in the collection *Die Serapions-Brüder* (The Serapion Brethren, 1819–1821), will develop this fusion of aesthetics and physiology. "Automata" is a highly speculative dialogue between two friends about the nature of the artifact in its relationship to life and nature. In addition, however, it is also a fantastic tale that elaborates the disturbing impact that an encounter with an automaton (taking the form of a speaking Turk) has on two friends. Finally, the story can be read as an analytical and rather perverse development of the Pygmalion myth. Hoffmann's narrative of an encounter with an automaton rewrites the neohumanist elaboration of Ovid's Pygmalion myth, in which a beautiful ivory statue comes to life under the caresses of an admiring artist, thus refiguring the interaction between the artwork and its beholder.

Puppets or paintings that come to life are indeed an integral element of Hoffmann's fantastic tales (such as "Der Sandmann," "Meister Martin der Küfner und seine Gesellen," "Signor Formica," "Die Elixiere des Teufels"). In these stories the artifact-come-to-life stands in the position of the female beloved and is often even in competition with an actual living woman. Furthermore, in some of them the lover/beholder of the artwork-come-to-life is also the artist/creator of the artifact. None of this is true for "Automata," and this difference is what underscores its analytical twist on the Pygmalion scenario. The roles of beholder, artist, creator, and beloved are not conflated as in the classicist and hermeneutic appropriations of the Ovidian scenario but instead are distributed among different actants and narrative programs.

"Automata" can be divided into three parts. First is the narration of the encounter between two friends, Ferdinand and Ludwig, and an automaton, the speaking Turk. The encounter triggers Ferdinand's confession of his innermost secret to Ludwig, which constitutes the second part, where Ferdinand recounts how he came to meet his mysterious beloved. The third part of the story narrates a sequence of encounters with Professor X, a local expert on automata, who seems to have played some mysterious role in constructing the speaking Turk.

Psyche and Automaton

Herder's essay of 1778 titled "Some Observations About Form and Gestalt from Pygmalion's Shaping Dream" (Einige Wahrnehmungen über Form und Gestalt aus Pygmalions bildendem Traume) is directed against the representational model of aesthetic illusion.[15] Sculpture, above all other art forms, endows the beholder with an ideal body that he or she internally recreates through an imagined sense of touch and feeling; the beholder/creator endows the sculpture with life through an erotic, sensual, warm response to that ideal body. The term *life* does not denote any possible confusion with an external reality. For Herder, sculpture is definitely an idealization and at the same time very real. Its ability to come to life has much less to do with the effects of *trompe l'oeil* than with the beholder's heightened, jubilatory feeling of embodiedness. The beholder is elated as he or she experiences the emphatically human, autonomous sense of the soul as an overall organized totality that, in apprehending both sensuous and spiritual reality, also constitutes these realities as world.

Herder makes the point that it is above all in the medium of sculpture that this neohumanist ideal of the autonomous totality of the soul is articulated; that painting, because it entertains an entirely different and dangerous relationship with the beholder's imagination, represents a threat:

> The magic of painting is altogether different. Because painting is not corporeal presentation [*Darstellung*], but only a depiction, fantasy, a re-presentation, painting opens a wide field for fantasy and lures it into its colored, perfumed gardens of lust. The sick gourmets of all periods would prefer to fill up their cabinets of lust with indecent paintings rather than sculptures: for with sculpture, not even in the sleeping hermaphrodite is there indecency . . . Fantasy desires only scent, appearance, alluring color; her wings are tied by the faithful nature of truth in its entirety, for it asserts itself too strongly. Sculpture remains always naked, but the beautiful Danae by Titian has to be wisely covered by a little veil: the magic screen for a corrupted sense that, once awakened, knows no limits. (my translation)[16]

Whereas sculpture by its very presence reminds man of an Edenic, prelapsarian innocence that asserts organic wholeness and independence from its environment, painting as representation always refers to something absent, and hence almost necessarily entails a disintegrating threat; the desires and fantasies it evokes lead away from the self and may end up in an unnatural, pathological alienation or the degradation of human into brute.

Herder distinguishes two kinds of erotic pleasure, one that disintegrates the self—the one associated with painting—and another that affirms and strengthens the self as an autonomous autoerotic system:

> A single spirit poured itself over the statue and held the hand of the artist, so that the work is held together and becomes a unity. Whoever—(to mention the most difficult immediately)—whoever stood next to the famous hermaphrodite and did not feel how in each oscillation and turning of the body, in all that he does and does not touch, there is a bacchic dream and hermaphrodism; how he is suspended by a torture of sweet thoughts and lust that penetrates the entire body with a gentle fire—whoever does not feel this and does not feel how he as the beholder senses in himself, involuntarily, the echo or the resonance of the same play of the strings; to whoever would be so insensitive, neither my words nor anybody else's words could explain it. That exactly is what is so unshakably certain in a sculpture. Because it is a human being and an entirely enlivened body, it can speak to us as an action. It holds us, penetrates our entire being and awakens the entire play of the cords of human sympathy.[17]

The sleeping hermaphrodite, as a figure that has overcome both sexual difference and the demands and stimuli of the external world, is offered as the ideal object of a narcissistic fantasy of an intensely autoerotic pleasure. Here the direction of the enlivening force is actually inverted with respect to the Pygmalion myth. In this case, the sculpture of the hermaphrodite ("suspended by a torture of sweet thoughts and lust that penetrates the entire body with a gentle fire") imposes its own sense of embodiedness on the beholder, so that the beholder sympathetically feels what the statue expresses. It is the beholder who is enlivened by this gentle fire, rather than the statue by the caresses of its admirer. Two further elements that guarantee this perfect match, without gaps or friction, between the statue's life and the beholder's soul are the unified and unifying spirit of the creator behind the statue, and the silence in which the entire transaction transforms us ("geht stumm und unbegreiflich in uns hinüber").

The encounter with the speaking Turk in Hoffmann's "Automata" builds on Herder's pivotal scenario of a hermeneutic, divinatory understanding by provocatively supplanting Herder's antirepresentational model of corporeal presentation (*Darstellung*) with a model of simulation. A long introductory description of the audience's fascination with the automaton both invokes the hermeneutic scenario of beholding an inspired work of art and perverts it by externalizing, concretizing, and literalizing the metaphor of inspiration.

The usual procedure was to whisper the question one wished to ask into the Turk's right ear, upon which he would turn first his eyes, and then his whole head towards the questioner; becoming aware of a gentle stream of air, proceeding from his lips, one believed that the soft reply that was given really did come from the interior of the figure.

From time to time, after a few answers had been given, the exhibitor would insert a key in the Turk's left side and wind up some clockwork with a good deal of noise. Here, also, he would, if desired, open a sort of lid, so that inside the figure you could see a complicated mechanism consisting of a number of wheels; and although you might not think it probable that this had anything to do with the automaton's speech, it was still evident that it occupied so much space that no human being could possibly be concealed inside, even if he were no bigger than August's dwarf who was served up in a pastry. . . .

People wearied themselves with conjectures concerning the medium of this marvellous message. The walls, the adjoining room, the furniture, everything connected with the exhibition was carefully examined and scrutinized, all completely in vain. . . .

Despite the tasteful arrangement and the most mysterious, marvellous nature of this work of art, perhaps the interest of the public might soon have grown fainter, if the artist had not succeeded in attracting the spectators in an ever-new way. The interest was kept alive by the nature of the answers the Turk gave, which were always formulated with a deep insight into the individuality of the questioner. Sometimes they were dry, sometimes rather rough and joking, then again they were full of spirit and wit, marvelously and even painfully to the point. Often a mystical gaze into the future startled by a reference to something that was accessible only to the questioner, cognizant of the hidden thoughts and questions that dictated the question. Furthermore, it often happened that the Turk, questioned in German, would reply in some other language that just happened to be known to the questioner, in which case it would be found that the answer could not have been expressed with equal point, force, and conciseness in any other language than that striking and ingenious answer of the wise Turk's becoming the subject of general remark.[18]

The speaking Turk differs from ordinary automata in its manner of simulating hermeneutic values. It breathes, and it speaks in oracles that address the most intimate desire of its interlocutors. As a moving entity independent of any direct mechanical link with the artist, the machine seems to have its own moving principle, a life or soul. Its exhalation of air suggests that the automaton has an inner life. The depth of its answers suggests a supernatural force or spirit. The automaton does not evoke these favorite categories of the hermeneutic enterprise (life, spirit, and individuality) by assuming the shape of an inspired artwork, such as the idealized representation of the human body in which Herder enthusiastically affirms the enlivening force of the spirit. Rather than invoking these humanist categories in a scenario of silent contemplation and enthusiastic identification with the beauty of Greek sculpture, the speaking Turk simulates, materializes, and externalizes the invocation of humanist and hermeneutic values. He is a clever installation that, on the one hand, functions like a dummy in that he provokes in the audience exactly those responses that "something real" would provoke, while on the other hand the description also insists on the Turk's artificial, mechanical character.

For Herder, the scenario of perfect understanding excludes language, in spoken or written form.[19] The exchange between beholder and statue is mute and culminates in a perfect mutual mirroring. The unifying spirit of the creator supports the identificatory embrace of the two. Whereas Herder's hermeneutic scenario, building on the radical discontinuity between animal and man (on account of the humanizing nature of language), has to exclude speech, the automaton's fascination derives precisely from its speaking abilities. Although the narrator suggests that it is the specificity of the Turk's answers that is at the bottom of its powers of fascination, he also gives away the secret of the hermeneutic lure: the language the Turk speaks is not at all transparent, but oracular and often a foreign language whose choice the interlocutor grasps only at the moment of listening to the automaton. Up to this point, the comparison with Herder's Pygmalion merely highlights the mechanisms of the hermeneutic lure by way of its material simulation in the form of the dummy of the Turk.

The second part of the narrative engenders discourse about the beloved woman in conjunction with the enlivening effects of the artwork. It is this aspect of the Ovidian tale that is radically altered in Herder's essay. Instead of transforming the ivory girl into a woman of flesh and blood, Herder depicts a self-sufficient autoerotic intensity in the image of the sleeping hermaphrodite. In Hoffmann's tale, Ovid is still recalled, but what was Pygmalion's good fortune becomes Ferdinand's trauma. Ferdinand's encounter with the automaton produces all the elements that Herder's Pygmalion excluded, elements that for Herder would disrupt and scatter the self-sufficient wholeness of the embodied soul. The automaton speaks, but it speaks in riddles, and the encounter with its mystery engenders precisely those elements that Herder condemned as "Unzucht," that indecent form of lust he associated with the centrifugal effects of painting and representation: absence, fantasy, and loss of self.

The Pleasures of Pain and the Mysterious Lover

The second part of "Automata," which narrates Ferdinand's encounter with the automaton, and which as a result brings about his confession of his most intimate secret, proceeds by replicating Ferdinand and Ludwig's experience for the reader, who is confronted with an unexpected and inexplicable event that is then elaborated retroactively. We learn about the shocking effect of the automaton's answer to Ferdinand's query even before we learn what it said. Furthermore, the effect of the encounter with the enigma is described in terms of its physical impact. Once we know the automaton's answer, the reader—like Ludwig—stands in need of further explanation. Ferdinand explains the automaton's response by relating his strange love story. The telling of this mysterious love is thus framed as an attempt to make sense of an intense physiological reaction. The effect of Ferdinand's confession is recursive in two regards: on the one hand, it is described as a pleasurable physical stimulation, the same that he mentions having experienced in narrating his encounter with the beloved; on the other hand, the confession places Ludwig in the position of the beloved with whom Ferdinand shares what is most intimate to him. Part two of "Automata" thus moves between states of physical excitation and an imaginary unity with an object of love.

Ferdinand's most intimate secret, "the beloved of his soul," is a response to the desire of another; this response is awakened by the sound of an aria expressing an invincible desire that issues from beyond death and corporeality. He tells how one night on a journey with several friends after an evening of drinking, having withdrawn to his room and in a state between wakefulness and sleep, he hears a female voice, accompanied by a piano, singing "Mio ben ricordati."[20] A beautiful girl enters his room and tells him that she has only to sing and he will remember her as the beloved of his early childhood. Upon awakening the next morning, however, he realizes that there was no real counterpart to this dream, no childhood memory that would match the image of the beloved from his dream. Interrupted in these musings, he looks out the window down to the street, where a postal chaise is preparing for departure. From another window close to his own, a woman has also been watching the street below. She soon leaves her place at the window; as she quits the house she turns around, whereupon he recognizes her as the singer from his dream. He tries neither to follow nor to find her; instead, never mentioning her to anyone, he fashions a miniature portrait of her, which he personally inserts into a setting he had commissioned for another picture of the same size, and wears it underneath his clothes, the face turned to his breast. He assures Ludwig that he made certain that nobody else ever saw the portrait.

Ferdinand's question to the Turk was "Will there ever again be a time for me like that which was the happiest in my life?" (English translation, 87; German, 408). After asking him to turn around the medallion he is wearing on his chest, the Turk finally answers that Ferdinand will lose her at the very moment he lays eyes on her again.

Ludwig is the first to know this most intimate secret of Ferdinand's, the story of how he found the beloved of his soul. The degree to which the encounter with the automaton draws the two friends into intimate communion is emphasized by a detail we learn further along in the narrative: at the moment of the automaton's reply, not only Ferdinand but also Ludwig can hear the melody of "Mio ben ricordati," which earlier transported Ferdinand into a state of physical tension, a mixture of pain and enjoyment, and which conjured up the image of his beloved. For the two friends, the encounter with the automaton produces intensification of friendship and intimacy, in both their conversation and their common sensations: "Just as your answer was being given to you, I happened to place my hand on the railing which surrounds the figure. I felt it thrill and vibrate in my hand, and I fancied also that I could hear a kind of musical sound" (English translation, slightly modified, 93; German, 416).

Ferdinand never made the least effort to follow and find the woman of his dreams; instead, he keeps her strictly to himself as an exclusively imaginary object. However, by merely mentioning her ("Unhappy man! At the moment when you will see her again you will have lost her forever!" [338]), the Turk has broken the hermetic closedness of Ferdinand's imaginary love relationship. Indeed, were Ferdinand to see her again, she would be another, she would no longer be identical with his imaginary dream beloved, hence he would indeed lose her. The automaton, quite unlike Herder's sculpture, disrupts the imaginary dyad between Ferdinand and his beloved by reintroducing language and representation.

Ferdinand's narrative departs from the myth of falling in love at first sight in various ways. For one thing, there is no original encounter, but only retroactive positing of one. Yet the conjecture that he has always known her—meaning that she is merely the product of his dreams—does not hold fully true either. Such would be the response of a psychology that presupposes a psychic entity or interiority that is neatly separate from a knowable external reality. Indeed, this is Ferdinand's first reaction when he wakes up. But as soon as he tells himself that the highest form of happiness is merely a product of his dreams, he recognizes his dream girl in the woman departing from his lodgings. What are we to make of this turn? What is the nature of Ferdinand's desire?

To pursue these questions we might look at his account of the moment of supreme happiness and enjoyment. The episode of his dream encounter is preceded by the strange nocturnal singing experience and concludes with his viewing the singer from his window. Both of these passages use the same imagery of intense stimulation as the dream encounter:

I had never imagined anything approaching the effect of those long-drawn swelling and dying notes upon me. The melody was marvellous—quite unlike anything I had ever heard. Oh, it was the deep, tender sorrow of the most fervent love itself. As it rose in simple phrases, the clear upper notes rang like crystal bells, and as it sank till the rich low tones seemed to die away like the sighs of a despairing plaint, now a rapture which words cannot describe made me tremble in my innermost being—I felt the pain of a boundless longing seize my heart like a spasm. I could scarcely breathe, my whole being was merged in an inexpressible, heavenly delight [*Wollust*]. (English translation, modified 85; German, 405)

It was the singer!—it was the dream image!—the gaze of the heavenly eye fell upon me and it was as if the beam of a crystal tone pierced my heart like the point of a burning dagger, so that I felt an actual physical ache; all my fibers and nerves trembled and I was petrified in unnamable bliss. (English translation, modified, 86; German 406–7)

Pleasure and pain become indistinguishable in these descriptions, which draw on a synesthetic mixture of sensory impressions all of which pierce, shake up, and finally drown the listener or beholder's enraptured self. Whether an opera aria issuing from an unseen source or the parting glance of a woman, these intense signals posit an other who is different from the self that they are shattering. In this sense, the beloved cannot be just the product of Ferdinand's imagination or dream. Furthermore, as the source of the voice or the gaze, this other threatens a purely imaginary beloved who can function as an integral part of a closed psychic economy. After the painful intensity of the aesthetic experience, therefore, the imaginary beloved becomes a protection against this shattering force of the real. In this sense, Ferdinand's secret portrait of the beloved becomes an attempt to shield himself against desire.

The automaton's mention of his secret love disrupts this guarded and private imagination. The reader has already been told, in the same language that Ferdinand used to describe his nocturnal arousal, about the automaton's penetrating answers and sharp insights into each individual's desire. To the extent that it threatens Ferdinand's impossible love object, the automaton embodies some evil, alien power. Along the same lines, however, we would have to add that it threatens him with a disruption that strongly resembles the physical, erotic excitation that led him to create the absent lover to begin with. After his encounter with the automaton, Ferdinand repeats his attempt to contain the sexualizing alterity within the dyadic set-up of their friendship, when he adds a conclusion to Ludwig's speculation about the mysterious powers of the automaton:

The fact that his beloved friend, too, had heard the sound, was to Ferdinand proof of the psychic rapport that existed between them; and as they further penetrated into the secrets of the psychic relationships between related spiritual principles, when ever more lively and marvelous results were produced, he began to feel the heavy burden lift away that had weighed upon his chest since he had received the answer. He felt encouraged and emboldened to meet whatever ominous fate might hold in store for him. "How could I lose her," he said, "she who rules eternally over my inner being and thus asserts such an intensive existence that she would only perish along with my own being?" (my translation; German, 369)

Ferdinand fuses the memory of his beloved with talk about arousal and excitement. The intimate and intense conversation between the two friends has become one solution for allowing enjoyment of the enlivening excitement without the shattering threat of an unknown other.

But the narrative does not end here. There is still a third part, which revolves around the two friends' pursuit of Professor X. By focusing on the function of this personage, we can begin to outline the transformation that the fantastic genre proposes in relation to the Pygmalion myth, and to understand a new model of the artwork, the artist, and the power of art over life.

Art and Power over Life

Professor X is first mentioned by an unnamed man who, interrupting a discussion of automata among bystanders, remarks that the man displaying the automata did not deserve to be called an artist: "You are wrong in supposing the commonplace person who exhibits it [the work of art] to be the artist. The truth is that he really has no hand at all in what are the truly remarkable features of it. The originator of them is a gentleman deeply experienced in all the arts—one who lives among us, and has done so for many years—whom we all know very well, and greatly respect and esteem. . . . The gentleman to whom I allude is none other than Professor X" (English translation, modified, 89; German, 411). In this shift from "artist" to "deeply experienced in all the arts," we witness a redefinition of the role of the artist: he is no longer the creator or maker of the work in its materiality but the impresario and orchestrator of its effects. His profound experience and knowledge of the arts defines his function and hence his title, Professor X. The plural *arts* emphasizes the disciplinary and technological aspect of art in the sense of "arts and sciences" and in the sense of technique, skill, and technology.

What, then, is Professor X's relationship to the automaton? He did not make it, but he intervened in the manner in which it was shown to the public. He is not the showman involved in a performance, but the man behind the scenes who has arranged the overall effect of the automaton's display. He could be described as a multimedia expert and public relations specialist of his day. Initially, the automaton did not fascinate its audience in any particular way. One day, the professor saw it and, having listened to its answers, whispered something into the showman's ear, which made the latter pale. The show was canceled for a fortnight. During that time, the professor spent several days at the hotel where the automaton was kept. When the show reopened, the automaton was transformed into the fascinating enigma it has been ever since. Thus the function of the artist here is redefined from that of maker of the artwork to producer of the enigma; he is the animating spirit behind the speaking Turk. His extensive scientific and technical knowledge allows him to present the automaton in such a manner that it becomes a marvelous enigma, a hermeneutic lure that simulates life.

In his status, he is somewhere between a professional scientist and a dilettante bricoleur and collector—we know neither if he actually is a professor of physics and chemistry, nor if he collects automata as part of his scientific and technological pursuits. He belongs with such typical Hoffmann characters as Professor Spalanzani,[21] the hypnotist, councillor Krespel, Lindhorst, and Drosselmeier, to mention only some of the best-known representatives of this group of eccentric, mysterious, and at times sinister and powerful helper figures. This class of Hoffmann characters shares two salient features. On the one hand, they hold a liminal position in relation to the symbolic order. All of these characters are associated with a highly respected group of professionals or administrators, but in their private lives and interests they are extremely idiosyncratic and eccentric. They are usually unmarried; somehow solitary; and involved with unorthodox pursuits of technological, artistic, pedagogical, or medical skills and knowledge. On the other hand, they hold a phantasmatically invested position for the other characters. Because of their specific position with respect to the symbolic order, as outsiders who seem above and beyond societal conventions and fictions, these characters are placed in the position of a presumed superior knowledge and the ability to control the fate of others; thus they can quickly become the focus of paranoid fantasy. Though not all of Hoffmann's fantastic tales deploy this kind of character, whenever one is present the fantastic features of the tale are developed as a function of this figure. It is also in view of this figure that the demarcation between a poetics of the fantastic (with its uncanny or sinister twist on the Pygmalion myth) can be distinguished from less unsettling accounts of the function of art.

The concluding part of "Automata" contrasts Professor X, this new figure of the artist behind the scenes, with models of aesthetic experience that seek a utopia of contemplative harmony and unity with the spirit, nature, or some other metaphysical entity. Both friends set out to question Professor X about the secret of the automaton. At his home, he shows them his collection of automata, but the two friends feel somehow disappointed and betrayed after he stages a concert performance by the automata for them; they are convinced that Professor X is concealing some ultimate secret. As Ludwig and Ferdinand take a final walk together, conversing about the nature of art, they catch sight of Professor X's secret garden.

The conversation between the two friends before the garden comes into view focuses on how music can approximate the mysterious sounds of nature. Ludwig tries to illustrate how a perfect tone can reestablish man's long-lost harmony with nature. To illustrate this primordial harmony, he quotes Gotthilf Heinrich Schubert's description of a state in which "the spirit of man did not embrace Nature, but in which Nature embraced the spirit of Man, a time when the Mother was still nourishing the marvelous being to whom she had given birth from the depth of her existence, when Nature moved Man to perpetual enthusiasm and, surrounding one with sacred music, and marvelous sounds revealed the secrets of her eternal activity" (my translation, 97; German, 421). This quote from Schubert's *Nachtseite der Naturwissenschaften* refers to a vital element that has recurred throughout Ludwig and Ferdinand's discussion about art and music: the search for the perfect natural sound as a way of accessing another state of being. In Schubert's formulation, however, the natural sound is explicitly characterized as access to a world of total maternal care. This scenario of almost uterine bliss is new; the mother has never been mentioned before in the story. Indeed, this vision of total appeasement and contentment stands in stark contrast to the scenes of pleasurable pain, tension, excitement, and enlivenment that so far have dominated all description of memorable experience. What distinguishes this scene from the others is its programmatic exclusion of alterity, desire, and the symbolic. Furthermore, it is marked as a regressive fantasy, a return to a long-lost realm. Schubert's fantasy of a return to preverbal bliss is the expression of an impossible desire not to desire, a vision of the end of desire as a way to escape from want.

Schubert's invocation of a state of primordial unity and harmony between man and nature is, of course, part of a popular Romantic philosophy of nature.[22] But Schubert's systematic reliance on a predifferential unity is also crucial to the much more extensive hermeneutic paradigm that governs Herder's reformulation of the Pygmalion myth—as for instance in Herder's description of his contemplation of the sleeping hermaphrodite. In the case of Herder, we have either the unifying soundscape of a maternal nature or the embrace of a paternal spirit to guarantee the humanist ideals of freedom and *Bildung*.

In Hoffmann's fiction, however, the wish to return to primordial unity with nature is revealed as fantasy. The theme of love is introduced by the exciting and destabilizing melody of "Mio ben ricordati." Whenever this melody recurs, it issues from an unlocated source, in an unknown voice. The words evoke a desire that defies death. As we have seen, Ferdinand's response to this melody is always a search for a loving partner, a stabilizing other, a plea for love as a defense against desire. In other words, the melody must be understood in contrast to Schubert's or Herder's utopia of a self-preserving unity. The function of the artist/creator/spirit as the stabilizing other is assigned to the professor/mechanic/dilettante, who is phantasmatically invested with the expectation that he shore up the symbolic order, that he give definite answers and end uncertainty and desire—a demand or an expectation that certainly exceeds his human powers. To the extent that he is always already associated with the symbolic order, the figure of Professor X comes to mark the impossibility of a return to preverbal bliss.

It is worthwhile to consider more closely how the two friends catch sight of Professor X's garden. As they continue their speculation about penetrating the secrets of nature, they suddenly hear a strange sound vibrating through the air, the melody of "Mio ben ricordati." As they look up, they see the entrance to an enclosed garden and observe a little girl playing and singing with her little sister.

What was their astonishment, what inner horror penetrated them when they saw Professor X, who was standing in the middle of the garden beneath a lofty ash-tree! Instead of the terrible ironic smile with which he had received them at his house, his face wore a deep melancholy earnestness, and his gaze in beatific transfiguration was fixed upon the heavens, as if he were contemplating that world hidden beyond the clouds, of which those marvellous tones floating in the air like the breath of a zephyr were telling. He walked up and down the central path, with slow and measured steps; but, as he passed along, everything around him seemed to waken into life and movement. In every direction crystal tones came scintillating out of the dark bushes and trees, and, streaming through the air like fiery flames, united in a wondrous concert, penetrating the inmost heart and inflaming it into the highest rapture of heavenly anticipations. Twilight was falling fast; the Professor disappeared among the hedges, and the tones died away in pianissimo. At length our friends went back to the town in profound silence; but, as Ludwig was about to separate from his friend, Ferdinand clasped him firmly and said: "Be true to me! Be true to me!—Oh, I can feel it too clearly that a foreign power has intruded into my innermost being and has grasped its hidden strings, making them resound at its pleasure. I am helpless to resist it, though it should drive me to my destruction!—" (English translation, modified, 99; German, 424–25)

To the extent that this shared vision of the professor is provoked by the two friends' intense conversation about the ultimate secrets of nature, the mysterious source of music, and the excitation of resonance, the vision seals or embodies an intense experience of sexualized talk that was initiated with Ferdinand's confession. Again, he seems to seek protection from the shattering of identity-securing barriers by clinging to his interlocutor and imploring him to remain faithful. What remains to be explained, however, is why the professor, who doesn't display any of his frequent sardonic or sarcastic expression but merely raises his eyes to the sky, becomes an object of horror. What in this vision might trigger intense anxiety? Why is this scene of perfect bliss and enjoyment cast in the affective register of a nightmare?

If the vision were merely a shared daydream within the two friends' conversation, the professor would have no place in it. For wasn't their fantasy borrowed from Schubert's? Doesn't it therefore exclude the representative of the symbolic order, the third element? But their vision includes the professor, so it contradicts the standing of their experience as daydream, hence marking it as reality. Nevertheless, the scene includes many supernatural features, and it significantly contributes to the tale's fantastic nature. The characteristic moment of indecision between what is real and what is fantasized is elaborated not just as a cognitive issue but as desire and fantasy. Already when Ferdinand—after having thought he could clearly separate the dream world of happiness from a deficient reality by having classified his mysterious love as a figment of his imagination—looks out the window and catches the parting glance of his beloved, Hoffmann's narrative, as we have seen, undermines traditional hermeneutic and rationalist assumptions about psychic interiority as distinct from an external reality. The scene with the departing lover strongly suggests that the opposition between an exclusive, private dream world and an intersubjective waking reality does not hold; a dream might be less the articulation of desire than an attempt to flee the reality of desire.

The professor seems to belong to a generally acknowledged intersubjective reality, a well-known inhabitant of the town whose sight should by no means disrupt or suspend the ordinary perceptual schemata. Nevertheless, in the quoted passage the sight of him becomes the occasion of shock and anxiety; it spoils the happiness and imagined bliss of the two friends. Hence, he appears in an ambivalent position that allows two interpretations. On the one hand, he marks the impossibility of perfect enjoyment; as a representative of the symbolic order he marks the perpetual reality of want, lack, and desire. On the other hand, however, Professor X can be mobilized as a disavowal of the impossibility of bliss and the perfect satisfaction of desire by being turned into an external and specific obstacle to enjoyment; by being the one who has it all, to the exclusion of others. Rather than the dead father of the symbolic law, he becomes the living father who has access to all enjoyment, to all women, who thus bars everybody else. This mythical figure of an obscene enjoyment—like Freud's archaic father of the horde in *Totem and Taboo*—becomes a denial of the reality of desire, of the fact that there is no Other behind the other and the fact that the speaking subject always remains split between desire and fulfillment.[23] The vision of the garden combines the harsh reality of the symbolic order that prevents a return to the imaginary totality envisaged by Schubert with an occasion for escape into the phantasmatic denial of this reality.

The vision of the two friends therefore contains two alternatives: a symbolic order that is neither controllable nor knowable by the speaking subject whom it subjects to desire; or the ability to give up desire in favor of enjoyment with the aid of a mythical father. The conclusion of the narrative disambiguates this vision with Ferdinand's choice of madness and happiness.

Although the two friends were planning to seek out the professor on the morning after their vision of the garden scene, "to approach Professor X and perhaps finally to solve the enigma that had such a deep impact on Ferdinand's life; . . . an unexpected letter from Ferdinand's father called him to B., [so] he could not afford the least delay" (my translation; German, 425–26). An absent father's command seems to prevent Ferdinand from solving the riddle of his life with the aid of the professor, the subject who knows how to explain and interpret the disturbing, sexualizing, and menacing enigma of the automaton. But ultimately Ferdinand ignores the desire of his father, replacing the absent father with the sight of the professor, who ultimately becomes the figure through whose agency he gives up desire and flees into madness and happiness.

Ferdinand leaves with the intent to visit his father for a fortnight, but he does not return from this journey. Two months later, Ludwig receives a letter from him recounting how on his journey he was led to visit a church and became the accidental witness of a wedding ceremony in which the enigmatic characters of his beloved and Professor X play a decisive role:

> Mechanically I went into the church and entered exactly at the moment when the clergyman was concluding the ceremony with the blessing. I looked, the bride was the singer. She looked at me, turned pale, and fainted. The gentleman who was behind her caught her in his arms. It was Professor X.—What happened further I do not know, nor have I any recollection as to how I got here; probably Professor X will tell you. But a peace and serenity, such as I have never known before, have now taken possession of my soul. . . . Have I lost her? Is she not mine forever in the glowing inner life? (English translation, modified, 101; German, 426–27)

Professor X is not the groom, nor is he a prohibiting agent; nevertheless, it is into his arms that the bride sinks. Had the professor been the groom, he would have been a rival, and Ferdinand would have remained in the order of desire, in this case the explicitly mimetic desire—of desiring another's object of desire. In Ferdinand's version, however, the professor takes the object out of circulation, which transforms the scene into a fantasy of the end of desire.

*

The figures of the speaking automaton and the mysterious Professor X focalize the many strands of Hoffmann's discourse on Romantic art that have been elaborated within this narrative. Even the moment within the diegetic context of the narrative that directly addresses the nature of the work of art, Ferdinand and Ludwig's dialogue discussing the passage from Schubert's *Ansichten*, cannot, as we have seen, be separated from the story of the automaton's functioning and the professor's agency that contextualizes and comments it. The work of art is neither the meaningful, inspired totality of the hermeneutic classicist model nor the vision of a return to Nature and a preverbal, presymbolic uterine bliss as envisioned by Romanticist scientists like Schubert; for Hoffmann it is an enigmatic simulation of life itself. Standing in contrast to the Pygmalion myth, the animation of the speaking Turk can be read as a critique of the hermeneutic scenario of an artwork-beholder interaction, for ultimately it is not the automaton that comes to life but the beholder, who is sexualized and seduced by the enigmatic encounter. As a disruptive and sexualizing encounter, therefore, the impact of the automaton in Hoffmann's tale is the precise opposite of the autoerotic and narcissistic scenario of aesthetic contemplation. Through the figure of the automaton, Hoffmann describes the nature of art as completely enigmatic but also entirely open, and invested with variable limits and frame. Hence the work of art is not a closed totality; if anything, it is a fragment. The automaton, though it does not itself become a model object of art, in effect replaces the Greek sculpture.

Throughout Enlightenment aesthetics, the image of the stringed instrument was used to explain the working of sympathy or pity as an excitation of resonance, as when one string, when plucked, causes another to vibrate sympathetically.[24] Interestingly, the same image also informed the emerging neurological discussion of sensory stimulation, pain, pleasure, and excitement.[25] Hoffmann's aesthetics takes this model of aesthetic reception from the culture of sensibility to its limits, to the point where the work of art and even the discussion of aesthetics as a separate sphere disappear or become indistinguishable from materialist discussion of nerve impulses and sensory data. We have seen an example of this in the impact of Scudéri's speech on the king, in the description of how she infuses her listener with the liveliest, most glowing life. Likewise in "Automata," Ferdinand sums up the lasting impact of the mysterious artwork of the speaking automaton in a final image: "Oh, I can feel it too clearly that a foreign power has intruded into my innermost being and has grasped its hidden strings, making them resound at its pleasure" (424–25). In Ferdinand's image, the beholder/audience is described like the actual instrument that is being touched. The aspect of mediation drops out as audience and artistic instrument become indistinguishable. We might extend the musical model and argue that the audience becomes part of the artistic performance. To the extent that the experience of being penetrated by a foreign power unalterably interferes with the consciousness of the audience/beholder, that consciousness is in the process of being transformed by the mysterious artist, the technician of the imaginary. To put this new model of the artwork-artist-beholder interaction in a nutshell: the role of the artist is defined in terms of his all powerful, life-shaping agency.

Unlike Scudéri's accomplished rhetorical performance, cast in the limelight of the court and at the center of power, which urges a reconfiguration on the conception of a defendant's subjectivity, making psychological considerations outweigh evidentiary proof in a court of law, Professor X exerts his power behind the scenes. His powerful status and ability to intervene so profoundly in Ferdinand's life is attributable less to his actual skill, knowledge, or position in a social hierarchy than to the role attributed to him as the subject who knows and can answer the ultimate questions that move an individual's desire—in brief, to his phantasmatic status.

Although often sinister and powerful, the artist is not the creator of a self-contained artifact. The artist as a technician of the imaginary is a radically modern phenomenon who makes conscious use of available media technologies. Although Hoffmann was a highly accomplished draftsman, musician, and writer, he did not fuse the "sister arts" into a total work of art in the manner of Wagner or the impresario modern multimedia event. His stories often appeared first in journals and only later were gathered and republished in book form. Music, theater, and painting, though thematically central to his stories, are left to the silent reader's solitary imagination. Unlike the earlier culture of sensibility that encouraged the reader's seamless identification with the fiction, Hoffmann's stories frequently contrast a hallucinatory, ersatz reality of an image with its material and medial support. Hoffmann's work examines the media-technological conditions of art and their constant assimilation into quasi-natural modes of perception, only to turn around and then draw attention to the fictionality of the construction of reality. Thus the characterization of the modern artist as the technician of the imaginary is accompanied by the mise-en-scène of the production and reception of art.

4

Artificial Paradise and the Medial Woman

"Serapion," "Rat Krespel," "La morte amoureuse," and "Ligeia"

In the Chapter One discussion of "The Elementary Spirit," we saw how Hoffmann's retelling of *The Devil in Love* emphasizes the dependency of the fantastic genre on the dominance of the print medium, and how the protagonist's seduction by the elementary spirit went hand in hand with his excited imagination, his identificatory, solitary, and hallucinatory consumption of popular fiction. This chapter further pursues the topic of mediation and the arts. Two of the stories I analyze in this chapter, E.T.A. Hoffmann's "Rat Krespel" (Councillor Krespel) and Théophile Gautier's "La morte amoureuse" (The Dead Leman) situate pleasure not in the verbal arts but in the realms of music and painting, almost as if those nonverbal art forms were more sensuous and more immediate. These sites of sensuous bliss are clearly marked within the fiction as lying beyond the boundaries of what is accessible to ordinary mortals, and they are intimately connected with a female figure, who permits access to them. The mysterious woman of these fantastic tales mediates a relationship to an art form and becomes the conduit to an artificial paradise, a site of sensuous enjoyment without a body.

Typically, the plot of those fantastic tales that belong to the thematic complex of the pleasures of artificial paradise resemble the story of Orpheus and Eurydice, involving a beautiful young woman who dies and then is mysteriously revived, only to die again.¹ Just as the vision of utter enjoyment and perfect sensual pleasure without a body is associated with beautiful music or a sensuous oil painting, the medial woman's function is compared to an extraordinary violin or a statue that comes to life. To the extent that she can profoundly affect and alter the protagonist's own perceptual reality and sense of embodiment, the mysterious woman functions as some kind of prosthesis for the protagonist or observer in the story. Additionally, since the nature of the medial woman is kept a mystery and it is never entirely clear whether she is a spirit, a ghost, or just an ordinary mortal woman with a particularly frail constitution, the question of her physicality or spirituality comes to represent the material conditions of the medium itself.

The fantasy of a bliss transcending the limitations of the human body can be related to certain idealist currents in early nineteenth-century culture. In the previous chapter, we observed how Hoffmann's "Automata" critically draws on Schubert's version of Schelling's idealism. Similarly, Poe's "Ligeia" makes explicit reference to transcendentalism, and Théophile Gautier's work shows the influence of neo-Platonism through his intensive study of Goethe's late work. Furthermore, all of these writers were fascinated by the then-popular and influential occultist observations and practices of Mesmerism.² Yet these intellectual trends and scientific fashions cannot explain the particular emplotment that the fantasy of enjoyment without a body receives in the fantastic tale. Once the problematic nature of this enjoyment without a body is emphasized, though, another contemporary context becomes relevant: the history of media technology, consumerism, and the rise of a self-satisfied bourgeoisie in the post-Napoleonic age.

Hoffmann, Gautier, and Poe all direct their fiction against bourgeois utilitarianism and moralism; they celebrate versions of pleasure and enjoyment that can be associated with the new sociocultural type of the dandy, aesthete, or bohemian, types that are generally discussed as representative of a slightly later modernist or decadent aesthetics. The forms and media of communication that these authors despise for fostering a philistine, moralist, and utilitarian bourgeois culture are primarily bourgeois and petit bourgeois clubs and associations that organize the pleasures of leisure time in the case of Hoffmann, and the expanding journals of a beginning mass and consumer culture in the case of the slightly younger Gautier and Poe. The form of pleasure and the type of escape into an artificial paradise that is modeled in their fantastic fiction are characterized in terms of its social liminality or of a conflict between a moral code and an aesthetic one. It is this problematic of pleasure and escape, this reflection on the costs and limits of the artificial paradise, that I examine in some detail.

This chapter begins with discussion of two stories from Hoffmann's collection *The Serapion Brethren*. The first, an untitled story from which the collection gets its name, is the story of Serapion, a late-eighteenth-century nobleman who believes he is a second-century Christian martyr. Serapion lives the life of a hermit in the woods, believing he keeps friendly company with thinkers of all ages and epochs. He couples a visionary intensity in storytelling with vehement denial of the mortality and corporeality of the human body. Going hand in hand with Serapion's denial of the body is a denial of any tangible means of mediation.

By contrast, the principal character in the second story of the collection, "Councillor Krespel," is dependent for his bliss on the mediation of musical instruments and the wonderful voice of his daughter.[3] Gautier's "The Dead Leman" is similar to "Councillor Krespel" insofar as it, too, escapes the medium of writing and the technology of print culture and explores the pleasures of an artificial paradise in the world of painting and color through commerce with the famous courtesan Clarimonde, a commerce that is depicted as total immersion in a world of visual beauty. The concluding section of this chapter shows how Poe's "Ligeia" can be read as a commentary on the entire thematic complex as it spells out the connection between the medial woman and the imaginary materiality of the signifier by focusing on the narrator/protagonist as a writer and reader in the realm of print technology.

Temporality, Ideal Beauty, and Mortality

In the preface to his anthology *The Serapion Brethren*, Hoffmann writes that the collection's frame narrative should be understood in the tradition of Tieck's *Phantasus*. Its conversational setting allows him to gather together previously published narratives and relate them to each other through an ongoing, serene exchange among like-minded friends about the nature of art and literature. The actual conversation in the frame narrative covers topics representing a spectrum of concerns, from discussion of various forms of entertainment to the advantages of different artistic media, to the relationship between madness and reality, and to that between spirit and mind. Hoffmann furthermore points out that, in contrast to Tieck's anthology, the company from his own frame narrative lacks the inspiring and colorful presence of lovely ladies and begs his reader not to hold this against his work.

At the beginning, however, the actual tone of the frame narrative's discussion among a group of companions, reunited after a twelve-year separation, is not one of easy and carefree conviviality. Lothar, among the group, bemoans a profound sense of loss in the wake of time's irretrievable passage. To overcome this feeling, Ottmar proposes institutionalizing their gatherings, an idea that Lothar finds as laughable as the practices of the petits bourgeois who, in their philistine clubs, need to regulate their boredom with elaborate codices intended to structure their banal pleasures. The mention of petit-bourgeois attempts at organizing leisure time nevertheless produces quite a bit of amusement, spiced with irony and sarcasm, as some of the group members anecdotally elaborate particularly ridiculous details of these philistine forms of entertainment, such as one club that chose as its symbol a rooster attempting to lay eggs.

During all of this discussion, only one member, Cyprian, remains silent, apparently lost in his own thoughts. When asked by the others about his silence, he tells his friends that he has been thinking all day about a curious encounter he had in his past. He points out that the philistine denial of the passage of time has, in his mind, something quite uncanny and sinister about it. It reminds him of two friends, who had been quite close when they both studied philosophy but then were separated for a good twenty years. At the moment of their accidental reunion, they resumed their intense philosophical discussions from former times as if nothing had happened in the interim. After a heated debate of about two or three hours, they separated, never to meet again. In light of this anecdote, Cyprian proposes a more measured approach. On the one hand, he agrees that the philistine clubs should not serve as a model for their gathering. On the other hand, he points out that they need not be afraid that regular meetings will necessarily turn them into anxious philistines. At this point, the group agrees that they should enjoy their punch and listen to the story that has been on Cyprian's mind. He obliges by telling them about his strange encounter with the mad hermit Serapion.

The story of Serapion stands in a complex relationship to its surrounding context. Initially, it draws a hostile, uneasy response among the group of friends, though eventually they choose him as their patron saint, seeing in him the representative of a poetic principle, of an intense inner vision that is to guide them in selecting texts to present to each other at their regular gatherings. What brings about this change of mind is a tale that Theodor tells, in an effort to dispel the feeling of unease occasioned by the Serapion story. He tells the tale of an encounter he had with the eccentric and half-mad violin maker Councillor Krespel. Far from softening the disturbing impact of the Serapion story, Theodor's tale produces exactly the opposite of its intended result. His listeners are so unsettled that they revise their attitude toward Serapion's madness and name their group after him. Hence, Serapion and the so-called principle of Serapion—of a radical idealism and exclusive commitment to the intensity of an inner vision—though it might very well represent the antithesis of the self-satisfied petit-bourgeois forms of entertainment and distraction, nevertheless also has to be seen as a cover up or defense against a far more disturbing complex that is invoked by the story about Krespel. In other words, the two stories have to be considered a unit, in which the latter casts a critical light on the former, by elaborating a set of concerns that are safely excluded or rejected by Serapion's serenely mad denial of temporality, mortality, mediation, and sexuality.

Serapion: Radical Visionary Bliss and the Denial of the Body's Mortality

Cyprian relates how, on a walk through a deep forest in southern Germany, he met a man who looked as if he had stepped out of a painting of a medieval hermit. This man, Cyprian has been told by the people of a nearby town, though not quite right in his head, is harmless and good natured. Curious to learn more, Cyprian learns from the local Doctor S. that this man had been a highly accomplished, poetically gifted nobleman who suddenly disappeared just as he was about to be sent to an important diplomatic post. Sometime after, he was observed dressed in a monk's habit, living in a solitary hut in the woods. The hermit's identity was confirmed by a relative, and he was brought to a psychiatric institution to be cured of his mad fury. The doctor, however, determined that if he were left in peace his madness would not erupt into violent action.

Piqued by the doctor's account, Cyprian studies the available psychiatric literature in the hope of finding a cure. After a personal visit, however, he realizes the futility of his efforts as a lay psychiatrist. The hermit, believing that he is the second-century martyr Serapion, argues quite rationally that the psychiatric belief in curing madness by engaging with the deranged mind through reason is rather mad in itself, for if madness were to be brought so easily under rational control there would be no mad people left. Serapion further argues that Cyprian, who refuses to accept the hermit's identity as that of the martyr, is in flagrant disregard of the relativity of time. To Serapion, barely three hours have elapsed since emperor Decius had him executed.

Serapion's madness is thus characterized as a radical idealism opposed to materialist determinism. He elevates his idealism into an ethical stance when he alerts Cyprian to his own tranquility and serenity:

"I too survived these tortures hell itself had ignited in my breast. When I woke up with torn limbs and a shattered head the spirit illuminated my interiority and allowed soul and body to return to health. O my brother, I wish that heaven will allow you, while still on earth, to partake of the enjoyment of the tranquility and serenity that refreshes and strengthens me. Don't be afraid of the shudders of deep solitude, for only therein will the pious heart gain such a life!"

Serapion, who had spoken the last words with true sacerdotal unction, was now silent as he directed his transfigured gaze towards the sky. How could I but feel the uncanniness of it all?[4]

The story leaves no doubt as to Serapion's actual identity: he is not the martyr Serapion but a contemporary of Cyprian's. Why, then, should Cyprian be unsettled by the hermit's words and the encounter? It seems less the content of Serapion's utterance that unsettles Cyprian than the position from which he is speaking, that of a person who died long ago. For Cyprian, Serapion's position is captured in the "transfigured gaze," the very same visible attitude in which Professor X in "Automata" appeared to the two friends Ludwig and Ferdinand. Exactly as in "Automata," this transfigured gaze becomes an occasion for dread, or an uncanny feeling. Again in this story, the quality of the gaze is used to indicate an impossible otherworldly enjoyment, to capture a vision of ultimate fulfillment that would end all desire, not given to ordinary mortals who are bound up in a world marked by temporality, loss, and material obstacles. Serapion's serenity is the blissful enjoyment of a purely unmediated intellectual or spiritual vision that denies the individual's corporeal embodiedness.

Nevertheless, Serapion's idealism is not all that outlandish. His spiritualist view of happiness, an intensely sensual but incorporeal vision, reflects a particular stage in the cultural history of the print medium that, by the late eighteenth century, thanks to the ready availability of books, not only encouraged the absorbed reader's hallucinatory identification with what appears on the printed page (a circumstance Hoffmann extensively explored in "The Elementary Spirit") but also—in developments ranging from copyright regulations to the inspirational model of the poetic genius of Romanticism and textual hermeneutics—led to the emphatic concepts of work and author.[5] If we bear this in mind, we understand that underlying Serapion's boasting of the wonderful company he keeps in his isolated woods—he tells Cyprian that just on the previous day he has received the visits of Ariosto, Dante, and Petrarch—is a personal history of engagement in a lively reading of texts by these authors. Cultivating an intense reading experience made possible by the ready availability of books, in this sense, replaces the temporal and spatial limitations of a mortal human being.

Serapion rejects those among his critics who would accuse him of confusing the constructs of his imagination with reality:

Isn't it the spirit alone that can grasp what happens around us in space and time?—What is it that hears, sees and feels in us?—Could it be the dead machines that we call eye—ear—hand etc. and not the spirit?—Should the spirit not form its world in space and time on its own in our interiority, and, leave these functions instead to another principle in us? That would not make sense. For if it is only the spirit that can grasp the events that occur before us, then that which the spirit has comprehended will have really happened. (33–34)

Serapion's radical idealist hermeneutics opposes the organs of sense perception—disjointed "dead machines"—to the forming activity of the living spirit, which alone can do the work of organizing sensory data into distinct phenomena. In contradistinction to a materialist determinism, the actuality of experience and hence the nature of reality depends on the spirit's faculty of apprehension alone. Serapion's belief in the supreme power of the spirit invokes the ideal of a purely mental or intellectual vision that, by means of its purity and intensity, can produce a reality of its own. The setting for this intellectual vision would be the private library, in which the hermeneutically inclined reader can experience reading not as a painstaking process of deciphering or decoding but as effortless, immediate, and transparent communication with the spirits of the authors whose works he studies. This fantasy of the library, however, denies the materiality of the signifier, which is to say, the fact that writing depends on some kind of material that encodes and preserves the differential markers of language. This externality of writing is what Serapion overlooks in his appeal to the exclusive power of the spirit.

Serapion's ability to overcome temporality, and with it a painful sense of loss and destruction, accords exactly with the desire articulated in the introductory framing conversation, yet his ability to transcend the limitations of temporal existence is achieved at the cost of madness, and ultimately denial of the mortality of the body. The manner in which Cyprian's story illustrates the power of the spirit over the opacity and limitation of material reality makes it clear that what is at stake is not a quasi-religious model of inspiration but rather a secular model of poetic production:

> Now Serapion told a novella, conceived and recounted as only the poet generously gifted with spirit and a fiery imagination could do. All the characters emerged in three dimensions and glowing with such life that one was carried away, charmed by its magic force; as in a dream, one was led to believe that Serapion had actually seen it all from his mountain. (34)

Because Serapion's visionary talent produces a convincing semblance of life that replaces an external, material reality, he would have to belong to the class of poet and artist figures of Hoffmann's poetics. Yet Cyprian does not retell any of Serapion's actual novellas. Instead, he is unsettled by the contrast between Serapion's irrefutable madness on the one hand, and his serenity, sociability, and narrative talent on the other.

That Serapion's madness, however, is not limited to mere disregard for the existence of the external world but self-consciously embraces a position outside the symbolic order is readily illustrated by a detail from Cyprian's conversation with Serapion. Cyprian refers to an episode in the life of the legendary medieval monk Serapion, who commanded a pious maiden to strip naked and walk with him through the streets of Rome as proof that she had truly renounced the world. When the maiden refused, the monk rebuked her in anger. In response to Cyprian's interjection, Serapion unabashedly declares that he, the martyr Serapion, had nothing in common with this legendary dirty, ascetic monk for whom proof of true renunciation of the world of the flesh had to be part of a public demonstration. Unlike the medieval monk, for whom sexual desire would have been neither a psychological nor a physiological matter but part of a social reality fully entrenched in the symbolic order, Cyprian's interlocutor violently rejects this episode from the life of the Serapion of legend as a repulsive form of asceticism. Hence, as the modern Serapion proposes his own isolated lifestyle as the purer and better expression of renunciation of the temptations of the flesh, he also identifies the realm of sexual difference, together with the symbolic order of which it is part, as a domain from which he considers himself entirely separate. This categorical erasure of an episode from the life of the appropriated identity points to the thematic field of feminine sexuality, made conspicuous by its abrupt dismissal. This thematic field, however, will recur in the tale of Councillor Krespel that follows.

Cyprian concludes his recollections of Serapion by relating how, happening to return to the hermit's hut, he finds Serapion stretched out, his hands folded, seemingly asleep but actually dead. Thus Serapion's idealism, marked by the highly attractive but paradoxical desire not to desire, is also fulfilled in his death, in which he resembles somebody who is peacefully asleep. Yet as an ultimate twist, the finality of his death concludes the whole story with a reminder of the inescapable mortality of the human body. Serapion thus comes to embody the world of madness and intense inner vision, as distinct from the world of external reality, temporality, and mortality.

At first the circle of friends attempts to ridicule Cyprian's narrative by making fun of his strange taste for Catholic mysticism, saints' legends, the occult, and madness. Then they speculate about the potential dangers of contact with madmen. Theodor in particular finds the idea of seeking happiness in Serapion's form of madness terrifying. It is in this context that he proposes to tell a story in which he sees a far less radical contrast between reason and madness.

"Councillor Krespel": Narration and Fantasy Between Two Deaths

It would be very difficult to summarize the plot of "Councillor Krespel" without reproducing the tale in its entirety. The most characteristic feature of this tale is how the sequence and order of narrated events and actions comment on and intervene in the personalized narrator's perspective, in this way undermining the distinction between plot and its narration. Indeed, it is not immediately clear whether its eponymous hero or the tale's narrator should be considered the protagonist. Though personalized, the narrator merely plays the marginal role of a curious witness attracted by rumor and hearsay to the title figure. Even so, until the very end of the tale the reader's access to the title figure is mediated by this narrator. Even the story's last section, Krespel's own autobiographical narrative, is told in indirect speech. Moreover, the sequence of the story's narrative segments does not follow a chronology of events centered on Krespel but rather the chronology of the narrator's encounters with Krespel.

Artificial Paradise and the Medial Woman 157

The text is clearly structured and can be divided into two parts. The first part encompasses the narrator's first visit to the town in which Krespel lives. Upon his arrival, he hears rumors about the eccentric figure of Councillor Krespel, whom he subsequently meets at a dinner party. After Krespel's departure from the dinner party, he learns more about him, and his curiosity is piqued by what he learns about the beautiful young singer Antonia, who lives under Krespel's jealous watch. Subsequently, he is invited to Krespel's own house for a few visits, of which he describes only the first and the last in any detail. Krespel shows him his collection of famous violins, including an especially prized one whose beautiful tone, he claims, competed even with Antonia's voice. Eventually the narrator meets Antonia. But one day, as he tries to seduce her into singing, a furious Krespel turns him out of the house, asking him never to return.

The second part of the story begins when the narrator, returning to town, accidentally encounters an apparently mad Krespel on his way back from Antonia's funeral. Bewildered by this sight and full of suspicion that Krespel must have been somehow responsible for Antonia's untimely death, the narrator pays Krespel an unexpected visit. Confronted with the narrator's accusation, Krespel tells him his life story, recounting details about his failed marriage and the circumstances under which he was united with Antonia, who, he now reveals, was his daughter.

Adding to the intricacy of the narration is the interplay of the perspectives and biases from which light is shed on the objects of Theodor's fascination, Krespel and Antonia. From the narrator's perspective, the bizarre Krespel appears in possession of some obscene source of enjoyment, a secret source of pleasure that is the result of criminal transgression. A second perspective is given by the character of the professor, a friend of the councillor's, who knows little more about Krespel than what was generally known by the townsfolk. He tells the narrator about Krespel's unusual domestic arrangement, living as he does with a mysterious and beautiful singer, Antonia, and his strangely jealous behavior toward her. The third perspective that completes the picture is Krespel's own account of his story, which Theodor retells in indirect speech. Finally, throughout the story there is an additional, impersonal perspective that appears not in the form of an omniscient external narrator but as occasional, sudden turns in the narrative that undermine the narrator's complacently youthful misinterpretation of the circumstances in the course of his personal encounters with Krespel and Antonia; it is in this undercutting of the narrator's narcissism and sense of control that the story's ironical and fantastic dimension unfolds.

The story begins with the narrator Theodor's arrival in a town where he hears of the notorious "Councillor" Krespel, a successful and wealthy diplomat and lawyer whose house, built in the most unconventional way, is guided by no pattern or plan other than those dictated by his own whims. The reader is invited to share the narrator's impatience to learn more about this extraordinary person. Soon after, the narrator personally meets Krespel at a dinner party at the house of Professor M. Krespel moves in a jerky, unpredictable manner, jumps onto furniture, speaks either in a loud and excited voice or a nasal singing one, meanders in conversation, and is given to unexpected and passionate outbursts. For dinner, the guests have been served rabbit. After collecting the bones from the dinner plates, Krespel sends the professor's five-year-old daughter to fetch the rabbit's feet from the kitchen. Pulling out of his pocket some miniscule tools, he fabricates little boxes and toys out of the rabbit bones for the children to play with.

Suddenly, the professor's niece asks Krespel of the whereabouts and health of "our dear Antonia." She appears to have committed a *faux pas*, and the professor attempts to rescue the situation by asking Krespel about his violins. This seems to mollify Krespel, and he recounts with satisfaction how he has cut open a wonderful antique Amati, and that he trusts Antonia will by now have completed the business of its dissection. When, soon after, Krespel rather abruptly makes ready to leave, the narrator catches sight of the councillor's face in the mirror and sees tears welling in his eyes.

After Krespel's departure, the narrator urges the professor to tell him all about the violins Krespel has spoken of with such animation, and especially about the mysterious Antonia. The professor reports that Krespel is an eccentric but excellent builder of violins. Whenever he succeeds in constructing a very good violin, he plays it with great intensity for about two hours and then hangs it on the wall, never to touch it again. He is also a collector of famous old violins, which he likewise plays once before taking them apart and throwing the pieces into a bin.

As for Antonia, the professor admits, he could easily be led to detest Krespel for the way he treats her, were it not for Krespel's gentle, almost effeminate ("bis zur Weichlichkeit") good heart. After this exculpatory preamble the professor relates how Krespel, when he first came to town, lived all by himself with the aid of a housekeeper. One day he left town for a few months. On the evening of his return, the windows of his house were brightly lit and a crowd gathered in front to listen to a magnificent impromptu concert of a wonderful female voice accompanied by Krespel on the violin. After the end of the concert, at around midnight, Krespel was heard in a heated argument with another man. A girl's loud scream interrupted them, followed by dead silence. Suddenly a young man stormed out onto the street, took the next postal chaise, and departed instantly.

Nobody dared to ask Krespel about these mysterious events, but the housekeeper reported that Krespel had returned from his voyage accompanied by the beautiful girl whose name was Antonia and the young man who appeared to be her fiancé. Krespel kept the girl under close watch and barely allowed her to show herself at the window. Whenever he let himself be persuaded to take her along into company, he would watch her jealously and prevent her from singing. Nevertheless, for the people in town, whether or not they had been present at the nighttime concert, Antonia's singing became the legendary standard of how a truly beautiful voice should sound.

The professor's narrative ends the introduction to "Councillor Krespel," which portrays the eponymous hero as an intriguing and extraordinary figure who acts as if he is untouched by the demands of rationality, etiquette, and morality. In other words, he acts as if he stands outside the symbolic order, the order of language, law, and reason that is at the foundation of all social interaction and that marks the individual human subject as desiring and lacking. In contrast to the character of Serapion, who actually lives as a hermit, Krespel acts out his denial of the social and symbolic order by means of the social isolation of Antonia. To the extent that Krespel is not entirely outside the social and the symbolic, this story is concerned with issues of mediation, narration, and artistic media in a far more direct manner than was the case in the Serapion story. What is more, Krespel is introduced through hearsay and rumor, and even the professor remarks that there must be some hidden secret that would explain it all. Thus the story, in contrast to Serapion's, focuses on Krespel's fantasy of paradisiacal bliss and his desire not to desire; it also draws attention to the mediation of this fantasy and the reader's investment in learning about it.

It is this kind of phantasmatic investment that the narrator explicitly mentions as he ironically inserts a critical commentary between the introduction of Krespel's character and circumstance, and the next part of the story:

You know how keen I am on such fantastic things, and you can easily imagine how imperative it was for me to become acquainted with Antonia. . . .

Naturally, I heard Antonia's marvelous singing in my dreams the following night, and when she most touchingly implored me to save her in a superb adagio (which, absurdly enough, I seemed to have composed myself), I determined, like a second Astolpho, to break into Krespel's house as into Alcina's magic castle, and deliver the queen of song from her shameful bonds.[6]

The narrator marks his own fantasy as the cliché of a hero who rescues the damsel in distress out of the bonds of the evil magician. He furthermore characterizes this fantasy as a narcissistic vision of omnipotence by adding the "absurd" detail that it was in an aria composed by him that Antonia implored him to rescue her. Indeed, the narrator's ironic commentary leads the reader to expect a more commonplace reality, one opposed to the narrator's narcissistic dream world. Although the narrator's model of reality and illusion opposes an adequate and neutral depiction of facts, reducing them to simple wish fulfillment and subjective dream, this simple opposition is contradicted in the subsequent events that launch directly into the realm of the fantastic.

On his first visit to Krespel's house, the narrator does not even meet Antonia, though he is shown Krespel's wonderful violin collection. When he eventually meets Antonia, he is surprised to notice that Krespel does not display the jealous watch over the young woman of which the professor had warned him; instead, Krespel seems rather pleased about his visitor's conversation with the young woman. Apparently it is not the young woman herself but merely her voice that constitutes the object of Krespel's jealousy. One evening, after Krespel has proudly shown to the narrator a Cremati he dissected, and as the three are engaged in an especially lively discussion expressing their disdain at overly mannered singing styles, the narrator plays the piano in an attempt to seduce Antonia into singing. At that moment Krespel bursts out in anger, curses him, and throws him out of the house with an injunction never to return.

Antonia, the object of Krespel's intense jealousy, is from the beginning metonymically associated with Krespel's other passion, his consuming interest in violins. Already at the professor's dinner invitation, Krespel would not submit to being questioned about the girl, though he was quite happy to talk about the pleasure he takes in dissecting violins. The violin is in turn metonymically associated with the rabbit that was served for dinner at the professor's house, for Krespel's skill as a violin builder is announced on the occasion of his virtuoso display of dexterity in fabricating toys out of the rabbit's bones and feet. Even in the conclusion of the story, when Krespel decides to give up forever his passion for violins, we see him still fabricating toys.

In the introductory phase of the narrative, the choice of the verb used to describe Krespel's taking a violin apart evokes an association with dissection, vivisection, or at least carving up a roast or game: literally, he "cuts open" the violin. The verb *aufschneiden* in German is a technical term used for cutting open a roast, a corpse, or a body. This verb literalizes the metaphor of the "body" of the violin. Subsequently the narrator refers to Antonia's careful taking apart of the violin as *zerlegen*, "carving up," a term used for dividing the pieces of roast game or poultry, where the bones are still left inside.

Initially, the reference to the body of the violin and its literalization through the two verbs *aufschneiden* and *zerlegen* places primary emphasis on the sacrilegious nature of Krespel's "research": he will not hesitate to destroy a unique and singular masterpiece like the Amati. He is willing to sacrifice the most precious art works for his private enjoyment and the pleasure he takes in prying into the hidden, secret, and mysterious body of the instrument. Now, as the narrator makes closer acquaintance with his host, Krespel shows him one special violin, intimately linked with Antonia, that he has never dared to cut open. As we learn later, playing this violin becomes the substitute for Antonia's singing. Through this metonymical association, Krespel's pleasure in cutting open famous violins becomes even more explicitly associated with his relationship to Antonia:

"This violin," Krespel said when I asked him about it, "this violin is a very remarkable and wonderful piece by an unknown master, probably of Tartini's time. I am completely convinced that there is something peculiar about its inner construction and that if I take it apart [*zerlege*] I will discover a secret I have been looking for for a long time, but—laugh at me if you like—this dead thing, which depends upon me for its life and its voice, often speaks to me by itself in the strangest manner. When I played it for the first time, it seemed as if I was but the hypnotist who so affects his somnambulist that she verbally reveals what she is able to see within herself. Do not suppose that I am foppish enough to attribute even the slightest importance to ideas so fantastic in nature, but it is nevertheless peculiar that I have never succeeded in convincing myself to cut open [*aufschneiden*] that dumb, dead object." (English translation, modified, 175; German, 48)

Krespel's argument works by means of denial. By insisting that the violin is a dumb, dead thing that can be cut open, he shows that in fact by not cutting it open he respects it as a living, sentient body. On the other hand, he claims that if one attributes life to this dead thing, this life is merely due to his own enlivening power as a good violinist. Thus in one and the same breath he maintains that the violin is no more than a dead object, while at the same time attributing life to it in a literal sense. He explains that the first time he played this violin it spoke to him, as if it had its own independence and alterity.

Krespel's comparison of himself with the "hypnotist" is extremely interesting. This enforces the metonymic relationship between the living body of a woman and the violin and also evokes the imagined power relationship. A comparable use of the charged scenario between hypnotist and patient can be found in the slightly earlier play by Heinrich von Kleist, *Käthchen von Heilbronn*, from 1807, the same year in which Schubert published his *Ansichten von der Nachtseite der Naturwissenschaften*, which also features a detailed discussion of somnambulism and sleepwalking. Kleist's memorable reference to the hypnotist-patient scenario occurs in two scenes depicting Graf Wetter von Strahl's interview of Käthchen, once as a witness during a secret trial and the other time in an intimate setting, while she is sleeping under an elderberry bush. Both scenes emphasize the same aspect that Krespel mentions: the fact that the hypnotized woman brings forth something of her own, her own secret, the truth—and not merely something being suggested to her by the hypnotist. In Kleist's text, the new and unusual power dynamic between interviewer and interviewee already stands in lieu of the sexual encounter between two bodies, in a hypnotist-patient interview that is ostensibly supposed to produce the woman's truth and secret but actually stands in for an erotic encounter. This substitution—far from being free of excitement, pleasure, and pain—becomes a new site of sexuality as a purely discursive, and perfectly perverse, encounter.[7] By calling on the analogy of the hypnotist's power over the female patient, Krespel too emphasizes the transgressive, occult, and sexualized nature of the relationship between himself and Antonia.

The metonymic chain that connects an erotic encounter to the discursive production of sexuality, the pleasurable talk about the woman's ultimate secret, is rather complex and circuitous. The narrator's expected encounter with a most lovely woman that would culminate in her courtship and rescue had been marked as a youthful, ridiculous, narcissistic dream by the narrator himself. In the subsequent narrative of the evenings spent at Krespel's home, there is no straightforward disillusionment on the part of the narrator; instead, the narrative shifts its focus onto Krespel's mysterious secret and the narrator's phantasmatic investment in it: the wish to participate in Krespel's imagined obscene enjoyment.

Indeed, the second and last section of the narrative shift from the narrator's interest in Antonia to his relationship with Krespel. Again, the narrator provides self-critical hints for the reader before he retells Krespel's story. He relates how upon his return to town he meets Krespel dancing madly on his way home from Antonia's funeral. Suspecting Krespel of having somehow caused Antonia's death, he confronts him, but after hearing Krespel recount the story of his life he realizes how wrong he was and leaves, feeling moved and shamed ("gerührt und beschämt," German, 56). Krespel's narrative recounts how he met an Italian singer, Angela, whom he married and then left while she was pregnant with their daughter, Antonia; how later, after her mother's death, he took in Antonia; and how his daughter had to be prevented from singing because of a life-threatening constitutional weakness. Once more, the narrator suggests a model in which his own expected, and somehow affectively invested, version of the story is undermined.

If we believe Krespel's story, Antonia died in her sleep while Krespel was also sleeping. Hence in technical legal terms Krespel can indeed not be accused of having murdered her. It is possible, however, to read Krespel's narrative in the light of the dream that he was having at the time Antonia must have been dying. In this dream, she was singing, and hence risking her life, but the sheer mesmerizing beauty of her song prevented Krespel from getting up and looking after her. If we take this dream into account in its full ambivalence, as both a wish and an anxiety, and furthermore consider some of the details of Krespel's narrative that lead up to telling this dream, then we might have to revise our interpretation of the narrator's confession of having left Krespel "moved and ashamed." Indeed, Krespel as much as our narrator seems somehow implicated in Antonia's death. In this sense, the narrator's shame would have to be read as the reaction to his investment in Krespel's secret, which reveals itself as a form of complicity.

To pursue this latter reading, which investigates the notion of a guilt that exceeds the purely legal definition of the term, we must consider the metonymic cluster around Antonia and the violin in greater detail. It is only in Krespel's final account that we learn more about Antonia as an artist and singer whose extraordinary voice is an index of a constitutional weakness. Krespel's suspicion about the source of her illness is confirmed by a doctor:

He presented her with a choice—she could either follow her fiancé and surrender to his and the world's allurements with the certainty of dying young, or give to her father in his old age a happiness and a peace he had never known, and thereby live for many years. Antonia collapsed sobbing into her father's arms, and he, aware of the agony the next few minutes might bring, did not want to hear anything more explicit. He spoke with her fiancé, but despite his assurance that no note would ever cross Antonia's lips, the Councillor was fully aware that B— himself [Antonia's fiancé] could never be able to resist the temptation to hear her sing—at least the arias he was composing. The musical world, even though it knew of Antonia's suffering, would surely never surrender its claim to her, for people like this can be selfish and cruel when their own enjoyment is at issue. The Councillor disappeared from F— with Antonia and arrived at H—. B— was in despair when he learned of their departure. (English translation, 185–86; German, 61)

The alternative he presents her with—either love or life—does not entail the option of a true choice, but only of a forced one. To live, she cannot but remain with her father; he makes sure that she does. He refuses to give in to her sobbing or to believe the assurances of her fiancé, Mr. B.; instead he abducts her. The suspicion arises that Antonia's physical safety is at best a welcome excuse for Krespel, who wants to keep his daughter exclusively to himself so that she can "give to her father in his old age a happiness and a peace he had never known." Nevertheless, B. finds them, and the daughter declares she would rather die than give up her love and her art. This critical confrontation leads to the singular, spectacular nighttime concert that gives rise to her local fame among the townsfolk and leads to speculation and gossip about Krespel's relation to her.

    The narrator describes Krespel's reaction to his daughter's assertion of her desire in these words: "His daughter, the only being in the wide world who could kindle in him a bliss he had never known, the one who could reconcile him to life, tore herself violently from his embrace; and he wanted this dreadful event to happen!" (ibid., translation modified). How else should we read this but that if Krespel is to be deprived of his daughter's presence, then she may just as well die. She has refused to give up her desire, she has chosen her love; hence he wants the unspeakable, he wants her death: they play, and she sings and suddenly collapses. Krespel gets what he wants. The fiancé leaves believing Antonia is dead, but she recovers, and Krespel has her all to himself. In a manner of speaking, Krespel has already killed her, having sacrificed her life for his own sake at the moment he manages to keep her in his house.[8]

At this point, Krespel's condemnation of the world and its willingness to sacrifice the life of the artist for its own enjoyment is at best hypocritical, for he too is equally guilty of having sacrificed his daughter's life as an artist and singer for his own "needs." Yet the two forms of enjoyment and the two types of guilt associated with it are not of the same kind; the audience selfishly sticks with its desire, whereas Krespel's behavior and choice try to deny the reality of desire by negating his daughter's alterity, mortality, desire, and adult life by instead making her into a dependent child with whom he can lead a strange, symbiotic existence: "She now clung to Krespel with a most devoted and daughterly affection and shared with him all of his favorite hobbies, his peculiar schemes and whims. She helped him take old violins apart and put new ones together. 'I will not sing anymore, but I will live just for you,' she often said to her father, smiling softly, after someone had asked for a song and she had refused" (English translation, 187; German, 62). In other words, he has forced his daughter to give up her own adult life to become the means of his happiness—a strangely medial woman, an instrument that must not sing.

The two final phases of Krespel's narrative are only logical within his phantasmatic denial of desire: to abolish any possible want in his self-enclosed universe, Antonia's renunciation of her art must also be abolished. As Krespel has to cancel lack and desire, Antonia too must feel no lack, and no desire of hers should remain unfulfilled. Luckily, they find the violin that can sing in her stead when he plays it. Hasn't he already made Antonia into a dead thing, his instrument? Hence her death appears as both her liberation from this life that was empty, and as the final consequence of his reducing her to a dead thing. In fact, the two alternatives become indistinguishable. Her passionate embrace of her fiancé, her singing for him of the song he composed for her, her blissful peace after she acquiesces and accepts her father's decision, and her death all coalesce in Krespel's dream of her death that coincides with her actual demise: "Krespel said that the state in which he found himself was incomprehensible, for an appalling anxiety was combined with a rapture he had never before experienced" (English translation, modified, 188; German, 63).

By way of concluding my reading, I glance briefly at how Krespel's narrative about his marriage to Angela serves as a contrastive background to his relationship with his daughter. Though she looks like an angel and sings beautifully, the capricious prima donna refuses to take Krespel's name or to acknowledge his marital authority. Instead she tortures him with her whims, from which he seeks refuge in his playing of the violin. Their tempestuous marital life comes to an end when finally, after Angela smashes one of his violins, Krespel, having thrown her out the window, flees back to Germany. Eight months later, he is informed of the birth of a healthy baby girl. Moreover, from a faithful friend he learns that Angela, who until then was a temperamental prima donna, is now, to the great satisfaction of the maestro, the most compliant of singers. Upon hearing this news, Krespel resigns himself to remaining an absent father and husband.

To some extent, both Angela and Krespel are musicians and artists. Yet only Angela is a famous professional, whereas Krespel is an amateur. Moreover, the singer inhabits her instrument in a manner inaccessible to the violinist. Her shattering of his violin in all of its willful violence also emphasizes the fact that his body is distinct and separate from his instrument. His act of retaliation—throwing her out the window—calls attention to the degree to which her instrument, her voice, is bound up with her life and her body, and moreover with her life-giving, her birthing capacity. Is his subsequent desperate search for a principle of life and art through dissection of famous violins then to be understood as a pathetic attempt at coming to terms with, at overcoming or compensating for, this fundamental difference?

Krespel learns that his daughter has grown up to be an extraordinary singer, but even when mother and daughter are on a tour through Germany he decides against meeting with them: "He would have loved seeing his daughter, who truly lived in his inmost being [*die recht in seinem Innersten lebte*], and who often appeared to him in his dreams; but as soon as he thought about his wife he had an uncanny feeling, and he remained at home among his dismembered [*zerschnittenen*] violins" (English translation, modified, 184; German, 59). Soon after, he learns about his daughter's engagement and Angela's death: "Despite the fact that the Councillor was deeply disturbed by this news of Angela's death, he nevertheless soon felt that a disturbing, uncanny principle had left his life and that now he could breathe freely for the first time" (English translation, modified, 184; German, 59). Obviously, Krespel was incapable of assuming the role of husband and father so long as the woman was present who did not entirely give up her desire for his sake. Angela, his strong-willed, independent wife, is associated with desire and a reality that he cannot control, hence she represents some disturbing and uncanny principle. Only after Angela's death can Krespel temporarily manage to construct for himself, in his isolated, contented relationship with his daughter, and by controlling and instrumentalizing this singer's life and body, a situation in which his daughter serves as his medial woman and means of access to an artificial paradise. Nevertheless, the story also reflects on the costs and limitations of this dubious ideal.

Whereas Serapion's happiness required vehement denial of sexual difference and mortality in terms of his mad identification with the martyr's life after his dismemberment and death, Krespel acts out the fantasy of the end of desire not by madness but by instrumentalizing his daughter as "the only being in the wide world who could kindle in him a bliss he had never known, the one who could reconcile him to life." Whereas Serapion's relationship to art is in asserting the primacy of a pure, intense mental or intellectual vision, unmediated by external reality, Krespel's artistic quest is found in the search for the elusive principle that determines the organization of the perfect instrument or medium capable of producing the most beautiful sound. He seems to have found this instrument or medium in his daughter and her proxy, the queen of violins. Although his dismantling of violins suggests he is in search of a mechanical principle of construction, both the association of this principle with his daughter's fragile constitution and the vocabulary of dissection suggest that what is at stake is an organism's principle of life. Without Antonia's mysterious constitutional weakness, which turns the exercise of her art into a life-threatening risk, she would be just another gifted prima donna like her mother. Her mysterious illness, however, makes her an object of fantasy. Her illness intimately fuses the principle of her beautiful song with the principle of her life, thereby situating her between two deaths—first, her death as an active performer and desiring young woman that she incurs as she becomes the victim of her father's protective prohibition, and then her actual physical death. Both Serapion and Antonia occupy a phantasmatic space separated from reality and the world of normal sociability for a limited time. In either case, this phase can be characterized first as a reversal of or flight from desire and mortality and ultimately as deferral of the finality of death.

*

When Theodor finishes recounting his tale, his friends are extremely agitated and upset. Lothar cannot bear the pathos and utter hopelessness of the tale's ending, the bleak desolation that is the outgrowth of the strange and fatal "sympathy" between Antonia and the violin. The friends, in other words, severely object to this explicit thematization of the medial woman and suddenly return to Serapion, who, now in the light of Krespel's creative destitution, seems to represent an infinitely more expedient poetic principle of mediation for attaining a glimpse of the artificial paradise of art. Having registered their profound unease with Theodor's tale about Councillor Krespel, they now agree to consider Serapion the patron saint of their gatherings.

From Serapion, they borrow the criterion by which they distinguish those poetic products that are worthy of being shared in their gatherings. As they understand it, no poet who is not entirely convinced of having actually seen what he recounts can produce the willing suspension of disbelief in his audience. In other words, only the authenticity and intensity of the poet's affective conviction of the reality of his vision can make a poetic product come to life; it is only those tales that have the aesthetic properties allowing them to be told in their gatherings.

In embracing Serapion as the model for the true poet, the friends do not, however, deny his madness:

Poor Serapion, was your madness anything other than the fact that some hostile star had robbed you of the knowledge of that duplicity on which all of our earthly being depends? There is an inner world and a spiritual force that can view this in full clarity, in the most perfect brilliance of the most animated life, but it is our earthly inheritance that it is the external world in which we are implicated, that works as the lever that sets this inner force into motion. (my translation; German, 68)

What Serapion's madness refutes—this "earthly inheritance," this dependence on the external world as the "lever" that sets forces into motion, thus allowing the perception of a brilliantly animated life (for Hoffmann, a typical image of reading qua perception)—is nothing other than the poet's dependence on the externality of writing and hence the materiality of the signifier. Finally, Cyprian's description of Serapion's madness as mere oversight of the fundamental duplicity of the world must be seen as a defensive, euphemistic reformulation of his first reaction to Serapion's mad vision of ultimate happiness and the end of desire. In his personal encounter with Serapion's visionary ability, he was struck by a feeling of uncanniness, not the pure admiration that would be due to an aesthetically powerful, convincing vision.

Thus we must conclude that Serapion's idealism represents an extremely defensive position. He emerges as a figure affording a relatively safe and clear distinction between sanity and madness. In this function, he is also used to cover up exactly those areas where this distinction cannot be so clearly drawn, as in Krespel's more sinister form of madness, a madness that Theodor surmises is not so far away from the norms of the mentally healthy. In terms of our concern with the fantasy of paradisiacal bliss, Serapion embodies the unsullied safety of an uncompromisingly idealist—albeit untenable—position that implies total denial of the body and mortality. Even so, Serapion's story, in spite of vehement idealism, does, like Krespel's story, demarcate access to otherworldly sensuous bliss as an artificial paradise that is situated between two deaths, between Serapion's or Antonia's symbolic death and their final corporeal demise.

In the next section, I show how both Gautier's "The Dead Leman" (1836) and Poe's "Ligeia" (1838) explore this phantasmatic site between two deaths as the space of a transcendent beauty and the locus of a highly intense sensual enjoyment without a (mortal) body. Gautier's fantastic tales pursue an ongoing critique of the Christian concept of the human body as the locus of personal identity, one that identifies in the Christian tradition the main obstacle to unfettered access to a world of sensuous bliss. Poe, by contrast, spells out the media-technological background that supports the fantasy of unlimited and unmediated access to the world of sensuous bliss and the construction of the medial woman.

"La morte amoureuse"

Among the tales of the Romantic fantastic, those by Théophile Gautier are most unequivocally invested in the pleasures of the artificial paradise of art.[9] In many of his tales, access to this timeless world of beauty and the senses is by way of a female lover who generally belongs to this other and often remote world of beauty.[10] Moreover, access to the pleasures of the artificial paradise and the manner in which the female lover can function as the medial woman have to do with the nature and status of her body's corporeality. There is nothing threatening or intrinsically problematic in Gautier's tales about succumbing to the pleasures of the artificial paradise, though a boundary or limit of some sort ultimately disturbs the attempt at wholesale escape into the world of the senses.

"The Dead Leman" is in every sense typical of Gautier's tales. The plot is in many ways indebted to Cazotte's *The Devil in Love* and Matthew Lewis's gothic novel *The Monk*. Romuald, an old priest and the first person narrator of the tale, recounts a strange episode from his youth. He relates how for a brief period, beginning on the day of his ordination into the priesthood, he found himself living a dual existence, and how, while living according to the limited and strict duties of his religious profession, he simultaneously led the life of an extravagant nobleman, lover of the recently deceased though mysteriously reanimated courtesan Clarimonde. In the first phase of the story, she is a living woman whom Romuald desires and knows he is unable to join. The second phase of the tale consists of his actual affair with Clarimonde, an affair that begins after her death, when he lays eyes on her beautiful corpse, and his entanglement in her phantasmatic world begins.[11]

The first part of the tale depends far less on narration than on evocative description of a vision of paradisiacal bliss that is a total immersion in a world of light and color. Romuald's involvement with Clarimonde is introduced as the sudden and radical transformation of the world he has known until then. Like a bride looking forward to her wedding, the young seminarian joyously and eagerly anticipates his ordination. He has never known temptation or regrets; his world has been limited and utterly closed off within the narrow confines of the seminary. During the ordination ceremony, he is suddenly overwhelmed as he catches sight of a regal and magnificently dressed woman:

> It was as if scales fell from my eyes. I experienced the sensation of a blind man suddenly recovering his sight. The bishop, but now so radiant, suddenly faded away, the candles turned pale in their golden sconces, like stars at dawn, and the whole church was enveloped in complete darkness. The charming creature stood out against that dark background like an angelic revelation; she seemed illuminated by herself, and to shed light rather than to receive it.[12]

Romuald's simple and stable reality is suddenly transformed by a vision of light and colors that invade the familiar surroundings. The perception of depth ceases when the distant woman appears in immediate proximity. Lowering his eyes in an effort to fend off the influence of "exterior objects" proves unsuccessful, "for through my lashes I could see her glistening with all the colours of the rainbow, and in a purplish penumbra as when one looks at the sun" (ibid.). His transformation, which he characterizes as a feeling of "being invaded by distraction," might also be characterized as an experience of being dispersed in the visual field, as if he were becoming part of a painting, losing both his focus and agency.

At the center of this new and radiant visual field are Clarimonde's eyes:

They shot forth rays like arrows, which I distinctly saw flying towards my heart. I do not know whether the flame which illuminated them came from heaven or hell, but it surely came from one or the other. That woman was an angel or a demon, perhaps both; she certainly did not issue from the loins of Eve, our common mother. (English translation, 181; French, 120)

Clarimonde's eyes are the focal point of an immensely transformative power. Her gaze indicates a desire that can annihilate all prior distinctions that define the order of creation, and of human existence within it.

At the same time as Romuald witnesses the world illuminated by Clarimonde, he is confronted with a nightmarish transformation of the ordination ceremony. He is caught between the radically new visual field that awakens both fear and desire in him and the rigid inexorability of the ordination ritual that forces him to make his vows before the altar.

The ceremony progressed, however, and I was carried very far from the world, the entrance to which my rising passions fiercely besieged. I said yes, however, when I longed to say no; when everything within me rose in revolt and protest against the violence my tongue exerted on my soul: a hidden [*occulte*] force tore the words from my throat against my will. It is the same feeling, perhaps, that makes so many maidens go to the altar with the firm resolution of refusing publicly the husband who is forced upon them, although not a single one fulfills her intention. . . . One dares not cause such a scandal before the world, or disappoint the expectation of so many people: all their wishes, all their glances seem to weigh upon you like a cloak of lead. (183–84, 121)

The ceremony removes Romuald not just from Clarimonde but from an entire world. He reiterates exactly the same comparison with the young maiden's marriage vows that he used to characterize his prior eagerness to enter the priesthood, only now the ordination is no longer a confirmation and culmination of his lifelong ideals, but a perception of himself as an object of scrutiny and fulfillment of the expectations of others. Most remarkably, his resistance to the ceremony is not described in terms of opposition between the external ritual and his internal state; rather, it is exclusively in terms of an external world of the senses: of Clarimonde's spellbinding presence and desire, and of the equally external order of the priesthood bearing down on him with all the rigidity and weight of a leaden cloak.

Instead of Romuald's interiority, it is primarily Clarimonde as an external observer who serves as an index of what happens to him: "The expression of the fair unknown changed as the ceremony progressed. Tender and caressing at first, it became disdainful and dissatisfied, as if because it had not been understood" (184, 122). She looks at him expectantly, a picture of utter desolation as he formally enters the priesthood:

> Never did human features express such poignant suffering; the maiden who sees her betrothed suddenly fall dead at her side, the mother by her child's empty cradle . . . the poet who has allowed the only copy of the manuscript of his finest work to fall into the fire, seem no more crushed and inconsolable. The blood entirely left her charming face, and she became as white as marble; her beautiful arms fell beside her body, as if the muscles had lost their power; and she leaned against a pillar, for her limbs trembled and gave way beneath her. As for myself, with livid cheeks and brow bathed in sweat more bloody than that of Calvary, I walked with tottering steps towards the door of the church; I was suffocating; the arches seemed to rest on my shoulders, and I fancied that my head alone bore the whole weight of the dome. (187, 123)

Clarimonde's gaze externalizes Romuald's subjectivity. She serves as the screen onto which he projects the expressions of an irretrievable loss that follow one upon the other, not in terms of psychological detail but as a series of dramatic tableaux. The expression of her loss of him externalizes and makes visible his loss of her in a manner that, in addition to being idealized and aestheticized, is also narcissistically invested. The image of the poet's loss of the only copy of his manuscript especially emphasizes the function of an idealizing, immortalizing agency that Clarimonde holds for him: it is he who would have been the unique copy of an artistic masterwork, at the same time an ideal of beauty and its concrete material embodiment. In response to her loss of him, Clarimonde appears to lose her own life, her color, her muscle tone, until her pallor matches the color of white marble. Romuald's own mortification, though not described along these aestheticizing lines, is likewise detailed from an external observer's position, and in terms of concrete bodily sensations. He does not become an immortal work of art but rather an aging or ill man who is staggering, barely in control of his body.

On his way out of the church, he feels Clarimonde touch his arm and reproach him. The imprint of her cold, serpentine hand seems to brand him like a red hot iron. On the way to the seminary, he receives a little note from a page: "'Clarimonde, at the Concini Palace'" (189, 124). The final stage of this strange and impossible courtship is described as a rage of despair over his separation from life:

> "Ah! if I had not been a priest, I might have seen her every day . . . instead of being wrapped in my dismal winding-sheet, I should have garments of silk and velvet, gold chains, a sword, and plumes, like the gallant young cavaliers. My hair, in-

stead of being dishonoured by a broad tonsure, would play about my neck in waving curls; I should have a fine waxed moustache, I should be a hero." But an hour passed in front of an altar, a few words barely spoken, had cut me off forever from the ranks of the living, and I myself had sealed the door of my tomb; I had shut with my own hand the bolt of my prison! (191–92, 125)

Romuald now sees himself as having consented to being buried alive, condemned to attend to the dying, to live in a world without beauty. This life of a priest, subject to chastity and poverty, which to him now appears as a form of death, is opposed not to the life of the bourgeois or the libertine but rather to the life of the dandy. The pleasure of being with Clarimonde means the pleasure of colorful fabrics, fanciful accessories, and elegant coiffure.

The object of his jealousy and envy, when he looks bitterly out of the window of his cell, is a scene of a young mother playing with her little child: "she kissed its little red lips, still empearled with drops of milk, and [*en l'agaçant*] indulged in a thousand of those divine puerilities which mothers alone can invent" (192–93, 125). Romuald's sexual fantasy is clearly not about sexual intercourse, nor about the ecstatic shattering of body and ego boundaries. Instead, it reveals a polymorphously perverse infantile eroticism that unfolds in the mother's attention to the child. He identifies, however, neither with the mother nor with the child; his erotic investment is in the entirety of the scene before him. In his later involvement with Clarimonde, it is the same kind of maternal caress, when she plays with his hair or helps him dress, that is for him the height of the pleasures of their "wild nights." At the end of the story, in his final glance at her, the drop of blood on her discolored lips echoes the pearls of milk on the child's rosy mouth.

Romuald's fantasy of total sensual bliss is not an Oedipal fantasy of desire for this or any mother. In fact, his fantasy of the joys of the world is the fantasy of a pagan, artificial paradise similar to the one that is celebrated by Gautier in his capacity of art critic, as expressed for instance in his praise of Veronese:

Men easily rediscover felicities more intoxicating than those shared by the solitary couple in old Eden. Do they not have women, flowers, perfumes, gold, marble, silk, wine, music, poetry, art, that flower of the mind? The exchange of ideas or feelings with a being similar to yet different from oneself; variety in harmony, admiration, that spiritual love, and love, that admiration from the heart which both exalts and prostrates you; the consciousness of belonging to that perpetual, collective man with whom God converses, in the silence of creation, in order to pass the time of eternity!

Glory then to Paolo Veronese, who brings the elements of happiness that divine benevolence has placed at our disposal shining before our eyes! An earth on which there are more than twenty thousand kinds of flower and plant purely for ornament, where the decoration of sunsets is changed every evening, where splendid form is so superbly clothed in colour, cannot be a vale of tears. Yes, if people wanted it, the water of *The Marriage at Cana* could turn into wine perpetually, and the harlot's perfumes into heavenly fragrances![13]

According to Robert Snell, Gautier's art criticism celebrates an observer position that (despite being highly subjective) is neither reflective nor sentimental nor psychologized. It is a subjectivity that, eluding any definite subject position, transcends personal identity: "A man for whom the visible world exists, Gautier himself sometimes hardly seems to exist at all outside the world of his own perceptions. The perceptions define the man, or rather allow him to elude definition, for in his pagan dream of sensual plenitude and repletion (his version of Winckelmann's *sufficienza*), personal identity is transcended."[14]

In the medium of the fantastic tale, Gautier appears to articulate exactly the same vision of an artificial paradise of sensuous enjoyment without a mortal body. Still, his fantastic fictions, by elaborating the strange corporeality of the medial woman, go beyond the concerns of his art criticism, problematizing the means of accessing this artificial paradise. From the start, Clarimonde's presence, described as an overpowering kaleidoscope of light and color, lends physical focus to Romuald's transcendence of personal identity. Not just the intensity of the sensory impressions emanating from her otherworldly presence but even her nature and origin defy categories in the young priest's captivated senses. In life, she stands as the embodied vision of indescribable beauty; in death, the materiality of her revived body becomes the conduit and medium for Romuald's entry to the sensual plenitude of an artificial paradise.

Unlike her literary predecessors, Cazotte's Biondetta and Hoffmann's elementary spirit, Clarimonde's physical presence is not an illusion; she remains present in the flesh, a partner to the protagonist in a sensuous, physical relationship: "She would have excited satiety itself and chained inconstancy. To have Clarimonde was to have twenty mistresses, she was so mobile, so changing, and so unlike herself [*dissemblable d'elle-même*]; a very chameleon! She would make you commit with her the infidelity you might have committed with others, by assuming the nature, the manners, and the style of beauty of the woman who seemed to please you" (231–32, 144). Her ever-changing nature, the fluidity that is crystallized in her sea-green pupils, is from the beginning associated with her particular ability to immerse Romuald in a world of limpid and luminous colors and alluring shapes in which opposition and contradiction easily coexist: "That woman was an angel or a demon, perhaps both" (181, 120); "Dead or alive, statue or woman, ghost or body, her beauty was still the same" (219, 138). It is through Clarimonde's dead body that this visually differentiated field becomes more than an insubstantial dream; it is her body that gives Romuald access to her world.

Shortly after the ordination, the dying Clarimonde sends for Romuald, but he arrives too late. Whereas the living Clarimonde existed in the world of light and color, the dead Clarimonde evokes the medium of sculpture, the art form that, according to Gautier, has the most direct, immediate, and transparent relationship to the ideal of beauty.[15] On the one hand, sculpture inhabits the same physical space as its beholder; it is utterly present to him in its three-dimensionality. On the other hand, it transports the beholder into a world of ideal beauty and form to the extent that both its shape and surface are purified of all imperfections and accidents. Clarimonde's death is carefully differentiated from actual decay and dying. When Romuald looks around her opulent chamber, "a broken black masque, a fan, and disguises of all sorts, were lying about on the chairs, and showed that death had appeared in that sumptuous abode unexpectedly and unannounced" (206, 132). While she was alive, Clarimonde's imposing beauty had been accentuated by her splendidly colored and textured clothes; now he sees her body, not stripped, naked, and vulnerable, but in its full ideal nudity:

> She was covered with a linen veil of dazzling whiteness, of which the dark purple of the hangings heightened the effect, and of such fineness that it did not at all conceal the charming outlines of her body, and enabled me to follow those lovely lines, as undulating as the neck of a swan, which death itself had not been able to stiffen. She was like an alabaster statue made by some clever sculptor to place upon the tomb of a queen, or like a slumbering maiden upon whom snow had fallen. (208, 132–33)

The thin white veil functions like a filter and a screen. It idealizes the imposing sculptural beauty of Clarimonde's dead body, transporting it from the world of living flesh. However, by not being an actual sculpture or funerary ornament, her dead body is not a sign that represents an absence but a full presence of its own.

When Romuald submitted to the ordination ceremony, he experienced the ritual as his own condemnation to a life cut off from the living. The effect of the ritual on Clarimonde was to turn her into white marble, the material of a sculpture. Her wake completes this process. As Romuald contemplates her aestheticized body and finally kisses her, she promises to return and give back to him the life he has given to her: the life of sensuous, primarily visual plenitude that exists entirely for its own sake.

"I waited for thee so long that I am dead; but now we are betrothed, and I shall be able to see thee and to come to thee. Adieu, Romuald, adieu! I love thee; that is all that I wished to say to thee, and I give thee back the life to which thou hast recalled me for an instant by thy kiss; we shall soon meet again." (212–13, 135)

Clarimonde's words during her return to life articulate the exchange that becomes possible through his animating contemplation and kiss of the beautiful corpse. He brings her back to life, and her visits return him to life, that is, to the fullness of life in the realm of the senses, the very life that Romuald vowed, in the ordination ceremony, to renounce.

Romuald's superior, Serapion, is aware of the strangeness of Clarimonde's death and tells the young priest of his fear that the famous courtesan might not remain confined to her grave, for Clarimonde seems not to be dead in the ordinary sense, and her body has shown no signs of decay. In all of the subsequent episodes, Clarimonde always appears to Romuald at night, when he is asleep; she seems to wake him out of a dream. In her first appearance, she is still clothed in her shroud, the thin white veil. She reports to him the travails she undertook to repossess her body and asks him to prepare himself to join her and become her lover. Only after some time, after they have been living their new life as lovers, does he accidentally find out that she has carefully taken some of his blood while he slept. Somehow, this does not seem to worry him; again, it is only Serapion's warnings that make him take heed.

At first glance, Romuald's new life of the senses seems merely a masquerade of luxurious clothing. On her second visit, Clarimonde helps Romuald put on the clothes she brought along for him and asks him to regard himself in a mirror.

I was no longer the same, and I did not know myself. I resembled myself no more than a finished statue resembles a block of stone. My former face seemed to be only the rough sketch of that which the mirror reflected. I was handsome, and my vanity was sensibly tickled by the metamorphosis. That elegant apparel, that richly embroidered vest, made of me a totally different person, and I marvelled at the power of a few yards of cloth cut in a certain way. The spirit of my costume penetrated my very skin, and within ten minutes I was reasonably conceited. (227, 142)

This passage, though, marks his new life as something more than a masquerade. His new clothes do not merely disguise the obscure country priest as a glamorous nobleman; they also effect the transformation of his entire personality as the "spirit of the costume" penetrates through the skin. His body in this passage is not the bearer of his uniqueness and identity over time, not the locus of an interiority that can preserve its distinction from the environment. This would have been the model for one of the primary functions of the human body that has dominated the entire Judaeo-Christian tradition, a tradition that has carefully avoided the possibility of genuine metamorphosis, or metempsychosis.[16] Instead of being a bearer and marker of identity, Romuald's body in this passage becomes the material that can be reshaped as a work of art.

Nevertheless, Romuald's old personality is not entirely extinguished by this transformation; it is split and made double by it. Part of him, his diurnal self, is a poor and obscure priest living in a remote parish; his other, nocturnal self is a glamorous nobleman and Clarimonde's lover, living a luxurious life in a Venetian palace. Although the two selves appear to exist entirely independently of each other, there is a slight mutual awareness in the sense that the nocturnal self suffers from the recurring nightmare that it has to live the life of a poor priest, whereas the diurnal self feels disturbed by the recurring dream of living the exuberant life of a proud and wealthy nobleman. In each case, it is the external décor that determines the nature of reality and its opposing nightmare or dream.

At this point, one might ask what in Romuald's new existence prevents his complete and radical transformation. What is the obstacle that prevents his becoming entirely integrated into the artificial paradise of the ideal world of beauty and immortality? What leads to the doubling of his existence rather than a total metamorphosis? Or indeed: What prevents his double existence from enduring? If he were truly and entirely transformed by Clarimonde's clothes, there would be no memory of his old self with which the new self can be compared. But even in the passage just quoted, the observing first person speaker is present, and it is he who announces "I was no longer the same, and I didn't recognize myself." Furthermore, Romuald notes the absurdity of the situation in which, despite his splitting into two mutually exclusive forms of existence, he somehow maintained a constant sense of the same self: "J'ai toujours conservé très nettes les perceptions de mes deux existences. Seulement, il y avait un fait absurde que je ne pouvais m'expliquer: c'est que le sentiment du même moi existât dans deux hommes si differents" (143) [I have always kept the perceptions of my two existences neatly separate. Yet, there has always been that absurd fact that I could not quite explain: the same feeling of self persisted in these two different men] (my translation). What is it that sustains the feeling of the same self, that leads to a split, but prevents the transformation of a true metamorphosis?

Within the diegetic universe of the tale, Romuald's superior, Serapion, is the agent who bars him from complete transformation. Serapion has warned Romuald of Clarimonde's dubious and dangerous nature, and Romuald remembers his words even while living an exuberant life of luxury in Venice. Serapion embodies a position that acknowledges both Romuald's obligations as a poor country priest and his relationship with the beautiful courtesan. Without Serapion's repeated warnings, Romuald may not be at all alarmed about giving some of his blood to sustain Clarimonde's vampiric existence. It is Serapion who asserts the power of history and temporality against the timeless eternity of art. It is also Serapion, well versed in the techniques of the examination of conscience, who condemns Romuald to his split existence; and again it is Serapion who "liberates" him by destroying the beautiful part of Romuald's double life. To the extent that the story blames Serapion, it is the Christian concept of personal identity and mortality that represents the main obstacle to entering into a pagan world of pure sensual enjoyment.

Serapion, however, is the obstacle to Romuald's total transformation into a timeless work of art only at the diegetic level. There, he is the observer of Romuald's split existence, the one who bridges the two worlds and finally closes the rift as he exorcises Clarimonde's world. At the level of the articulation of the narrative qua narrative—for Clarimonde's world does not lend itself to narration, but merely to description—it is the speaking position of the first person narrator (Romuald) that is the placeholder for the consistent "same feeling of self" that accompanies both the impoverished priest during his daily routine and the glamorous nobleman during his nightly excursions. In this respect, the identity of the first person narrator both prevents Romuald's complete metamorphosis and allows the story to be told as a fantastic tale. Thus, at a formal level the equivalent to Serapion's model of a coherent personality that relies on the Christian concept of the mortal body is the set of narrative conventions that posit a coherent, embodied, personalized narrator.

Whereas Hoffmann introduces and elaborates the uncertainty of the observer position of the fantastic through multiple frames and by alternating between first and third person, personal and impersonal narration, Gautier's fantastic tales generally condense the frame into a personalized first person narrator whose narrative focuses on a limited escape from the constraints of his contemporary reality into a timeless world of sensual plenitude. The "impossible speaking position" of the dead martyr that was emphasized by Hoffmann's Serapion tale is foreclosed for Romuald. On the narratological level, the *jouissance* of Serapion's madness (in Hoffmann's story indicated by Serapion's splendid but unrecounted tales) is traded in for the pleasure afforded by the "recountability" of Romuald's coherent first person narrative. The drive to enjoy this privilege brings Romuald back from the brink—just as, in commercial terms, the same drive continues to organize, restrain, and guarantee popular success for the genre of the fantastic tale. To put Gautier's fantastic into a nutshell: better sensationalist escapism than madness.

In the programmatic preface to *Mademoiselle de Maupin* (1836), Gautier advocates his *l'art pour l'art* as the poet and artist's refusal to engage in a contemporary world marked by technological progress, the new railway, belief in utility, and the dictates of a prudish Christian moralism propagated by the mass publication of journals. Opposed to this contemporary reality, Gautier's romanticism, like that of other French romantic Hellenists, celebrates classical antiquity as "a primitive age when in almost childlike simplicity men lived under sunny skies in harmony with nature, rejoicing and unashamed in their physical beauty, and when death was represented by a laughing genius pointing his torch down rather than by tombs, skeletons, and the gnawing worm."[17] The artist must not subject himself to any kind of moralist or didactic agenda. If his art is to be of any use at all, it is merely to generate some income for the artist and to be a temporary means of escape from a tedious contemporary reality.

In the next section, I turn to Edgar Allan Poe's tale "Ligeia" (1838), which examines and radically destabilizes Gautier's world (defined by the sinister juxtaposition of a principle of reality anchored in the Christian notion of the mortal human body and the imaginary bliss of a purely spiritual sensual enjoyment). The question about the nature of personal identity and the soul's dependence on an individualized body that furnishes the parameters for the observer position in Gautier's tale is addressed both in terms of the medial function of the female body and the defiance of mortality. Poe's text, by contrast, analyzes the escapist fantasy of entering into an artificial paradise of sensuous bliss beyond the constraints of the mortal human body by examining the material conditions of its production—that is, by examining what it might mean to be writing and reading in the realm of the senses.

Ligeia: "Her Large and Luminous Orbs"

Poe's "Ligeia" has been read as a philosophical tale about the nature and limits of the mind, the human body, thought, and the will (Dayan); as a satirical take on the contrast between German idealism and English Romanticism (Griffith); and as a tale that exemplifies Poe's famous dictum from "The Philosophy of Composition" (1846) that "the death . . . of a beautiful woman is, unquestionably, the most poetical topic in the world,"[18] be it in terms of a psychoanalytical dimension (Bronfen) or resonance with sentimental mass culture (Elmer).[19] In my analysis, I pay particular attention to the poetological dimension of "Ligeia," to the manner in which this text can be discussed not only as a fantastic tale but also as a reflection on the production of the fantastic, in view of the hallucinatory sensualities of print culture.[20]

The generic nature of "Ligeia" is not immediately obvious. Long, descriptive passages as well as the narrator's reflection on his mnemonic and linguistic limitations punctuate, interrupt, and fragment the narration. Two separate plots—one about the narrator's remembrance of his first wife (Ligeia) and her death; the other about his second wife (Rowena), her death, and the return of Ligeia—raise the question as to what would provide the connection, the unity for the piece of writing. The title, though, immediately suggests that Ligeia somehow constitutes this unifying element. But what or who is Ligeia: a text, a word, a name, a woman, a ghost, a spirit, an image or an idea, something material or immaterial, a medium or a message? The word *Ligeia* serves as both the title of a text and the name of a woman. However, this name does not come from a mortal woman but from a dryad, a tree nymph in Virgil's *Georgics*. Although the Greek etymology of the word suggests the medium of sound, a loud call, Poe's story quickly shifts from an imaginary aurality to a visual register: a shift that is motivated by the silence of print culture.

If we bear in mind the multiple options of who or what Ligeia might be and still approach this text as a narrative, we see in its plot not merely the telling of some past event but also the narrator's presence as a writer who attempts to conjure up the presence of his lost beloved in the act of writing. "Ligeia" then comes to stand for embodiment of the medium of writing, that element by which this particular text and shaped artifact achieves its coherence; she is the mediating instance by which writing becomes transparent; the spiritual guide, the muse, the beloved woman who turns a piece of writing into an effortless reading, and finally into a metaphor for the imaginary materiality of the signifier.

Before the actual narrative commences, the first person narrator calls Ligeia in a manner that resembles the traditional invocation of the muse:

Ligeia! Ligeia! Buried in studies of a nature more than all else adapted to deaden impressions of the outward world, it is by that sweet word alone—by Ligeia—that I bring before mine eyes in fancy the image of her who is no more. And now, while I write, a recollection flashes upon me that I have *never known* the paternal name of her who was my friend and my betrothed, and who became the partner of my studies, and finally the wife of my bosom. Was it a playful charge on the part of my Ligeia? or was it a test of my strength of affection, that I should institute no inquiries upon this point? or was it rather a caprice of my own—a wildly romantic offering on the shrine of the most passionate devotion? I but indistinctly recall the fact itself—what wonder that I have utterly forgotten the circumstances which originated or attended it? And, indeed, if ever that spirit which is entitled *Romance*— if ever she, the wan and the misty-winged *Ashtophet* of idolatrous Egypt, presided, as they tell, over marriages ill-omened, then most surely she presided over mine.[21]

The "sweet word" Ligeia is opposed to the deadening surroundings, the sensory deprivations of the scholar. Not her voice but her name is sweet; the narrator evokes the sweet sound by calling her name. The story commences with an elegiac tone, with the narrator's narcissistic enjoyment of his lament. It is notable that her name is not a signifier that would partake of the symbolic order; indeed, it is opposed to the realm of writing qua law and name of the father. She stands for a kind of love that isolates lovers from all social context and consideration. Likening the radical exclusivity and absolute nature of this passion to the sin of idolatry, the narrator offers a further gloss on Ligeia's function for him. Not the representation of a divinity but an idol, the full presence of the divinity in the material object, she comes to stand for the identity between signifier and signified. Ligeia is introduced as an object that can be entirely possessed and worshipped. She is not a speaking subject, not a signifier for other subjects.

This object that is supposedly fully present and possessable, however, is a lost object. The writer/scholar has to struggle to evoke her presence, a struggle that seems particularly hard since he has no context for her, and hence has very little to narrate. He calls this isolated idol her "person," and this is the only thing the narrator can attempt to remember and describe. With this switch from her name to her person, the narrator leaves the initial aural register in favor of a visual one. From then on, his primary concern becomes evocation of sights: first the appearance of his beloved Ligeia, then the contrasting features of his second wife, and finally the scenario of his second wife's death and Ligeia's return in the bridal chamber of the old English abbey.

The purpose of these descriptions is to make an existentially absent object present to the narrator's mental sight, to give shape to her imaginary presence. To the extent that he attempts to depict her extraordinary beauty, the narrator is both dependent on and limited by his own language, which draws on the traditional blazon with its conventionalized catalogue of beauties. Initially, the description of Ligeia recalls some elements of an antique statue—for instance, the marble luster of her hand and her tall slender stature. However, to the extent that he wants to evoke the unique beauty of her person, he can only say what she is not: not a dead artifact, nor just one example in a series of such artifacts.

Yet her features were not of that regular mould which we have been falsely taught to worship in the classical labors of the heathen. "There is no exquisite beauty," says Bacon, Lord Verulam, speaking truly of all the forms and *genera* of beauty, "without some *strangeness* in the proportion." Yet, although I saw that the features of Ligeia were not of a classic regularity—although I perceived that her loveliness was indeed "exquisite," and felt that there was much of "strangeness" pervading it, yet I have tried in vain to detect the irregularity and to trace home my own perception of "the strange." I examined the contour of the lofty and pale forehead—it was faultless—how cold indeed that word when applied to a majesty so divine!—the skin rivalling the purest ivory, the commanding extent and repose, the gentle prominence of the regions above the temples. . . . I scrutinized the formation of the chin—and, here, too, I found the gentleness of breadth, the softness and the majesty, the fullness and the spirituality, of the Greek—the contour which the god Apollo revealed but in a dream, to Cleomenes, the son of the Athenian. (250)

Although he expects to find a "strange" feature that might allow him to pin down the element that marks her departure from classical regularity, he can single out nothing. Informed by an enthusiasm reminiscent of Winckelmann or Herder for the beauties of Greek antiquity, the narrator avoids turning her into a dead artifact by emphasizing the spirituality of her beauty, not in terms of concrete features but by evoking aspects of her form in their immateriality, not as made or shaped but as a purely mental process, a process of formation and divinely inspired revelation.

When in a second step the narrator attempts to locate Ligeia's strangeness, and the beauty and singularity in her eyes, he departs from classicist aesthetics but encounters another limit to his powers of description. First, he hastens to point out that, once it comes to the eyes, classicist models of beauty have nothing to say. But then he also realizes that the strangeness of Ligeia's eyes is not a physical, optical feature.

The "strangeness," however, which I found in the eyes, was of a nature distinct from the formation, or the color, or the brilliance of the features, and must, after all, be referred to the *expression*. Ah, word of no meaning! behind whose vast latitude of mere sound we intrench our ignorance of so much of the spiritual. The expression of the eyes of Ligeia! How for long hours have I pondered upon it! How have I, through the whole of a midsummer night, struggled to fathom it! What was it—that something more profound than the well of Democritus—which lay far within the pupils of my beloved? What *was* it? I was possessed with a passion to discover. Those eyes! (251–52)

The narrator leaves the regime of description, dependent upon classicist notions of beauty as well as a textual model of representation, as he turns to Ligeia's ineffable, unique, individualizing feature: "the expression of her eyes." The expression of a person's eyes traditionally stands for the person's alterity, individuality, and psychic interiority. Yet the narrator does not switch from the representational paradigm to an expressive paradigm of language; he chooses not to turn Ligeia's uniqueness into a hermeneutic issue of the specificity of her interiority, or a psychological depth that can be expressed. Nevertheless, the narrator insists on his inability to name or comprehend this unique feature by pointing out that the term *expression* is an empty signifier, a mere sound. Note that the narrator does not articulate his separation from her as his distance or lack of understanding of her person, but in terms of his being confronted with the opacity of language. Indeed, it is in this passage that Ligeia assumes the position of the medium; that her eyes stand for the virtual materiality of the signifier.

The expression of Ligeia's eyes becomes not something that can be represented, described, understood, or consciously remembered. It becomes the object of a spiritual quest and the subject matter of a story. As long as the narrator remains within the regime of description, the absent Ligeia must be represented by analogy to a dead object or artifact. With the shift of focus to the expression of her eyes, however, Ligeia's person, her mortal corporeality, and her relationship to temporal change emerge. It is here that a narrative program begins to take shape as the writer is faced with his blockage, his lack of access to the expression of her eyes. The agenda has been altered with respect to the first attempts at invoking Ligeia's presence. Before, the narrator tried to conjure up her looks, her ideational presence, through a description of her physical appearance. Now, he approaches her person through an opaque expression, a meaningless phrase, "the expression of her eyes." By means of foregrounding the enigmatic expression, the opaque, undecipherable phrase, he evokes the desire for transparency and insight. The object of desire is no longer just the appearance of the absent beloved as a concrete embodied woman. Rather, he longs for the kind of effect her presence would have on his confrontation with the materiality of writing.

The object of the writer/narrator's quest now is no longer just his lost beloved but the kind of knowledge and insight that he was able to gain in her presence: "we often find ourselves *upon the very verge* of remembrance, without being able, in the end, to remember. And thus how frequently, in my intense scrutiny of Ligeia's eyes, have I felt approaching the full knowledge of their expression—felt it approaching—yet not quite be mine—and so at length entirely depart! And (strange, oh strangest mystery of all!) I found, in the commonest objects of the universe, a circle of analogies to that expression" (252). The narrator ceases to grasp for the meaning of the single enigmatic term and instead searches for the "many existences in the material world" that might awaken in him a sentiment analogous to the one aroused by "her large and luminous orbs" (ibid.). By moving from "the expression of her eyes," which he had glossed as an unintelligible term to "her large and luminous orbs," that is, by shifting away from the register of hermeneutics and unintelligibility to the physics of luminosity, to her eyes as physical objects that emit light, the narrator has situated Ligeia between a meaningless, illegible signifier and an embodiment of light—*the* medium of transparency.

Although he cannot represent, define, or analyze the uniqueness of the expression of Ligeia's eyes, he can inventory a paradigmatic set of phenomena that have given him a similar sentiment. The narrator modifies the object of his quest and also changes from a metaphorical procedure to a metonymical one, from the attempt to invoke the hidden signified by way of the right comparison to an attempt at invoking it through a string of similarly mysterious expressions:

> I recognized it, let me repeat, sometimes in the survey of a rapidly-growing vine—in the contemplation of a moth, a butterfly, a chrysalis, a stream of running water. I have felt it in the ocean; in the falling of a meteor. I have felt it in the glances of unusually aged people. And there are one or two stars in heaven. . . . I have been filled with it by certain sounds from stringed instruments, and not unfrequently by passages from books. Among innumerable other instances, I well remember something in a volume of Joseph Glanvill, which (perhaps from its quaintness—who shall say?) never failed to inspire me with the sentiment; "And the will therein lieth, which dieth not. Who knoweth the mysteries of the will, with its vigor? For God is but a great will pervading all things by nature of its intentness. Man doth not yield him to the angels, nor unto death utterly, save only through the weakness of his feeble will." (252–53)

The first set of examples, especially the series of the moth, the butterfly, and the chrysalis, suggests that he is concerned with metamorphosis, with a natural force that induces a radical change and still preserves some kind of identity that is not bound up with material decay or the shape of a particular body. A second set of examples involves human artifacts or expressions. In particular, the "glances of unusually aged people" and the citation from Glanvill suggest that the narrator senses some mysterious force of being able to overcome the finality of death: "Length of years, and subsequent reflection, have enabled me to trace, indeed, some remote connection between this passage in the English moralist and a portion of the character of Ligeia. An *intensity* in thought, action, or speech, was possibly, in her, a result, or at least an index, of that gigantic volition which, during our long intercourse, failed to give other and more immediate evidence of its existence" (253). Thus, beginning with the musings on the expression of her eyes, Ligeia's mysterious beauty also becomes an index "of that gigantic volition," of a mysterious natural force or cosmic connection that only appears in her approach to death. Throughout the first part, Ligeia's status has been shifted back and forth between some kind of signifier (a name, a meaningless expression, an index) and an affectively highly charged lost object and elusive, transcendent signified (the beloved, the muse, the spiritual guide, a cosmic force or idea).

The narration of the first part of "Ligeia" focuses on the writer's experience of her death. Her waning health and vitality is not integrated, nor connected to any external events; rather, it is exclusively portrayed, in view of her medial function, in the narrator's relationship to transcendentalist knowledge. Whereas her approaching death appears as the return of the opacity of the medium of writing, her state of health is depicted as her magical power to make unreadable texts transparent to him. "With how vast a triumph—with how vivid a delight—with how much of all that is ethereal in hope—did I *feel*, as she bent over me in studies but little sought —but less known—that delicious vista by slow degrees expanding before me, down whose long, gorgeous, and all untrodden path, I might at length pass onward to the goal of a wisdom too divinely precious not to be forbidden!" (254) Her medial function, which consists in enabling him to gain access to a "higher," "transcendent," or "spiritual" sight, is described in terms of the literalization and concretization of her role for him, captured in the metaphorical expression that she was able to *illuminate occult passages for him*. The light of her eyes makes him see through a textual passage onto an untrodden path to knowledge.

However, the status of this "vista" is more complex, for the expanded concretized image is overdetermined and calls up disparate traditional images of the woman as both seductress and spiritual guide. First, there is the schema of the spiritual quest and the likening of Ligeia's role to that of Dante's Beatrice. Yet, by the enigmatic claim that these vistas of divine knowledge are "too precious" and hence forbidden, the dark Lady Ligeia is dissociated from Beatrice and the positively coded spiritual guide. Likewise, with respect to the neo-Platonic version of spiritual sight as the ultimate insight into the last truths, a tradition suggested also through the Glanvill quotation, the vision of Truth and Beauty is dissociated from the Good. Finally, there is the concrete media-historical image that associates Ligeia with the print medium. Her eyes can turn a page of a book into a window that opens up a view into a new world, into an "untrodden" landscape. This image of the page that opens up onto a "delicious vista by slow degrees expanding before me" was typical of the Renaissance celebration of its new media technologies: linear perspective and the printing press.[22] Ligeia comes to stand for an illuminating presence behind the print medium. The writer remembers how in her presence he was an inspired reader who could access esoteric, transcendentalist insights or a spiritual vision almost immediately, without having to decipher what he was reading.

Ligeia's fatal illness, as her eyes begin to show less of their radiant luster, is described in terms of the emergence of writing's opacity. Instead of the look through the page onto the landscape of the mind, the narrator focuses on the look of the letters on the opaque page: "Without Ligeia I was but as a child groping benighted. Her presence, her readings alone, rendered vividly luminous the many mysteries of the transcendentalism in which we were immersed. Wanting the radiant lustre of her eyes, letters, lambent and golden, grew duller than Saturnian lead. And now those eyes shone less and less frequently upon the pages over which I pored. Ligeia grew ill" (254). In the previous image of reading, writing was rendered transparent to a quasi-immediate mental sight of the signified; now the image of reading focuses on the imaginary materiality of the signifier, the changing look of the letters: from golden brilliance to dull lead. When the narrator adds the adjective *Saturnian* to the "weighty" opacity and materiality of the lead, he evokes the traditional emblematics of melancholia: dull, brooding, lead, and Saturn. As Ligeia's vitality diminishes, the print medium loses its transparency. Her waning powers seem to transport the narrator backward into an earlier phase of the history of media technology. In contrast to print technology's tendency to render writing invisible, here we witness the waning of the realm of "illuminated" manuscripts with lambent, golden letters.

Poe's Arabesque, or Death by Drapery

The first part of "Ligeia" elaborates the imaginary materiality of the signifier in view of the ideal of transparency. The narrator invokes Ligeia's person by staging the effects of her vanishing. He narrates her death, the extinction of her luminous orbs, as his own repositioning toward the print medium. By contrast, the second part of "Ligeia" is dominated by images of the opacity of writing. Whereas the first part began with an attempt to describe the beautiful beloved woman, the second part commences with an elaborate description of the "unforgettable" bridal chamber, which the narrator furnished as he was grieving for Ligeia and in which he received his second wife, Rowena. This exuberantly luxurious interior space takes the place of the hallucinated presence of the beloved woman:

I gave way, with a child-like perversity, and perchance with a faint hope of alleviating my sorrows, to a display of more than regal magnificence within.—For such follies, even in childhood, I had imbibed a taste and now they came back to me as if in the dotage of grief. Alas, I feel how much even of incipient madness might have been discovered in the gorgeous and fantastic draperies, in the solemn carvings of Egypt, in the wild cornices and furniture, in the Bedlam patterns of the carpets of tufted gold! I had become a bounden slave in the trammels of opium, and my labors and orders had taken a coloring from my dreams. But these absurdities I must not pause to detail. Let me speak only of that one chamber, ever accursed, whither, in a moment of mental alienation, I led from the altar as my bride—as the successor of the unforgotten Ligeia—the fair-haired and blue-eyed Lady Rowena Trevanion, of Tremaine.

There is no individual portion of the architecture and decoration of that bridal chamber which is not now visibly before me. Where were the souls of the haughty family of the bride, when, through thirst of gold, they permitted to pass the threshold of an apartment *so* bedecked, a maiden and a daughter so beloved? I have said that I minutely remember the details of the chamber—yet I am sadly forgetful on topics of deep moment—and here there was no system, no keeping in the fantastic display, to take hold upon the memory. (258–59)

Clearly the interior of his abbey in England is the materialization of a phantasmatic scenario. The narrator associates this interior space with an entire list of mental abnormalities: a childhood perversity, institutionalized madness, melancholia with a vague hope of overcoming the grief, and finally the dreams of an opium addict. In this passage the interior of the abbey becomes indistinguishable from his psychic interiority; or does it actually take its place? In the vocabulary of clinical psychology, dissociation would describe the narrator's abdication of responsibility for his actions and his externalized, distanced view of the irresponsible family members of his bride who let their daughter marry somebody who was so clearly mad and potentially dangerous. The narrator, however, describes this phenomenon not in the clinical terms of dissociation but in terms of his observer position in relation to the external organization of memory. His exotic collections and strange decorations prevent controllable retrieval of information. He has only the detailed visual memory of the individual objects, no sustained memory of his actions, thoughts, or reflections that would force him to take responsibility for the fate of his second wife. The narrator's agency, memory, and consciousness have been handed over to the furniture and decorations. Indeed, as mad or fantastic as it might sound, it is the decoration of the bridal chamber that ultimately kills Rowena and reanimates Ligeia.

The window of the bridal chamber is the source of an unnatural, distorted, and distorting light: "an immense sheet of unbroken glass from Venice—a single plane, and tinted of a leaden hue, so that the rays of either the sun or moon, passing through it, fell with a ghastly lustre on the objects within. Over the upper portion of this huge window, extended the trellicework of an aged vine, which clambered up the massy walls of the turret" (259). This "trellice-work of an aged vine" replaces what otherwise—without the lead tint—could be a view into the open landscape. In part one, the narrator listed a "rapidly growing vine" among those "material existences" that evoked for him a feeling analogous to the expression of Ligeia's eyes. Now a slightly different vine will also, by the end of the narrative, evoke the actual vision of Ligeia's eyes. Instead of the vine's rapid growth, there is the combined image of the constructed, segmented elements of the trellis, which distributes the growth across the plane. The lead-tinted window resembles the opaque surface of a sheet of paper, or a page in a book that is decorated by an ornamental vine. By distributing the vine over this surface, the trellis draws attention to the vine's ornamental aspect. Indeed the trellis analyzes the ornament by isolating repeatable, serially combinable, geometrically constructed elements of serpentine lines and leaves. This analytical intervention transforms the organic entity into an image of mechanical reproducibility.

The vine on the trellis serves as an image of the type of reproduction that informs print technology's usage of movable letters, that involves breaking up the serpentine line of handwriting into the isolated, combinable letters on the printed page. In this function, the image of the vine from Poe's text verbally picks up the pictorial tradition of that ornament that became known as the arabesque. Beginning with Albrecht Dürer and his thematization of print technology, the arabesque—situated at the threshold between the linearity of the two-dimensional composition of an image and the three-dimensional perspectival illusion of space—has been used to illustrate the imaginary materiality of the signifier.[23] In this sense, the arabesque is in an exact contrast to the complementary image of the open vista or view through the window, which quite frequently on the title page of a book was used to thematize transparency, that is, the imaginary *immateriality* of the signifier.[24]

There are further cues that Poe's text traces this function of the arabesque as an image that illustrates the imaginary materiality of the signifier. Immediately after the description of the window follows a description of the internal source of light: "From out the most central recess of this melancholic vaulting, depended, by a single chain of gold with long links, a huge censer of the same metal, Saracenic in pattern, and with many perforations so contrived that there writhed in and out of them, as if endued with a serpent vitality, a continual succession of parti-colored fires" (259–60). Both the Saracenic pattern and the "serpent vitality" invoke the aesthetics of the arabesque. Whereas outside, on the lead-tinted window, there is the dark arabesque of the vine, inside the bridal chamber there is the golden arabesque of the burning censer. The colors, gold and metal, recall the image of the lambent, golden letters that the narrator remembers from the phase of Ligeia's declining vitality, that phase of their relationship when she was about to leave him in her function as his spiritual guide, when she was no longer going to illuminate dark passages for him and open up his reading to new vistas and insights. Then, in the first part of "Ligeia," the narrator's imminent loss of immediate transcendentalist insight was captured by reference to a different, older technology of writing that invoked manuscript culture, with its golden letters turning into a dull Saturnian lead. Consequently, the arabesque as illustration of the virtual materiality of the signifier appears at the threshold of new media technologies, such as the transition from the culture of the illuminated manuscript to the new print technology of standardized, movable letters.

The narrator, however, also includes in his use of the arabesque its better-known, more familiar sense of referring to an orientalizing ornament that aestheticizes an enigmatic writing. The two senses—aesthetization of an enigmatic writing and ornamental illustration of the virtual materiality of the signifier at the threshold between seeing and reading, deciphering and interpreting, signifier and signified—are clearly related. The narrator's melancholia for his idolatrous love is translated into nostalgia for the culture of illuminated manuscripts, for the sensuous, external, ornamental features of an unknown Arabic script. To these traditional uses of the arabesque, which stem primarily from the pictorial tradition of art history, Poe's text adds a specifically literary aspect, one that is most centrally related to the transition from description to narration in this specific text and to the poetics of the fantastic tale:

The lofty walls, gigantic in height—even unproportionably so—were hung from summit to foot, in vast folds, with a heavy and massive-looking tapestry of a material which was found alike as a carpet on the floor, as a covering for the ottomans and the ebony bed, as a canopy for the bed, and as the gorgeous volutes of the curtains which partially shaded the window. The material was the richest cloth of gold. It was spotted all over, at irregular intervals, with arabesque figures, about a foot in diameter, and wrought upon the cloth in patterns of the most jetty black. But these figures partook of the true character of the arabesque only when regarded from a single point of view. By a contrivance now common, and indeed traceable to a very remote period of antiquity, they were made changeable in aspect. To one entering the room, they bore the appearance of simple monstrosities; but upon a farther advance, this appearance gradually departed; and step by step, as the visitor moved his station in the chamber, he saw himself surrounded by an endless succession of the ghastly forms which belong to the superstition of the Norman, or arise in the guilty slumbers of the monk. The phantasmagoric effect was vastly heightened by the artificial introduction of a strong continual current of wind behind the draperies—giving a hideous and uneasy animation to the whole. (260–61)

When the narrator refers to "the true character of the arabesque" he seems to mean the ornamental use of an aestheticized mysterious linearity that resembles writing. To this traditional use of the arabesque, the drapery in the bridal chamber adds another aspect when the lines turn into changing shapes and forms in relation to the changing position of the observer. To a certain extent, one might argue that the draped bridal chamber can also be compared with a printed page: the ubiquitous and uniform use of the heavy tapestry, covering most of the interior space and furniture, would have the effect of removing the perspectival aspect of the room and the plasticity of individual pieces of furniture. Individual forms and shapes that would have their own colors, textures, and position in space are covered over, hidden under one bicolor, gold-and-black surface. In addition, the narrator emphasizes the thick, heavy, voluptuous fabrics of the tapestry and the curtains appealing to the senses of touch and feeling in all of their opacity. In contrast to the printed page, however, the observer is not faced with a uniform, plane surface of inscription bearing distinct characters but rather is enveloped or surrounded with an entirely disorienting environment in which the distinction between figure and ground vanishes. What emerges in this description stands in stark contrast to the richly detailed surface textures of the painters of the Northern Renaissance as well as to the classical and neoclassical understanding of drapery as a means of making the idealized human body, in all of its plasticity, perfectly transparent. Indeed, the description of the bridal chamber is anything but a vision of visual plenitude and bliss of the kind Gautier's fantastic tales would evoke. And, as opposed to Gautier's fantasy of visual plenitude in "The Dead Leman," Poe's phantasmagoria does not take its cues from the medium of painting but from the decorative genre of the arabesque, a genre that is associated with all kinds of technology of serial reproduction, especially with print technology.

Poe's text establishes an intimate link between the print medium and the fantastic. However, as was already indicated, the draped bridal chamber does not resemble just any printed page. Additional features need to be added to the printed text to make it oscillate, to produce the effect of a "hideous animation." Besides the hidden mechanism by which a stream of air moves the drapes in such a way that they give rise to fantastic shapes and figures to match superstition and guilty, obscene dreams, there is also a crazed, unstable observer/narrator. In other words, the unstable observer/narrator position—which is the defining feature of the fantastic tale—is linked to a mechanism that moves the opaque decorative fabric of the text such that the linear ornaments seem to acquire a soul or life of their own. Thus the supernatural intrusion of the fantastic tale is explained in terms of an optical illusion that arises exactly at the threshold of the imaginary materiality of writing. The climax and closure of the actual narrative, the narrative about Rowena's death, the watch at her corpse, and Ligeia's return can then be characterized as the actual emplotment of this hideous animation and as an illustration of the generic mechanism that has been outlined in terms of its media-technological conditions.

"Hideous Animation"

Immediately after the description of the drapery, the narrator talks about the first two months of his marriage to Rowena. During the first month, he takes pleasure in frightening his bride with his moodiness, his hatred for her, and his ardent love and yearning for Ligeia, "the beloved, the august, the beautiful, the entombed" (261), for whom he calls aloud at all hours. The only function left to Rowena is as the painfully tortured observer. During the second month of their marriage, she falls ill, briefly recovers, and then relapses into a fatal illness characterized by nervous irritation and excitability: "She spoke again, and now more frequently and pertinaciously, of the sounds—of the slight sounds—and of the unusual motions among the tapestries, to which she had formerly alluded" (262). Whereas the narrator knows all about the hidden mechanism by which the tapestry moves and thus creates the illusion of animation, he observes how his new wife is mortally terrified by it. The narrator does nothing to console or remove her from the terrors of the bridal chamber. When she is about to faint with fright, he merely hurries across the room to fetch a goblet of wine for her. Nor does he trust and act upon his own perceptions of an "invisible object" that he felt passing him, of a "faint, indefinite shadow of angelic aspect—such as might be fancied for the shadow of a shade," "a gentle foot-fall upon the carpet," and finally "three or four large drops of a brilliant and ruby colored fluid" which fell "within the goblet, as if from some invisible spring" (263). Although the narrator attributes these perceptions to his opium dreams, he nevertheless has to admit that immediately after Rowena drinks "a rapid change for the worse took place . . . on the third subsequent night, the hands of her menials prepared her for the tomb, and on the fourth, I sat alone, with her shrouded body, in that fantastic chamber which had received her as my bride" (264).

The last formulation of this passage sharply articulates the result of Rowena's sojourn in the obscenely decorated room not in terms of her death nor his loss of her but in terms of a new scenario, one in which the bride is received and integrated into the fantastic chamber, in which she, like the draped furniture, has become part of this entire environment by way of her shrouded body—or in which her shrouded body, like the arabesque figures of the drapery, can give rise to superstition, guilty dreams and a hideous animation. For the narrator, the watch at Rowena's body becomes an occasion to think with utter intensity and passion "of that unutterable woe with which I had regarded *her* thus enshrouded. The night waned; and still, with a bosom full of bitter thoughts of the one only and supremely beloved, I remained gazing upon the body of Rowena" (264). Within the uniformity of the arabesque, ornamental bridal chamber (the perfect externalization of the imaginary materiality of the signifier), the shrouded body of Rowena presents the narrator/observer with one definite shape and site, the female corpse that is not covered by the ornamental drapery but merely by a shroud. The white shroud becomes a screen that allows him to hallucinate another body, the one of his beloved Ligeia, who stands for the imaginary immateriality of the signifier, the medial woman who can render writing transparent.

Within the constellation of this new scenario, a grotesque narrative program is played through, not just once but repeatedly, which lends to the whole action an even more horrifying, mechanical, automatic, and compulsive aspect: the narrator hears some faint noise, some sigh, watches the shrouded body intently, finally discovers a bit of color, some blood beginning to circulate along "the sunken veins of the eyelids." Horrified, awed and mortified, the narrator summons all of his energy, obeying some sense of duty that compels him "to call back the spirit still hovering," only to realize that his efforts are in vain, that he has in front of him nothing but a repulsive, clammy, and stiff corpse. Thereupon "I fell back with a shudder upon the couch from which I had been so startlingly aroused, and again gave myself up to passionate waking visions of Ligeia" (265).

In spite of the strong contrast between the body coming back to life and the increasingly disgusting, shriveled dead flesh, both the dead and the waking or reanimated body are dreadful to the narrator. Whereas the body trying to come back to life fills him with terror and mortifies him, the recently dead body is at the same time an object of sheer disgust and even indifference, to the extent that it does not require his attention and intervention but allows him to dream of Ligeia, to give himself up to "passionate waking visions of Ligeia." Thus the main contrast is not between the living body and the dead one, but between Rowena's body as capable of physically living and dying and Ligeia as the object of a mental sight and a purely mental passion. Yet, especially as the repetition of this narrative program makes clear, the two poles, Rowena's shrouded body and the mental vision of Ligeia, are intimately related. Only when Rowena is dead and the narrator is at her watch can he fully indulge in his recollections of Ligeia and project his "waking vision of Ligeia" onto the shrouded body. But the intensity of his passionate desire seems to be also the force that interrupts it, that brings Rowena's body back to life, such that he has to abandon his vision of Ligeia and engage his attention in the repeated, futile attempts at reanimation of a disgusting, horrifying corpse.

The last section of "Ligeia," about Rowena's wake and the narrator's passionate waking visions of Ligeia, draws its fantastic narrative program from an alternation between the two senses of *wake*, the watch kept at the side of a corpse and waking or awaking as rousing from sleep. The narrative moves back and forth between the narrator's horrified attempt to reanimate Rowena's corpse and his passionate vision of his beloved Ligeia. However, this narrative does not reach the conclusion desired by the narrator; Ligeia's illuminating presence never does return. Instead, the corpse suddenly gets up, shows itself in its full, tall stature; and as the shroud falls from its head, Ligeia's black hair and eyes becomes visible. It is when Ligeia's eyes return the narrator's gaze that the narrative has reached its abrupt end. In part one the expression of Ligeia's eyes was not merely an undefinable signifier; it was what guided the narrator's quest, his metonymical association of quotations, observations, perceptions—what reminded him of the secret of her individuality and her beauty, her particular intensity and willpower. In the last phrase of part two, her black eyes are merely physical marks that identify the walking, reanimated shrouded corpse as Ligeia's rather than Rowena's body. In this very last instance, Ligeia's black eyes do not stand out in terms of their ineffable expression but have become purely physical markers, like a scar or deformity that identifies the body of a particular individual.

By introducing the thematic complex of the arabesque, Poe's text is an extremely insightful commentary on the kind of fantastic tale that focuses on the fantasy of sensuous bliss without a body. "Ligeia" is built around the narrator's account of two distinctly different sets of encounters with an enigmatic signifier. In the first, the shape of Ligeia's eyes has an illuminating function and holds out the promise of access to a transcendent signified, which the story foregrounds as the vista into the valley, a concretization of a traditional image for the imaginary immateriality of the signifier. For the second set, the narrator's imagined illuminating presence of the beloved's gaze is replaced by his abandonment in an environment of the arabesque, of enigmatic and opaque writing, which cancels all transcendentalist prospects as well as the observer's memory and ability to distinguish what is within himself from what lies outside. The way out of this arabesque immanence appears to be through the shrouded corpse of his second wife. It is the one element in the bridal chamber that is not part of the disorienting, illegible ornamental writing; instead it becomes a screen, an occasion to hallucinate the absent beloved. But once Ligeia actually returns and takes possession of Rowena's corpse, her eyes are no longer large and luminous orbs; now they are merely indices of her physical identity and corporeal presence, which put an end to reading and signification. Her eyes are no longer an expression but merely black markers, like two dots. Full stop. The end.

Hoffmann's tale of the visionary hermit Serapion articulates a desire for escape into a realm of sensual and spiritual delights beyond the limitations of the mortal human body: a desire for the end of desire. Yet the programmatic status of this tale is problematic to the extent that Serapion's madness is characterized as the emphatic denial of all forms of mediation of the order of writing and sexuality. None of his supposedly wonderful tales are given, and indeed, any tale told by an unequivocal madman could not achieve the dimension proper to the fantastic tale. The stories of Councillor Krespel, Gautier's "The Dead Leman," or Poe's "Ligeia," by contrast, engage with the fantasy of an escape into the sensual delights beyond the limits of the mortal body. They address precisely those obstacles and limits of mortality, sexuality, the symbolic order, and the various aspects of mediation and media technologies that Serapion, in his madness, denies.

What makes these texts into fantastic narratives is the manner in which they make use of the personification of the medium—the figure of the medial woman suspended between life and death—as an extraordinary means of access to an aesthetic experience that is more than mere description. In each case, the medial woman represents the state of a temporary suspension of death and decay, and a temporary escape from a normal world of social interaction with its restrictions and restraints. Clarimonde is most clearly situated between two deaths: between her initial death following Romuald's ordination, and the final destruction of her body by the resentful advocate of Christianity. Antonia is equally trapped between two deaths. Her removal from the social world, from expression and love, and her sequestration in the isolation of her father's household, is a kind of suspension, an early death of which her final, physical death is the consummation. Her death, however, appearing as a terrifying wish fulfillment both in her father's dream of her wonderful singing and in the narrator's fascination with her voice and the frailty of her body, is removed from any easy moralizing access.

As if to comment on how we are to imagine the site for this kind of escape from the mortal body within the history of reading and writing, Poe's narrative specifies the strange suspension of, or escape from, a normal temporal and spatial order, through the details of the first person narrator's decoration of Rowena's sumptuous bridal chamber, which will be the locus of his contact with the medial woman, Ligeia. In the elaborate description of the arabesque interior, the cultural site of the fantastic is indicated as the space between the imaginary immateriality of the signifier—the transparency of the library that gives way to imagined vistas—and the imaginary materiality of the signifier: the ornamental and opaque, potentially three-dimensional characters of illegible signs.

5

Fantastic Encounters with the Marvels of History

"Isabella von Ägypten" and "La Vénus d'Ille"

The nineteenth century was marked by a profound interest in the nature of history and by reconstruction (and construction) of local and national traditions. Especially after the French Revolution and the Reign of Terror, interest in the general nature and direction of history was greatly heightened. Philosophers of history were concerned with the status of metahistorical narratives and the condition of the possibility of progress. The academic world witnessed the institutionalization and formalization of the disciplines of historiography, archaeology, and historical philology. Beyond those scholarly areas of inquiry, in the fields of literature, poetry, and the fine arts the question of the past—particularly as it was supposed to entail alternate or forgotten traditions—also acquired a new sense of urgency in the context of early-nineteenth-century nationalisms. Many Romantic poets and writers contributed to constructing a national tradition through collections and editions of vernacular oral literatures, legends, fairy tales, and folk songs. Moreover, the poets and writers of that era did not limit themselves to the curatorial role of collectors and preservers of the past; they were also actively engaged in constructing national traditions that spurned new literary forms. Sir Walter Scott's historical novels, Wordsworth's lyrical ballads, and even ingenious "fake" antiques (such as Mérimée's *La Guzla* of 1827) are examples of this intensified relationship with the past.

Whereas the poetic, dramatic, and literary production of the Enlightenment was geared toward universal truths and hence was generally indifferent to the realm of historical reference, for many writers and poets of the early nineteenth century past events and traditions were suddenly no longer irrelevant or dead. But how and why should past events matter to the present? Why should historical facts or finds not just be part of history, in a safely distant past? Why instead should they be incorporated as an integral, important, shocking, or inspiring element of the living present?

As I have already indicated, the answer to this question entails many possible directions having to do with how the past is found and to what ends, whether it is a preserved past or a constructed one, and whether it is integrated to the present or distinguished from it. Among the most pressing reasons for a survival of the past, and its continued actuality or revival, is the early-nineteenth-century concern with establishing or asserting local, ethnic, or national group identities, conceived in opposition to modern, rationalist, and hence universalist models. To the extent, however, that these constructions are undertaken in the service of contemporary interests, the nature of the contemporaneous present itself is fundamentally altered through them, since a presumably rationalist, enlightened, uniform modernity is confronted with its antitheses, with representatives of irrational traditions, superstitious practices, or magical forces that disrupt the homogeneity of the present.

The nineteenth century's renewed and intensified literary, artistic, and poetic concern with history and a national past spawned a great variety of poetic programs, literary genres, and artistic innovations that range from discovery of medieval epics and preparation of editions of folk song and oral poetry to the invention of the historical novel and the lyrical ballad.

Yet this sketch of early-nineteenth-century preoccupation with historical reference and national traditions also sets a new and additional context for the marvelous and its close relative, the fantastic tale. As we have seen, both are literary modes that explore the limits of reason and understanding, be it in the wonder reaction to something that cannot be accommodated by the known and familiar, or the reaction of shock that is due to suspension of the principles of the Enlightenment that undergird a modern, rationalist universe.

The focus of Chapter Five is on the fantastic tale as a literary genre that not only participates in this heightened concern with historical reference and national traditions but also reflects on a contemporaneous modernity that, as a result of this preoccupation with history, has lost its homogeneity. This kind of "contextualization" of the fantastic tale, however, should not be applied indiscriminately. Rather, it is primarily indicated for those fantastic tales that code their generically decisive "alien" element (the irrational, incomprehensible event or occurrence that intrudes into the rationalist diegetic universe) as an "historical other" pertaining to a different historical epoch, and appearing in the form of an archaism or a metonymic instantiation of a history or tradition. This subgroup of fantastic tales can be read as a reflection on the change from a homogeneous modern universalist and rationalist present to a multilayered, heterogeneous contemporaneity for which the distinctions between past, present, and future have become destablilized.

For the last chapter of this study on the emergence of the fantastic tale, I have chosen to focus primarily on two stories by Achim von Arnim (1781–1831) and Prosper Mérimée (1803–1870). The fictions of both writers confront the reader with the undifferentiation of historical periodization, the lack of distinction between the past and the present, and a fundamental—either euphorically utopian or deeply disturbing—doubt as to whether the past is really past or actually part of the present or future.

The differences between these two writers can be related to the specific historical and political contexts in which they were working. Arnim's early fiction is profoundly informed by the pre–nation-state nationalism of the Prussian reformers during the period of the Napoleonic occupation of German speaking territories. Mérimée, on the other hand, wrote his fiction while he was a civil servant of the French nation state of Louis Philippe, charged with establishing an inventory of those antiquities that were pertinent to the national past. Consequently, for the Prussian poet preoccupation with the past and construction of a national or ethnic tradition was opposed to the interests of a modern state, especially if the latter was associated with the Napoleonic code, the legal equivalent of the modernist, universalist, and assimilationist politics of the French Emperor. By contrast, Mérimée, one generation later, took the modern French nation state as a given and investigated the modern tension between the capital and the provincial periphery; and between supposedly archaic local, ethnic traditions and the homogenizing cultural hegemony of the nation state.

Bella's Blood

Achim von Arnim's tale "Isabella von Ägypten" (Isabella of Egypt), published in 1812 as part of a loosely connected cycle of four novellas, has a long and involved plot. A bare outline would have to highlight these features: set in the early sixteenth century, the narrative begins *in medias res* with the young and beautiful Isabella, who has learned about her father's death and is about to attend to his last rites. Isabella lives with her old guardian, Braka, in an abandoned, supposedly haunted house close to the river Schelde in what today would be Belgium. Her father, the Gypsy leader Michael, was accused of theft and has been hanged in the aftermath of anti-Gypsy persecution. After her father's corpse is taken down from the gallows, she consumes a ritual meal as he is given over to the river that will, according to Gypsy belief, take the deceased leader back to Egypt, his people's legendary land of origin.

Immediately after Michael's death by hanging, the group of Gypsies around Isabella learns of the young prince Charles V's plan to come to their neighborhood and stay overnight at the house in which Isabella lives. The prince, feeling challenged by the rumors that the abandoned house is haunted, wants to debunk the commonly held superstition by spending the night there. On the night of the prince's visit, Braka persuades Isabella to appear to him as he sleeps, disguised as a ghost. Immediately in that first nightly encounter, the two fall in love with each other. The following morning, the prince leaves in the belief that he has met a hauntingly beautiful ghost. Isabella pines after him and is willing to do anything to rejoin him. Braka tells her that to pursue her beloved she will need money, which she can obtain with the aid of a magical mandrake root.

Many of the supernatural events of the narrative are related to procuring wealth. Isabella follows Braka's advice and seeks the magical root that sprouted from the tears of her hanged father, an adventure fraught with danger. The root, if properly tended, will grow into a small being with an insatiable desire for wealth and an uncanny ability to track down hidden treasure. Having found the root, Isabella then takes on the task of rearing the ugly little creature as if it were her baby.

In their efforts to unearth hidden treasures, the mandrake, Isabella, and Braka are helped by the Bearskinner. An equally legendary figure, he is an undead servant, whom Braka, by recounting his story, resurrects from the grave. The Bearskinner and the mandrake become the means by which Isabella can leave her rural existence and enter into the society of Ghent, the city of Charles's residence. Braka supports Isabella in her plans to win Charles because she wants her to fulfill the ancient Gypsy prophesy by which she is destined to conceive a son from the emperor. Isabella, however, pursues her plans out of pure, disinterested love for the prince.

Charles and Bella find each other at the home of Braka's friend, Nietken, in the fictional city of Buik during the Kirmess festival. To distract the jealous mandrake, who attempts to prevent Charles and Bella's union, the prince's tutor commissions a golem, a copy of Bella. The mandrake falls in love with the Golem Bella, and even Charles cannot tell the two Bellas apart and is thus led to sleep with the golem. Finally, after a maze of intrigue and misunderstanding, Charles and Bella become estranged from one another.

Ultimately, Bella realizes that the future emperor does not really love her because he is far too concerned with wealth and power. Charles has even gone so far as to encourage a sham marriage between the mandrake and Bella, to profit from the mandrake's wealth-procuring skills. Her father appears to her in a vision and reminds her of her calling to lead her people back to Egypt. One night, she abandons the sleeping Charles and leaps out of his window into the arms of the Gypsies below. She leads her people back to Egypt and there gives birth to a son.

Charles and Isabella never meet again. Both become rulers in their separate lands, leading separate lives, but they die at the same time. She expires surrounded with the praise and love of her people; he, with a vision of his beloved Isabella. The story closes with the narrator's prayer to the holy Isabella to bestow grace upon him and to grant protection in a future announced by an ominous comet.

The story begins with the separate trajectories of the two political figures, and concludes with their divergent careers as political leaders and then their separate deaths. The main part of the narrative, the love story of their youth, begins with their accidental encounter and separation; it is followed by Isabella's overcoming extreme obstacles to find him again, the short period they spend together, and their final separation. There are two decisive turning points in the narrative. The first is when Isabella departs from the haunted house to move to the city to find her beloved; the second is when Isabella deliberately leaves Charles, leaping out of the window to join her people. Both turning points are crucial to the political dimension of the story. Whereas the first marks Isabella's crossing of the threshold from childhood to adulthood and her dark realization of her adult identity and political mission, the second turning point, her conscious departure from her lover to join her people, marks the irreconcilability of the two very different political figures and the types of political leadership they stand for.

Arnim's story is unlike most of its contemporary fantastic tales, which center around a single mysterious encounter that makes the reader doubt what has really happened. Instead, Arnim's story weaves in and out of the register of the marvelous as it freely mixes both realistic and historical accounts and characters with supernatural and legendary occurrences and figures. There is, as a result, simultaneous deployment of mutually contradictory reading conventions, such as those pertaining to the realm of history and those that operate within an allegorical domain. Whereas initially the story is framed as being based on textual sources and historical documents, in the end its narrator appears as the tale's author and inventor. Thus the story poses as fact and fiction, derived from both the collective tradition and individual invention.

My analysis of "Isabella of Egypt" highlights three aspects of this marvelous tale. The first is its mixture of historical and legendary material, which informs the contrast between the two rulers, the historical figure of Charles V and the legendary figure of Isabella. Then I turn to the construction of Isabella's femininity and sexuality, representing the key to her special status as a new kind of political leader, which the tale prepares and elaborates in view of Isabella's relationship to the mandrake and to the contrast between the real Isabella and the Golem Bella. Finally, I trace how the category of blood emerges in this story, as a key to defining both individual and group identity. Moreover, I show how blood for Arnim is the key to an alternate model of signification and representation, a model of symbolization and communication that Arnim associates with Christian elements. I conclude with consideration of the first, unpublished frame narrative that Arnim wrote for the novella collection. It is this earlier frame that reveals the poetics of the marvelous and Arnim's semiotics of blood in its sinister racist and antisemitic aspects.

The Political Mixture of Legend and History

In the dedication of his novella collection to Wilhelm and Jacob Grimm, Arnim acknowledges the contrast between the Grimms' approach to legendary and historical material and his own. Whereas the Grimms were devoted to studying and preserving German folklore, which they believed had to be done with the respect due to genuine antiques that embody the spirit of the German nation, Arnim sees unification of the German national spirit as a task that still remains to be accomplished rather than as something completed in the past. In a letter written in December 1812, Jacob Grimm objects to Arnim's distortion of the character of Charles V. Couldn't

Arnim just as well have taken a fictional prince for his tale? Arnim, however, disagrees. The sixteenth century of Charles V in Arnim's story is not just the backdrop to a historical costume play; nor is the tale's appropriation of the historical king the occasion for a nostalgic invocation of the past. For Arnim, the sixteenth century of Charles V marks the beginning of modernity in the shape of a deplorable capitalism. Moreover, the figure of Charles V is not just a stand-in for any royal character but represents the last embodiment of the Holy Roman Empire. The young prince is contrasted with the Egyptian princess: he, the bearer of a doomed imperial hope; she, the icon of a future national unity. Here is a particular political dimension that needs the specificity of historical reference. This political dimension involves the contrast between the old idea of empire and the new idea of a nation that derives its strength from its unified people.[1]

Charles V represents a particular kind of emperor. On the one hand, his empire, which brought such vast territories under his rule by the Hapsburg dynastic marriage policy, was short-lived. On the other hand, in spite of the transitory character of his empire, it was under his rule that the imperial idea witnessed a great iconological revival.[2] In 1811, when Arnim chose to explore the imperial idea associated with Charles, he was confronting yet another incarnation of it in Napoleon. It would be misleading, though, to argue that Charles V in Arnim's story merely stands in for Napoleon; the relationship to the political situation in German territories under Napoleonic occupation in Arnim's own time is more complex than that.

Rather than just focusing on one emperor with his particular characteristics, Arnim's story draws on the whole model that was used to explain and justify a Christian emperor's return to the Augustan model of rulership over the world. The key to this idea of the Holy Roman Empire was the allegorical figure of the virgin Astraea. In Arnim's story, it is the images and symbols associated with Astraea that inform the utopian character of the legendary gypsy princess Isabella. Just as Astraea is the key figure that explains the transfer of the empire from Augustus to the Christian era, Isabella becomes the key figure in Arnim's story of how the traditional imperial model of power is to be transformed into an altogether new model of political power and leadership.

According to Greek mythology, Astraea, the holy and just virgin, left earth and was transformed into a heavenly constellation. According to Virgil, she could also return from heaven and bring about a renewal of the golden age. From Charlemagne on, until Charles V, the revival of the imperial model relied on the figure of Astraea; indeed, the transfer of the Augustan imperial model to the Christian emperor referred to the authority of Virgil. In the words of Frances Yates: "Virgil was believed to have spoken with the inspired voice of a prophet when he proclaimed in the Fourth Eclogue that the golden age was about to return, and with it the reign of the Virgin Astraea, or Justice, and that a child would be born destined to rule a reconciled world. These words were understood to refer to the birth of Christ in the golden age of Augustus. Through such associations, it was possible to use pagan imperial rhetoric concerning . . . Christian emperors" (4). In brief, Astraea can be seen as embodying both the end of the golden age and the promise of the possibility of its return.

From the beginning of Arnim's tale, the mythological figure of Astraea is invoked in the character of Isabella, who is an oriental beauty associated with the night, the moon, and the stars. She resembles the Virgin Mary and is destined to bear a new political leader. Both aspects of the Astraea myth—the Greek version, where the heavenly constellation marks the end of the golden age; and Virgil's, where she descends to earth from the heavens—figure prominently in Arnim's narrative. Indeed these two aspects are the key to the narrative climax and conclusion of Arnim's tale.

The reader merely has to visualize the crucial scene of Isabella's final departure from Charles to realize how this nocturnal scene offers a memorable staging of the Astraea myth. Charles and Isabella, the two lovers, having lost their former intimacy are depicted at night in their bedroom. Charles is dreaming about gold and treasures. Bella is awakened by the wonderful sounds of her people, the Gypsy leaders, who are gathered underneath her window to serenade their recognized princess and ruler. The dance of the Gypsies becomes wonderfully visible to the princess, who is looking into the night from Charles's window, because they have drenched their hands and clothes with a secret phosphorous solution that produces a marvelous glow on contact. Right after Charles, who is dreaming that he will get entangled in a golden chain, pushes Isabella away from him, she jumps out of his window into the arms of the Gypsies.

Seen from Charles's window, this leap out into the night to join the glowing bodies parallels Astraea's departure from earth and her joining a constellation of stars: *pax* and *justitia* have left the emperor-to-be. Charles's empire is doomed. Seen from the perspective of the Gypsies, however, the holy virgin comes down from the sky, into their arms, to lead them back to Egypt. Here Isabella's leap mirrors Astraea's return from heaven to earth, the commencement of a new golden age.

In Isabella's trusting leap into the arms of her people, we encounter a distinctly different vision of political power and leadership. Whereas Charles has no interest in the many peoples he will rule, Isabella's position as a political figure is primarily defined in terms of the mutual relationship of love and loyalty between herself as the charismatic leader and her people.

The fact that a modern nation cannot be defined in terms of territory alone but must in addition be united to its ruler as a membership organization becomes especially important in the context of occupied territories and disputes over how legitimate rulership and governance should be defined. This was the situation in 1811 in the German-speaking territories that were under Napoleonic occupation, where there was a lively debate first as to how an effective resistance could be shored up, and second as to what form a new government and constitution would have to take once the occupational force was ousted. It was in these debates that Arnim was involved while he wrote "Isabella of Egypt."[3]

Already the bewilderingly strange expository introduction of the character of Isabella borrows narrative details from the Astraea myth. Staring at the moon, Isabella is introduced as an oriental beauty and a creature of the night. As the narrative commences, she and her dog are led to the river Schelde, in which her father's dead body floats toward their home in Egypt. As Yates notes about Astraea's genealogy: "The parentage of the virgin is obscure; some . . . call her Erigone daughter of Icarus, a pious virgin whose little dog led her to her dead father's body. She has affiliations with several deities . . . and like Isis [she is associated] with the moon" (Yates, 32–3). Arnim borrows these details from the Astraea myth to incarnate the idea of a just and peaceful rule in the specific character of the legendary Isabella. By focusing on how Isabella has to leave the future emperor Charles, he dissociates the utopian dimension of the Astraea myth from the old idea of empire.

Only as long as Astraea is a fairly abstract, highly codified allegorical figure like Justice can she be mobilized by all kinds of rulers—Charlemagne, Charles V, or Elizabeth I. Achim von Arnim, however, constructs his narrative such that for most of the narrative Astraea is exclusively associated—in fact, identical—with the distinctly individualized, living female character Isabella. Thus the allegorical Astraea is no longer available to the inheritor of the imperial title, Charles V, who historically made use of the Astraea imagery. At the very end of the story, Isabella is reintegrated into the allegorical dimension of the Astraea myth, when the dying Charles has a vision of the beloved of his youth, and Isabella becomes the name of the hope for a better future.

For Arnim, the future hope for just and peaceful rule is programmatically associated with women, not men. Right after concluding the narrative of "Isabella of Egypt," he inserts a brief passage that is supposed to constitute the bridge to the next story, "Maria Melük," which also prominently features a powerful female character.[4] He alerts his reader to the comet of 1811, which he interprets as a political portent, adding this verse: "Wo große Zeichen hin zur Zukunft deuten,/Da wollen wir nicht stets nach Männern schauen,/Es ändern sich auch einmal wohl die Zeiten:/Vielleicht beginnt nun bald die Zeit der Frauen! [Where great signs signify the future/We shall not always look towards men/Times are changing/Perhaps finally the time of women is about to commence!]"[5] The "time of women" means a radical rethinking of models of power and sovereignty. By way of gendering access to Astraea, Arnim dissociates the political utopia from the figure of the male emperor-to-be and reserves it as the exclusive domain of Isabella the Gypsy princess. The precise nature of the new model of power and political leadership is elaborated through Isabella's femininity, sexuality, and ethnicity.

Isabella's Sexuality and Femininity

How does Isabella's femininity and sexuality matter? Throughout the story, she is defined in terms of her capacity to remain true to her desire, to love forcefully and loyally. Although for a long time the leadership that she is to assume is mentioned exclusively in view of her destiny to bear the child of the emperor, her capacity as a loving and caring mother is not elaborated in view of her biological son but instead through her relationship to the mandrake, as it is part of the pure desire that marks her maidenhood. What is at stake in terms of Isabella's femininity has all the force of an instinct or drive. However, unlike animal instinct, it is not defined in terms of a clear aim or object; it is radically open and malleable. This drive unfolds in the story as the singular feature that sets Isabella apart from everybody else; it defines her identity and imbues her with her leadership qualities.

First of all, Isabella's femininity is depicted as a particular form of virginity and innocence—namely, her ignorance of anything concerned with an instrumental rationality, and along with it the uses of sexuality and marriage in the service of the power politics of alliances. The narrator points out that she is utterly stunned when Charles accuses her of having used him to gain a promotion for the mandrake on whom Bella lavished extraordinary maternal tenderness and care: "Bella burst into tears and swore that it was not so; her love was genuine. Indeed, it was her fondest wish to have his child, who would bring her people glory and freedom. This candor embarrassed the archduke somewhat (She was innocent in her whole being; he was innocent only out of pride). Stammering, he swore that he would do everything possible to grant her wish, so long as it did not conflict with his political circumstances."[6] Charles may never have slept with a woman, but Isabella's innocence, the narrator emphasizes, is a much more profound quality.

In the end, Charles loses Bella precisely because he cannot let go of his political instrumentality, because he proposes a sham marriage between the mandrake and Bella to draw on the mandrake's wealth-producing powers. (It is after Charles proposes this ceremony, to which Bella refuses to give her consent, that she leaps out of the window.) In case the reader has not quite caught on to the story's strong condemnation of this kind of politically calculating traffic in women, a colorful image is added. Charles's most influential advisor, Chièvres, suggests that the mandrake be promoted to minister of finance. The narrator adds that Chièvres was nursing the hope that Charles would take Mme. de Chièvres as his mistress, thereby expanding his own political influence over the prince. During the sham marriage ceremony, Bella, clothed in royal robes, is immediately taken for a foreign princess. By contrast, Mme. de Chièvres wears a bridal dress, "in white damask embroidered with a picture of Adam and Eve under the apple tree" (English translation, 81; German, 725). The iconography could not be clearer: sexual relations as part of calculated alliance politics are equated with the fall. Bella is pure of this sin.

Bella's femininity is furthermore explored in terms of her contrast with the golem. To distract the possessive mandrake, Charles's tutor commissions a simulacrum of Bella from an old Jew:

While speaking, the Jew finished his work. He breathed onto the column, wrote the word on her forehead, hidden under her bangs, and before them stood a second Bella, who from the mirror had knowledge of everything that Bella had experienced up to that point, but desired nothing for herself [*die aber nichts Eignes wollte*], only that which existed in the mind of her Jewish creator, namely pride, lust, and greed—like all sins, the perversion of fine and spiritual inclinations. That she exhibited these traits without any spiritual striving distinguished her from even the Jew, but also from all other people, who, incidentally, were as taken in by her illusion as were the birds by the old painting of fruit, so that they flew at the canvas and tried to eat from it." (English translation, 54; German, 688)

Golem Bella looks exactly like Isabella but lacks Isabella's decisive character trait. If Isabella is defined in terms of her pride, her ability to love and her frugality, Golem Bella is exactly the debased caricature of Isabella's virtues. Note that the narrator relates Isabella's spirituality, and hence virtuous potential, to one definite, identity-defining feature: not her shape, looks, or body; nor her experience, knowledge, and history; but exclusively her ability to want, to desire in an utterly pure and disinterested manner. It is this quality that gives her authority, sovereignty, and independence of will. The golem knows merely debased, materialist wants and demands, and this turns her into a creature of pride, greed, and lust.

Nevertheless, this passage is strangely overdetermined as to what exactly distinguishes Bella from Golem Bella. Is it exclusively Bella's ability to desire that sets them apart, or is it also the fact that the golem's maker, the old Jew, has transferred some of his own qualities to his creation? The narrator asserts the latter, while at the same time denying it. Yes, Golem Bella has inherited her thoughts from the old Jew. But no, the Jew is distinctly human, whereas the golem, as a mere simulacrum of a human, lacks even the potential for spirituality. We will return to the subject of Arnim's anti-Semitism; what is important to retain for the present is the fact that Golem Bella, as a simulacrum, is representative of a narrowly defined heterosexual genitality, of which Isabella is the opposite.

Long before Isabella is contrasted with Golem Bella, when she expresses her desire to find the wonderful prince with whom she has fallen in love, the narrative focuses on Isabella's innocent sexuality as her most distinguishing character trait. She learns from Braka that to pursue the prince she will need money, which she can obtain through the magical mandrake, in a risky and scary operation. Not just anybody can obtain this magical root:

A girl is required who loves with her whole soul, without the carnal desires of her sex [ohne Begierde zur Lust ihres Geschlechts], for whom her beloved's mere proximity suffices: a primary, essential condition, perhaps for the first time truly realized in the person of Bella, because all the Gypsies she had met until now had treated her like a higher being, and she recognized herself as such. The physical appearance of the prince [die Erscheinung des Prinzen] was so holy and pure to her, like the body of the host during mass, that has passed too quickly to awaken her consideration [wie der Körper des Allerheiligsten in der Messe, vorübergegangen, zu schnell um ihre Betrachtung zu wecken]. In such a girl, whose sails billow with the powerful winds of imagination, must also dwell the more-than-manly courage to go with a black dog to the gallows in the eleventh hour, where an innocently hanged man has shed tears upon the grass. There she must carefully stuff her ears with cotton and search with her hands until she finds the root and then—in spite of all the cries of the root, which is in no way natural, for it is the child of the hanged man's innocent tears—lay bare its head, lay a noose of her own hair around it, hitch that up to the black dog, and then run away, so that the dog, in its desire to follow her, will pull the root from the ground, and, in so doing, will inevitably be struck down in a flashing convulsion of the earth. Whoever at this moment—the most crucial one—has not properly stuffed her ears can be driven mad on the spot by the screaming. (English translation, slightly modified, 15–16; German, 636–37)

This recipe for obtaining a mandrake highlights some of the distinguishing features of Bella's femininity: her specific innocence is her ability to desire without any narrowly conceived heterosexual genital objects and aims; she is hence susceptible to a powerful imagination and capable of more-than-manly courage (*übermännlicher Mut*).

The unique purity of her desire for the prince is illustrated by a curious religious analogy: her relationship to his visual appearance and physical presence is compared to her relationship to the host during mass. The consecrated host is elevated as an offering for spiritual communion, as the object of a vision that must see through the mere physical appearance to the real substance, the body of Christ. By adding the detail that her relationship to this sight was of such a short duration that it did not awaken her contemplation, the narrator marks her relationship to the prince as one not yet consummated.

The comparison with the host introduces a unique model of representation. To Isabella, the appearance of the prince is not of the same order as the appearance of Golem Bella is to its maker, the old Jew. Golem Bella, an object of lust, is compared to Zeuxis's illusionistic painting, a mimetic representation and perfect trompe l'oeil, in which painted grapes even deceive the birds, who come to pick at them. She is mere surface, mere looks, mere appearance, made of clay and of borrowed thoughts; she has no flesh, no blood, nor a desire and will of her own. There is nothing behind the looks of the golem. By contrast, the appearance of the prince is compared to the host during the service—to the transubstantiated body of Christ. This means that Golem Bella's lack of substance, her status as simulacrum of a human, is contrasted with the Christian sacramental model of embodiment and transformation, which posits a real presence. It is Isabella's exceptional purity that knows how to desire this kind of presence, how to love, how to relate to the real thing rather than a simulacrum.

Whereas initially Isabella's love of the prince is so pure and sublimated that its substance—the prince's body, his flesh and blood—cannot even enter her consciousness, it is through maternal love for the mandrake that her ability to love acquires a physicality that becomes a vital component of her self-awareness, identity, and political calling. In other words, the narrative phase that focuses on Isabella's procuring and raising of the mandrake deals with the kind of transformation that she has to undergo before rejoining the prince. The mandrake might be considered as Bella's offspring, the shoot, that has its roots in this nonreproductive, not-yet-genital desire. To unfold the mandrake's humanoid potential, his adoptive mother has to create his face: "The rosehip was first pressed onto the right spot, but she did not notice that her loving kisses soon pushed it askew. Next, she set in the two juniper berries. The little fellow seemed to look at her. That so filled her with joy that she would have gladly put in a dozen, if she could have found a good place for them. . . . Finally she presented him with a second set of eyes on the back of his neck, and we have to admit that this invention was not entirely without merit" (English translation, 20; German, 642). Hence Isabella's radical aimless and objectless sensuality is transferred to how she endows the little creature with sensory organs.

Whereas Isabella's love for the prince was explicitly void of any physical desire, it is through an uninvited, tempestuous, willful kiss by the mandrake that she is physically aroused for the first time. This scene of seduction and sexualization happens right after she has realized that the mandrake is quickly developing qualities that will need to be checked. The mandrake mocks her efforts to educate him, saying: "'I have a feeling that you have something evil in mind for me, but I'll make everything well again.'—With that he climbed down, jumped into her lap, and kissed her so heartily that his millet-beard almost rubbed her skin raw. In spite of that, she felt a strange stirring of her blood [dennoch fühlte sie eine sonderbare Bewegung ihres Blutes] that she could not understand, and to which she gave no thought. However, at that moment the little fellow was so dear to her and she expected she knew not what of him [und sie erwartetete und wußte nicht was von ihm]" (English translation, slightly modified, 24; German, 647). Suddenly, but only for a moment, she is alerted to what until then has been her unnoticed, unproblematized sexuality, her own physical response to him, described as "a strange stirring of her blood."

So far I have argued that Isabella's character as a charismatic, strong leader is derived from her virginal sexuality, her ability to desire, and the purity of this desire. Nevertheless, her desire is shaped and embodied, and furthermore related to models of representation and creation. We can distinguish several stages of Isabella's sexual and political maturation. In the very beginning, she appears to the young prince as a spectral apparition, while he appears to her as a real presence and as a body (one that does not elicit her contemplation, as will be remembered from the analogy with the host during the service). The second stage encompasses her relationship to the mandrake, the phase of a polymorphously perverse sexuality, of which the mandrake is the embodiment. This relatively long and complex narrative phase entails Isabella's "creation" of the mandrake, his transformation through her endowing him with senses and sensuality, in a grotesque, tragicomic analogy to the divine processes of the creation of man.

The narrative phase centered around the mandrake comes to an end as both the mandrake and Isabella reach a state of maturity. The mandrake has grown up to his final height of three feet, is sprouting a beard, lusting for wealth, and finally capable of detecting hidden treasures. Isabella is ready to enter the world and seek out the prince; however, she does not quite know this. It is Braka who makes the plans for them to leave their haunted house in the country and suggests to Bella that she is ready to take a man. Bella's outlook on the new phase in her life is quite different:

She was happy to be setting out into the world, but she was afraid of the people around her, and the feeling that they were not worthy of her overwhelmed her in a sudden rush of pain. She was ashamed of them because she had known her father, and all her gratitude toward Braka, all the joy she felt at the flourishing of the little root-man that she had so fortuitously and boldly created, could not suppress this shame.

The grandeur of her Egyptian tribe was in her blood, and she looked at the stars as if to her ancestors, and, in the middle of this cold October, she felt her country's summer, when the Nile recedes and everyone sets to work, but she was also aware of her people's ancient transgression, that they had not wanted to give the Holy Mother Mary shelter on her flight to Egypt, when she rode there with her blessed child in the pouring rain: He, however, had raised His hand and described a circle with it, and above them there stood a rainbow, which did not allow a single drop to fall upon them. "Is our sin still unatoned!" sighed Bella, and around the moon she spied a marvelous colored ring, so that her heart rejoiced and prayed without words. (English translation, 32; German, 659)

This paragraph describes Bella's outlook on her passage into the world as composed of memories of her personal past, the legends of her people, and

New and Old Testament iconography (namely, the Christ child and Noah's rainbow), as well as elements from the mythology of Isis and the Astraea legend. All of these heterogeneous elements come together in a hopeful picture or vision of the future and a new covenant that will finally allow her wandering people to repossess their territory. The vision serves to mark Isabella as the new leader of her people, ready to assume that role, even though she might not know it yet.

This passage connects the narrative of Isabella's sexual maturation with the narrative of her social and political maturation; the connective element is in the term *blood*. Mention of it appears exactly at that threshold in the narrative when she becomes an adult who can go out into the world and fulfill her destiny. Hence Isabella's sexual maturation is indicated in the phrase that describes her physical arousal as a "strange stirring of her blood," even as reference to blood marks a sudden but still somehow latent awareness of her leadership position as both above and part of her people. This connection is addressed in the phrase "the grandeur of her Egyptian tribe was in her blood."

The Uses of Blood

The term *blood* connects the two narrative programs of this tale, first of the female protagonist's maturation, her transition from the last days of her childhood into womanhood, and later of initiation into her calling, her mission to assume a role of leadership of her own people. It is noteworthy that what is at issue in her sudden sexual arousal is not a desire to act on this sensation. Her arousal is important exclusively in terms of the new sense of self, identity, and individuality that she attains. This new sense of self, alluded to as "the grandeur of her Egyptian tribe [that] was in her blood," is accompanied by sudden awareness of a sense of shame as she looks at the bizarre "family" surrounding her: Braka, the Bearskinner, and the mandrake.

The several meanings of blood in Arnim's tale fuse distinct concepts of an individual's identity: Isabella's strong ethnic identity as an Egyptian; isolation in consequence of her superior social standing; and identification with her father, whom she suddenly remembers. She does not inherit her royalty by way of being part of a dynastic line; her royalty is in her blood as part of her Egyptianness. Her sovereignty is derived from something she shares with her people. Blood, in both cases, indicates a latent awareness of her identity that is somehow physiologically grounded and essential to life processes.

It is in this particular semantic field of blood that the phantasmatic dimension of the transition from an older European dynastic model of alliance politics is indicated, both to a new model of political leadership and to a modern construction of sexuality and individuality. In the introductory first volume of his *The History of Sexuality*, Michel Foucault suggests that in the nineteenth century obsession with sexuality and hereditary degenerative diseases—the concern with "blood"—played the same role for the bourgeois family in matters related to procreation as careful alliance politics played for the older European aristocracy in their concern about optimizing accumulation of power and wealth.[7] In Arnim's tale, we see the new political leader of the future, Isabella of Egypt, as an alternative to Charles, the inheritor of a doomed empire that owed its momentary but fragile power exclusively to clever alliance politics. We can also see how this new ruler assumes her role of political leadership by responding to the call of her blood. Isabella's initiation into her political mission is depicted as the realization of her sexuality ("a strange stirring of her blood") marking her entry into the world, and her self-realization in terms of recognizing her superior position, her destiny as a leader, which is defined not merely in patrilineal terms but also in ethnic identity (her Egyptian tribe). In Arnim's tale, we witness a redefinition of marriage and sexuality in the transition from alliance politics to a focus on sexuality as a crucial but latent identity-defining characteristic. Arnim's tale shares this elaboration of a new concept of sexuality with the majority of fantastic tales of its time. What sets Arnim's story apart from the fantastic tales of his period is his poetics of the marvelous, connecting this modern concept of sexuality with a concept of leadership, political representation, and ethnic identity.

In the contrast between Charles and Isabella, we observe two distinct concepts of political power: on the one hand, the concept of a ruler's power over a territory, and on the other the concept of the ruler's power over a people. The latter form of leadership, where the ruler looks after each and every one of the members of his or her people, is strongly characteristic of the Judaic tradition, as opposed to the Greek and Roman models of power, which take the form of control over a bounded territory. Of course, nowhere in actual history would either model of power exist in its pure form and isolated from the other. Certainly, for the modern nation state rule over a defined territory and over this territory's inhabitants are relevant. However, the distinction between the two concepts can be helpful in defining certain trends of modernization. According to Foucault, the model of power that involves each individual subject as well as the totality of a population acquires new relevance in the sixteenth and seventeenth centuries with the expanding bureaucracy and new policing sciences of the absolutist state. Especially after the French Revolution, during the phase of the Napoleonic occupation, this model of leadership and government received new emphasis and inflection in conjunction with highly politicized concepts of national identity in some of the German-speaking territories.[8]

In the context of anti-Napoleonic politics in the Prussia of 1811, efforts were made to shore up resistance to the occupational army. Military reformers such as Gneisenau and Scharnhorst claimed that a successful overthrow of the Napoleonic army would be possible only with the aid of voluntary militias, or even a general draft. To make this come true, political leaders would have to rely on the people's investment in their fate as a united entity transcending local interests and class barriers. Gneisenau appealed to the Prussian king to involve preachers in this effort to raise a patriotic spirit.[9] In the same year, Achim von Arnim founded the Christian German Roundtable, a group of poets, members of the landed gentry, and legal historians engaged in an exercise of imagining a constitution. Their hope was to conjure up ways of creating a national unity that would sustain the patriotic effort, conceived in contrast to those presumably French models of citizenship and state that relied on principles of universality and practices of assimilation.[10] The Romantic collections and editions of medieval literature, popular legends, fairy tales, and folk songs belong to the same larger historical and political context.[11] However, as opposed to the brothers Grimm, Arnim (who, together with Brentano, had also edited a collection of folk songs and poetry) was acutely aware that the unity of the people could not just be resurrected from a legendary past but rather had to be constructed as an ongoing work that involved certain aspects not only of the past but also of the present and the political future.[12]

With his tale of Isabella of Egypt—indeed, with his entire novella collection from 1812—Achim von Arnim addresses a number of aspects of this project of national unity regarding the people and their relationship to their leader. The model of government and leadership that cares for each one and the totality of a people is introduced by way of the diaspora of the Gypsies and Isabella's relationship to them in terms of pastoral care. The climax and closure of the story in conjunction with the actualization and gendering of the Astraea myth (that is, the dissociation of the imperial idea from Charles) make it clear that it is to Isabella's style of leadership that the future is given. The populist, patriotic model of power and representation is staged in the scene of the Gypsies' "election" or "recognition" of Isabella as their rightful leader, the scene that concludes with her trusting leap into their arms to unite herself with her people. Finally, there is the aspect that emphasizes the sexualized individual qua individual, which removes sexuality from its immediate association with reproductive genital heterosexual practices and instead makes it primarily into a latent source of power and knowledge. It is this model of sexuality that describes Isabella's extraordinary strength and courage, her determination and distinction as a leader.

In addressing the question of Arnim's anti-Semitism,[13] the concept of the unity of a people and the contrast between Gypsies and Jews is relevant. Whereas the Gypsies remain distinctly apart from the culture and life style of whatever country they live in, the Jewish diaspora has undergone phases of intense assimilation. In other words, the glorification of Gypsy culture and Isabella's "Egyptianness" implicitly entails a polemical opposition between a good form of leadership and ethnic identity that is incarnated by this distinctly different young woman on the one hand, and Jewish cultures and communities in the German-speaking territories who had not preserved an ethnic identity on the other. As I show later, Arnim's anti-Semitism is both systemic to his patriotic vision and new with respect to a more traditional anti-Semitism. Ultimately, Arnim makes Jewishness no longer an external ethnic or religious marker but rather a hidden racial marker, a somehow mysterious and powerful quality of the "blood."[14]

The role that the assimilated Jew plays in Arnim's political thought, as the figure triggering anxiety over a people's identity and unity and hence needing to be turned into a scapegoat, can be shown exceptionally well in the unpublished frame narrative for the novella collection of 1812. For publication, this frame narrative, set right after the Tyrolian uprising against Bavarian rule, was replaced by the much shorter introduction and dedication to the Grimm brothers. For the present reading of Arnim's political uses of history, the two frames belong to the same paradigmatic set.

The much shorter, published introduction to the 1812 collection primarily emphasizes the unfinished, open-ended nature of the world of sagas and legends, stating Arnim's position that constructing the unity of the people's tradition and heritage is the task of the present and the future. The unpublished frame addresses Arnim's patriotic concern with ethnic tradition and local culture far more openly in its polemical opposition to the utopia of universal understanding and brotherhood. It spells out how his concept of the individuality and untranslatability of ethnic and local particularity is based on an emphatic notion of embodiment or incarnation on the one hand, and related to a critique of modern uniformity, habituation, and ennui (or "empty" time) on the other. Arnim's assessment and critique of a modern loss of genuine, firsthand experience seeks a cure in revitalization of our ability to wonder, in a poetics of the marvelous that would restore life and blood to past tradition. Thus the category of blood figures prominently in a poetics of the marvelous that conjoins the political goals of the marvelous, in the manner of a magical fluid helping to infuse legends from the past with a vitality that makes them support the political future of national unity.

The title of the unpublished frame narrative to Arnim's collection of novellas, "Die Versöhnung in der Sommerfrische" (The Reconciliation in the Summer Resort), marks the utopian hope of a universal brotherhood, of an enlightened cosmopolitanism, or of a Christian reconciliation beyond national and class identity.[15] It refers to the joint efforts of the narrator and a mountain hermit, Andreas, to reconcile their friends, the stubborn Tyrolian patriot Sebastian and the enlightened and assimilated Jew Raffael Rabbuni, with one another. The obstacle to this reconciliation is entirely on the side of Sebastian, who violently objects to his daughter Therese's love for Rabbuni, despite the latter having miraculously saved her from madness after the loss of her first fiancé. Although Sebastian agrees to make peace with Rabbuni and share a meal with him, sending Therese to fetch wine and bread, he cannot join the hermit Andreas in his utopian hope:

> Like the first people on earth we shall enjoy everything in peace as if it had been created for us. In these lovely saturnalia of nature, in this golden age, we shall forget who we are, like angels we shall contemplate human stories and educate our hearts in view of them.—Sebastian said: Should I forget who I am, I would find it inscribed on my belt, and should I lose my belt, it is inscribed above my door with my own blood, for when the construction of the house was finished, I was shot, and thus did not have to buy expensive paint. Otherwise I would be happy to imagine myself to be Andreas, and if I could have my wife in addition, I would indeed want to live like an angel in heaven.[16]

Sebastian declares himself constitutionally incapable of sharing the hermit's vision of universal peace and brotherhood; his identity is what makes him oppose Andreas's vision of angelic, prelapsarian bliss. This identity is his name, his house, his masculinity and love of his wife—that is, his mature male sexuality. As opposed to the hermit who chose to leave his wife and family, Sebastian is bound to them, as he is bound to the house he constructed and defended at the risk of his life, and these are ties he declares himself incapable of ever forgetting. His identity is inscribed with his blood, shed in defending his home against a foreign force; this blood marks his address, his name, and where he belongs. He rejects the hermit's angelic, utopian existence as something that in its asexual, otherworldly nature is inaccessible as well as undesirable for him. His identity is earthy and locally bound. *Blood* is the term Sebastian introduces to reject the utopian vision of universal reconciliation. Blood is a marker of identity, of individuality and of group allegiance, a sign of embodiment, sexuality, masculinity, representative of an indelible bodily memory that exceeds consciousness itself. Finally, Sebastian's blood above his door alludes to the sacrificial blood from the Passover in the Exodus, in the same way as the name of Isabella's guardian (the old Gypsy woman, Braka), the name that opens the story, is the Hebrew word for the thanksgiving liturgy, the blessing at the Passover ritual.

To the extent that blood marks what is real, authentic, or substantial, it sets aside a particular kind of sign that can constitute and communicate individual and group identity. In this magical capacity, it seems to be primarily sacrificial blood. But then Arnim also repeatedly refers to the Christian doctrine of incarnation and redemption, and the Eucharist through which the distant historical event of Christ's crucifixion and resurrection can be made present for each individual and the whole of the Christian community. However, the blood in the frame as well as in the story are not Eucharistic wine, but blood. Indeed, in the paragraph that comes just after Sebastian's declaration of his resistance to a universal concept of reconciliation, the hermit speculates on how traditions can pale and lose in the immediacy of an appeal, though they can also be revivified through new bloodshed. The immediate occasion is Therese, who brings wine and bread to the company. Andreas wonders why his contemporaries no longer understand how the disciples at Emmaus recognized the resurrected Jesus Christ from the manner in which he was breaking the bread:

Why is so much no longer understood and therefore rejected? Because we experience very little first hand. As social life gets increasingly comfortable and structured, many impressions become entirely an issue of tradition, which gets paler and paler until violent events once again lend blood to the picture. Habit and daily exposure gnaw at the wonders of the world like rain at the monuments of a great past. But it merely takes the freshness of felicitous circumstances, a great deed, and everything will reemerge in its original youthful beauty, the burden of empty times disappears and everything is again new and marvelous to us. (575)

In "Isabella of Egypt," the Eucharist was invoked to distinguish a particular relationship to the appearance and presence of another person (the specific purity of Isabella's love for the prince) from the primitive lust that is elicited and experienced by the superficial, insubstantial simulacrum of Golem Bella. There the Eucharist represented the potential for communicating with a real presence, the body of Christ, which nevertheless for that stage of Isabella's development is not fully realized because Isabella has not yet experienced the strange stirring of her blood. In comparable fashion, the introductory narrative also refers to the Eucharist as both an ideal model of communicating with a real presence and a ritual that has lost its force and vitality. It is important to note in this context that Arnim's semiotics and semantics of blood do not mean the circumscribed Christian doctrine of incarnation, of Christ's sacrifice and redemption; he uses these allusions to validate an antimimetic model of representation, a certain appreciation of violent events and their power to break with the numbing, desensitizing influences of daily routine and habit. In this case, there is little distinction between the quasi-modernist aesthetics of violence and defamiliarization on the one hand and the belief in the rejuvenating forces of violence and war on the other.

In my analysis of Arnim's "Isabella of Egypt," I have tried to show how this story proposes and explores a newly mobilized and modified model of leadership, patriotism, and national identity through Isabella's femininity, sexuality, and love. The old idea of empire is transformed into a new model of popular sovereignty embodied by the Gypsy leader Isabella. What connects her to her people (as well as what distinguishes her from them and leads her to assume and execute her leadership) comes to her through her blood. "The Reconciliation in the Summer Resort" presents a more systematic picture of the multiple but related functions of this magical fluid. Blood works as the conveyor of substance, of a vital force; it is a guarantor of presence and authenticity. Furthermore, blood can define a collective and an individual identity below the markers of culture—below consciousness, memory, or convention. It is both a sign and a real thing, as it is also the trace of violence and sacrifice. In this last function, in its ability to return life, power, and a sense of wonder to cultural monuments,

Arnim quite literally spells out a poetics of the fantastic as a modern use of the marvelous actualizing historical and legendary material.

The Living Past and Its Resistance to Modernization

Prosper Mérimée (1803–1871) published his most famous fantastic tale, "La Vénus d'Ille" (The Venus of Ille) in 1837 in the *Revue des Deux Mondes*, three years after he was appointed "inspecteur général des monuments historiques." He held that position for some twenty years, traveling extensively all over France, documenting, assessing, and establishing an inventory of monuments of the Roman and especially the medieval past, deciding what needed and deserved restoration and what should go to museums in the provinces or be taken to the capital. The post of inspector general of historic monuments was created in 1830, after the state began to take responsibility for upkeep of old buildings in response to the movement of the 1820s that accompanied the revival of historical studies and the campaign against the neglect of the country's architectural heritage, expressed primarily in Hugo's and Montalembert's vehement outcry against vandalism.[17]

As inspector general, Mérimée quickly established his reputation as a conscientious, erudite, and careful judge, and a shrewd protector of historical monuments. During the same period, he also began to publish extensively on ancient and medieval antiquities and history—works that finally gained him admission into the French Academy. In his biography of Mérimée, A. W. Raitt speculates that in his early period as inspector general, during which time the aspiring author published "The Venus of Ille," "Colomba" (1840), and "Carmen" (1845), Mérimée became increasingly disenchanted with works of the imagination, such that he finally repudiated this kind of writing in favor of documenting historical, philological, and archaeological facts.[18]

It is not within the scope of this study to pursue Raitt's thesis about the tension between fiction and fact throughout Mérimée's career; rather, to take a more detailed look at his fiction, especially the fantastic tale "The Venus of Ille," and trace the instability of the distinction between fact and fiction.

"The Venus of Ille" is recounted by a first person narrator who travels to the south of France, apparently in a function comparable to that of an inspector general. He spends a weekend with a provincial antiquarian, who proudly shows him a huge bronze statue of Venus that he has recently unearthed in his garden. The time of the narrator's visit to the provincial town happens to coincide with the nuptials day of his host's son, which comes to a tragic end when the young man is found dead after his wedding night. There is no reliable witness to the murder. The narrator leaves the possibility open as to whether there has been a supernatural intrusion into the complacently prosaic provincial universe. The traumatized young wife claims that a dark giant entered the room in the middle of the night and smothered her husband. The traces on the corpse seem to confirm her account, as do the aural perceptions of the narrator, who heard heavy footsteps approaching and departing from the room of the newlyweds during the night.

Even this brief plot summary of "The Venus of Ille" shows how Mérimée works into his fiction, into the very fabric of the fantastic tale, his experience as inspector general and his concern with archaeological discoveries and historical facts. Moreover, the generically decisive element—the hesitation over the supernatural event of the statue's murderous appearance—is dependent on the fiction of the narrator's status as an objective, trustworthy witness and reporter of facts. If, however, an archeological find, an ancient statue, can accomplish a murder, then we are no longer safe from the antiquities we study. Presumably, ancient and inanimate objects can suddenly burst into violent action, so that the separation between some remote past and the present is no longer guaranteed.

Before continuing to examine how historical, antiquarian, and archaeological issues play into the very construction of the fantastic tale, a brief glance at two of Mérimée's later tales, "Colomba" and "Carmen," is instructive. Mérimée frames these two stories by staging a clash between the rational universe of the cosmopolitan traveler or the enlightened scholar, and the irrational, potentially supernatural universe of ancient cultures and peoples. Though these two later works are not fantastic tales, thematically they too unfold Mérimée's concern with a presumably archaic ethnicity clashing with modernity. Furthermore these two tales, like "The Venus of Ille," link an occult and archaic potential for violence to a powerful image of femininity.

"Colomba," based on Mérimée's travels in Corsica and told by an impersonal narrator, focalizes the events through two English tourists, a father and his unmarried daughter, who try to cure their boredom with the typical tourist attractions in Italy by embarking on a journey to far more exotic Corsica. On the boat, they encounter Orso, an attractive young man, educated in the capital; having completed his service as lieutenant in the Napoleonic army, he is on his way back to his ancestral home. Although his father was assassinated in the course of a long-standing feud between his family and another eminent one, the young man has come to reject the local customs of vengeance. His sister, Colomba, who has never left the island and who is an eminent bard in the local tradition of the lament (steeped in its incitement to violence), uses all of her charisma and sinister scheming to drag her brother back into the vendetta. When she finally succeeds in bringing her brother into a situation in which he is ambushed and fires two fatal shots at his assailant, the killing satisfies both the local blood thirst and a scenario of self-defense.

Reminiscent of Arnim's statement about the power of blood to restore ancient monuments to new vigor and life, "Colomba" thrives on the picturesque attractions of local color and violent customs, which become a magical antidote to modern ennui. The story's focus is not just on the strange beauty, the antiquity and authenticity of the Corsican landscape, architecture, and lore, but also on their personification in the tale's eponymous heroine and her power to reawaken the intense passion and violence that appear to belong to a more primitive layer of history. In and through the setting of the island and in the figure of Colomba, the ancient past is utterly present and can be made to erupt at any moment. Unlike the heroine of Arnim's tale, however, the powerful female ethnic figure is tinged with evil, as is evident, for instance, in this passage describing her departure with her brother from the inn where the English tourists are staying: "From the window of the sitting room Miss Lydia saw the brother and his sister mount their horses. Colomba's eyes were shining with a malicious joy that she had not noticed before. This tall and strong woman, fanatic in her barbaric ideas of honor, pride inscribed on her forehead, and lips curved by a sardonic smile as she led the young man, armed as if for a sinister expedition, reminded her of Orso's fears, and she thought she could see him being led to perdition by his evil genius."[19]

Though this story does not draw on the supernatural, it suggests that Colomba's sinister character is related to some occult force or agency. Colomba's evil nature appears in her eyes and facial expression as she is about to vanish out of sight of Miss Lydia in her sitting room window. The ominously occult nature of Colomba emerges at the limits of the modern observer's field of vision. Yet we must also note that Miss Lydia's perception— though cast into the perspective of the modern, rational observer—is also informed by her fascination and desire for this exotic alterity, a desire that thoroughly questions the neutrality of the observer. It is this gaze, this witnessing of the presumably neutral modern observer and its relation to some mysterious evil, that we consider in much greater detail with regard to "The Venus of Ille."

"Carmen" can also be read as a story that explores a modern observer's encounter with alterity. The story is told by two first person narrators. The narrator of the frame tells how on a research trip to Spain, in search of the true site of the battle of Munda in Andalusia, he accidentally encounters a dangerous looking man with whom he shares his cigars. Later on, the narrator meets a young Gypsy woman of savage beauty who offers to read his fortune and who the reader later learns is Carmen. After a few months, upon his return from his quest, the narrator is taken by a Dominican friar to visit an outlaw and deserter imprisoned on death row. This prisoner turns out to be Maria-José, the stranger with whom the narrator shared cigars at the rest stop. The main part of the story, embedded in the frame narrator's tale, comprises Maria-José's powerful confessional narrative about his love for Carmen, the beautiful, irresistibly seductive, but unfaithful Gypsy woman whom he is finally driven to murder. Though more beautiful and sexually attractive, Carmen in many ways resembles Colomba, a creature unencumbered by law or convention but fiercely loyal to her people. As opposed to Colomba, however, Carmen's character is highly ambiguous, for she is both the figure of a fascinating and distinct exotic ethnicity and a chameleonlike figure of passing. Carmen's mysterious power and sexual attraction is part of her ethnic identity, which, though operative and somehow perceptible, is nevertheless not entirely manifest. Thus Carmen becomes a figure of the fascination with latent alterity and difference.

To the frame narrator, Carmen stands out as an unconventionally beautiful example of a Gypsy, an observation that leads him to speculate that she is not of pure race. He sees in Carmen a savage, inhuman creature comparable to a wolf or cat: "Her eyes above all had an expression that was at the same time voluptuous and savage, which I have never since found in any human gaze. Eye of Gypsy, eye of wolf, this is a Spanish saying that shows good observation. If you don't have the time to go to the Botanical Gardens in order to study the gaze of a wolf you should look at your cat when it lies in wait for a sparrow."[20] Carmen is marked by some quasi-inhuman cruelty and potential for violence that is expressed in her gaze; moreover, this unbridled volatility seems somehow related to her racially understood ethnicity.

The word *black* in "Carmen" constitutes a racial self-designation, a distinction that sets the Gypsies apart in terms of an incommensurate alterity, marking this people's refusal to subject themselves to any law other than their own, or to enter any ulterior, common, or mediating ground between their group identity and that of anyone belonging to another group. The notion that the Gypsies' blackness is not a descriptive designation that would be situated on the continuum of a color spectrum, but rather a sheer marker of difference, is further elaborated in the frame narrator's final appendix on Gypsy language and culture: "The physical characteristics of the Gypsies are easier to distinguish than to describe. Once one has seen a single one of them, one can recognize an individual of this race from thousands. The physiognomy, the expression, this is what primarily separates them from other people that live in the same region. Their skin is very dark, always darker than that of the populations among whom they live. From this stems the name *Calés*, the blacks, by which they refer to themselves" (my translation; German, 660).

The diverse Gypsy dialects, all greatly influenced by the respective languages of the host countries, operate along the same indexical register as their physique, but they do not constitute a positive unity. Generally, the Gypsies don't even speak Romany in addition to their respective host languages, nor do they possess a lingua franca in common with Gypsies from other regions. Rather, the Gypsy dialects mark their identity and unity by setting them apart from their hosts, indicating only the traces of some ancient common source. The Gypsies embody the ultimate resistance to the modern, Napoleonic model of citizenship that is based on assimilation.

The frame narrator of "Carmen" does not end up discovering the precise site of the battle of Munda—a clearly datable ancient layer of history—as he originally intended; instead, he finds a more or less latent trace of a primitive past, embodied by the Gypsies and their language(s). This means that the narrator's scholarly position vis-à-vis a safely distant past is challenged by the living ethnic tradition. The text begins with an archaeological field trip, but it ends with a philological essay. The title heroine, Carmen, incarnates the seductive power, menace, and danger of coming into contact with this living ethnic alterity. She is the one who refers to herself as the devil with whom José-Maria slept without noticing it, an event that eventually leads to their violent deaths. The savagely different, even diabolical Carmen is comparable to Colomba, who also can conjure up archaic violent passions that are associated with a premodern ethnicity. The antimodern thrust of Carmen's and Colomba's ethnicity is shown as active resistance or opposition to the institutions of the modern nation state. Both women display their utter disregard for the agents and institutions of the state: the police, the army, and the judicial system. Whereas Carmen encounters Maria-José when he is called to the tobacco factory to arrest her after she has cut another woman's face in a fit of vengeance, Colomba makes a mockery of the provincial prefect who comes to her house to settle the ancient conflict between the two feuding clans.

In Achim von Arnim's "Isabella of Egypt," the tribal loyalty and ethnically based group identity of the gypsies becomes crystallized and transfigured in the person of Isabella and acquires a utopian character, serving as a positively coded model of popular sovereignty and the embodiment of a future style of leadership. Thus for Arnim, engaged in the patriotism of the anti-Napoleonic resistance, glorifying ethnic group identity becomes a means of forging a modern national unity. In Mérimée's tales, by contrast, ethnic traits serve to mark resistance to modernization. They indicate a reservoir of savage, inhuman passion and violence. Whereas Arnim makes use of the peculiar license of the fantastic tale to forge a visionary utopia out of historical and legendary material, and whereas "Isabella of Egypt" qua marvelous tale culminates in an inspired, visionary grasp of the future, Mérimée's tales are not oriented toward a utopian future. Instead, Carmen's and Colomba's ethnic identity represents a threat both to the universalist principles of a modern nation state and to the neutrality of an enlightened, rationalist observer. Moreover, as I hope even this cursory discussion of these two tales has shown, the modern observer is not entirely indifferent to this threat. Indeed, it might be part of the observer's desire to be startled out of her state of ennui, as in Miss Lydia's case; or it might be the kernel of an intense erotic attraction, as in the case of José's and the narrator's fascination with Carmen.

"The Venus of Ille"

In Mérimée's fantastic tale "The Venus of Ille," an inexplicable, presumably supernatural event connected with the archeological find suddenly and violently intrudes into the rational, enlightened universe of the observer/narrator. The story's supernatural feature depends on the violent agency of this inanimate object, a statue of Venus. Despite its inanimate nature, the statue shares with Colomba and Carmen a status representative of a powerfully attractive premodern alterity. In contrast to Colomba's ties to Corsica or Carmen's loyalty to the Gypsies, however, the Venus statue does not stand out in terms of a tie to one specific ancient tribe or ethnic group; it emerges as a figure that can bring out different traits in different people, a figure that brings out a certain competitiveness and appears to fuel a great deal of phantasmatic investment.

Indeed, as a first overview indicates, the Venus statue is riddled with contrasting attributes. It is black or dark green, colors that in the course of the narrative associate her (in the context of a tennis match that fuels ethnic rivalry between the locals and a visiting group of Spanish challengers) with the ethnic group of the Spanish tennis player, the outsider. In the same context, however, she is also associated with the local tennis champion, to whom she appears to lend her own physical energy. Not only is she likened to those masculine figures, but equally she shares attributes with the young bride.

In spite of her initial designation as "une idole en terre," the Venus statue is not an archaic clay idol that can be dated and identified in relationship to the archeological layer in which it was found. Instead, she is clearly associated with historical times since she bears partly legible Latin inscriptions and is made of bronze. Nevertheless, her initial designation, which the narrator misunderstands to refer to a terra-cotta idol (which would suggest a chthonic, archaic mother or fertility goddess in many ways), circumscribes the phantasmatic dimension she holds for all those who come into contact with her. Monsieur de Peyrehorade, the provincial dilettante antiquary who has found her in his yard, uses her to distinguish himself as a scholar. His philological speculations are supposed to date his find and determine its provenance and possibly its maker and artist. The provincial scholar treats the statue as part of the living present. In terms of his scholarship, he associates her with philology, the science of living sources, in contrast to archeology, the science of dead finds. Though clearly inanimate, the statue insinuates herself as a living presence in multiple ways in his daily life; he worships her as an idol of Venus.

The competing descriptions of the statue echo some of the debate surrounding the study of antiquities—namely, how much and what can be drawn from developments in the fields of history, geology, philology, and archeology. It was in the 1820s and 1830s that stratificatory dating methods from the field of geology were first applied to archaeological finds that included in one and the same site human bones, those of extinct animal species, tools, and artifacts. This method decisively altered the concept of the antiquity of the human species. If indeed humans had existed together with extinct animal species, then the human species was much older than had been hitherto assumed. As paleontology, geology, and comparative ethnology joined archeology, prehistory emerged as a scientific field of study. Against the prevalent theory of the great flood, it became possible to conceive of a continuity between ancient and modern times, between prehistoric and modern man.[21] This is not to assert that Mérimée uses his tale to advocate new methodologies from the emerging field of scientific archaeology over and against the dominant paradigms of eighteenth-century archaeology, nor that he would situate the Venus statue in a precisely datable layer of history or prehistory that stands in a continuum with modern times. But his story does explore competing theorems, paradigms, and models in the study of objects from antiquity to elaborate the nonsynchronicity of the contemporary present tense. Presumably archaic traits and primitive passions are—like the elements of an ancient but still spoken language—no longer part of a safely distant past but a powerful component of a heterogeneous modernity.

Apart from the distinctions and nondifferentiations between an enlightened modernity and a presumably archaic or tribal past, "The Venus of Ille" explores another set of differences and their potential undoing. In their naïve efforts to impress the authority from Paris, both M. de Peyrehorade (the eager antiquarian scholar) and Monsieur Alphonse (his son, a would-be dandy) represent not merely the slightly backward region with its own local customs and traditions but also the province in its relationship to the capital—the tension between center and periphery that is, in its own way, highly modern. The provincials are subjected to the Parisian narrator's condescension when he shows how, though they try to imitate the ways of the capital, they continue to suffer from the stigma of their provincial inferiority. The contrasts between the observer position of the inspector from the capital and the provincial amateur scholar contribute a great deal not just to the tale's ironical tone but also to the essential hesitation with respect to the possibility of supernatural intrusion; the provincial scholar seems to believe in the agency of the goddess, whereas the Parisian narrator appears to remain neutral in his judgment. Even so (and this is the focus of my last section on the story), the Parisian narrator is also implicated in the poor provincial's naïveté. But first I turn to the statue's strange status as representation.

The Idol's Looks and the Idol's Look

From the moment the statue is first mentioned until the violent ending of the tale, the Venus statue is associated with two sets of ambiguities. First is the matter of her historical ambiguity. There is no unequivocal date or place for her. Her antiquity and archaic features become part of the living present. This much has already been discussed. More than this, however, her semiotic status is radically unstable. This semiotic instability is worked out along such questions as: How does she represent divinity? How does she represent human form? Does she merely depict the physical likeness of the goddess of love, or does the statue somehow make the goddess miraculously present? If the statue is more than a mere allegorical representation, how does she personify the violent powers of love? This ambiguity of the Venus statue is also expressed in the inscription, *Cave amantem*, which M. de Peyrehorade understands to mean "Beware of the one who loves her," a translation that locates the danger with her lover. The Latin, however, might also mean the opposite: "The one who loves her has to be on his guard," in the narrator's translation. These ambiguities surrounding the statue become even more complex if we consider the epigram of the story, a quotation from Lucian (125–192 C.E.): "May the statue be favorable and well meaning, since she so closely resembles a human being." What exactly is meant by this cryptic phrase? Does the statue's potential evil emanate from a deceptive resemblance to the human? Or, as I argue below, does her proximity to the human also demarcate a relationship of radical nonidentity? For as close as she is to the human form, she is by no means human; indeed, she is inhuman.

Much of the statue's fundamental ambiguity (especially its semiotic aspects) is immediately marked by the term *idol*, used by the local guide who leads the Parisian visitor to M. de Peyrehorade in the village of Ille. Their ensuing dialogue deserves to be quoted at some length:

> "I'll bet that you have come to Ille to see the idol. I guessed that when I saw you drawing pictures of the saints at Serrabona."
>
> "The idol! What idol?" The word had aroused my curiosity.
>
> "What! Did nobody tell you at Perpignan that Monsier de Peyerhorade had found an idol in the earth [une idole en terre]?"
>
> "Do you mean a statue in terra-cotta, in clay [une statue en terre cuite]?"

"No, I don't. It's made of copper, and there's enough of it to make hundreds of coins. It weighs as much as a church bell. It was a good way down, at the foot of an olive tree, that we dug it up...."

"'What's that?' I said. We went on picking away, and a black hand appeared, which looked like the hand of a dead man coming out of the ground. I felt frightened; I went up to Monsieur and I said to him: 'There's dead folk, master, under the olive tree; you'll have to send for the priest.' 'What dead folk?' he asked. He came along, and he'd no sooner seen the hand than he cried out: 'An antique statue!' You might have thought he'd found a buried treasure...."

"And what did you find in the end?"

"A huge black woman, more than half naked, saving your presence, sir, all in copper, and Monsieur de Peyrehorade told us it was an idol of pagan times ... you know, when Charlemagne was alive."

"I see what it is ... a statue of the Virgin in bronze which belonged to a convent that has been destroyed."

"The Blessed Virgin? Not on your life! ... I'd have known straightaway if it had been the Blessed Virgin. I tell you it's an idol; you can see from her appearance. She looks straight at you with her great white eyes ... Anybody'd think she was trying to stare you out, because you daren't look her in the eyes."

"White eyes, were they? No doubt they are inlaid in the bronze; it might be a Roman statue."

"Roman! That's it! Monsieur de Peyrehorade said that it was Roman. Ah! I can see that you're a learned man like him."

"Is it whole and in good condition?"

"Oh, she doesn't lack anything, Monsieur. It's much more beautiful and better finished than the painted plaster bust of Louis-Philippe in the town hall. But for all that, I can't recall the idol's face. She looks wicked ... and she is wicked, too."[22]

Whereas the Parisian archaeologist associates with the phrase "idole en terre" an archaic, prehistorical terra-cotta figurine, the native guide tells him that she is of copper. It turns out that she is very large, taller than a human being and made of bronze. The "earth" is the material that surrounds her, not what she is made of. As the diggers accidentally discover their find, they first expect to unearth a human corpse. However, she is increasingly dissociated from anything human, especially with respect to her powerfully malignant gaze. The local guide completes his narrative by telling the visitor that the statue has broken his friend's leg, which might prevent him from ever again being one of the best tennis players in town.

In the dialogue, the statue's characterization proceeds negatively by unfolding what this idol is not rather than presenting a catalogue of its positive features. The dialogue presents multiple layers of information to the reader of the story about the statue and people's attitude towards it. Indeed, the actual data about the statue are intricately interwoven with the commentaries of the naïve local guide, and the speculations and questions of the Parisian scholar, who does not pay much attention to his local informant but pursues his own train of associations. Whereas the narrator conjectures that she might be a statue of the Virgin, the local guide insists on her pagan features and her evil look. The narrator ventures this suggestion even though his guide has described her as seminude and as an object from pagan times, the times of Charlemagne. Obviously, situating her within the Christian era does not necessarily rule out her pagan nature but brings out the heterogeneity of any given epoch of the past and present.

What makes the statue into more than a mere dead object is not primarily an issue of verisimilitude or trompe l'oeil realism that would cause her to be confused with a real human or divine being; it is not her visage, her looks, but rather her *look*. What animates her is the stare of her white eyes, her disfiguring, fixating gaze: "Elle vous fixe avec ses grands yeux blancs . . . On dirait qu'elle vous dévisage. On baisse les yeux, oui, en la regardant." (411). Her eyes are not a matter of a realistic representation but rather an index of her animation. The statue's realism is introduced as an afterthought (by way of contrasting her with the realistic bust of Louis Philippe in the mayor's office). The statue's realism is framed in terms of her "completeness." Whereas the narrator wants to know whether she is well preserved, the local guide's answer shifts this concern with decay and the destructive effects of time into the quasi-atemporal aesthetic domain by pointing out that she is extremely well finished, that she doesn't "lack anything," that she is more beautiful than the painted plaster bust. In spite of (or rather because of) her completeness in every realistic detail, the guide cannot recall her face. There is no split between her as an object and her status as a representation. Signifier, signified, and referent are united without difference and lack. Thus, semiotically speaking, the statue is indeed an idol.

The statue's status as idol as well as its association—albeit false—with a statue of the Virgin recalls the rich folkloric tradition associated with the gothic idol. In the twelfth and thirteenth centuries, popular legends proliferated, in view of increasingly "naturalistic" representations, about the actual appearance of the Virgin or a saint, or the sudden animation of a painting or statue. Christian theologians of that period felt that the representations of the Virgin had to be protected from confusion with pagan statues of Venus, which indeed had been venerated and caressed as concrete, material idols in the past. To keep Christian worship of saints distinct from pagan idol worship, theologians of the those centuries insisted on a distinction between the saint's ideational presence and the actual physical statue or painting.[23] The same distinction between the actual representation and what is being represented could very well be applied to the ideational presence of Louis Philippe and his naturalistic bust in the mayor's office. By contrast, for the Venus statue—somehow because of her animating look—this distinction collapses; the physical statue and the ideational presence are inextricably intertwined, and it is this that makes her into an idol.

It is important, though, to note that despite Mérimée's conscious use of the gothic idol, his story does not suggest a return to the concerns of the twelfth century. When, later on in the narrative, the issue of idolatry is brought up as M. de Peyrehorade faces his Catholic wife's protests against his worship of the statue, the issue of idol worship is framed as a perfectly modern phenomenon. De Peyrehorade insists, referring to the Charter of 1814 guaranteeing religious freedom, on his liberty to subscribe to the cult of the idol as he describes his plans to venerate her by sacrificing doves and offering roses and incense to her on the day of his son's wedding. His position implies the differentiation between secular and canonical law, between church and state. Idol worship in the modern sense is not therefore some regression to an archaic cult but an expression of religious freedom, and the exercise of a private, basic right protected by the modern state.

Whereas veneration of statues of saints could be legitimated by arguing that it was not the realistic art object but the ideational presence of the saint itself that was the object of adoration, thus distinguishing the saint's cult from pagan idolatry, the Venus statue in her full presence has the status of an idol. She is not just a representation; indeed, she cannot be represented. Just like the local guide who cannot remember her face, the narrator too is incapable of drawing it. The guide mentions having seen the visitor "drawing portraits" of the saints of Serrabona, but when on the morning after his arrival, on the day of Alphonse's wedding, the narrator attempts to do the same with the Venus statue, his efforts are in vain:

Fantastic Encounters with the Marvels of History 231

As early as eight o'clock, I was sitting in front of the Venus, pencil in hand, beginning again for the twentieth time the statue's head, without being able to seize the expression. Monsieur de Peyrehorade bustled about, giving me advice and repeating his Phoenician derivations. Then he placed some Bengal roses on the pedestal of the statue and addressed to it, in a tragicomical voice, supplications for the couple who were going to live under his roof. He went in to change about nine o'clock, and at the same time Monsieur Alphonse appeared, wearing a close-fitting suit, white gloves, patent-leather shoes, chased buttons, and a rose in his buttonhole.

"You must do my wife's portrait," he said, leaning over my drawing; "she is pretty, too." (English translation, 79; French, 425)

This passage confirms the statue's status as an idol, a physical object that serves as an object of veneration, as it reiterates its resistance to being reduced to mere representation, in this case a drawing, or in the previous case a remembered face that can be described. The roses that M. de Peyrehorade lays down in front of the statue are echoed in the rose the bridegroom wears in his buttonhole. Already then, M. Alphonse appears in a structurally ambiguous position with respect to the statue; he could also be her bridegroom. This ambiguity is further elaborated by his request that the visitor attempt a portrait of his wife, a request that places his bride into the same paradigmatic class as the statue. This move, making the two not only comparable but also exchangeable is later echoed in M. de Peyrehorade's speech during supper after the wedding:

"Yes," continued Monsieur de Peyrehorade, "there are two Venuses under my roof. One I found in the earth, like a truffle; the other came down to us from the heavens to share her girdle with us."

He meant, of course, her garter.

"My son, choose between the Roman and the Catalan Venus. The rascal chooses the Catalan, the better part, for the Roman is black and the Catalan is white; the Roman is cold, and the Catalan sets on fire all who come near her." (English translation, 83; French, 429)

Little does the father know then that the idol has already chosen his son, that his son is actually "affianced" to the statue, in the sense that it is she who wears the diamond ring, the family heirloom intended for Alphonse's wife.

The scene that "affiances" M. Alphonse to the statue occurs on the morning of the wedding day, before the wedding ceremony has taken place. Following the visitor's aborted attempts to portray the statue and M. de Peyrehorade's presentation of offerings to the idol, there is a crucial shift of focus in the narrative sequence that leads to the Venus's appropriation of the status of bride to the young Alphonse. This shift is indicated when the narrator gives up his focus on the Venus statue as an object of representation, abandoning his vain attempts to "seize her expression" and instead turns his attention to the village square that adjoins Peyrehorade's estate—the site of a fierce tennis match in which some transient Spanish muleteers are about to beat the local youth. Despite his wedding costume, determined to save the honor of his country, Alphonse intervenes in the tennis match. When he misses the first ball, he throws away his racquet and blames that "'damned ring . . . which is too tight on my finger and made me miss a sure thing!' With some difficulty he took off his diamond ring, and I went over to him to take it, but he forestalled me, ran to the Venus, slipped the ring on her third finger, and resumed his position at the head of his fellow villagers. He was pale, but calm and determined. From then on he made no more mistakes and the Spaniards were soundly beaten" (English translation, 80; French, 426).

The shift of focus from the Venus statue's looks to looking at the tennis match entails the visitor's change of perspective, but it also means a shift in the function of the statue itself, from an object to be looked at to the bearer of a powerful gaze and an agent of superhuman, evil forces. It is under her gaze, her evil eye, that the tennis match unfolds, bringing violent passions into view. The entire tennis game is framed as a competition between ethnicities, the local "Illois" and their Spanish opponents. The narrator refers to the locals' "national" pride, their local patriotism, terms that denote the precise opposite to the modern concept of the nation state. He makes similar remarks with reference to the Spaniards, between whom he immediately differentiates according to local ethnic groups: "C'étaient des Aragonais et des Navarrois, presque tous d'une adresse merveilleuse. Aussi les Illois, bien qu'encouragés par la présence et les conseils de M. Alphonse, furent-ils assez promptement battus par ces nouveaux champions. Les spectateurs nationaux étaient consternés" (425–26) [They were Aragonians and Navarrians, almost all marvellously skilled. Although the people from Ille were encouraged by the presence and the advice of M. Alphonse, they were quickly beaten by these new champions. The patriotic onlookers (spectateurs nationaux) were aghast] (English translation, modified, 79).

Although the statue is not mentioned until M. Alphonse puts the bridal heirloom on her hand, her look is reflected in the two central players of the opposing sides. The narrator's description of the leader of the Spanish team and Alphonse borrows some of her key attributes. Alphonse undergoes a metamorphosis from a vacuous, foppish dandy into a beautiful athlete: "At that moment I found him really beautiful. He was passionate. His clothes, which a little earlier had filled his thoughts to the exclusion of everything else, were completely forgotten. A few minutes before he would not have dared turn his head, for fear of disturbing his cravat. Now he no longer gave a thought to his curled hair or his beautifully pleated jabot" (English translation, slightly modified, 79; French, 48). Alphonse's sudden beauty is due to an intense patriotic passion that makes him lose his usual awkwardness and stiffness. The statue's beauty is equally one of passion and suggested movement. When the narrator describes her, he marks the contrast with classical Greek works of art: "It was not at all the calm and austere beauty of the Greek sculptors, whose rule was to give a majestic immobility to every feature" (English translation, 79; French, 426).

Whereas, however, the young athlete's passion is not elaborated in terms of a moral code, the statue's enlivening passion finds its articulation in her evil expression: "I noticed with astonishment that the artist had deliberately set out to express ill-nature raised to the level of wickedness. Every feature was slightly contracted: the eyes were rather slanted, the mouth turned up at the corners, and the nostrils somewhat distended" (English translation, 72; French, 418). The statue's malignant features are transferred to the Aragonian opponent of Alphonse, the Spanish tennis player who also assumes her dark color and stature: "He was a man of about forty, six feet tall, slim and wiry; and his olive skin was almost as dark as the bronze of the Venus" (80, 426). Beaten in the match and subjected to Alphonse's condescending remarks, his suppressed anger and thirst for vengeance become a specification of the statue's generalized evil looks, when the narrator again associates him with the statue by way of reference to his skin color and his height: "The Spanish giant felt the insult keenly. I saw him go pale under his tanned skin. He looked miserably at his racquet and ground his teeth; then in a choking voice he muttered: 'Me lo pagarás'" (80, 427).

The term *giant* ("géant") is otherwise reserved for the statue, and its use culminates in the bride's presumably crazed account of her traumatic wedding night: "Then she turned her head . . . and saw, so she says, her husband on his knees by the bed, with his head on a level with the pillow, in the arms of a sort of greenish giant who was embracing him with all its might" (English translation, 88; French, 434). Although the narrator suspects Alphonse's opponent of the horrible deed, upon interrogation the Spaniard insists that had he indeed intended to avenge himself he would have stabbed him immediately and not waited until the next day. An investigation confirms that he has an alibi for the fateful night. Indeed, the impossible seems to have happened: the murder seems to have been committed by the Venus statue.

Here at the young couple's bedside, on their wedding night, the now mysteriously animate statue enacts her function, albeit in a disturbingly violent fashion, of signifying love and marriage. In the legend, as in this story, the statue asserts her rights to prevent the groom from marrying his human bride. The traditional medieval legend, however, knows little of murder or revenge. Mérimée's tale, by contrast, associates her with aggression and violent revenge rather than love, from the very first mention of the statue. The local guide considers the statue's breaking of his friend's (Jean Coll's) leg the proof of her evil nature. His account personifies the dead object as an agent of castration or emasculation, since this accident prevents the young man from ever again standing out as the excellent runner or tennis player he used to be. Likewise, during the visitor's first night at the Peyrehorade home he witnesses two local youths passing by the tennis court, apostrophizing the statue. Whereas one of them threatens to avenge Jean Coll, the other questions his prowess, suggesting that she is so hard that nothing could attack her, that their peer, Etienne, had already broken his file on her trying to cut into her. The self-styled avenger, apparently a locksmith apprentice, suggests that if he only had his cold chisel with him he could "knock out her big white eyes" (English translation, 70; French, 416). Not having their special tools on hand, one of them picks up a stone and throws it at the statue; the stone rebounds and hits him on the head.

The Parisian visitor frames this as an act of just retribution: "Yet another vandal punished by Venus! Would that all destroyers of our ancient monuments could have their heads broken like that!" (English translation, 70; French, 416–17). M. de Peyrehorade, to whom he reports the incident the following morning, gleefully embraces this interpretation of the vandals' just punishment. The statue's agency thus is a function of her having become the site of male rivalry and male bonding, of challenging masculine pride by way of her hardness, completeness, and indestructibility.

The Inspector's Investment

What are we to make of the fact that the goddess of love appears first of all as a threat of castration, as an indestructible and self-sufficient femininity, which lacks nothing, which brings out male vulnerability as it thwarts any attempt to assert masculine prowess and pride? Certainly, the narrator's position as observer is greatly invested in this fantasy of a powerful phallic female in both scenarios of her violent intervention. The relatively trivial stoning incident as well as the fatal wedding night cast the narrator in the position of an invisible, solitary, voyeuristic witness. He seems to project the statue into the role of both avenger of the barbaric vandals and avenger of love. In both cases, her intervention strengthens the presumed superiority of the sophisticated, ironical Parisian scholar and outsider over the provincials.

The narrator invokes the statue's malicious energy and evil eye to express his disdain not just for the local youths' disrespect for historical monuments but also for M. Alphonse's mercantile approach to his marriage. Thus he points out that Alphonse shows considerably less interest in his fiancée than in his horses or his clothes. He is shocked "to see a young man appear more affected by the dowry than by the beautiful eyes of his future wife" (English translation, modified, 76; French, 423). When the narrator describes his first reaction to the young woman, he contrasts his own appreciation of her with the fiancé's neglect of her. Moreover, he seems to appeal to the goddess of love to avenge the thwarted beauty:

> Mademoiselle de Puygarrig was eighteen years old, and her lithe, delicate figure was a great contrast to the bony frame of her sturdy fiancé. She was not just beautiful: she was enchanting [*séduisante*]. I admired the perfect naturalness of all her replies. Her expression was kindly, but nevertheless was not devoid of a slight touch of maliciousness which reminded me, in spite of myself, of my host's Venus. While making this comparison to myself, I wondered if the superior beauty which the statue undoubtedly possessed was not largely due to her tigerish expression, for strength, even in the evil passions, always arouses wonder and a sort of involuntary admiration.
>
> What a pity, I reflected, as we left Puygarrig, that such a charming person should be so rich, and that her dowry should be the cause of her being courted by a man unworthy of her! (English translation, 77–78; French, 424)

Whereas the statue's eyes, above everything else, endow her with an evil beauty, he perceives in the beautiful young woman's responses a veiled tendency toward maliciousness. As avengers with beautiful features but malignant energy, the Venus of Ille and the Venus of Puygarrig (note that the young woman's patronym is also the name of her town!) become interchangeable.

Actually, both the young man and young woman assume features of the statue in this passage. During the tennis match the young man turned into a beautiful athlete, full of passion and animation, but here it is the young woman who is beautiful and animated. Similarly, the statue's weight, height, hardness, and indestructibility are invoked with regard to the Spanish player's extraordinary height and M. Alphonse's very large and bony frame. Thus the statue combines a cluster of attributes that normally would be considered mutually exclusive or contradictory. It is indestructible, huge, and hard, and yet extremely flexible, athletic, and animate. Since it embodies both male and female features, some commentators of Mérimée's story have identified the statue with the preoedipal narcissistic fantasy of the phallic mother.[24] The visitor's observations and his story, with its actants, their roles, and their functions, all arise out of the matrix of the Venus of Ille's set of contradictory attributes. One might also characterize this story in terms of how it focalizes the events, how the narrator borrows his perspective from the statue, how this perspective severely compromises his objectivity, and ultimately how it implicates him in the tragic climax of the tale.

We need to trace how the story unfolds the narrator's investment in the violent ending of the interrupted wedding night, and how the story connects the narrator's sense of urban superiority and condescension toward his provincial hosts with the Venus statue, which comes to occupy the phantasmatic place of the phallic mother. From the beginning, when his guide mentions the upcoming wedding, the visitor has an exaggerated aversion: "This wedding, of which I now heard for the first time, would upset all my plans. I said to myself that I was going to be a killjoy; but I was expected, and as Monsieur de P. had written to say I was coming, I should have to present myself" (English translation, 63–64; French, 409). On the night of his arrival, before the narrator has actually seen the statue, M. de Peyrehorade leads him to the guest room upstairs, pointing out to him with a wink that the room reserved for the young couple is at the opposite end of the corridor, for, as he certainly knows, newlyweds have to be isolated. The visitor is struck by the height and enormous length of the bed in his room, almost seven feet long—a narrative detail that prepares his voyeuristic position as witness to the imminent wedding. Because of the remoteness of his own room from the wedding chamber, his observer position is compromised as to the accuracy and completeness of the data. He might only hear rather than see something, which leaves plenty of room for speculation and hallucination. Indeed, his observer position is situated on the stage or theater of fantasy, if we designate by this term the imagined scenario or mise-en-scène of satisfaction.

Whereas the narrator has an almost phobic reaction to the idea of being around a wedding, his host does everything to play down the significance of this event, by calling it a trifle (*une bagatelle*) and by apologizing for its simplicity: "To a Parisian who has had his fill of festivities . . . And a wedding without a ball too! However, you will see a bride . . . a bride . . . who will take your breath away . . . But you are a serious man, and you are no longer interested in women. I have better things to show you. I'm going to give you something to feast your eyes on! I've a fine surprise in store for you tomorrow" (English translation, 67; French, 413). On the one hand, the Parisian visitor is referred to as an expert with sophisticated tastes, as somebody whose very high standards might, at best, be met by the beauty of the bride. On the other hand, he is apostrophized as a serious man who is no longer interested in the simple pleasure of women, one to whom the host hopes to offer a delectable surprise. The scopophilic pleasure of being taken to look at the Venus statue takes the place of enjoying beautiful women. Thus the visitor seems to be destined for the Venus statue, just as M. Alphonse is destined, through his engagement, for Mlle. de Puygarrig. In neither case are we to think of love as an essential component to the engagement; instead (and this makes the two comparable), each man's self-image seems to motivate his object choice. As we know, however, the narrative program gets more complicated. M. Alphonse is not only to be married to Mlle. de Puygarrig but he is also claimed by the statue, the visitor's woman, to whom he has accidentally affianced himself when his athletic ambition and local patriotism stir him into passion.

When Alphonse displays his horses and fashionable tastes to the visitor, he appeals, like his father, to the interlocutor's Parisian sophistication. Though he mentions his fiancée only in passing, he makes much of the diamond-studded wedding ring that has been handed down to him from his grandmother. The visitor points out that in the capital the customary choice would be a far simpler wedding band, usually composed of two metals, like the other ring Alphonse is wearing on his hand: "'That little ring,' he added, . . . 'was given to me one Shrove Tuesday by a woman in Paris. Ah, what a time I had when I was staying there two years ago. That's the place to enjoy oneself, and no mistake!' . . . And he sighed regretfully" (English translation, 77; French, 423). Ironically, it is this token of an intensely pleasurable but transitory affair that Alphonse is forced to place on the hand of his bride during the actual ceremony, since he has left the other ring on the hand of the Venus statue. The woman whom Alphonse marries for purely mercenary reasons thus joins ranks with the woman he enjoyed in Paris. Both are ultimately exchangeable, merely relevant to him for his self-centered use and pleasure, comparable to his status symbols, possessions, consumer objects, and fashion accessories.

The wedding band as the sign of an indissoluble, exclusive tie is not the object of M. Alphonse's concern. This would have been represented by the other ring, bearing the engraving "Ever thine [Sempr' ab ti]" (English translation, 77; French, 423). The narrator, however, critical of Alphonse's approach to marriage, disapproves of this ring for aesthetic and functional reasons. He deems it too big and cumbersome; the diamonds distract from the original design. After all, it is his advice that Alphonse ends up following when he gives his bride the wedding band of the Parisian fashion. Thus, in spite of the visitor's disdain for the young man, they are both in a comparable position with respect to their attitude toward marriage: both narcissistically invested in their dandyish or scholarly freedom, bachelordom, and independence. Neither wants to be attached to one woman in any more serious fashion than for purposes of distraction, pleasure, and convenience. The narrator's repeated expression of disdain for Alphonse's wedding is not, however, just the righteous indignation against this man's superficial and mercenary attitude toward his bride. After all, he dislikes all marriages: "I had a splitting headache; besides, I don't know why, a wedding always makes me feel melancholy. This one, moreover, disgusted me slightly" (English translation, slightly altered, 83; French, 429).

The alternative to this marriage of convenience—the one indicated by the diamond ring and consummated by the Venus statue—also undermines a crucial aspect of marriage: the law of the father, the rule that the spouse has to replace an incestuous object choice. The diamond ring was handed down from Alphonse's mother: "My mother gave it to me. It was an old family ring ... from the days of chivalry. It was worn by my grandmother, who had it from her grandmother. Goodness knows when it was made!" (English translation, 77; French, 423). To place this ring onto the finger of his wife would make Alphonse the placeholder of his grandfather and his wife the incarnation of a grandmother. This phantasmatic regression to an indistinct, archaic past echoes the narrator's first thought, when, upon hearing about "l'idole en terre," he expects the term to refer to a chthonic mother goddess.

Clearly, M. Alphonse's unconscious engagement to the Venus statue does not represent an oedipal object choice in the narrow sense. There is no question of the idol's resemblance to Mme. de Peyrehorade. Yet his unconscious choice repeats his father's passionate attachment to the statue, just as the consummation of his relationship to the statue entails a fatal conclusion to his father's desire: "'Look here, wife,' said Monsieur de Peyrehorade in a determined voice, as he stretched his right leg out towards her, clad in a shadowed silk stocking, 'if my Venus had broken this leg I wouldn't have complained'" (English translation, 68; French, 414). M. de Peyrehorade's demonstrative display of his passionate love of the statue accomplishes more than he intended. He wants to prove to the visitor his antiquarian knowledge and connoisseurship in an effort to bond with the Parisian scholar, but wishing to be elevated above the provincial ignorance and superstition of his wife and fellow villagers he betrays the fact that his scholarly pretensions are on a continuum with a foppish vanity that he shares with his son and their visitor. Indeed, the fetishistic overtones of this scene ultimately reveal and implicate the narrator's own investment in the idol to the extent that he is the one who isolates and focuses on the fashionable details of the silk stocking.

Thus, in actuality all the three men of the story—M. de Peyrehorade, his son, and the narrator—in their mimetically interconnected vanities are attached to the preoedipal, narcissistic fantasy of the phallic mother. The idol responds to the fantasy of the phallic mother, a fantasy that denies castration and supports the narcissistic image of a self-sufficient, whole masculinity—a masculinity that can freely choose and pursue its pleasures, fashions, consumer objects, and scholarly fame; one that is an embodiment of the modern, liberal individualist. To uncover the underlying fantasy of this kind of male narcissism, however, is one thing; to account for the murder and address the question of the statue's presumed agency is quite another. Clearly, this is the question that the story provokes and refuses to answer, which alone makes it a fantastic tale.

Signature, Event, Context: The Narrator's Blind Spot

Narratologically, the narrator's blind spot is in the distinction between the story as a composite whole, in which the narrator is one of several characters, and the narrator's function for the telling of the story, his linear performance. We could also situate the narrator's blind spot in the distinction between the story as a piece of fiction and the story as a fact-based travel account. This opposes, on the one hand, the narrator who is identical with the maker of an artifact and who in consequence resembles the extrafictional author, and on the other hand a narrator or Parisian scholar or reporter who attends to something that is independently given, who merely represents an event he witnessed. Additionally, the story raises questions about the identity and difference between a first person narrator and the author of the piece.

Objet trouvé, travel report, or artifact and fiction? Apart from the question about the referential dimension of the artifact, there is the matter of the artifact's relationship to its maker. One version of this is addressed within the story—not the referential dimension of an artifact, but instead the question about the artifact's dependence or independence from an artist or maker is addressed with respect to the statue's presumed maker. When M. de Peyrehorade translates the inscription "Myro fecit," he first claims that the statue is a product of the famous Greek sculptor Myron, then that it was made by one of his descendants, and then by a member of his school. The narrator, however, contradicts him and insists that *fecit* should be understood as *consecravit*, that this Myron was not the maker of the statue but rather an unknown lover who had been commanded in a dream to consecrate a bracelet to Venus, which was subsequently stolen, leaving bare holes in her arm where it used to be attached. This conjecture, which is supposed to fill in the gaps, the holes, where nothing is to be seen, according to M. de Peyrehorade, merely marks his Parisian visitor as an author of fictions: "Ah, it's easy to see that you have written some novels!" (English translation, 75; French, 422). This commentary is laden with irony, especially if we take into account that it also underlines the biographical parallels between the Parisian scholar of the fiction and its author (Prosper Mérimée), who is also both inspector general and writer of fiction. According to Peyrehorade, the distinction between a scholarly account of reality and the fabulations of a fiction writer parallels that between the scholar who is aware of the fabrication of the objects of external reality and the writer of fiction who mistakes his own creation as having an independent reality. Thus ironically, Peyrehorade points out the investment of the fiction writer in the fantasy of the phallic mother, since the visitor gives primacy to the goddess and her placeholder the statue, rather than to a human agent as its originator. It is noteworthy, however, that it becomes increasingly difficult for Peyrehorade to hold on to the model of a singular, unique author; he is forced to move from Myron as the name of an individual to Myron as a family name, and finally to Myron as the name of a school, a set of artistic techniques and the statue's style.

To the extent that Peyrehorade is invested in asserting the statue's supreme artistic value, and to the extent that his vision of its artistic origin is exclusively coded in terms of an originary masculinity, it seems to ward off the threat of another version of how an artifact could have come into being: the notion of birthing, phrased as a donation from a female agency. This alternative model is evoked and rejected in Peyrehorade's vehement insistence on the statue's status as a master work: "Do you know my wife wanted me to have my statue melted down to make a bell for our church? She would have been its godmother. A masterpiece of Myron's, Monsieur!" (English translation, 68; French, 414) A bell has no author, but merely a donor; it has a distinct shape and form, but no style. Considering this opposition to his wife, M. de Peyrehorade's notion of the originary author who is responsible for the statue's style finally reveals the affective and phantasmatic side of his emphatic model of the great artist as the fantasy of the godlike, all-controlling, shaping, inventing force.

Although the two men are engaged in some competition about scholarly competence and erudition, and in spite of the fact that M. de Peyrehorade has come up with the most obscure, minute interpretations and philological investigation about other aspects of the inscriptions on his cherished statue, there is a glaring oversight or omission of a word that apparently escaped his scholarly zeal. Neither of the two scholars attempts to translate or comment on the word from the statue's inscription that qualifies Myron as "Eutyches Myro," which in Latin would read "Prosper Myro," that is, it would give to the presumed "lucky" artist Mérimée's own first name. This discovery is left to the attentive reader of the tale as the final pointer that marks the narrator's blind spot. If *Eutyches* is read as part of Mérimée's proper name, its referential dimension distinguishes the realm of fiction from a reality external to this imagined world. Then Mérimée is the one who has made the artifact, the story, "The Venus of Ille," and in it has invented the Venus statue. The irony to which both the pompous provincial scholar and the would-be distant Parisian observer were subjected, and that was applied to their shared male fantasies, now spills over into the realm of nonfiction. Ultimately, the Venus of Ille, the statue and artifact, made by some lucky artist, has the same status as the story that shares the name of the statue. It is through this artifact that the Parisian observer, losing his stance as objective narrator, is reinscribed in the fiction: he encounters his blind spot as he becomes a witness to the fantasy ("a bridegroom is being crushed to death"). The huge hermaphroditic figure of desire and male rivalry prevents the marriage from being consummated. Thus it both justifies the narrator's horror of marriage and reveals the savage and violent component of his presumed neutrality and individualism. Prosper Mérimée self-ironically signs this fantastic tale as he also marks it with his distinctive style.

*

By way of concluding this chapter, it might be useful to cast a comparative glance at Arnim's "Isabella of Egypt" and Mérimée's "The Venus of Ille." Though different in their political outlook (Arnim was quite devoted to an anti-Napoleonic nationalist agenda; Mérimée, by contrast, was not particularly interested in politics) and style (Arnim's tales stand out for their metaphorical exuberance, luxurious use of hyperbole, and frequent excursions; Mérimée's tales are extremely concise and sparse), both writers explore the heterogeneity and nonsynchronicity of a given historical or contemporary situation. In either case, the nonhomogeneity of a given historical epoch, be it the modern period of the early nineteenth century or the period of modernization in the sixteenth century, is faced with occult forces, which only apparently belong to the past. For both writers, these occult forces have to do with some version of love, women, and female sexuality on the one hand and with versions of the folk, the people, and ethnic identity on the other. But this is where their similarity ends.

Although Arnim's story makes use of the supernatural in an otherwise rational universe, it does not quite fit the generic features of the fantastic tale. The nonrealistic features in his tale do not become an occasion for doubt or hesitation but are accepted in their facticity and as mere invention, legend, or allegorical figures. In this sense, Arnim's poetics constitutes a distinctly modern version of the marvelous. His poetics of the marvelous might also be characterized as a poetics of hybridization, of fusing seemingly incompatible categories that blur the distinction between fact and fiction. Arnim's vision of a better political future is intricately related to a political theory of representation, and to the charismatic and powerful leader Isabella as a metonymic instantiation of her people—as well as to a particular aesthetic theory of representation and signification. Through the figure of Golem Bella, it criticizes a model of descriptive representation as a superficial mimetism and deceptive cult of simulacra. This sort of representation is related to all kinds of corruption—to greed, lust, and avarice, the vices that flow from the early capitalist cult of simulacra—and is contrasted with an emphatic notion of representation and incarnation positing a real presence that takes its clue from the central Christian mystery and miracle of the Eucharist. Thus Arnim's tale develops a highly politicized use of historical reference within a poetics of the marvelous that could be labeled a secularized version of a Eucharistic semiotics. Like its Christian template and model, it affirms the actuality, transformative power, and concrete presence of the past event for the present and future. Nevertheless, to the extent that the narrator reveals himself as the inventor or creator of Isabella, he also inserts himself into the continuum of the more-or-less pathetic, grotesque, or comical Pygmalion figures that attempt to incarnate a creature, be it the mandrake's efforts (a detail I have not pursued in my analysis of the story) to recreate Golem Bella, or Isabella's own "creation" of the mandrake as a humanoid creature. In this respect, the pathos of the power of the transformative past is at least somewhat ironically broken.

In Mérimée's "The Venus of Ille," the fantastic event is constituted by an instant of a sudden and violent intrusion of the distant past into the present. Whereas Arnim constructs the vision of a better political future, one based on a political leadership that draws on direct contact with (even the love of) the people, and whereas he glorifies the power of blood as a marker of individual and group identity, Mérimée explores the destructive violence of tampering with seemingly archaic, chthonic forces. In this fantastic tale, to an even lesser extent than in "Colomba" and "Carmen," the pseudoarchaic element and its resistance to modern universalist principles is not clearly separated off as a decisive and exclusive component of the premodern, ethnic local tradition that appears as a beautiful, threatening and seductive violent female sexuality. Rather, it is revealed as the phantasmatic adumbration and the blind spot of a distinctively modern male sexuality. The violent forces appear as an acting out of the narcissistically invested modern individualist observer.

Mérimée's exploration of the figure of the presumably neutral, rational, and enlightened observer, strangely poised between the position of a mere reporter of facts, and that of the emphatic artist figure and creator of fictions that exist in their own right, leads us into a consideration of how the fantastic tale can be positioned with regard to the poetics and representational claims of realist fiction. Whereas I began this study by situating the fantastic tale's concern with the semiotics of the marvelous in the context of a Romantic philosophy of language, I conclude, in the Epilogue, with an attempt to outline how this new genre partakes in, and departs from, the larger context of realist art.

Epilogue, or Turning the Screw from Shock to Fascination

This selection of fantastic tales written between 1772 and 1847 shows the emergence of a new literary type that, though impossible to characterize in terms of a unified ideological agenda or a singular historical context, nevertheless registers a curious awareness of and engagement with multiple historical trends that were to shape the history of subjectivity. Exploring an aesthetics of intensity and shock, it can be formally captured as the staging of a new text-audience relationship, while pragmatically it can be characterized in view of its exploration of a new kind of subjectivity embedded in the history of sexuality.

The "new" sexuality of the fantastic tale has nothing to do with the pleasurable encounter between bodies, but much with the problems of relating to an other, the fear and yearning that accompany the desire to escape from the confines of the self by seeking to communicate with an other. In this sense, the fantastic tale builds on and departs from the underlying assumptions and values of the Enlightenment culture of sensibility, with its belief in transparent communication and sympathetic understanding. For the early fantastic tale, these ideals and values are still upheld, but any attempt at their realization reveals the opacity of language and the disastrous, often fatal and violent effects of total openness from whence issues a genuinely fantastic poetics and aesthetics, as a concern to explore those potentially shocking and exhilarating areas of perception and experience that emerge once the all-too-familiar and apparently obvious is revealed in its strangeness and constructedness. In this problematic relationship to desire and pleasure, the sexuality elaborated by the fantastic tale might indeed (albeit in hindsight) be considered a far-reaching historical event.

Modern sexuality, especially as articulated in the fantastic tale, is a deeply mysterious phenomenon, situated at the limits of what can be known and understood. It challenges traditional psychological models of the human faculties; it also challenges what were then the newly emerging psychiatric theories of mental health insofar as it depicts some occult force operating like an instinct but disregarding all of the teleologies that are usually associated with instinctual behavior. Long before the advent of psychoanalysis, we find fantastic tales exploring violent types of behavior that not only challenge all available rational psychological and psychiatric models but also suggest alternative ones instead. These fantastic tales posit a repressed trauma as the pathogenic cause of violent behavior; they depict mysterious obsession as the compulsive acting out of an illicit sexual encounter.

If the fantastic tale proposes and elaborates a new sexuality in terms of a model of an individual's motivational deep structure that cannot be matched up with contemporary extraliterary discourse, then the innovative thrust must be situated within the realm of the aesthetic. There is an aesthetics of shock and seduction that is germane to the fantastic tale. What was then the dominant model of representation tends to be if not replaced then at least supplemented by a model of simulation; one might say that there is a shift in emphasis away from exclusive focus on the content of a perception or representation to its effect and transformative power. The typically fantastic hesitation over the ontological status of certain events or phenomena, the question as to whether these are merely imagined by the protagonist or narrator or are real, whether they constitute elaborate deception or an actual challenge to the makeup of the depicted universe in terms of an intrusion of supernatural forces—this question is less an issue of cognitive disorientation than the occasion of shock, pleasure, or excitement, an intensification of sensuality and experience for the protagonist or narrator and also for the reader of the fantastic tale.

The emphasis on physiology over mental images, on intensity over nuance and quality, and on the transformation of pain into pleasure or pleasure into pain, as well as the exploration of the aesthetics of shock and overstimulation, is a key concern of an aesthetics of reception that emerges against the background of the cultural history of reading. The model of a hallucinatory, absorptive, and identificatory silent reading has become the standard for the reception of fiction, as a way of accessing and consuming ersatz sensuality and reality. Later fantastic tales explore this media climate more self-consciously, developing the earlier exploration in the fantastic tale of the issue of animation and the strange life-giving powers of the artist—the artist as seducer and technician of the imaginary.

The fantastic tale's challenge to the seemingly neutral and objective observer deploys the conventions of verisimilitude in realist fiction by juxtaposing a representational and a constructivist model of reality. On the one hand, this kind of fiction works with a model according to which a narrative or description can depict or represent a reality for the reader, to make the reader believe that he or she is actually perceiving external phenomena. On the other hand, the fantastic tale draws attention to the construction of reality and to the observer's blind spot, to the fact that any kind of observation entails a set of distinctions that make it impossible to represent and observe the totality of the world, insofar as these observations both necessarily exclude certain aspects of the world in their specific construction of an observable phenomenon, and generate the blind spot of the observer. To the extent that the fantastic tale engages with this fundamental paradox of observation, it can never aim at better observation of the world than the model offered according to scientific, occultist, psychological, or psychoanalytical principles, but instead only an alternative kind of observation, holding one kind of reality construction at bay by offering a set of equally valid alternatives, encouraging its reader to engage in observing phenomena and observing the activity of observation. Hence the fantastic tale can neither be reduced to an isomorphism with one specific extraliterary discourse nor explained in view of a single set of historical references that would figure as its defining context.

To the extent that the fantastic tale's characteristic feature—its hesitation between two mutually incompatible approaches to reality (a commonplace, everyday, familiar reality on the one hand, and a reality that appears to be determined by supernatural or occult forces on the other) draws attention to the activity of observation, it emphatically participates in what Niklas Luhmann discusses as the emergence of "world art."[1] Luhmann introduces this term to distinguish the more traditional "object art," which represents objects of the world, from an art that presents itself as an art object distinguished from other art objects—that is, art that presents itself as a distinct form no longer "representing" the world but merely positing the world insofar as it invokes the world as an unmarked state, a necessarily unobservable unity preceding the distinction that produces the observer and the observed. Thus Luhmann characterizes art's attention to commonplace, everyday reality, whether in seventeenth-century Dutch genre paintings, or the realist novel, or *Ulysses*, as a "universalizing" and "self-reflexive" trend in the evolution of modern art insofar as it provides its audience with the opportunity to make observations that become independent of the objects represented and instead directed at observing the activity of observation. Luhmann situates in this trend the emergence of a distinctly aesthetic experience, as well as attention to how an object is constructed in this and no other way, which also implies attention to how the object could have been constructed otherwise (say, if another stylistic feature were to be used) (25). In contradistinction to realist art, the fantastic tale not only implicitly invokes the world as the unmarked state but also explicitly directs its reader's attention to a set of occult or supernatural phenomena that are necessarily excluded from any realist construction of a diegetic universe.

Within Luhmann's approach to realist art, one might hence characterize the fantastic tale as a specific subspecies of realism, one that exceeds the perspectivalism of realist literature by bringing into relief the realist reality construction as form. Insofar as form constitutes not a distinct shape but, in its fundamentally two-sided aspect, also produces, together with a positive inside or shape, an adjoining excluded, undifferentiated, and radically open outside, one might see in the fantastic tale's portrait of occult or supernatural forces an attempt at giving shape to what is excluded from the realist portrait of everyday reality. In this respect, the fantastic tale can be considered a significant contribution to the development of art's heightened self-reflexivity and hence autonomy.

Yet an observation-theory approach that immediately inscribes the fantastic tale into the rather abstract and long-term development of an autonomous art system can only pay attention to a subset of features of the aesthetics of the fantastic tale—namely, those that partake in elaborating a self-reflexive, self-referential system. Although such features can be found already in the emergence of this genre (for example, Tieck's semiological approach to the marvelous, or Poe's poetics of the arabesque), the aesthetics of the early fantastic tale seeks just as much to explore and elaborate art's transformative impact on its beholder or audience in how it attempts to give definite shape to an otherwise unobservable and occult aspect of the world. It is the appearance of the supernatural that provokes a lasting shock to the stability of the boundary between an observer's psychic system and the external environment. Moreover, the aesthetic of shock and seduction tends to be coupled with that aspect of the self-reflexive dimension of the fantastic tale that reflects its position within the history of media technologies, especially in its awareness of the effects of a silent, absorptive, and escapist reading culture. The fantastic tale's aesthetics of shock and seduction is cast with a view toward its pragmatic dimension in terms of the overpowering impact on the reader/observer, and as a reflection on the nature and power of art, substituting art's representational model of reality with a model of art's ability to simulate life. It is with regard to the early fantastic tale's programmatically pragmatic dimension that this study has sought to delineate the fantastic tale's contribution to the history of sexuality.

Despite its limitations with regard to the genesis of the fantastic tale, the teleological Luhmannesque perspective can illuminate the further development of the fantastic tale, for if we look ahead from the early emergence of the fantastic tale to its reappearance in Henry James's famous *The Turn of the Screw* (which was first published in twelve serialized installments in *Collier's Weekly* in 1898), we can register a new twist to the genre, which ultimately might indeed be best described along the lines of the fantastic tale's reflection on the evolution of "world art."

The introductory frame narrative to *The Turn of the Screw* announces the story as an attempt to trump the traditional ghost story. In the context of telling ghost stories and commenting on their effects, Douglas, one of the characters from the frame narrative, asks whether there would be something uniquely chilling about a ghost story in which the apparition is seen by a child. The gathered company agrees as to the uncanny effect this would produce, and Douglas continues: "If the child gives the effect another turn of the screw, what do you say to two children—?"[2] Having excited the curiosity of his listeners, he proceeds:

"Nobody but me, till now, has ever heard. It's quite too horrible." This was naturally declared by several voices to give the thing the utmost price, and our friend, with quiet art, prepared his triumph by turning his eyes over the rest of us and going on: "It's beyond everything. Nothing at all that I know touches it."

"For sheer terror?" I remember asking.

He seemed to say it wasn't so simple as that; to be really at a loss how to qualify it. He passed his hand over his eyes, made a little wincing grimace. "For dreadful—dreadfulness!"

"Oh how delicious!" cried one of the women.

He took no notice of her; he looked at me, but as if, instead of me, he saw what he spoke of. "For general uncanny ugliness and horror and pain." (1–2)

The fantastic tale is thus framed in light of a narrative challenge that can outbid the typical effects of a ghost story, as Douglas artfully stages his own position as one who knows of an exceptionally gruesome tale. Ignoring the woman who revels in the anticipated *frisson* of hearing it, he focuses instead on the first person narrator, appearing to look through him onto the "uncanny ugliness and horror and pain" of the as-yet-unheard tale.

The first person narrator appears as a placeholder for the external reader of the fiction. Moreover, this position is marked as a site from which it is possible to observe and to be observed. Yet, rather than switch to a second-order observation or, in a 180 degree turnaround, focus on the observer as an object within the visible world, Douglas looks through the first person narrator and appears to stare at what is by definition unobservable. The signified of his speech is situated on the other side of all prior distinctions that make observation possible; in that sense, it is designated as the unmarked state of the world. This unobservable world becomes the source of Douglas's affect, which he describes in the sensory register as an overpowering horror and pain and in the aesthetic register as a "general uncanny ugliness." Thus before the actual telling of the tale, its content and its effect are collapsed into one.

In the transition to the story itself, the autobiographical tale of the unnamed governess that Douglas reads to the gathered company from a "thin old-fashioned gilt-edged album" (6), the first person narrator again comes into focus, but this time his position is associated with the margins of the text, with the absent title of the tale, and with the imaginary materiality of writing that produces beauty as an effect engendered by the actual telling of the tale as it unfolds over time:

"What's your title?"
"I haven't one."
"Oh *I* have!" I said. But Douglas, without heeding me, had begun to read with a fine clearness that was like a rendering to the ear of the beauty of his author's hand." (6)

The telling of the tale is presented as the activity of listening to the reading of a beautifully written manuscript. Beauty in this passage becomes a matter of connoisseurship as it is related to an autonomous realm of art objects that are distinguished in terms of their individual styles, captured in the metaphor of the "author's hand." It appears less as the character of one distinct object and more as the result of an elaborate process of differentiation, translation, and transcoding, captured in the switch between the imaginary, visual, and aural registers; between the finely differentiated manuscript letters and the clearly articulated sounds, which are both, of course, merely to be imagined by the external reader.

The introductory frame narrative of *The Turn of the Screw* offers two radically opposed takes on the fantastic tale's reception by suggesting on the one hand that the fantastic tale is an object of utter shock and horror, and on the other hand an object of pure aesthetic delight. The difference is constituted in the contrast between a focus on the signified—(the object of utter horror, ugliness, and pain, Douglas's yet-untold story that appears as the thing he looks at in lieu of the first person narrator on whom he rests his gaze) and the first person narrator's experience of listening to Douglas's reading of the manuscript (which is depicted as the perception of a finely differentiated signifier). One might also capture this difference as constituted in the distinction of a reference to the signified as a totality from a process of signification over time. The actual tale thereby is situated in the space and time of the in-between, the oscillation between the signified and the signifier.

This oscillation is captured by the frame narrative in the figure of the beautiful hand, more precisely in the text's movement through the various uses of this term: as a metaphor for handwriting, as the body part that enables a moment of physical intimacy, and finally as a metaphor for a particular authorial style in the phrase "his author's hand." Douglas explains that the unforgettable tale is forever contained in his heart, but he hastens to add that it is preserved in "old faded ink and in the most beautiful hand . . . A woman's [hand]" (2). Right away, the reference to the hand marks the transition from the unmediated and not-yet-communicated signified to the conditions of the possibility of its mediation and communication. This shift in focus to the materiality of communication is accompanied by introduction of the topic of love and intimacy, which is marked as a new signified from which the text recoils with renewed attention to the materiality of communication.

Douglas recounts how as a youth on vacation from school he met his sister's governess and how an intense mutual liking developed between them. During a stroll in the garden on a hot summer's day, she told him her story. Douglas's narrative does not recount what the governess told him in their intimate conversation, which he frames as a confession of love; it breaks off with his remembrance of his shudder at hearing her tale. At this point, the frame narrative shifts back to the timing of the arrival of the governess's manuscript package and the gathered company's speculation about Douglas's love. After the package has finally arrived, he introduces his reading with a brief introductory narrative that is supposed to establish the background for the text he is about to read. He tells how the governess's new employer held her hand in gratitude for agreeing to take up the ominous task of caring for the two children, a gesture that, according to Douglas, was her only reward for her dedication. This fleeting moment of ever-so-slightly eroticized intimacy contained in the handshake between the master and the governess is furthermore adumbrated in terms of the "beauty" of her passion for her stern master, to whose "seduction" she succumbs by agreeing never to involve him in the affairs of the children.

The introductory frame narrative of *The Turn of the Screw* thus proposes a model that inserts the fantastic tale within an aesthetic program that transforms an aesthetics and poetics of shock into an aesthetics of fascination. As it elaborates the setting for the tale of unheard-of shock and horror, the frame posits the beautiful as what arises in the temporal process of the telling—as the audience's attention is drawn to the specifics of its style, and focused on its specific manner of representing something as something, which also implicitly calls attention to how it could have been represented differently. In this respect, James's tale programmatically captures exactly the self-reflexive turn to world art that Luhmann associates with realist art.

Even so, as a fantastic tale *The Turn of the Screw* also adds a particular aspect to the aesthetics of fascination, for it calls attention both to style and form and also to the negative form of the unsaid and the unobservable. The shifting blind spot of the observer is thus highly charged, inasmuch as it is coded as radical evil emerging through observation of dangerous and seductive spectral apparitions. In the unfolding of the governess's tale, what and how something is said and observed also entails attentive fascination with what cannot and must not be said and observed with regard to the two children.

The governess, initially perceiving the children as embodiments of utter innocence and beauty, takes the position of a filter or censor as she protects, educates, and forms them: "They had nothing but me, and I—well, I had *them*. It was in short a magnificent chance. This chance presented itself to me in an image richly material. I was a screen—I was to stand before them. The more I saw the less they would. I began to watch them in a stifled suspense, a disguised tension, that might well, had it continued too long, have turned to something like madness" (28). Indeed, this tension does not last, for another twist is added to it. The governess begins to suspect that little Flora sees the ghosts but dissimulates her perception of them. This perception, cast into the register of second-order observation, radically challenges the governess's attitude toward her charges as it calls into question her view of them as the embodiment of innocence and beauty. She tells the housekeeper of "what she got hold of," observing: "Why of the very things that have delighted, fascinated and yet, at bottom, as I now so strangely see, mystified and troubled me. Their more than earthly beauty, their absolutely unnatural goodness. It's a game, . . . It's a policy and a fraud!" (48).

The children are no longer the authentic, spontaneous, naïve, and innocent observers of their surroundings; instead, they are aware of being observed as observers. The governess can no longer assume that she is the only filter and control of the children's perceptions; she realizes that the children are aware of her perceptions and capable of manipulating her. Both beauty and innocence are revealed as skillfully staged. On the one hand, the governess's insight entails recognition of what it is that constitutes and conditions the attraction of something beautiful as an object of fascination, rather than an object of indifference; for what holds the attention of an observer is the specific attention to *this* form, *this* kind of observation rather than another kind of observation. On the other hand, the governess's insight specifies the nature of the beautiful and the object of fascination as a fake and applies it to her own subjectivity when she perceives the inauthentic, constructed, clever lure's ability to implicate her into the order of desire.

The Turn of the Screw frames the fantastic tale as an enigmatic signifier and highlights all the technical, narratological challenges involved in producing an artifact that fascinates its beholder or audience, that captivates attention on specific observations as form. Yet, to the extent that the vague, ill-defined, fleeting appearance of the ghosts is coded as an instance of radical evil, utter temptation, and dangerous seduction, the story's gesture of indicating (if only negatively) the unmarked state of the world in its undifferentiated, unfiltered state—the other of world art, which has been excluded from art's self-reflexive attention to stylistic beauty—is also the occasion for overwhelming shock, as it is in the early fantastic tale, while it is also framed and indicated as part of art's power of seduction and fascination. This is how Henry James concludes the "New York Preface" to the tale:

There is not only from beginning to end of the matter not an inch of expatiation, but my values are positively all blanks save so far as an excited horror, a promoted pity, a created expertness—on which punctual effects of strong causes no writer can ever fail to plume himself—proceed to read into them more or less fantastic figures. Of high interest to the author meanwhile—and by the same stroke a theme for the moralist—the artless resentful reaction of the entertained person who has abounded in the sense of the situation. He visits his abundance, morally, on the artist—who has but clung to an ideal of faultlessness. Such indeed, for this latter, are some of the observations by which the prolonged strain of that clinging may be enlivened! (123)

REFERENCE MATTER

Notes

INTRODUCTION

1. See Pierre Georges Castex, *Le conte fantastique en France de Nodier à Maupassant* (1951): "Indeed, the fantastic cannot be confused with the conventional fabulation of mythological narratives or fairy tales, which implies the transport of the mind into another world. On the contrary, the fantastic is characterized by a brutal intrusion of mystery into the realm of real life; it is generally associated with morbid states of consciousness, which, in the phenomena of nightmares or delirium, projects the images of its own anxieties or terrors before itself" (p. 8, my translation). See also Tzvetan Todorov, *The Fantastic* (1975): "In a world which is indeed our world, the one we know, a world without devils, sylphides, or vampires, there occurs an event which cannot be explained by the laws of this same familiar world. The person who experiences the event must opt for one of two possible solutions: either he is the victim of an illusion of the senses, of a product of the imagination—and laws of the world then remain what they are; or else the event has indeed taken place, it is an integral part of reality—but then this reality is controlled by laws unknown to us ... The fantastic occupies the duration of this uncertainty. Once we choose one answer or the other, we leave the fantastic for a neighboring genre, the uncanny or the marvelous" (p. 25). For a historical overview of the term and the concept, see Reimer Jehmlich, "Phantastik—Science Fiction—Utopie" (1980).

2. Marianne Wünsch, in *Die Fantastische Literatur der Frühen Moderne (1890–1930)* (1998), makes this point forcefully; see esp. pp. 63–68.

3. Bynum, "Wonder" (1997): "All theories of wonder saw it as a significance-reaction: a flooding with awe, pleasure, or dread owing to something deeper, lurking in the phenomenon. The wonderer was situated, wonder was perspectival (even if miracles were not). ... Wonder was a response to something novel and bizarre that seemed both to exceed explanation and to indicate that there might be reason (significance—not necessarily cause) behind it" (p. 24).

4. Ludwig Tieck, "Über Shakespeare's Behandlung des Wunderbaren" (1991), pp. 703–4. All translations from this essay are mine.

5. Heinrich Bosse, "The Marvelous and Romantic Semiotics" (1975).

6. Tieck, "Shakespeare's" (1991), p. 719, my translation.

7. See Tieck, "Shakespeare's," " . . . denn eben darin besteht der Probierstein des echten Genie's, daß es für jede verwegene Fiktion, für jede ungewöhnliche Vorstellungsart, schon im voraus die Täuschung des Zuschauers zu gewinnen weiß; daß der Dichter nicht unsre Gutmütigkeit in anspruch nimmt, sondern die Phantasie, selbst wider unsern Willen, so spannt, daß wir die Regeln der Ästhetik, mit allen Begriffen unsers aufgeklärteren Jahrhunderts vergessen, und uns ganz dem schönen Wahnsinn des Dichters überlassen; daß sich die Seele, nach dem Rausch, willig der Bezauberung von neuem hingibt, und die spielende Phantasie durch keine plötzliche und widrige Überraschung aus ihren Träumen geweckt wird" (p. 685).

8. See David Wellbery, *The Specular Moment* (1996), esp. chapter five, "Genius and the Wounded Subject of Modernity," pp. 121–83.

9. English translation quoted from Cazotte, *The Devil in Love* (1991), p. 108. The original passage is in Cazotte, *Le diable amoureux* (1979), p. 124.

10. Todorov, *The Fantastic*, p. 33.

11. See especially Friedrich Kittler's discussion of E.T.A. Hoffmann's "The Golden Pot" in his *Discourse Networks 1800/1900* (1990).

12. The tale's last sentence reads: "Believe me, you must form legitimate bonds with a person of the fair sex; let your estimable mother preside over your choice; and even should the one she has chosen have talents and charms divine, never would you be tempted to take her for the Devil" (Cazotte, *The Devil in Love*, 1991, p. 125).

13. Johann Gottfried Herder, "Abhandlung über den Ursprung der Sprache" (1985), esp. pp. 711ff.

14. Immanuel Kant, "Mutmaßlicher Anfang der Menschengeschichte" (1977b), pp. 87–88.

15. Philippe Pinel (1745–1826), governor of Bicêtre and director of the Salpêtrière, who, under the name of "traitement moral," had introduced a pedagogical approach to madness, describes the "aliénation mentale" primarily in Lockean terms as a chain of association that has taken a wrong course from a cognitive point of view. Johann Christian Reil (1759–1813), to argue for the "psychische Kurmethode" as opposed to physical or chemical intervention, believed that madness is the result of an imbalance between the faculties, a dominance of the active imagination over sensory perception. See Reil, *Rhapsodien über die Anwendung der psychischen Kurmethode von Geisteszerrüttungen* (1803): "daß Gefühle und Vorstellungen, kurz Erregungen der Seele, die eigenthümlichen Mittel sind, durch welche die Intemperatur der Vitaliät des Gehirns rectificiert werden müsse (p. 49) [that emotions and representations, in brief, excitations of the soul are the proper means by which the imbalance of the vitality of the brain can be rectified]," for "Je thätiger die Phantasie des Verrückten ist, desto weniger kommen die Eindrücke der Sinnorgane zum klaren Bewußtsein (p. 47) [The more active the fantasy of the mad person the less the impressions of the sensory organs will come to a clear consciousness]."

16. My understanding of the basic conceptual changes in the nineteenth-century understanding of perversion is primarily based on Arnold I. Davidson's

groundbreaking essay "How to Do the History of Psychoanalysis" (1987a). Davidson cites Dunglinson's *Medical Lexicon* after the *Oxford English Dictionary* in his essay, p. 259.

17. Krafft-Ebing, *Der Conträrsexuale vor dem Strafrichter* (1894): "In general one can say that pederasty, apart from the aforementioned conditions, is alien to homosexuality and develops, wherever else it occurs, on the ground of moral depravation, and not on the ground of neurotic degeneration, and hence is to be considered as a vice (perversity), not as an illness (perversion)" (p. 9, my translation).

18. Foucault has made the point that the modern, medicalized notion of sexuality found its first expression in the influential essay "On the Contrary Sexual Sensation," by the neurologist and psychiatrist Carl Westphal (1833–1890). In the article, Westphal analyses primarily cases of men who are attracted to the same sex and argues that same-sex desire constitutes a special type of perversion of the sexual instinct, one that is independent of any specific sexual activity but rather consists of a fundamental orientation, a specific type of desiring. See Michel Foucault, *The History of Sexuality* (1980), p. 43.

19. I am following here Davidson's argument.

20. *Herculine Barbin*, edited by Foucault (1980). See also Davidson, "Sex and the Emergence of Sexuality" (1987b).

21. My proposition that fantastic texts work with a model of subjectivity much closer to that of twentieth-century psychoanalysis than to late-eighteenth- and early-nineteenth-century psychology and psychopathology is amply supported by a wealth of psychoanalytic readings of fantastic texts, which certainly are among the most sophisticated and subtle analyses of that literary genre. See especially the readings of *Der Sandmann*, *The Purloined Letter*, and *The Turn of the Screw* by Freud, Lacan, Friedrich Kittler, Barbara Johnson, and Shoshana Felman.

22. Todorov, *The Fantastic* (1975): "[P]sychoanalysis has replaced (and thereby has made useless) the literature of the fantastic. There is no need today to resort to the devil in order to speak of an excessive sexual desire, and none to resort to vampires in order to designate the attraction exerted by corpses: psychoanalysis, and the literature which is directly or indirectly inspired by it, deal with these matters in undisguised terms. The themes of fantastic literature have become, literally, the very themes of the psychological investigations of the last fifty years" (pp. 160–61).

23. Tobin Siebers, *The Romantic Fantastic* (1984): "Fantastic representation seeks to make different and to defer human violence, to render the question of human violence irrelevant and irresolvable, and yet to maintain it in aesthetic form" (p. 74). "The fantastic cannot exist without human violence and desire, for it represents their marriage and elaboration. Exactly like the imposition of the *signum diaboli* in actual cases of historical persecution and witchcraft, fantastic representation begins by robbing the victim of her humanity" (p. 75).

24. Rosemary Jackson, *Fantasy, The Literature of Subversion* (1981), p. 176.

25. José B. Monléon, *A Specter Is Haunting Europe* (1990), p. 14.

26. Deborah A. Harter, *Bodies in Pieces* (1996), p. 2.

27. Harter's analysis of this thematics has recourse to psychoanalytical models, especially to Jacques Lacan's seminal essay on the mirror stage, without however pursuing Todorov's claim that ultimately the fantastic tale held a functionally analogous position to psychoanalysis.

28. This feature of the culture of sensibility could also be illustrated by looking to a neighboring genre of the fantastic tale: the gothic, especially the gothic novel appearing in English literary history at the same time as German literature witnessed the emergence of the fantastic tale and the *Schauerroman*, the German equivalent of the gothic novel. The gothic novel shares many features with the fantastic tale, such as flirtation with the supernatural in an otherwise realistic frame and fascination with dark secrets and criminal heroes. For the gothic novel, these features are an issue of setting, plot, and atmospherics; for the fantastic tale, they are key elements of its framing of a text-audience relationship. See also my "'To Love a Murderer'—Fantasy, Sexuality, and the Political Novel" (1996).

CHAPTER I

1. See Castex, *Le conte fantastique* (1951), pp. 36–41.

2. Dietmar Rieger, Jacques Cazotte (1969); see esp. p. 15 on the review of Cazotte's novella in *L'Année littéraire*, vol. 2, pp. 99–122 (March 7, 1772).

3. Gérard de Nerval's preface from his 1845 edition is reprinted as Appendix I in Cazotte, *Le diable amoureux*, pp. 131–76.

4. See Rieger, *Jacques Cazotte*, p. 151.

5. Cazotte, *Le diable amoureux*, p. 128, my translation. In the following pages, I cite from Judith Landry's English translation, *The Devil in Love*. This translation is based on the revised edition of 1776, but it omits Cazotte's epilogue. Page references are given immediately after a citation in parentheses, first to the translation and then to the original.

6. Lacan's models of the subject's position in the symbolic order shifted throughout his career as he also altered his models of what the psychoanalytic cure could and should achieve. For a schematic overview, see Slavoj Žižek, *The Sublime Object of Ideology* (1989), p. 133.

7. Lacan, "The Subversion of the Subject and the Dialectics of Desire" (1977), p. 312.

8. For a detailed analysis of the antitheatrical conventions of mid-eighteenth-century genre painting, see Michael Fried, *Absorption and Theatricality* (1980).

9. It is noteworthy that Lacan also distinguishes the intersubjective other from the Other (the "pure subject of modern games theory"): "But it is clear that Speech begins only with the passage from 'pretence' to the order of the signifier, and that the signifier requires another locus—the locus of the Other, the Other witness, the witness Other than any of the partners—for the Speech that it supports to be capable of lying, that is to say, of presenting itself as Truth" (pp. 304–5).

10. E.T.A. Hoffmann, "Der Elementargeist" (1992), p. 674, my translation. In

the following analysis, page references are given to this edition in parentheses, following the page reference to the English translation of "The Elementary Spirit," in *Tales from the German* (1844), although, if needed, I will substitute with my own translation.

11. See the only careful comparative study of Cazotte and Hoffmann, "Cazotte lu par E.T.A. Hoffmann," by Markus Winkler (1988), pp. 113–132. Winkler's essay points out this allusion to Kant's distinction between Enlightenment as a process and Enlightenment as a finished product. He argues that when the captain appeals to "this enlightened age," we can hear the echo of Kant's answer to the question "What is Enlightenment?" (1784; 1983). Kant begins this famous essay by answering the question "whether we now live in an enlightened age" with an emphatic "no, but in an age of Enlightenment" (p. 130).

12. The first section of Chapter Four focuses on this tale.

13. Peter von Matt, *Die Augen der Automaten* (1971), pp. 94–97.

14. See Wellbery, *The Specular Moment*, pp. 3–26, the poem, and Wellbery's translation, pp. 4–6.

15. For a discussion of Goethe's "Prometheus," see Wellbery, *The Specular Moment*, pp. 287–345.

16. D. W. Winnicott, *Playing and Reality* (1971), esp. pp. 1–52 and 95–118.

17. See von Matt, *Die Augen* (1971), p. 103.

18. Isabel Hull shows that it was not until the early nineteenth century that the second sons of the landed gentry, bureaucrats, and men of the military could choose to remain unmarried: *Sexuality, State, and Civil Society in Germany 1700–1815* (1996).

19. See Otto W. Johnston, *The Myth of a Nation* (1989), esp. chapter four, pp. 85–102.

20. Klaus Günzel, *E.T.A. Hoffmann* (1979), pp. 262ff, my translation.

21. Ibid., pp. 373–408.

22. To quote only a few examples from the "argument" in which he condemns the fact that French language and culture has been partially adopted by German speakers. See Arndt, "Über deutsche Art und das Welschtum bei uns" (n.d.): "Let us go ahead and hate the French afresh, let us hate our Frenchmen, the defilers and destroyers of our force and innocence, where we feel that they are softening and enervating our virtue and strength" (p. 139). He calls French sentiment a most dangerous, infectious plague that weakens the force of the German man (p. 148), and then he compares the teaching of French to the daughters of German citizens with a most corrupting form of whoredom and miscegenation (p. 152). See also the essay "Was müssen die Deutschen tun?" (What Must the Germans Do?) from volume three of the same edition. Whereas the earlier essay from before the liberation wars situates the French enemy outside, in the French territory, the later essay from 1818 situated the French enemy among the "Frenchified" Germans themselves.

23. Arndt, "Über deutsche," p. 139.

CHAPTER 2

1. Tieck, "Über Shakespeare's Behandlung" (1991).

2. Heinz Hillmann, "Ludwig Tieck" (1971): "Tieck, like all of his romantic fellow poets, gradually drives a certain kind of reader, the enlightened bourgeois subject, into madness. They want to make him lose the use of the only kind of approach to the world that allows him to assert himself in a reality in order to habituate him to a world in which he loses all orientation such that he lets himself be driven merely by affects like lust and horror, or even the delight in horror" (p. 120, translation mine).

3. De Quincey's translation was first published in 1825 in an extra number of *Knight's Quarterly Magazine*. It was not reprinted by De Quincey in the collective edition of his writings. In my analysis, I refer to this translation, which was reprinted together with De Quincey's praise of Tieck's achievements in *The Collected Writings of Thomas De Quincey* (1890). Frequently, though—especially in the analysis of the poems—I offer my own more literal translation.

4. The introduction to the framing narrative of Tieck's collection *Phantasus*, vol. 6, *Schriften in zwölf Bänden* (1985), pp. 11–101. All translations are mine.

5. See Thorsten Unger, "'Romantisierte Welt' als ästhetische Überwindung des Gartens" (1991).

6. See David Wellbery, *Lessing's Laocoön* (1984).

7. Tieck's early essay "On the Use of the Marvelous in *The Tempest*" (Über Shakespeare's Behandlung des Wunderbaren) demonstrates how the concept of allegory is transformed by gradual distancing from the concept of illusion that was the key to the poetics of the Enlightenment. Whereas initially this essay praises a closed, homogeneous semiotic universe as central to the poetic and dramatic illusion, it ends with praise of Shakespeare's mixed repertoire of signs that manage, especially in comedy, to combine the low and individualizing—that is, the "markers of reality"—with the supernatural and the marvelous. For the Romantic and Tieck's concept of allegory, see also Bosse, "The Marvelous and Romantic Semiotics" (1981).

8. See Ingrid Kreuzer, *Märchenform und individuelle Geschichte* (1983), pp. 157–87. Kreuzer analyses the fairy-tale form especially from the point of view of the individual character's spatial trajectory and the function of place. On the basis of this analysis, she disagrees with overly psychologizing trends in the literature on "Blond Eckbert" and asserts its generic affinity with Goethe's highly complex *Märchen*.

9. Tieck, "Der blonde Eckbert" (1985), p. 127. Page references to this edition are given in parentheses; translations are mine, unless noted otherwise. For an English translation, see Tieck, "Fair-haired Eckbert" (1983), pp. 30–46.

10. Freud, "Psycho-Analytic Notes on an Autobiographical Account of a Case of Paranoia (Dementia Paranoides)" (1959), p. 63.

11. Ibid., pp. 59–60.

12. See also Eve Sedgwick's analysis of the paranoid gothic in her *Between Men* (1985), pp. 83–117; and my "'To Love a Murderer'" (1996).

13. My translation of Freud's "Psychoanalytische Bemerkungen übereinen autobiographisch beschrieben Fall von Paranoia (Dementia paranoides)," p. 193. Or, to

invoke Freud's model of projection: the external world that is perceived as reality serves as a defense against a repressed affect, or as a coping mechanism for dealing with the results of this repression.

14. Freud, "The Uncanny" (1959).

15. Kreuzer discusses these interpretations in *Märchenform*, pp. 158–59 and notes 146 and 147.

16. For masturbation debates and theories in the eighteenth century, see Hull, *Sexuality, State, and Civil Society* (1996).

17. See Kant, "Mutmaßlicher Anfang" (1997b).

18. See Jean Laplanche, *New Foundations for Psychoanalysis* (1989), pp. 89–151.

19. To a certain extent, Laplanche's intervention is comparable to Lacan's take on castration, in which model castration is to be understood in terms of the human subject's position in language.

20. Tieck, *Schriften in zwölf Bänden*, vol. 6 (1985), p. 209. Subsequent page reference to the frame and to the story "Liebeszauber" are to this edition, in parentheses. Translations are mine unless otherwise indicated.

21. See also Jörg Born, *Texttaumel* (2000). This study analyzes Tieck's poetics of *Schwindel*, of "dizziness," and the sensation of losing firm ground in the context of Tieck's thorough familiarity with Moritz's psychology; with psychiatric, anthropological, and philosophical models of madness of its time. In comparison with certain psychoanalytic models of the unconscious, it interprets Tieck's poetics as a critical intervention in the hermeneutic dilemmas of self-observation. Born primarily engages with "Blond Eckbert" to show how this fantastic tale fundamentally undermines the program of affording comprehensive and understandable access to the human soul's particularity through a coherent autobiographical story. In spite of his references to Tieck's surprise strategies, his "suddenness," and even a discussion of shock and trauma, Born does not analyze Tieck's assessment of the reorganization of an economy of pain and pleasure.

22. According to Manfred Frank's commentary, the passage is one of the earliest uses of the term individual in its new meaning, which de Quincey translates quite appropriately as "different and distinct."

23. Andreas Gailus, "A Case of Individuality" (2000). This essay is especially pertinent to my argument for showing the impact of Moritz on the development of modern notions of the individual in terms of particular narrative genres and strategies. Gailus concludes his essay by comparing Tieck and Moritz and arguing that in some of Moritz's later texts the possibility of self-knowledge and self-narration is as seriously questioned as it is challenged by Tieck's tales.

24. See also Leo Bersani, "Sexuality and Aesthetics" (1984).

25. The connection between trauma and sexuality is discussed by Jean Laplanche and Jean-Bertrand Pontalis in "Fantasy and the Origins of Sexuality" (1986).

26. See Laplanche, *Life and Death in Psychoanalysis* (1985).

27. For an excellent discussion of this phase in the discursive history of perversion, see Davidson, "How to Do the History of Psychoanalysis" (1987a).

28. Edgar Allan Poe, "The Imp of the Perverse" (1976), p. 268. In notes and chapter, references to this text are given in parentheses.

29. For a discussion of Poe's intervention in the sensationalism of his contemporaries, see Jonathan Elmer, chapter two, "Poe, Sensationalism, and the Sentimental Tradition" in *Reading at the Social Limit* (1995), pp. 93–125; for specific discussion of "The Imp of the Perverse" as a destabilization of the Cartesian model of the subject by way of the clash between the I of the utterance and the I of the statement, see chapter three of the same book, "Confessing the Crime of Confession," pp. 126–73.

CHAPTER 3

1. For the legal debate in German-speaking territories, see Ylva Greve, "Die Unzurechnungsfähigkeit in der 'Criminalpsychologie' des 19. Jahrhunderts" (1998).

2. See Wulf Segebrecht, "E.T.A. Hoffmanns Auffassung vom Richteramt und vom Dichterberuf" (1967), p. 98. References to this article are given in parentheses. All translations are mine. See also Jutta Kolkenbrock-Netz, "Wahnsinn der Vernunft—juristische Institution—literarische Praxis" (1985).

3. Segebrecht, who published this material in the interest of demonstrating continuity in Hoffmann's perspective as poet and judge, sees proof in the statement quoted in text that Hoffmann's career does not exhibit a split between the rationalist, pragmatic judge on the one hand and the artist who seeks out the complexity and ambiguity of reality on the other. Instead, Segebrecht emphasizes that for Hoffmann the judge, reality is just as problematic as it is for Hoffmann the artist.

4. Translated from the Latin: "amentia occulta est nisus et conatus animi oppressi ad actionem violentam, hanc actionem secreto appetentis et molientis tanquam suae oppressionis levamen et liberationem." The part of the document written by Schmolling's defense lawyer also cites Platner from Merzdorff's expertise: "Est quoddam genus amentiae, reconditum quidem et imo pectore inclusum, inopinato ac subito erumpens, atque tum a memoriae et judicii usu, tum ab omne reliqua vitae actione ita quasi disjunctum et separatum, ut nullis externis notis, scilicet causa et vis morbi, profundius latet, neque futurum provideri, neque praesens cognosci queat. Sed tamen vera haec insania est, quae in causa capitali necessarium argumentum afferat absolutionis etc." (Segebrecht, p. 108).

5. Hoffmann's refusal to concede to the opinion of the medical expert in this case, though not entirely unusual for its time, was nevertheless already perceived as highly problematic. Julius Hitzig, a personal friend of Hoffmann's, a fellow lawyer and legal scholar, and also his first biographer, felt that Hoffmann clearly overstepped the boundaries of his office by engaging in lengthy debate over the validity of psychiatric models. This criticism led Hitzig to publish all the documents of the Schmolling case in his journal on criminal law. One might say the Schmolling case became a symptom of how the juridical system was about to lose some of its territory to the truth-finding methods of the emerging science of psychiatry.

6. See Segebrecht's conclusion, pp. 134–8.

7. My analysis of "Das Fräulein von Scuderi" is greatly indebted to Friedrich A. Kittler, "Eine Detektivgeschichte der ersten Detektivgeschichte" (1991). In the secondary literature about this tale, there has been ongoing debate over whether Hoffmann's tale should be counted as a detective story or whether Poe should be considered the first writer of detective fiction, since Scudéri's conviction of the chief suspect's innocence relies entirely on her intuition and since she does not deploy the methods of detection and rational reconstruction that become the typical markers of the detective. See, for instance, Christopher A. Lee, "E.T.A. Hoffmann's 'Mademoiselle de Scudéry' as a Forerunner of the Detective Story" (1994), and Sheila Dickson, "Devil's Advocate? The Artistic Detective in E.T.A. Hoffmann's 'Das Fräulein von Scuderi'" (1993).

8. In this context, see Yvonne Holbeche, "The Relationship of the Artist to Power" (1980). Holbeche argues that Hoffmann's story exemplifies the Romantics' yearning to leave the position of the socially isolated artist.

9. Hoffmann, "Das Fräulein von Scuderi: Erzählung aus dem Zeitalter Ludwig des Vierzehnten" (1992), pp. 818–19. References to this edition are given in parentheses, along with references to "Mademoiselle de Scudéri" in *Selected Writings of E.T.A. Hoffmann* (1969); the extract appearing here is on pp. 243–44, the translation slightly modified.

10. It is primarily in this respect that my analysis of the story departs from Friedrich Kittler's seminal reading. Whereas he depicts Scudéri primarily as a maternal figure and plays down her role as an artist, I emphasize this role as essential to the transformation she undergoes from witty and précieuse courtier to insightful psychologist to the fully fledged embodiment of the catalyzing power of the artist.

11. In his commentary on the tale, Lothar Pikulik also isolates this passage and remarks that the old lady's speech renders the king into a helpless victim of her magical poetic power, just as he is seduced by the magical image of the beautiful Madelon at the end of her speech. See Pikulik's *E.T.A. Hoffmann als Erzähler* (1987), p. 172.

12. This aspect is of particular interest to readings that portray Hoffmann's story as an artist's novella. For a psychoanalytical interpretation along these lines, see Peter Schneider, "Verbrechen, Künstlertum und Wahnsinn (1980).

13. This, however, is exactly the model of sexuality and the emergence of the unconscious proposed by psychoanalytic theory and most succinctly formulated by Jean Laplanche in his "General Theory of Seduction." See Laplanche, *New Foundations* (1989), pp. 89–151.

14. See K. E. Rothschuh, *Geschichte der Physiologie* (1953), pp. 68–123; and Elizabeth Williams, *The Physical and the Moral* (1994).

15. For a detailed discussion of the Pygmalion myth, see Inka Mülder-Bach, "Im Zeichen Pygmalions" (1995). See also my "Pygmalion's Dream in Herder's Aesthetics, or Male Narcissism as the Model for Bildung" (1989).

16. Herder, "Plastik" (1892), p. 25.

17. Ibid., p. 60.

18. Hoffmann, "Die Automate" (1992), pp. 397–99. Quoted from "Automata" in *The Best Tales of Hoffmann* (1967), pp. 79–80, translation slightly modified. Page numbers to the English translation, followed by the German, are provided, although sometimes I will offer my own translation.

19. This is, moreover, perfectly in accord with Herder's philosophy of language. To be more precise, what is excluded is the materiality of the signifier. Herder states elsewhere that even the lonely man in the woods, without ever having uttered a single word, would have had language, because for him language means the soul's ability to function as an organized system that apprehends and creates its environment through its ability and freedom to perceive it.

20. "Remember well, when I have to die, how much this faithful soul has loved you. If the cold ashes can still feel love I shall still love you in the urn."

21. There was an actual historical Lazzaro Spallanzani (1729–1799), a famous physiologist at the University of Padua. He might well have informed Hoffmann's character of the professor in "Der Sandmann." In the same tale, in the optician's advertisements of spectacles as "Oken," there might be a reference to Lorenz Oken (1779–1851), the founder of the German society of physiology.

22. On Hoffmann's reception of Schelling's, and Schubert's, idealism, see William Arctander O'Brien, "E.T.A. Hoffmann's Critique of Idealism" (1989).

23. See Slavoj Žižek, *Looking Awry* (1992).

24. See, for instance, Gotthold Ephraim Lessing, Moses Mendelssohn, and Friedrich Nicolai, *Briefwechsel über das Trauerspiel* (1972), pp. 103ff. Lessing uses the model of resonance excitation to distinguish between "contact" (Berührung) and "movement" (Bebung), between direct physical contact and the affect of pity. Precisely this distinction drops out for Hoffmann.

25. On eighteenth-century theories of nerve stimulation, see G. J. Barker-Benfield, *The Culture of Sensibility* (1992), pp. 1–36.

CHAPTER 4

1. See Klaus Theweleit, *Orpheus und Eurydike* (1989).

2. For Gautier's relationship to Mesmerism, see Georges Poulet, *Études sur le temps humain* (1949), pp. 291–317.

3. See William Crisman, "E.T.A. Hoffmann's 'Einsiedler Serapion' and 'Rat Krespel' as Models of Reading" (1986). Crisman presents an extensive overview and discussion of the secondary literature on these two tales. According to him, it is neither the mad narrator of the novellas (Serapion) nor the accomplished raconteur Krespel who serves as a particular poetic ideal but rather the actual narrators in the stories, Cyprian and Theodor (named only in the frame narrative)—more precisely, their learning process as narratees—that is to be understood in a programmatic fashion, defining the collection *Die Serapions-Brüder*.

4. The tale has no title. I refer to it as "Serapion" and translate and give page references to the German edition, *E.T.A. Hoffmann: Die Serapions-Brüder* (1992); here, p. 33.

5. Friedrich Kittler, "Autorschaft ist Liebe" (1980). See also Heinrich Bosse, *Autorschaft ist Werkherrschaft* (1981).

6. "Rat Krespel," in *Sämtliche Werke in Sechs Bänden*, vol. 4 (1992), p. 47. Page references to this edition are given in parentheses, following the page reference to the English translation of "Councillor Krespel," in *Selected Writings of E. T. A. Hoffmann* (1969), here p. 174.

7. For a detailed analysis of *Käthchen von Heilbronn* along these lines, see Chris Cullens and Dorothea von Mücke, "Käthchen von Heilbronn" (1997).

8. Gabriele Brandstetter argues that this story exemplifies Hoffmann's model of the artist's muse. Krespel uses Antonia's illness as an excuse to prevent her from being an active artist on her own terms and in her mother's footsteps, to keep her all to himself and to substitute his instrument, the violin, for her voice. See Brandstetter's "Die Stimme und das Instrument" (1988), pp. 15–38.

9. See Georges Poulet's chapter on Gautier, which emphasizes the particular escape from temporality and historicity that Gautier's fiction and aesthetics aim at. Poulet also traces how Gautier was influenced by the translation of Hoffmann into French in the 1830s, the translations of Goethe's *Faust I* and *Faust II*, de Quincey's *Confessions of an Opium Eater*, and his own experiments with drugs and interest in Mesmerism.

10. Since she is frequently likened to a work of art, one might be tempted to read Gautier's tales in the context of the Pygmalion thematics. See, for instance, Ross Chambers, "Gautier et le complexe de Pygmalion" (1972); and Annie Ubersfeld, "Théophile Gautier ou le regard de Pygmalion" (1989).

11. In an excellent chapter on Gautier's use of the fantastic, Pierre-André Rieben characterizes Gautier's typical plot structure in terms of a tripartite schema: (1) a stable order of reality; (2) perturbation of this stable order, involving a new order of perception or transformation of the prior order; and (3) a return to the first stable reality, frequently accompanied by a sense of loss or resignation. See Rieben, *Délires Romantiques* (1989), pp. 95–96.

12. Gautier, "La morte amoureuse" (1901), p. 119. Page references to this edition are given in parentheses, following the page references to the English translation of Gautier, "The Dead Leman" (1970), here pp. 179–80.

13. *La Presse*, Feb. 10, 1849, quoted in Robert Snell, *Théophile Gautier* (1982), p. 147.

14. Snell, pp. 145–46.

15. On Gautier's admiration for sculpture, see Snell, pp. 111–21.

16. See Caroline Walker Bynum, chapter two, "Metamorphosis, or Gerald and the Werewolf," pp. 77–109, and chapter four, "Shape and Story," pp. 176–81, in *Metamorphosis and Identity* (2001).

17. See Raymond Giraud, "Winckelmann's Part in Gautier's Perception of Natural Beauty" (1967), p. 172.

18. Poe, "The Philosophy of Composition" (1965), p. 201.

19. See Elisabeth Bronfen, "Risky Resemblances" (1992); Joan Dayan, "Con-

vertibility and the Woman as Medium" (1987); Elmer, "Poe, Sensationalism, and the Sentimental Tradition" in *Reading at the Social Limit* (1995) pp. 93–125; and Clark Griffith, "Poe's 'Ligeia' and the English Romantics" (1985), pp. 71–80.

20. For a study of Poe's literary production and his attitude toward the changing book and magazine culture in America, see Kevin J. Hays, *Poe and the Printed Word* (2000). Though Hays does not mention "Ligeia," the text was written in that period during which Poe radically revised his position toward book culture: "The year the *Tales of the Grotesque and Arabesque* appeared, pamphlet novels began being published. The importance of the pamphlet novel to Poe's literary career cannot be underestimated. The new format forced Poe to question the value of separately published books[. . . .]Poe's disgust with the pamphlet novel coincided with his growing uncertainty about the aesthetic value of the book-length narrative[. . . .]Early on, Poe eschewed periodical publication, which others, including his own brother Henry Poe, took advantage of, but Poe eventually came to champion the periodical. To him, the magazine, not the book, became the vehicle for serious, important literature[. . . .]" (p. 114).

21. Page references in text are to Poe, "Ligeia" (1965); this passage is on pages 248–49.

22. Gerhart von Graevenitz, *Das Ornament des Blicks* (1994), pp. 13–19.

23. Whenever writing is understood as a cultural technique of preserving and transmitting meaning, the materiality of writing is merely virtual materiality; although some material support is certainly needed to inscribe and preserve writing, its actual concrete nature is largely irrelevant. For writing to mean anything, it suffices that it partake of an internally coherent system of differential marks that can be read. Whether we are dealing with printed letters on paper, painted signs on silk or parchment, electromagnetic signals, or engravings in stone seems to matter little. Moreover, as soon as writing is linked with reading, as soon as the differential marks make sense, the external sensory perception of the characters can be replaced by merely imagined sense perception. The question of writing's material sensuousness is displaced when we attend to the sight, sound, taste, or feeling of the immaterial signified. One realm of senses gives way to another, and the text as such disappears. But this transparency is historical. It is especially within the domain of print culture that the activities of reading and sense-making tend to render the medium of writing transparent.

Oddly, perhaps, it is only when the materiality of the textual surface is flawed, wounded, or interrupted that we can think about it. Whenever writing is undecipherable, owing to some physical distortion or damage done to the characters or the surface of inscription, or thanks to the reader's ignorance of the code, the elements of writing are foregrounded in terms of their physical features. The written text might appear as a pattern or differentiated surface that nevertheless remains an enigma. In the case of undecipherability, when a particular artifact resists a decoding effort, we encounter writing as a specific instance. This particularity is, indeed, the materiality of the script. The aesthetic domain shares with the domain of the undecipherable a tendency to foreground instances of the medium's opacity. Under certain historical circumstances, this opacity becomes available for its own elaboration.

24. I owe this insight to the brilliant study by von Graevenitz about Goethe's poetics of the arabesque in his West-östlicher Divan. Von Graevenitz traces the history of the ornament and the arabesque in the visual arts and relates it to the history of print technology. Whereas the first part of his book demonstrates how this history illustrates the imaginary materiality of the signifier, the second part proceeds to show how Goethe's poetics of the arabesque draws on and elaborates this history. See von Graevenitz (1994), pp. 19–24.

CHAPTER 5

1. For a very different reading of why and how Arnim constructs a political utopia with the aid of historical references to Charles V, see Friedrich Strack, "Das 'Wunder' der Geschichte und die 'Wahrheit' der Sagen" (1994). According to Strack, the key to the utopian/historical aspect of the story lies with Charles and the son of Charles. He makes much of the fact that Isabella's son, Lrak, is merely mentioned but not of further relevance. Instead there is mention of a late love affair of Charles with a harpist. Strack traces this reference and argues that the son of that liaison, Don Juan d'Austria, can be considered a figure of redemption because in the battle of Lepanto in 1571 he freed the Occident of the Turkish threat.

By contrast, Ludwig Völker, "Naturpoesie, Phantasie, Phantastik" (1979), clearly situates the utopian aspect with Isabella. However, according to Völker, Isabella embodies primarily an idealized vision, the purity of love, the redemptive potential of fantasy that was crucial for the early Romantics. For Völker, Isabella does not embody any concrete political ideas.

2. Frances A. Yates, in *Astraea* (1993), describes the importance of Charles in these words: "It is precisely as a phantom that Charles's empire was of importance, because it raised again the imperial idea and spread it through Europe in the symbolism of its propaganda, and that at a time when the more advanced political thinking was discrediting it" (p. 1).

3. For Arnim's concern with constitution making, see Jürgen Knaack, *Achim von Arnim—Nicht nur Poet* (1976), pp. 45–54, and also 35–38.

4. See also Gisela Henckmann, "'Vielleicht beginnt nun bald die Zeit der Frauen'" (1994).

5. Arnim, "Isabella von Ägypten" (1990), pp. 743–44, my translation.

6. Arnim, "Isabella of Egypt" (1997), pp. 53–54; German, p. 688.

7. Foucault, *The History of Sexuality* (1980).

8. Foucault, "Omnis et singulatim" (1981).

9. See Hans Kohn, *Prelude to Nation-States* (1967), especially his chapters "Romanticism and the Rise of German Nationalism," pp. 168–86; "The Romantic Concepts of History, State, and Liberty," pp. 187–93; and "Adam Müller and Heinrich von Kleist," pp. 194–202. Kohn tells a wonderful anecdote: "When Gneisenau

submitted to the King plans for a popular insurrection and suggested in his memorandum of August 8, 1811, that the clergymen in the countryside, recalling the religious struggles of the Maccabees, should preach a crusade against France, the King noted in the margin of the memorandum, "good as Poetry'" (p. 218).

10. For discussion of the politics and goals of the "Christlich-Deutshe Tischgesellschaft," see Knaack (1976), pp. 35–38. Knaack corrects the traditional cliché of the Tischgesellschaft as an assembly of reactionary forces of the old aristocracy opposed to the reforms of Stein. He shows that Arnim had invited a varied group of men having very divergent political outlooks. The purpose of the Tischgesellschaft, according to Knaack, was not a sort of party assembly but rather a model or experiment as to how a diverse group of people can freely write themselves laws and found a constitution. Knaack does not address Arnim's anti-Semitism at all.

11. See Knaak, p. 43.

12. This is how Arnim (1990) draws attention to the contrast between the Grimms' approach and his own to legendary and historical material:

> In Eurem Geist hat sich die Sagenwelt
> Als ein geschloss'nes Ganze schon gesellt,
> Mein Buch dagegen glaubt, daß viele Sagen
> In unsern Zeiten erst recht wieder tragen,
> Und viele sich der Zukunft erst enthüllen,
> Nun prüfet, ob es Euch das kann erfüllen. (616)

[In your spirit the world of legends/has gathered itself into a closed whole./My book however believes that many legends/are especially appropriate for our times/ and many are only revealed to the future/now you should see whether it can fulfill this for you.]

13. Knaak's account of the political agenda of the Tischgesellschaft entirely ignores the extraordinary force and violence of Arnim's anti-Semitism, expressed in what was then an unpublished speech to the Tischgesellschaft about "The Hidden Markers of the Jews." For analysis of this speech, see Heinz Härtl, "Romantischer Antisemitismus" (1987). Although Härtl calls Arnim's speech at the Tischgesellschaft the most extreme and worst kind of anti-Semitism of its time, he sees a stark contrast between Arnim's position in the Tischgesellschaft, with its intended political model, and the position Arnim holds in his fiction at the same time. My reading differs in this respect, since I want to argue that there is a systematic connection between the Tischgesellschaft politics and the novella collection, one that has to do with the pseudoEucharistic model of representation that also informs the political model of representation of the constitution of the people in terms of an ethnic, racial, and blood connection or bond. For another, rather apologetic account of Arnim's anti-Semitism, see Henckmann, "Das Problem des 'Antisemitismus' bei Achim von Arnim" (1986).

14. For the history of the proto-national socialist uses of the folk, of race, and of the nation in the nineteenth century, see also Günter Hartung, "Völkische Ide-

ologie" (1987). Hartung argues that even though in the 1850s nationalist uses of the idea of the folk had their anti-Jewish tendencies, this form of discrimination and defamation of Jews still constructed Jewishness primarily as a religious and cultural identity. Gobineau's theory of racism from the 1850s had no anti-Semitic elements. Hartung situates the racial definition of Jews in the 1870s. In this sense, Arnim's obsession with the "hidden markers of the Jews" can be called indeed a racist anti-Semitism *avant la lettre*.

15. For an analysis of Achim von Arnim's anti-Semitism as an integral aspect of his national patriotism, see also Ethel Matala de Mazza, "Brot und Wein" (1999).

16. Arnim, "Versöhnung in der Sommerfrische" (1990), pp. 574–75. Not in English translation.

17. See A. W. Raitt's chapter eight, "Inspector-General," in his biography *Prosper Mérimée* (1970), pp. 137–54.

18. See Raitt, p. 197.

19. Prosper Mérimée, "Colomba" (1957), pp. 477–78, my translation.

20. Mérimée, "Carmen" (1957), p. 622, my translation.

21. Alain Schnapp, *The Discovery of the Past* (1996), p. 294.

22. Mérimée, "The Venus of Ille" (1995), pp. 64–65, translation slightly modified; "La Vénus d'Ille" (1957), pp. 410–11.

23. See Michael Camille, *The Gothic Idol* (1989). He concludes his analysis of Gothic representations of Mary, "Virgin or Venus? The Gothic Goddess 'Comes to Life'," with a discussion of the multiple versions of the legend that also underlie Mérimée's story, a crucial episode in Lewis's gothic novel *The Monk* and another fantastic tale, Eichendorff's "Das Marmorbild" (The Marble Statue): namely, the story about a young man affianced to a statue that came to life. In some versions of the story (the older ones), the statue in question is a Venus; in others it is the Virgin Mary. The young man puts his ring onto her hand while he is playing football. On the young man's wedding night, the older version has the demonic love goddess (the younger ones have the Mother of God) interposing herself between bride and bridegroom (p. 239).

24. For the most extensive psychoanalytical reading along these lines, see Jacques Chabot, *L'autre moi* (1983), pp. 121–58. See also the introduction by Antonia Fony to her edition of *La Vénus d'Ille et autres nouvelles* (1982), pp. 5–24.

EPILOGUE

1. Niklas Luhmann, "Weltkunst" (1990).
2. Henry James, *The Turn of the Screw* (1966), p. 1.

Works Cited

Arndt, Ernst Moritz. "Über deutsche Art und das Welschtum bei uns." In *Sämtliche Werke*, ed. August Leffson and Wilhelm Steffens, vol. 11, *Geist der Zeit* 4, 129–57. Berlin: Deutsches Verlagshaus, 1912.

———. "Was müssen die Deutschen tun?" In *Sämtliche Werke*, ed. August Leffson and Wilhelm Steffens, vol. 3, 261–311. Berlin: Deutsches Verlaghaus, 1912.

Arnim, Achim von. "Isabella of Egypt: Emperor Charles V's First Love (A Narrative)." In *Ludwig Achim von Arnim's Novellas of 1812*, trans. Bruce Duncan, 5–95. Lampeter, Wales: Edwin Mellen Press, 1997.

———. "Isabella von Ägypten, Kaiser Karl des Fünften erste Jugendliebe." In *Werke in sechs Bänden*, ed. Roswitha Burwick et al. Vol. 3, *Sämtliche Erzählungen 1802–1817*, ed. Renate Moering, 622–744. Frankfurt am Main: Deutscher Klassiker Verlag, 1990.

———. "Versöhnung in der Sommerfrische." In *Werke in sechs Bänden*, ed. Roswitha Burwick et al. Vol. 3, *Sämtliche Erzählungen 1802–1817*, ed. Renate Moering, 541–609. Frankfurt am Main: Deutscher Klassiker Verlag, 1990.

Barker-Benfield, G. J. *The Culture of Sensibility*. Chicago: University of Chicago Press, 1992.

Bersani, Leo. "Sexuality and Aesthetics." *October* 28 (1984): 27–42.

Born, Jörg. *Texttaumel: Poetologische Inversionen von "Spätaufklärung" und "Frühromantik" bei Ludwig Tieck*. Heidelberg: Winter 2000.

Bosse, Heinrich. *Autorschaft ist Werkherrschaft: Über die Entstehung des Urheberrechts aus dem Geist der Goethezeit*. Paderborn: Schoningh, 1981.

———. "The Marvelous and Romantic Semiotics." *Studies in Romanticism* 14, no. 3 (1975): 211–36.

Brandstetter, Gabriele. "Die Stimme und das Instrument—Mesmerismus als Poetik in E.T.A. Hoffmann's 'Rat Krespel.'" In *Jacques Offenbachs "Hoffmanns Erzählungen." Konzeption—Rezeption—Dokumentation*, ed. Gabriele Brandstetter, 15–38. Laaber: Laaber Verlag, 1988.

Bronfen, Elisabeth. "Risky Resemblances." In *Over Her Dead Body*, 324–48. New York: Routledge, 1992.

Bynum, Caroline Walker. "Metamorphosis, or Gerald and the Werewolf." In *Metamorphosis and Identity*, chap. 2, 77–109. New York: Zone Books, 2001.

———. "Shape and Story." In *Metamorphosis and Identity*, chap. 4, 176–81. New York: Zone Books, 2001.

———. "Wonder." *American Historical Review* 102, no. 1 (February 1997): 24.

Camille, Michael. *The Gothic Idol*. Cambridge: Cambridge University Press, 1989.

Castex, Pierre Georges. *Le conte fantastique en France de Nodier à Maupassant*. Paris: José Corti, 1951.

Cazotte, Jacques. *The Devil in Love*, trans. Judith Landry, intro. by Brian Stableford. London: Dedalus, 1991.

———. *Le diable amoureux*. Paris: Garnier Flammarion, 1979.

Chabot, Jacques. *L'autre moi: Fantasmes et fantastique dans les nouvelles de Mérimée*. Aix-en-Provence: Édisud, 1983.

Chambers, Ross. "Gautier et le complexe de Pygmalion." *Revue d'Histoire Littéraire de la France* (72e Ann.), 72 (1972): 641–58.

Crisman, William. "E.T.A. Hoffmann's 'Einsiedler Serapion' and 'Rat Krespel' as Models of Reading." *Journal of English and Germanic Philology* 81, no. 1 (January 1986): 50–69.

Cullens, Chris, and Dorothea von Mücke. "Käthchen von Heilbronn: Ein Kind recht nach der Lust Gottes—oder die Macht und Religion der Sexualität." In *Kleists Dramen: Neue Interpretationen*, ed. Walter Hinderer, 116–43. Stuttgart: Reclam Verlag, 1997.

Davidson, Arnold I. "How to Do the History of Psychoanalysis: A Reading of Freud's *Three Essays on the Theory of Sexuality*." *Critical Inquiry* 13, no. 2 (winter 1987a): 252–77.

———. "Sex and the Emergence of Sexuality." *Critical Inquiry* 14, no. 1 (autumn 1987b): 16–48.

Dayan, Joan. "Convertibility and the Woman as Medium." In *Fables of Mind*, 133–92. New York: Oxford University Press, 1987.

De Quincey, Thomas. *Confessions of an Opium Eater*. In *The Collected Writings of Thomas De Quincey*, ed. David Masson, vol. 3, *Tales and Romances*, 207–449. Edinburgh: Adam and Charles Black, 1890.

Dickson, Sheila. "Devil's Advocate? The Artistic Detective in E.T.A. Hoffmann's 'Das Fräulein von Scuderi.'" *Forum for Modern Language Studies* 29, no. 3 (July 1993): 246–56.

Elmer, Jonathan. *Reading at the Social Limit: Affect, Mass Culture, and Edgar Allan Poe*. Stanford: Stanford University Press, 1995.

Fony, Antonia. "Introduction." In *La Vénus d'Ille et autres nouvelles*, by Prosper Mérimée. Paris: Garnier Flammarion, 1982.

Foucault, Michel. *The History of Sexuality*, trans. Robert Hurley. New York: Vintage, 1980.

———. "Omnis et singulatim: Towards a Critique of 'Political Reason.'" In *The Tanner Lectures on Human Value II*, ed. Sterling McMurrin. Salt Lake City: University of Utah, 1981.

———, ed. *Herculine Barbin*. New York: Pantheon, 1980.

Freud, Sigmund. "Psycho-Analytic Notes on an Autobiographical Account of a Case of Paranoia (Dementia Paranoides)." In *The Standard Edition of the Complete Psychological Works of Sigmund Freud*, trans. James Strachey, vol. 12, 3–82. London: Hogarth Press and Institute of Psycho-Analysis, 1959.

———. "Psychoanalytische Bemerkungen über einen autobiographisch beschrieben Fall von Paranoia (Dementia paranoides)." In *Studienausgabe*, ed. Alexander Mitscherlich et al., vol. 7, *Zwang, Paranoia und Perversion*, 135–203. Frankfurt am Main: Fischer, 1982.

———. "The Uncanny." In *The Standard Edition of the Complete Psychological Works by Sigmund Freud*, trans. James Strachey, vol. 17, 218–52. London: Hogarth Press and Institute of Psycho-Analysis, 1959.

Fried, Michael. *Absorption and Theatricality: Painting and Beholder in the Age of Diderot*. Berkeley: University of California Press, 1980.

Gailus, Andreas. "A Case of Individuality: Karl Philipp Moritz and the *Magazine for Empirical Psychology*." *New German Critique* 79 (2000): 67–105.

Gautier, Théophile. "La morte amoureuse." In *Récits fantastiques*. Chronology, introduction, and notes by Marc Eigeldinger, 117–50. Paris: Garnier Flammarion, 1901.

———. "The Dead Leman." In *Théophile Gautier's Short Stories: The Fleece of Gold, The Dead Leman, Poems, etc.*, trans. George Burnham Ives, 173–244. First publication 1903; Freeport, N.Y.: Books for Libraries Press, 1970 (reprint).

Giraud, Raymond. "Winckelmann's Part in Gautier's Perception of Natural Beauty." *Yale French Studies* 38 (1967): 172–82.

Graevenitz, Gerhart von. *Das Ornament des Blicks: Über die Grundlagen des neuzeitlichen Sehens, die Poetik der Arabeske und Goethes "West-östlicher Divan."* Stuttgart: Metzler, 1994.

Greve, Ylva. "Die Unzurechnungsfähigkeit in der 'Criminalpsychologie' des 19. Jahrhunderts." In *Unzurechnungsfähigkeiten: Diskursivierungen unfreier Bewußtseinszustände seit dem 18. Jahrhundert*, ed. Michael Niehaus and Hans-Walter Schmidt-Hannisa, 107–32. Frankfurt am Main: Peter Lang, 1998.

Griffith, Clark. "Poe's 'Ligeia' and the English Romantics." In *Edgar Allan Poe*, ed. Harold Bloom, 71–80. New York: Chelsea House, 1985.

Günzel, Klaus. *E.T.A. Hoffmann: Leben und Werk in Briefen, Selbstzeugnissen und Zeitdokumenten*. Berlin: Claasen, 1979.

Harter, Deborah A. *Bodies in Pieces: Fantastic Narrative and the Poetics of the Fragment.* Stanford: Stanford University Press, 1996.
Härtl, Heinz. "Romantischer Antisemitismus: Arnim und die 'Tischgesellschaft.'" *Weimarer Beiträge* 33, no. 7 (1987): 1159–73.
Hartung, Günter. "Völkische Ideologie." *Weimarer Beiträge* 33, 7 (1987): 1176–85.
Hays, Kevin J. *Poe and the Printed Word.* Cambridge: Cambridge University Press, 2000.
Henckmann, Gisela. "Das Problem des 'Antisemitismus' bei Achim von Arnim." *Aurora* 46 (1986): 48–69.
———. "'Vielleicht beginnt nun bald die Zeit der Frauen': Zum emanzipatorischen Aspekt der Frauengestaltung und Geschlechterdifferenz im Werk Achims von Arnim." In *Grenzgänge: Studien zu L. Achim von Arnim*, ed. Michael Andermatt, 79–102. Bonn: Bouvier, 1994.
Herder, Johann Gottfried. "Abhandlung über den Ursprung der Sprache." In *Johann Gottfried Herder Frühe Schriften 1764–1772*, ed. Ulrich Gaier, 695–810. Frankfurt am Main: Deutscher Klassiker Verlag, 1985.
———. "Plastik: Einige Wahrnehmungen über Form und Gestalt aus Pygmalions bildendem Traume." In *Herders Sämmtliche Werke*, ed. Bernhard Suphan, vol. 8, 1–87. Berlin: Weidmannsche Buchhandlung, 1892.
Hillmann, Heinz. "Ludwig Tieck." In *Deutsche Dichter der Romantik: Ihr Leben und Werk*, ed. Benno von Wiese, 111–34. Berlin: Schmidt, 1971.
Hoffmann, E.T.A. "Automata." *The Best Tales of Hoffmann*, ed. E. F. Bleier, 78–102. New York: Dover, 1967.
———. "Die Automate." In *Sämtliche Werke in sechs Bänden*, ed. Wulf Segebrecht et al., vol. 4, *E.T.A. Hoffmann: Die Serapions-Brüder*, 396–429. Frankfurt am Main: Deutscher Klassiker Verlag, 1992.
———. "Councillor Krespel." In *Selected Writings of E.T.A. Hoffmann*, ed. and trans. Leonard J. Kent and Elizabeth C. Knight, vol. 1, *The Tales*, 168–88. Chicago: University of Chicago Press, 1969.
———. "Der Elementargeist." In *Sämtliche Werke in sechs Bänden*, ed. Wulf Segebrecht et al., vol. 5, *E.T.A. Hoffmann: Lebens-Ansichten des Katers Murr, Werke 1820–1821*, ed. Hartmut Steinecke, 659–707. Frankfurt am Main: Deutscher Klassiker Verlag, 1992.
———. "The Elementary Spirit." In *Tales from the German*, trans. John Oxenford and C. A. Feiling, 268–98. London: Chapman and Hall, 1844.
———. "Das Fräulein von Scuderi: Erzählung aus dem Zeitalter Ludwig des Vierzehnten." In *Sämtliche Werke in sechs Bänden*, ed. Wulf Segebrecht et al., vol. 4, *E.T.A. Hoffmann: Die Serapions-Brüder*, 780–853. Frankfurt am Main: Deutscher Klassiker Verlag, 1992.
———. "Mademoiselle de Scudéri: A Tale of the Times of Louis XIV." In *Selected*

Writings of E.T.A. Hoffmann, ed. and trans. Leonard J. Kent and Elizabeth C. Knight, vol. 1, *The Tales*, 213–71. Chicago: University of Chicago Press, 1969.

———. "Rat Krespel." In *Sämtliche Werke in sechs Bänden*, ed. Wulf Segebrecht et al., vol. 4, *E.T.A. Hoffmann: Die Serapions-Brüder*, 39–64. Frankfurt am Main: Deutscher Klassiker Verlag, 1992.

———. "Serapion" [untitled]. In *Sämtliche Werke in sechs Bänden*, ed. Wulf Segebrecht et al., vol. 4, *E.T.A. Hoffmann: Die Serapions-Brüder*, 23–37. Frankfurt am Main: Deutscher Klassiker Verlag, 1992.

Holbeche, Yvonne. "The Relationship of the Artist to Power: E.T.A. Hoffmann's 'Das Fräulein von Scuderi.'" *Seminar* 16 (1980): 1–11.

Hull, Isabel. *Sexuality, State, and Civil Society in Germany 1700–1815*. Ithaca: Cornell University Press, 1996.

Jackson, Rosemary. *Fantasy, The Literature of Subversion*. New York: Methuen, 1981.

James, Henry. *The Turn of the Screw*, ed. Robert Kimbrough. New York: Norton, 1966.

Jehmlich, Reimer. "Phantastik—Science Fiction—Utopie: Begriffsgeschichte und Begriffsabgrenzung." In *Phantastik in Literatur und Kunst*, ed. Christian W. Thomsen and Jens Malte Fischer, 9–33. Darmstadt: Wissenschaftliche Buchgesellschaft, 1980.

Johnston, Otto W. *The Myth of a Nation: Literature and Politics in Prussia under Napoleon*. Columbia, S.C.: Camden House, 1989.

Kant, Immanuel. "An Answer to the Question: What Is Enlightenment?" In *Perpetual Peace and Other Essays on Politics, History, and Morals*, trans. with intro. by Ted Humphrey, 41–48. Indianapolis: Hackett, 1983.

———. "Beantwortung der Frage: Was ist Aufklärung?" In *Werkausgabe*, vol. 11, *Schriften zur Anthropologie, Geschichtsphilosophie, Politik und Pädagogik 1*, ed. Wilhelm Weischedel, 51–61. Frankfurt am Main: Suhrkamp, 1977a.

———. "Mutmaßlicher Anfang der Menschengeschichte" (Speculative Beginning). In *Werkausgabe*, vol. 11, *Schriften zur Anthropologie, Geschichtsphilosophie, Politik und Pädagogik 1*, ed. Wilhelm Weischedel, 85–102. Frankfurt am Main: Suhrkamp, 1977b.

———. "Speculative Beginning of Human History." In *Perpetual Peace and Other Essays on Politics, History, and Morals*, trans. with intro. by Ted Humphrey, 49–60. Indianapolis: Hackett, 1983.

Kittler, Friedrich A. "Autorschaft ist Liebe." In *Die Austreibung des Geistes aus den Geisteswissenschaften: Programme des Poststrukturalismus*, 142–73. Uni-Taschenbücher 198, Paderborn Schöningh, 1980.

———. *Discourse Networks 1800/1900*, trans. Michael Metteer, with Chris Cullens. Stanford: Stanford University Press, 1990.

———. "Eine Detektivgeschichte der ersten Detektivgeschichte." In *Dichter—Mutter—Kind*, 197–218. München: Fink Verlag, 1991.
Knaack, Jürgen. *Achim von Arnim—Nicht nur Poet: Die politischen Anschauungen Arnims in ihrer Entwicklung*. Darmstadt: Thesen Verlag, 1976.
Kohn, Hans. *Prelude to Nation-States: The French and German Experience, 1789–1815*. Princeton: Van Nostrand, 1967.
Kolkenbrock-Netz, Jutta. "Wahnsinn der Vernunft—juristische Institution—literarische Praxis: Das Gutachten zum Fall Schmolling und die Erzählung 'Der Einsiedler Serapion' von E.T.A. Hoffmann." In *Wege der Literaturwissenschaft*, ed. Jutta Kolkenbrock-Netz et al., 122–44. Bonn: Bouvier, 1985.
Krafft-Ebing, Richard von. *Der Conträrsexuale vor dem Strafrichter*. Leipzig: Franz Denticke, 1894.
Kreuzer, Ingrid. *Märchenform und individuelle Geschichte: Zu Handlungsstrukturen in Werken Ludwig Tiecks zwischen 1790 und 1811*. Göttingen: Vandenhoeck und Ruprecht, 1983.
Lacan, Jacques. "The Subversion of the Subject and the Dialectics of Desire." In *Ecrits: A Selection*, trans. Alan Sheridan, 292–325. New York: Norton, 1977.
Laplanche, Jean. *Life and Death in Psychoanalysis*, trans. with intro. Jeffrey Mehlman. Baltimore: Johns Hopkins University Press, 1985.
———. *New Foundations for Psychoanalysis*, trans. David Macey. Oxford: Basil Blackwell, 1989.
———, and Jean-Bertrand Pontalis. "Fantasy and the Origins of Sexuality." In *Formations of Fantasy*, ed. Victor Burgin, James Donald, and Cora Caplan, 5–43. London: Methuen, 1986.
Lee, Christopher A. "E.T.A. Hoffmann's 'Mademoiselle de Scudéry' as a Forerunner of the Detective Story." *Clues* 15, no. 2 (fall-winter 1994): 63–73.
Lessing, Gotthold Ephraim, Moses Mendelssohn, and Friedrich Nicolai. *Briefwechsel über das Trauerspiel*, ed. Jochen Schulte-Sasse. München: Winkler, 1972.
Lewis, Matthew G. *Ambrosio, or, The Monk*. London: J. Bell, 1798.
Luhmann, Niklas. "Weltkunst." In *Unbeobachtbare Welt: Über Kunst und Architektur*, ed. Niklas Luhmann, Frederick Bunsen, Dirk Baecker, 7–45. Bielefeld: Verlag Cordula Haux, 1990.
Matala de Mazza, Ethel. "Brot und Wein: Zu Achim von Arnim's 'Versöhnung in der Sommerfrische.'" In *Der verfaßte Körper. Zum Projekt einer organischen Gemeinschaft in der politischen Romantik*, 389–418. Freiburg im Breisgau: Rombach, 1999.
Matt, Peter von. *Die Augen der Automaten*. Tübingen: Max Niemeyer, 1971.
Mérimée, Prosper. "Carmen." In *Romans et nouvelles*, 609–66. Monaco: Bibliothèque de la Pléiade, 1957.

———. "Carmen." In *Carmen and Other Stories*, trans. with intro. by Nicholas Jotcham, 1–53. Oxford: Oxford University Press, 1989.
———. "Columbia." In *Carmen and Other Stories*, trans. with intro. by Nicholas Jotcham, 162–290. Oxford: Oxford University Press, 1989.
———. "Colomba." In *Romans et nouvelles*, 437–564. Monaco: Bibliothèque de la Pléiade, 1957.
———. "La Vénus d'Ille." In *Romans et nouvelles*, 409–35. Monaco: Bibliothèque de la Pléiade, 1957.
———. "The Venus of Ille." In *Tales of the Fantastic, Madness, and the Supernatural from Nineteenth-Century France*, ed. and trans. Joan C. Kessler, 63–90. Chicago: University of Chicago Press, 1995.
Monléon, José B. *A Specter Is Haunting Europe: A Sociohistorical Approach to the Fantastic*. Princeton: Princeton University Press, 1990.
Mücke, Dorothea von. "Pygmalion's Dream in Herder's Aesthetics, or Male Narcissism as the Model for Bildung." *Studies in Eighteenth-Century Culture* 19 (1989): 349–65.
———. "'To Love a Murderer'—Fantasy, Sexuality, and the Political Novel: The Case of Godwin's *Caleb Williams*." In *Cultural Institutions of the Novel*, ed. Deidre Lynch and William Warner, 306–34. Durham: Duke University Press, 1996.
Mülder-Bach, Inka. "Im Zeichen Pygmalions: Die lebendige Statue und die Entdeckung der 'Darstellung' im 18. Jahrhundert." Habilschrift Fachbereich Germanistik der Freien Universität Berlin, June 1995.
O'Brien, William Arctander. "E.T.A. Hoffmann's Critique of Idealism: Psychology, Allegory, and Philosophy in 'Die Automate.'" *Euphorion* 83 (1989): 369–406.
Pikulik, Lothar. *E.T.A. Hoffmann als Erzähler: Ein Kommentar zu den "Serapions-Brüdern."* Göttingen: Vandenhoeck and Rupprecht, 1987.
Poe, Edgar Allan. "The Imp of the Perverse." In *The Short Fiction of Edgar Allan Poe: An Annotated Edition*, ed. Stuart and Susan Levine, 268–71. Urbana: University of Illinois Press, 1976.
———. "Ligeia" (1838). In *The Complete Works of Edgar Allan Poe*, vol. 2, *Prose Tales of Edgar Allen Poe*, reprint of 1902 ed. (Crowell), 248–68. New York: AMS Press, 1965.
———. "The Philosophy of Composition." In *The Complete Works of Edgar Allan Poe: Essays and Miscellanies*, ed. James A. Harrison, 193–208. New York: AMS Press, 1965.
Poulet, Georges. *Études sur le temps humain*. Edinburgh: Edinburgh University Press, 1949.
Raitt, A. W. "Inspector-General." In *Prosper Mérimée*, chap. 8, 137–54. New York: Scribner, 1970.

Reil, Johann Christian. *Rhapsodien über die Anwendugn der psychischen Kurmethode von Geisteszerrüttungen*. Halle: Curtsche Buchhandlung, 1803. Reprint, 1818.

Rieben, Pierre-André. *Délires Romantiques: Musset-Nodier-Gautier-Hugo*. Paris: José Corti, 1989.

Rieger, Dietmar. *Jacques Cazotte: Ein Beitrag zu erzählenden Literatur des 18. Jahrhunderts*. Heidelberg: Carl Winter, 1969.

Rothschuh, K. E. *Geschichte der Physiologie*. Berlin: Springer Verlag, 1953.

Schnapp, Alain. *The Discovery of the Past*. N.p. (Spain): British Museum Press, 1996.

Schneider, Peter. "Verbrechen, Künstlertum und Wahnsinn: Untersuchungen zur Figur des Cardillac in E.T.A. Hoffmanns 'Das Fräulein von Scuderi.'" *Mitteilungen der E.T.A. Hoffmann Gesellschaft* 26 (1980): 34–50.

Sedgwick, Eve Koussevitsky. *Between Men: English Literature and Male Homosocial Desire*. New York: Columbia University Press, 1985.

Segebrecht, Wulf. "E.T.A. Hoffmanns Auffassung vom Richteramt und vom Dichterberuf: Mit unbekannten Zeugnissen aus Hoffmanns juristischer Tätigkeit." *Jahrbuch der deutschen Schillergesellschaft* 11 (1967): 62–138.

Siebers, Tobin. *The Romantic Fantastic*. Ithaca: Cornell University Press, 1984.

Snell, Robert. *Théophile Gautier: A Romantic Critic of the Visual Arts*. Oxford: Clarendon Press, 1982.

Strack, Friedrich. "Das 'Wunder' der Geschichte und die 'Wahrheit' der Sagen." In *Zwischen den Wissenschaften: Beiträge zur deutschen Literaturgeschichte; Bernhard Gajek zum 65. Geburtstag*, ed. Gerhard Hahn, 292–303. Regensburg: Pustet, 1994.

Theweleit, Klaus. *Orpheus und Eurydike*. In *Buch der Könige*, vol. 1. Basel: Stroemfel/Roter Stern, 1989.

Tieck, Ludwig. "Der blonde Eckbert." In *Schriften in zwölf Bänden*, ed. Manfred Frank et al., vol. 6, *Phantasus*. Frankfurt am Main: Deutscher Klassiker Verlag, 1985.

———. "Fair-Haired Eckbert." In *German Literary Fairy Tales*, ed. Frank G. Ryder and Robert M. Browning. German Library, 30, 30–46. New York: Continuum, 1983.

———. "Liebeszauber." In *Schriften in zwölf Bänden*, ed. Manfred Frank et al., vol. 6, *Phantasus*. Frankfurt am Main: Deutscher Klassiker Verlag, 1985.

———. "The Love Charm." In "The Love Charm: A Translation from Tieck," by Thomas De Quincey. In *The Collected Writings of Thomas De Quincey*, ed. David Masson, vol. 12, *Tales and Romances*, 434–67. Edinburgh: Adam and Charles Black, 1890.

———. "Über Shakespeare's Behandlung des Wunderbaren." In *Schriften in zwölf*

Bänden, ed. Manfred Frank et al., vol. 1, *Schriften 1789–1794*, ed. Achim Hölter, 685–722. Frankfurt am Main: Deutscher Klassiker Verlag, 1991.

Todorov, Tzvetan. *The Fantastic: A Structural Approach to a Literary Genre*, trans. Richard Howard. Ithaca: Cornell University Press, 1975.

Ubersfeld, Annie. "Théophile Gautier ou le regard de Pygmalion." *Romantisme* 66 (1989): 51–59.

Unger, Thorsten. "'Romantisierte Welt' als ästhetische Überwindung des Gartens: Überlegungen zum Gartenmotiv in den Rahmengesprächen von Ludwig Tiecks *Phantasus*." *Journal of English and Germanic Philology* 90, no. 4 (October 1991): 467–90.

Völker, Ludwig. "Naturpoesie, Phantasie, Phantastik: Über Achim von Arnims Erzählung Isabella von Ägypten." In *Romantik*, ed. Ernst Ribbat, 114–37. Königstein T/s.: Athenäum, 1979.

Wellbery, David E. *Lessing's Laocoön: Semiotics and Aesthetics in the Age of Reason*. Cambridge: Cambridge University Press, 1984.

———. *The Specular Moment: Goethe's Early Lyric and the Beginnings of Romanticism*. Stanford: Stanford University Press, 1996.

Williams, Elizabeth. *The Physical and the Moral: Anthropology, Physiology, and Philosophical Medicine in France, 1750–1850*. Cambridge: Cambridge University Press, 1994.

Winkler, Markus. "Cazotte lu par E.T.A. Hoffmann: Du *Diable amoureux* à *Der Elementargeist*." *Arcadia* 23, no. 2 (1988): 113–32.

Winnicott, D. W. *Playing and Reality*. London: Tavistock, 1971.

Wünsch, Marianne. *Die fantastische Literatur der frühen Moderne (1890–1930): Definition, denkgeschichtlicher Kontext, Strukturen*. München: Fink Verlag, 1998.

Yates, Frances A. *Astraea: The Imperial Theme in the Sixteenth Century*. London: Pimlico, 1993.

Žižek, Slavoj. *Looking Awry: An Introduction to Jacques Lacan Through Popular Culture*. Cambridge: MIT Press, 1992.

———. *The Metastases of Enjoyment: Six Essays on Woman and Causality*. In series Wo es war. London: Verso, 1994.

———. *The Sublime Object of Ideology*. Phronesis, ed. Ernesto Laclau and Chantal Mouffe. London: Verso, 1989.

Index

aesthetic code vs. moral code, 107, 149–50, 179, 186. *See also* art, autonomy of
aesthetic experience, 196, 247
aesthetic hypersensitivity, 59, 81, 84–87, 92–93
aestheticization, 172, 175–76
agency, 3, 70, 72, 98, 109–10, 170. *See also* freedom
alienation, 61, 63, 68, 132
allegory, 4, 8, 19, 63, 75, 77, 202–3, 205, 227, 242, 262n7
alterity: access to, 61–64, 107–8; confrontation with, 25–26, 28, 45, 47, 91, 95; containment of, 38, 138–39, 142–43; desire for (*see* fascination); ethnic, 223; exclusion of, 97, 141, 144; historic, 199, 222, 225–26, 242; sacrifice of, 164–66; seduction by, 9–10, 19–20, 22, 34, 97, 223
amentia occulta, 110–12, 114–15, 127, 264n4
amorality, 104–5, 159, 188
animation, 38, 40, 141, 149, 176, 243, 246; of beholder, 131–33, 135, 145; "hideous," 192–93; of work of art, 130–33, 135, 140, 145, 162, 229–30, 233. *See also* life
anthropology, 10, 67, 76–77, 98–99
antiquity, 179, 183, 220, 225–26, 233
anti-Semitism. *See under* Arnim, Achim von
antitheatricality. *See* authenticity

arabesque, 189–93, 195–96, 247
archaeology, 197, 220, 223, 225–26
Arndt, Ernst Moritz, *Geist der Zeit* (Spirit of the Times), 50–54, 56, 261n22
Arnim, Achim von: and anti-Semitism, 202, 207–8, 215–16, 270n13, 270n14; and political debates, 205–6, 214. Works: "Isabella von Ägypten" (Isabella of Egypt), 199–215, 218, 221, 224, 242–43; "Maria Melük," 206; "Die Versöhnung in der Sommerfrische" (The Reconciliation in the Summer Resort), 216–19
art: autonomy of, 80, 146, 179, 247, 249 (*see also* aesthetic code vs. moral code); and performance, 103, 105–6, 119, 125–26; power of, 112, 139–40, 247–48; production of, 39–43, 48, 63, 147, 155, 192; reception of, 146–47, 244; sister arts, 131–32, 148, 150, 175. *See also* artist
artificial paradise, 130, 148–50, 155, 159, 164, 167–70, 173–77, 180, 195
artist: as technician of the imaginary, 16, 35, 112, 139–40, 146–47, 246; transformative role of, 111, 119, 122–27, 129, 146. *See also* art
assimilation. *See* universalism
Astraea, 203–5, 212, 214–15
authenticity, 29–31, 125, 168, 217–18, 252
authorship, 6, 8, 154, 239–43, 249–51

Index   283

"Die Automate" (Automata) [Hoffmann], 111–12, 130, 133–46, 149, 153

bachelorhood, 20, 36, 49–50, 56, 238
battlefield account, 51–52, 54–55
beauty, 42–43, 48, 87, 175, 182–83, 185–86, 235; harmonizing notions of, 62–64, 79, 85–86, 89, 91–93, 183; pathology of, 81, 84, 86, 93, 107
Bildung, 142
biopower, 110–11, 119, 124–25, 127, 214
blind spot, 67, 106, 239–41, 243, 246, 251
"Der blonde Eckbert" (Blond Eckbert) [Tieck], 58–60, 64–79, 81, 97–99, 105
blood, 43, 82, 93, 176, 178; semiotics of, in Arnim, 202, 210–12, 215–18, 221, 243
body: of Christ (*see* Eucharist); corporeality of, 32, 161, 166, 169, 174, 184; of a dead woman, 170, 172, 174–76, 193–95; and identity, 169, 177–78, 180; of a man, 172, 177–78; memory of, 217–18
bourgeoisie, 74, 122, 124–25, 149, 151–52, 213
bourgeois tragedy, 80, 124
bureaucracy, 38, 214
Bynum, Caroline, 4

capitalism, 14, 149, 203, 242
capital vs. province, 199, 226, 235–37, 239
carnival, 81–83, 85–88, 91, 95–96
Castex, Pierre Georges, 13–14
castration, 26, 74, 234, 239
Cazotte, Jacques, *Le diable amoureux* (The Devil in Love), 6–10, 18–35, 169, 174; and Hoffmann, "Der Elementargeist," 36–38, 40–43, 45–46, 48, 57
Charles V, 202–3, 205
Christliche Deutsche Tischgesellschaft (Christian German Roundtable), 214, 270n10, 270n13
classicism, 56, 97, 131–35, 138, 141–43, 154, 191
confession, 13, 59, 104; as declaration of love, 69–71, 250; desire for, 81, 95, 98–99, 102–7; effects of, 59–61, 64–65, 67–72, 135–36, 244; as work of art, 99, 103, 105–6, 108. *See also* individuality, hermeneutics of
connoisseurship, 125, 237–39, 249
contemplation, 84–85, 87–89, 91, 97, 134, 141, 145
conventionality, 29–30, 63, 87, 160, 182–83. *See also* authenticity
copyright regulations, 154
creativity, 40–43, 48

dandy, 149, 173, 176–77, 226, 233, 235, 238–39
Dante Alighieri, 186
Davidson, Arnold, 258n16
death, site between two deaths, 167, 169, 175–76, 179–80, 196
defense, 22, 25, 48, 69, 98, 168; beauty as, 64, 85–86, 88, 91, 93–94; imaginary beloved as, 138, 142
demographics, 110, 124
De Quincey, Thomas, 105
description, 178, 183–84, 190, 196
desire: for alterity (*see* fascination); of another, 21–22, 27–32, 48, 91, 94, 136, 171; denial of, 141, 144–45, 153, 156, 159, 165, 167, 195; indeterminacy of, 11–12, 35, 76–77; pure, 48, 98–99, 110, 122, 126–27, 206–11, 215
detective story, 111, 117, 119, 123, 265n7
devil, 36–37, 54. See also *Le diable amoureux*
Le diable amoureux (The Devil in Love) [Cazotte], 6–10, 18–35, 169, 174
diaspora, 214–15
dissection, 158, 160–61, 165–66

dissociation, 188
Dürer, Albrecht, 189

"Der Elementargeist" (The Elementary Spirit) [Hoffmann], 20, 35–57
emotion, ambiguity of, 69, 71, 97, 163. *See also* painful pleasure
empire, 203, 205, 213, 215, 218
empiricism, 100
enigma, 67, 77–79, 99, 116, 128–29, 135, 140, 144–46, 184–85, 252. *See also* arabesque
enjoyment: obscene, 28, 32–33, 35, 47, 144, 157, 163; perfect, 142, 144, 148–49, 169, 194–95
epistolary novel 23–24, 214
escapism, 2, 9, 16, 56, 144, 179–80, 248
ethnicity: and identity, 199, 212, 215–16, 221–24, 242; and political leadership, 206, 212–13; and rivalry, 225, 232; and tradition, 199, 215–16, 221, 223; and violence, 220–24
ethnology, 226
Eucharist, 209, 211–12, 216–18
eye, 170–72, 183–95. *See also* gaze

fairy tale, 19, 64–67, 70, 72–75, 98, 197, 214
fall, the. *See* original sin
fantastic, poetics of, 8, 62, 64, 107, 140, 219, 244
fantastic tale, 1–2, 13–15
fascination, 10, 16, 26, 28, 221–22, 224, 244; aesthetics of, 251–52
father, 144, 181, 212, 238
femininity. *See* woman
fiction vs. fact, 202, 219, 239–42
Foucault, Michel, 12–13, 110, 129, 213–14
"Das Fräulein von Scuderi" (Mademoiselle de Scudéri) [Hoffmann], 111–12, 117–29, 146
freedom, 10–11, 13, 76, 98, 101–2, 107, 113, 142. *See also* agency

Freud, Sigmund, 11–12, 25–26, 71, 73–74, 110, 144, 259n21
friendship. *See* intimacy
functionalism, 99–101, 106

garden, 61–62, 141–44
Gautier, Théophile: art criticism, 173–74; "La morte amoureuse" (The Dead Leman), 148–50, 169–80, 191, 195–96
gaze: evil, 221–22, 229, 232–35; reversal of, 27–28, 47–48, 79, 82, 87–88, 91–92, 94, 138, 194; "transfigured," 142, 153. *See also* eye
Geist der Zeit (Spirit of the Times) [Arndt], 50–54, 56, 261n22
generic hybridity, 100–3, 180–81, 202, 219, 224, 242; and subjectivity, 66–67, 70, 72, 74–75
genius aesthetics, 6, 40, 45, 49, 125, 154
geology, 225–26
ghost story, 248–49
Goethe, Johann Wolfgang von, 6, 37, 40, 44–46, 51, 149
golden age, 203–4, 206, 211–12
gothic novel, 260n28
Graevenitz, Gerhart von, 268n22, 269n24
Grandier, Urbain, 80
Grimm, Jacob and Wilhelm, 202, 214–15, 270n12
Gypsy. *See* "Isabella von Ägypten"; Mérimée, "Carmen"

Haller, Albrecht von, 129
harmony: of the faculties (*see* beauty, harmonizing notions of); with nature (*see under* nature)
Harter, Deborah, 15, 260n27
Herder, Johann Gottfried, 10, 79, 183, 266n19; "Einige Wahrnehmungen über Form und Gestalt aus Pygmalions bildendem Traume" (Some Observations About Form and Gestalt from

Pygmalion's Shaping Dream), 131–35, 141–42
hermeneutics: idealist (*see* classicism); of individuality (*see under* individuality). *See also* Pygmalion
historical reference, 198, 202–3, 219, 224, 242–43
historiography, 197, 202, 220, 225
history, 197–98, 214, 219; heterogeneity of, 198–99, 220–21, 225–27, 229, 242–43
Hoffmann, E.T.A., 1, 53, 131, 149, 179; battlefield account, 51–52; as civil servant and judge, 53, 110, 113–17, 264n5. Works: "Die Automate" (Automata), 111–12, 130, 133–46, 149, 153; "Der Elementargeist" (The Elementary Spirit), 20, 35–57; "Das Fräulein von Scuderi" (Mademoiselle de Scudéri), 111–12, 117–29, 146; "Rat Krespel" (Councillor Krespel), 148, 150, 152, 156–68, 195–96; [untitled] ("Serapion"), 40, 150–56, 159, 167–68, 179, 195–96; *Die Serapions-Brüder* (The Serapion Brethren), 130, 150–52, 167–68
homosexuality, 11, 71, 74, 97
Hugo, Victor, 219
humorology, 85
hypersensitivity, aesthetic. *See* aesthetic hypersensitivity
hypnosis, 162

idealism, 52, 149, 152–54, 156, 168–69
idée fixe, 111, 114
identity of a character with a literary prototype, 37, 42
identity of multiple characters, 68, 72–73, 92, 96, 152–53
ideology, 14–15, 57, 244
idol, 41, 43, 45–48, 181–82, 225, 227, 229–31, 239, 241
illness, physical, 149, 163–64, 167, 185–87
illumination, 184, 186–87, 190
illusionism, 34, 63, 131, 209

imaginary, technician of the. *See under* artist
immediacy, 34, 84; fantasy of, 146, 150, 152–53, 170, 175, 195–96
immortality, 51–52, 150–55, 167–68, 172, 180, 184–85, 196
imperial idea. *See* empire
"The Imp of the Perverse" [Poe], 60, 99–108, 110
incest, 65, 68, 72–75, 238–39
individualism, 239, 242–43
individuality, hermeneutics of, 12–13, 85, 98, 118–19, 121–24, 162, 178, 183–84
individualization. *See* allegory; individuality, hermeneutics of
innocence, 118–19, 121–24, 200, 206–7, 209–10, 252
insanity. *See* madness
insanity defense, 109–15
inspiration, 39, 45, 51–52, 55, 133, 155
instinct, 10–11, 13, 60, 76, 98–100, 103, 106, 110, 206, 245
intensity, aesthetics of, 13, 64, 79, 81, 94, 98, 105, 107, 125, 244–45, 247–48, 251
interiority, psychic: absence of, 171–72, 174, 177; vs. exterior reality, 24, 28–31, 34–35, 42, 137, 143, 183, 188, 247
interpellation, 20, 22, 24, 29, 43, 123
intimacy: codification of, 45, 49, 61, 150–52; and communication, 58–61, 65, 67–68, 70–72, 79, 81, 97, 135–37, 250; exclusive, 38, 138–39, 142–43, 159, 164, 166–67
irrationality, 100–102, 104
"Isabella von Ägypten" (Isabella of Egypt) [Achim], 199–215, 218, 221, 224, 242–43
Isis, 212
isolation: of another (*see* intimacy, exclusive); of oneself (*see* melancholia)

Jackson, Rosemary, 14
Jahn, Friedrich Ludwig, 52–53

James, Henry, *The Turn of the Screw*, 248–53
journalism, 105, 149, 179
juridico-discursive system. *See* legal system

Kant, Immanuel, 10–11, 76, 86
Kittler, Friedrich, 259n21, 265n7, 265n10
Kleist, Heinrich von, 162
Krafft-Ebing, Richard von, 11, 259n17

Lacan, Jacques, 26, 28, 259n21, 260n6, 260n7, 260n9, 263n19
language: exclusion of, 133–34, 137, 159; opacity of, 63, 184, 244; philosophy of, 3, 59, 64, 97, 107; representational model of, 60, 67; and subjectivity, 10, 26, 61–62, 64, 66–67, 72, 74, 78–79, 97, 107, 144, 180, 184
Laplanche, Jean, 77–78, 263n19, 265n13
latency. *See* unconscious
leadership, political, 201–6, 210, 212–15, 218, 243
legal system, 103, 109–11, 115–16, 118–19, 122–24
legend, 197, 214, 219, 224, 234, 242
Lessing, Gotthold Ephraim, 128
Lewis, Matthew, 169
library, 154, 196
"Liebeszauber" (The Love Charm) [Tieck], 59–60, 79–98, 105
life: search for principle of, 129–30, 167; of work of art, 130–31, 133–34, 161–62. *See also* animation
"Ligeia" [Poe], 149–50, 169, 179–96
love, 44, 87, 122–24, 181, 209. *See also* innocence
Lucian, 227
Luhmann, Niklas, 246–48, 251

madness, 59, 144, 150, 153, 155–56, 168–69, 179, 188, 195; theories of, 3, 11, 109–11, 113–15, 258n15 (*see also* amentia occulta)

magical thinking, 25, 27
manuscript, 187, 190
marriage, 33, 57; of convenience, 235, 237–38; as normalization strategy, 21–22, 33, 96; political notion of, 203, 206–7, 213
marvelous: in Arnim, 198, 202, 213, 216, 219, 224, 242–43; in Tieck, 4–6, 8, 58, 65, 247
masculinity, 36, 217, 234, 239, 241. *See also* bachelorhood; military
masturbation, 46, 76
materialism, 129, 153–54
Matt, Peter von, 40–43, 48
mechanical reproducibility, 189, 192
medial woman, 148–50, 165, 167, 169, 174–76, 179–81, 184, 186–87, 193, 196
media technology, 9, 25, 32, 34–35, 43–45, 139–40, 147, 169, 192, 196; history of, 149, 186–87, 190, 248. *See also* print culture
melancholia, 60, 65, 68–69, 72–74, 81, 84–85, 96, 187–88
memory, 180, 184, 188, 195, 217–18
Mérimée, Prosper, 197, 199, 219–20, 240–41; Works: "Carmen," 219–20, 222–24, 243; "Colomba," 219–24, 243; "La Vénus d'Ille" ("The Venus of Ille"), 219–20, 224–43
Mesmerism, 149
metamorphosis, 177, 179, 185
metempsychosis, 177
metonymy, 160–63, 165, 184–85, 194
military, 36–38, 50–52, 214, 224
mirror. *See* specular moment
modernist aesthetics, 64, 149, 218
Monléon, José, 14–15
Montaigne, Michel de, 128
Montalembert, Charles de, 219
Moritz, Karl Philipp, 38, 85
"La morte amoureuse" (The Dead Leman) [Gautier], 148, 150, 169–79, 191, 195–96

mother, 125, 141–42, 173, 206, 210
motive, 99–100, 112–27
muse, 181
music, 141, 143, 148–50; abhorrence of, 59, 81, 83, 85–86

Napoleonic Wars, 50–52, 55–57
Napoleonic occupation of Germany, 199, 203, 205, 213–14
narcissism, 122, 172, 181; and fantasy of integrity, 94, 132, 145, 236, 238–39, 243; of narrator (*see under* narrator)
narrator, 5, 23–24; blind spot of, 67, 239–41; and identity, 178–79; and madness, 155, 179; narcissism of, 157–58, 160, 162–63. See also observer
national identity, 197–99, 212, 214–16, 224
nationalism, 52–54, 56–57, 197, 199, 242, 261n22
nation-state, 199, 203, 205, 213, 224, 230, 232–33
nature, 60–63, 95, 100, 110, 130; harmony with, 141–43, 145, 246
Naturmärchen (fairy-tales of nature), 62–63
neo-Platonism, 149, 186
normalization, 10, 12, 47, 49, 96, 110. See also marriage, as normalization strategy
normal vs. pathological, 11–13, 20, 48, 106, 115–16
novelty, 104–7
nuptial imagery, 50, 55–56, 170–72

object relations theory, 46–47
observation, 246–47, 252
observer, 4–5, 7–8, 27, 29–35, 40, 48, 86, 94; blind spot of, 106, 246, 251; deindividualized, 102, 106–7, 174; in Mérimée, 220–22, 224, 235–37, 239, 243; position of, in fantastic tale, 59, 64, 105–6, 179, 192. See also narrator; outside observer
occultism, 13–14, 56–57
omnipotence fantasy, 160
opium, 188, 193
original sin, 11, 75–77, 207
Orpheus and Eurydice, 148–49
Other. See alterity
outside observer, 78–79, 171, 178
overstimulation, aesthetics of. See intensity, aesthetics of
Ovid, 130

painful pleasure, 9, 88–89, 91, 136, 138, 141, 245
painting, 132, 135, 148–50. See also tableau
paleontology, 226
paradise, artificial. See artificial paradise
paranoia, 31, 66–74, 140
patriotism, 50–54, 56–57, 214–16, 218, 224; local, 232–33
pedagogy, 67, 76–77, 110
penetration, 95–97
performance. See *under* art
perversion, 3, 10–12, 60, 99, 110; sexuality as, 13, 22, 33, 60, 76, 95, 97–99, 106–7, 129, 211
phallic mother, 235–36, 239–40
Phantasus [Tieck], 59–63, 80, 150–51
philology, 197, 223, 225, 241
phrenology, 99–101, 106
physiology, 41–42, 129–30, 146, 245
Pinel, Philippe, 114, 258n15
pleasure: organization of, 60, 81, 94–95, 97–98; painful (*see* painful pleasure)
Poe, Edgar Allan: "The Imp of the Perverse," 60, 99–108, 110; "Ligeia," 149–50, 169, 179–96; "The Philosophy of Composition," 180
police, 111, 117, 122–23, 125, 127, 224
presence, 176, 182, 187, 194–95, 209, 218
primal scene, 128–29

288   Index

print culture, 186–87, 189–92, 268n23; hallucinatory sensuality of, 180–81, 246. *See also* reading
Prometheus, 45–46, 125
psychiatry, 3, 11–12, 60, 85, 99, 109–11, 113–17, 152–53, 245
psychoanalysis, 3, 11–14, 58, 60, 74–75, 77–78, 98, 107, 110, 128, 245, 259n21; and paranoia, 67, 71; and repression, 71, 78
psychology, 3, 60, 107, 109–11, 115–16, 245, 258n15. *See also* realism, psychological
Pygmalion, 130–35, 139, 141–42, 145, 243, 265n15

rationalism, 3, 14, 28, 68, 80, 113, 116, 143, 198, 224
"Rat Krespel" (Councillor Krespel) [Hoffmann], 148, 150, 152, 156–68, 195–96
reading, 2–3, 6, 8–10, 19–20, 37–38, 45–46, 50, 56, 147–48, 150, 153–54, 245–46, 248; and sexualization, 38, 41–43, 48, 57, 75–77. *See also* print culture
realism, 15, 80, 229, 243, 246–47, 251; and fairy-tale, 65–67, 70, 72, 72–75; psychological 4, 19, 23–24, 58
Realitätsverlust, 25, 70
reality: construction of, 5–7, 28, 59, 63–64, 67, 73–74, 79, 97, 131, 147, 244, 246–47; vs. illusion, 5, 19, 21, 25, 27–29, 32, 34–35, 96, 177–78, 209; vs. imaginary, 6–7, 86, 143, 154
regression, 141, 238
Reil, Johann Christian, 114, 258n15
renunciation, 155, 165, 172–73, 175–76
representation: antimimetic model of (in Arnim), 209, 218, 242–43; Enlightenment paradigm of, 42, 58–59, 67, 183; political, 211, 213, 215, 242; vs. *Darstellung* (presentation) (in Herder), 132–33, 135, 137. *See also* Eucharist; simulation
repression, 69–71, 74–75, 77–79, 83–84, 93–98
resonance, 132, 143, 146
Restoration, 52–53, 56–57, 149
Rieger, Dietmar, 18–19
ritual 43, 82–83, 92–94, 96–97, 218
Romanticism, 6, 9, 37, 44, 56, 97, 127, 141, 145, 154; French, 179; German, 37–38, 50, 197, 214; and philosophy of language (*see under* language)

Schiller, Friedrich, 37–38, 40, 51, 97
Schmolling, Daniel, 110–13, 115–17, 127, 264n5
scholar, 181, 223, 225–26, 238, 240–41
Schubert, Gotthilf Heinrich, 141–45, 149
Scott, Sir Walter, 54–55, 197
Scudéry, Madeleine de, 111, 117, 125
sculpture, 131–35, 142, 145–46, 149; and woman's dead body, 172, 175–76. *See also* statue
secret. *See* confession; individuality, hermeneutics of
seduction, aesthetics of, 245, 247–48
self-referentiality, 37, 143, 247–48, 251
sensationalism, 54, 105, 179
sensibility, culture of, 16, 24, 33, 38, 42, 49, 59, 68, 80, 125, 146–47, 244
[untitled] ("Serapion") [Hoffmann], 40, 150–56, 159, 167–68, 179, 195–96
Die Serapions-Brüder (The Serapion Brethren) [Hoffmann], 130, 150–52, 167–68
Shakespeare, William, 4–6, 8
shock, aesthetics of. *See* intensity, aesthetics of
Siebers, Tobin, 14
signifier: (imaginary) materiality of, 150, 154, 168, 180, 184, 187, 189–93, 195–96, 249–50, 268n23; and signified, 182,

229, 250; transparency of, 181, 184, 186–87, 189–90, 193, 195–96, 268n23
simulacrum, 208–9, 242
simulation, 7, 9, 35, 133–35, 140, 145, 245, 248
sovereignty, 109–10, 118–19, 121–27. *See also* leadership, political
specular moment, 42–45, 49–50, 62–63, 134
spiritism, 20, 23, 26, 34, 38–43, 45
split personality, 177–78
statue, 224–25, 227, 229–31, 233, 241; and humans, 231–33, 235–37. *See also* sculpture
Sturm und Drang (Storm and Stress), 38, 40, 49, 56, 125
style, 241–42, 249, 251
substitution, 57, 95, 162, 238–39
suicide, 101–3
symbolic order, 31, 112, 140–44, 155, 159, 181, 196
synesthesia, 34, 138, 147

tableau, 29–30, 32, 47, 55, 122, 170, 172. *See also* painting
Tasso, 19, 128
taste. *See* connoisseurship
Tieck, Ludwig: "Der blonde Eckbert" (Blond Eckbert), 58–60, 64–79, 81, 97–99, 105; "Liebeszauber" (The Love Charm), 59–60, 79–98, 105; *Phantasus*, 59–63, 80, 150–51; "Über Shakespeare's Behandlung des Wunderbaren," 4–9, 58, 262n7
Todorov, Tzvetan, 8–9, 13–14, 73–74
tradition 197–99, 215–19, 221, 223
transcendentalism, 149, 186–87, 190, 195
transgression, 13, 70–72, 74, 77, 127–29, 157, 162
transitional object, 46–47
transparency: of communication (*see* intimacy); of signifier (*see under* signifier)

transubstantiation. *See* Eucharist
trauma, 74, 83–84, 91–92, 94–95, 111, 119, 125, 127–29, 233, 245
The Turn of the Screw [James], 248–53

unconscious, 11, 13, 26, 58, 60, 67, 73–75, 77–79, 97–98, 115–16, 128
universalism, 198–99, 214–17, 220–21, 223–24, 242–43
unmarked state, 246–47, 249, 252
utilitarianism, 149, 179

vandalism, 219, 234–35
veil, 175–76, 191–95
"La Vénus d'Ille" (The Venus of Ille) [Mérimée], 219–20, 224–43
"Die Versöhnung in der Sommerfrische" (The Reconciliation in the Summer Resort) [Achim], 215–19
violence, aesthetics of, 105, 218
Virgil, 181, 203–4
Virgin Mary, 204, 211, 229–30
vision, spiritual, 142–43, 151–54, 156, 168, 186–87, 194
vista, 186, 189–90, 196
vitalism, 129
vivisection. *See* dissection
voice, 30, 82, 84, 87–88, 136, 138, 142; and violin, 159–63, 165–66
voyeurism, 81, 235–37

Wellbery, David, 45
Winnicott, D.W., 46–47
woman: and political leadership, 202, 206–9; and violence, 220–21, 223, 242–43; and work of art, 131, 182–83, 231, 234–35, 237. *See also* medial woman
world art, 246, 248, 252
Wünsch, Marianne, 13–14

Yates, Frances, 204–5

Cultural Memory in the Present

Jean-Luc Nancy, *A Finite Thinking*, edited by Simon Sparks

Theodor W. Adorno, *Can There Be Life after Auschwitz?: A Philosophical Anthology*, edited by Rolf Tiedemann

Patricia Pisters, *The Matrix of Visual Culture: Working with Deleuze in Film Theory*

Talal Asad, *Formations of the Secular: Christianity, Islam, Modernity*

Dorothea von Mücke, *The Seduction of the Occult and the Rise of the Fantastic Tale*

Eric Michaud, *An Art for Eternity: The Cult of Art in Nazi Germany*

Marc Redfield, *The Politics of Aesthetics: Nationalism, Gender, Romanticism*

Emmanuel Levinas, *On Escape*

Dan Zahavi, *Husserl's Phenomenology*

Rodolphe Gasché, *The Idea of Form: Rethinking Kant's Aesthetics*

Michael Naas, *Taking on the Tradition: Jacques Derrida and the Legacies of Deconstruction*

Herlinde Pauer-Studer, ed., *Constructions of Practical Reason: Interviews on Moral and Political Philosophy*

Jean-Luc Marion, *Being Given: Toward a Phenomenology of Givenness*

Theodor W. Adorno and Max Horkheimer, *Dialectic of Enlightenment*

Ian Balfour, *The Rhetoric of Romantic Prophecy*

Martin Stokhof, *World and Life as One: Ethics and Ontology in Wittgenstein's Early Thought*

Gianni Vattimo, *Nietzsche: An Introduction*

Jacques Derrida, *Negotiations: Interventions and Interviews, 1971–1998*, ed. Elizabeth Rottenberg

Brett Levinson, *The Ends of Literature: Post-transition and Neoliberalism in the Wake of the "Boom"*

Timothy J. Reiss, *Against Autonomy: Global Dialectics of Cultural Exchange*

Hent de Vries and Samuel Weber, eds., *Religion and Media*

Niklas Luhmann, *Theories of Distinction: Redescribing the Descriptions of Modernity*, ed. and introd. William Rasch

Johannes Fabian, *Anthropology with an Attitude: Critical Essays*

Michel Henry, *I Am the Truth: Toward a Philosophy of Christianity*

Gil Anidjar, *"Our Place in Al-Andalus": Kabbalah, Philosophy, Literature in Arab-Jewish Letters*

Hélène Cixous and Jacques Derrida, *Veils*

F. R. Ankersmit, *Historical Representation*

F. R. Ankersmit, *Political Representation*

Elissa Marder, *Dead Time: Temporal Disorders in the Wake of Modernity (Baudelaire and Flaubert)*

Reinhart Koselleck, *The Practice of Conceptual History: Timing History, Spacing Concepts*

Niklas Luhmann, *The Reality of the Mass Media*

Hubert Damisch, *A Childhood Memory by Piero della Francesca*

Hubert Damisch, *A Theory of /Cloud/: Toward a History of Painting*

Jean-Luc Nancy, *The Speculative Remark (One of Hegel's Bons Mots)*

Jean-François Lyotard, *Soundproof Room: Malraux's Anti-Aesthetics*

Jan Patočka, *Plato and Europe*

Hubert Damisch, *Skyline: The Narcissistic City*

Isabel Hoving, *In Praise of New Travelers: Reading Caribbean Migrant Women Writers*

Richard Rand, ed., *Futures: Of Derrida*

William Rasch, *Niklas Luhmann's Modernity: The Paradox of System Differentiation*

Jacques Derrida and Anne Dufourmantelle, *Of Hospitality*

Jean-François Lyotard, *The Confession of Augustine*

Kaja Silverman, *World Spectators*

Samuel Weber, *Institution and Interpretation: Expanded Edition*

Jeffrey S. Librett, *The Rhetoric of Cultural Dialogue: Jews and Germans in the Epoch of Emancipation*

Ulrich Baer, *Remnants of Song: Trauma and the Experience of Modernity in Charles Baudelaire and Paul Celan*

Samuel C. Wheeler III, *Deconstruction as Analytic Philosophy*

David S. Ferris, *Silent Urns: Romanticism, Hellenism, Modernity*

Rodolphe Gasché, *Of Minimal Things: Studies on the Notion of Relation*

Sarah Winter, *Freud and the Institution of Psychoanalytic Knowledge*

Samuel Weber, *The Legend of Freud: Expanded Edition*

Aris Fioretos, ed., *The Solid Letter: Readings of Friedrich Hölderlin*

J. Hillis Miller / Manuel Asensi, *Black Holes / J. Hillis Miller; or, Boustrophedonic Reading*

Miryam Sas, *Fault Lines: Cultural Memory and Japanese Surrealism*

Peter Schwenger, *Fantasm and Fiction: On Textual Envisioning*

Didier Maleuvre, *Museum Memories: History, Technology, Art*

Jacques Derrida, *Monolingualism of the Other; or, The Prosthesis of Origin*

Andrew Baruch Wachtel, *Making a Nation, Breaking a Nation: Literature and Cultural Politics in Yugoslavia*

Niklas Luhmann, *Love as Passion: The Codification of Intimacy*

Mieke Bal, ed., *The Practice of Cultural Analysis: Exposing Interdisciplinary Interpretation*

Jacques Derrida and Gianni Vattimo, eds., *Religion*

The authorized representative in the EU for product safety and compliance is:
Mare Nostrum Group
B.V Doelen 72
4831 GR Breda
The Netherlands